lonely planet

# IRELAND'S
# BEST TRIPS

## 34 AMAZING ROAD TRIPS

This edition written and researched by

**Fionn Davenport**
**Isabel Albiston**
**Catherine Le Nevez**

## SYMBOLS IN THIS BOOK

 Top Tips

 Link Your Trips

Tips from Locals

Trip Detour

 History & Culture

 Family

Food & Drink

 Outdoors

 Essential Photo

Walking Tour

 Eating

 Sleeping

📞 Telephone Number
@ Internet Access
🕐 Opening Hours
🛜 Wi-Fi Access
Ⓟ Parking
🚭 Nonsmoking
❄ Air-Conditioning

✒ Vegetarian Selection
🏊 Swimming Pool

📖 English-Language Menu
👪 Family-Friendly
🐾 Pet-Friendly

## MAP LEGEND

**Routes**
Trip Route
Trip Detour
Linked Trip
Walk Route
Tollway
Freeway
Primary
Secondary
Tertiary
Lane
Unsealed Road
Plaza/Mall
Steps
)= = Tunnel
Pedestrian Overpass
Walk Track/Path

**Boundaries**
--- International
State/Province
Cliff

**Hydrography**
River/Creek
Intermittent River
Swamp/Mangrove
Canal
Water
Dry/Salt/Intermittent Lake
Glacier

**Highway Markers**
E44 E-Road Network
M100 National Network

**Trips**
1 Trip Numbers
9 Trip Stop
Walking tour
Trip Detour

**Population**
✪ Capital (National)
◉ Capital (State/Province)
● City/Large Town
○ Town/Village

**Areas**
Beach
Cemetery (Christian)
Cemetery (Other)
Park
Forest
Reservation
Urban Area
Sportsground

**Transport**
✈ Airport
Cable Car/Funicular
Ⓟ Parking
Train/Railway
Tram

*Note: Not all symbols displayed above appear on the maps in this book*

## PLAN YOUR TRIP

Welcome to Ireland .......................... 7
Ireland Highlights ........................... 8
If You Like... .................................. 20
Need to Know ................................ 22
City Guide .....................................24
Ireland by Region ......................... 30
Ireland Classic Trips ..................... 32

## ON THE ROAD

**1** Iconic Ireland .................. 7 Days    35

**2** The Long Way Round ............ 14 Days    49

**3** Tip to Toe ....................... 10 Days    63

### DUBLIN & EASTERN IRELAND ........................... 77

**4** A Long Weekend Around Dublin ........ 3 Days    81

**5** East to West ...................... 7 Days    89

**6** The Boyne Valley ...................... 2 Days    97

**7** Ancient Ireland .................... 4 Days    105

# CONTENTS

**8** Monasteries, Mountains & Mansions ................ 3 Days  113

**9** Wicklow Mountains ............... 3 Days  121

**10** Carlow Back Roads ............ 3 Days  129

**11** Kilkenny's Treasures ................ 3 Days  137

**12** Wexford & Waterford ............... 5 Days  145

**13** Blackwater Valley Drive ......................... 2 Days  153

**14** Family Fun ............................. 3 Days  161

## CORK & SOUTHWEST IRELAND... 173

**15** Ring of Kerry ........................ 4 Days  177

**16** Dingle Peninsula ............. 3–4 Days  189

**17** Southwest Blitz ........................... 4 Days  199

**18** Southwestern Pantry ...................... 5 Days  211

**19** West Cork Villages .................... 7 Days  219

**20** Shannon River Route ........................ 4 Days  227

**21** The Holy Glen ..................... 2–3 Days  235

Belfast & the North of Ireland
p313

Galway & the West of Ireland
p245

Dublin & Eastern Ireland
p77

Cork & Southwest Ireland
p173

# Contents cont.

## GALWAY & THE WEST OF IRELAND ........ 245

**22** Best of the West ................. 6 Days  249

**23** Musical Landscapes ............. 5 Days  261

**24** Mountains & Moors ....................... 6 Days  271

**25** Loughs of the West ............. 3–4 Days  279

**26** North Mayo & Sligo ........................ 4 Days  287

**27** Sligo Surrounds ................ 5 Days  295

**28** County Clare ......................... 7 Days  303

## BELFAST & THE NORTH OF IRELAND ....... 313

**29** The North in a Nutshell .............. 10 Days  317

**30** Delights of Donegal .................... 7 Days  329

**31** Inishowen Peninsula ................. 3 Days  337

**32** Northwest on Adrenalin ................. 4 Days  345

**33** From Bangor to Derry .................... 4 Days  353

**34** The Antrim Coast ......................... 3 Days  361

# ROAD TRIP ESSENTIALS

**Ireland Driving Guide** ................... 373

**Ireland Travel Guide** ..................... 378

**Language** ..................................... 386

**Index** ........................................... 389

**Aran Islands** Castle ruins on Inisheer

**Kenmare River** A boat floats on tranquil waters

# WELCOME TO
# IRELAND

Your main reason for visiting? Most likely to experience Ireland of the postcard – the captivating peninsulas of the southwest, the brooding expanse of Connemara and the dramatic wildness of County Donegal. It can also be uncovered in the lakelands of Counties Leitrim and Roscommon and the undulating hills of the sunny southeast.

Scenery, history, culture, bustling cosmopolitanism and the stillness of village life – you'll find all of these along the 34 road trips in this book. You'll visit blockbuster attractions and replicate famous photo ops. But there are plenty of surprises too – and they're all within easy reach of each other.

Whether you want to drive through the wildest terrain or sample great food while hopping between spa treatments, we've got something for you. And if you only have time for one trip, make it one of our eight Classic Trips, which take you to the very best of Ireland.

# IRELAND HIGHLIGHTS

**Classic Trip**

**2** **The Long Way Round**
Ireland's crenellated coastlines, vibrant port cities and island treasures. **14 DAYS**

**Classic Trip**

**29** **The North in a Nutshell**
Big cities, big-name sights, hidden beaches, tiny islands – an epic drive. **10 DAYS**

**Classic Trip**

**22** **Best of the West**
Enjoy epic landscapes on this tour of Ireland's best westerly sights. **6 DAYS**

**Iconic Ireland**
The best of Ireland's five-star cultural and natural attractions.  **7 DAYS**

*Classic Trip* **1**

**Tip to Toe**
The ultimate pan-Irish experience.  **10 DAYS**

*Classic Trip* **3**

**Southwest Blitz**
The best of the southwest coast, countryside and cosmopolitan city life.  **4 DAYS**

*Classic Trip* **17**

**Musical Landscapes**
A ride round County Clare's hottest trad music spots.  **5 DAYS**

*Classic Trip* **23**

**Ring of Kerry**
Pass jaw-dropping scenery as you circumnavigate the Iveragh Peninsula.  **4 DAYS**

*Classic Trip* **15**

*ATLANTIC OCEAN*

*St George's Channel*

50 km
25 miles

9

Ireland's best sights and experiences, and the road trips that will take you there.

# IRELAND
## HIGHLIGHTS
★

### Dublin

It's likely that your Irish visit will begin and end in Dublin, Ireland's capital and largest city by far. On **Trip 1: Iconic Ireland**, you can visit some of the city's best-known attractions, while **Stretch Your Legs: Dublin** gives you a chance to explore the city in greater depth, especially its rich Georgian heritage.

**Trips** 1 2 5 14

**Dublin** Ha'penny Bridge over the River Liffey

**Connemara** Accommodation on the shore of Kylemore Lake

# Connemara

A kaleidoscope of rusty bogs, lonely valleys and enticing hamlets laid across a patchwork of narrow country roads punctuated by the odd inviting country pub: welcome to Connemara, yours to discover on **Trip 24: Mountains & Moors**. Connemara evokes the very best of Irish scenery and the country itself, unsullied by centuries of history and transformation.

Trips

# Galway

Storied, sung-about and snug, Galway is one of Ireland's great pleasures. So much so that it's full of people who came, saw and still haven't managed to leave. Wander the tuneful streets and refuel in any of the city's great pubs on **Trip 23: Musical Landscapes** – it *could* keep you busy for a whole month of nights out.

Trips

# Belfast

There's far more to Belfast than its troubled past, as you can discover for yourself on **Trip 29: The North in a Nutshell**. But you can learn about Northern Ireland's recent history on our walking tour, **Stretch Your Legs: Belfast**, on which you'll explore the political murals and peace lines of West Belfast's divided neighbourhoods of the Falls and the Shankill.

Trips

**Connemara** Boats moored at Roundstone Harbour

## BEST ROADS FOR DRIVING

**R560, County Kerry** Drive the spectacular Connor Pass. **Trips** 1 16 22

**R115 (Old Military Rd), County Wicklow** The loveliest, loneliest road of the east. **Trip** 9

**Ring of Kerry** Ireland's most famous circular route. **Trips** 1 2 15 17

**Beara Peninsula** Magnificent views and lovely villages. **Trips** 1 2 19 22

**N59, Connemara** Mountains, moors and broody boglands. **Trips** 22 24 25 26

# Cork

An appealing waterfront location, some of the best food you'll find anywhere in the country, lively craic and a liberal, youthful and cosmopolitan dynamic make Ireland's second city, Cork, hard to resist. Foodies can taste the best of the city's (and county's) eateries and markets on **Trip 18: Southwestern Pantry**, and take in the key sites on our designated walking tour.

**Trips** 2 17 18 22

13

**Glendalough** Round tower and the ruins of St Kevin's settlement

# Glendalough

Once one of Ireland's most dynamic universities, the monastic ruins of Glendalough, founded by St Kevin as a spiritual retreat, are now among the country's most beautiful ruined sites. They're easily visited from Dublin on **Trip 4: A Long Weekend Around Dublin**. The remains of the settlement (including an intact round tower), coupled with the stunning scenery, are unforgettable, and are the perfect spot for a mountain hike.

Trips  **4** **7** **9**

## BEST TOWNS FOR TRADITIONAL MUSIC

**Dingle** A handful of bars with nightly music. **Trips** **1** **2** **16** **22**

**Miltown Malbay** Come for the Willie Clancy Festival in July. **Trip** **23**

**Ennis** The capital of music country. **Trips** **1** **23** **28**

**Doolin** Three pubs host some of the country's best sessions. **Trips** **2** **5** **23**

**Dingle Peninsula** Slea Head

**Rock of Cashel** The Rock of Cashel overlooks the ruins of Hore Abbey

# Dingle Peninsula

It seems that everybody wants to go to Dingle – join them on **Trip 16: Dingle Peninsula**. Luckily, this is one place that transcends the crowds with its allure. Sure you may be stuck behind a bus, but this rocky, striated land has a history as compelling as its beauty, not to mention prehistoric monuments, scenic spots and fabulous pubs.

Trips  1 2 16 22

# Brú na Bóinne

The vast neolithic necropolis of Brú na Bóinne in County Meath is 600 years older than the pyramids, 1000 years older than Stonehenge, and designed with a mathematical precision that would have confounded the ancient Greeks. You can visit on **Trip 7: Ancient Ireland**, especially to see the simulated winter sunrise that illuminates the main burial chamber.

Trips 4 6 7 14

# Rock of Cashel

The Rock of Cashel, a highlight of **Trip 21: The Holy Glen**, never ceases to startle when you first see it rising from the otherwise mundane plains of Tipperary. And this ancient fortified home of kings is just the tip of the iceberg; moody ruins are hidden in the surrounding green expanse, set neatly atop a rock overlooking pretty Cashel town.

Trips 7 21 3

# Ring of Kerry

Yes, it's popular. And yes, it's always choked with bus traffic, especially in summer. But there are about 1000 reasons why the Ring of Kerry is the tourist charm bracelet it is – and gets its own designated itinerary (**Trip 15: Ring of Kerry**). You'll find most of the reasons around the Iveragh Peninsula just west of Killarney; do it anti-clockwise unless you want to get stuck behind a caravan of tour buses!

**Trips** `1` `2` `15` `17`

# Giant's Causeway

The grand geological flourish of the Giant's Causeway is Northern Ireland's most popular attraction and one of the world's iconic natural wonders. Clamber across the 40,000 unique hexagonal basalt columns on **Trip 34: The Antrim Coast**, then decide whether you prefer the scientific explanation or the far more colourful legend that explains them.

**Trips** `2` `29` `33` `34`

(left) **Ring of Kerry** View of the Ring of Kerry from near Waterville

(below) **Giant's Causeway** Fused hexagonal columns of basalt

# Cliffs of Moher

Bathed in the golden glow of the late afternoon sun, the iconic Cliffs of Moher are one of the west coast's splendours. Witnessed from a boat bobbing below or from dry land as you would on **Trip 1: Iconic Ireland**, the towering stone faces have a jaw-dropping, dramatic beauty that's enlivened by scores of sea birds, including cute little puffins.

**Trips**

## BEST ANCIENT RUINS

**Carrowkeel** A megalithic tomb atop a scenic hill. **Trip** `27`

**Dún Aengus** A prehistoric fort abutting a sea-lashed cliff. **Trips** `2` `4` `23` `28`

**Clonmacnoise** Ireland's most important monastic university. **Trips** `5` `7` `8`

**Loughcrew Cairns** A 'forgotten' neolithic passage grave. **Trip** `7`

**Cruachan Aí** Europe's most significant Celtic royal site. **Trip** `7`

19

# IF YOU LIKE...

**Paragliding** Killiney Hill, near Dublin

## Ancient Monuments

Ireland is old – as in, older-than-the-pyramids old. Everywhere you go you can find a historic castle, the ruins of a 1500-year-old monastery or a collection of stones with faded carvings done by prehistoric people so ancient that archaeologists talk of eras rather than centuries.

**7 Ancient Ireland** The big stars of Ireland's ancient past.

**16 Dingle Peninsula** Slea Head is littered with prehistoric monuments.

**21 The Holy Glen** Visit County Tipperary's collection of monastic treasures.

**27 Sligo Surrounds** A wealth of prehistoric sites within easy reach of each other.

## Great Views

What do you fancy? A jagged coastline pounded by the waves? A desolate mountain range with a brooding, low-slung sky? Or perhaps an emerald valley stretched out below you, dotted with clusters of sheep and criss-crossed by stone walls? In Ireland, keep your camera close by.

**9 Wicklow Mountains** Mountain passes and glacial valleys are the scenic highlights.

**15 Ring of Kerry** Virtually every corner on this iconic drive reveals a postcard view.

**24 Mountains & Moors** A trip through broody, beautiful Connemara.

**30 Delights of Donegal** The stunning scenery of Ireland's northwestern corner.

## Hidden Treasures

Exploring the best of Ireland is not just about five-star attractions or the bustling crowds that won't get out of your perfect picture. Beyond the tourist chart-toppers there's a host of sights and towns that have escaped mass attention, but are just as worthy of your time.

**10 Carlow Back Roads** A marvellous county untouched by mass tourism.

**20 Shannon River Route** Ireland's mightiest river has a host of little-visited delights.

**25 Loughs of the West** The west's lesser-known backwaters.

**31 Inishowen Peninsula** Remote and hard to get to, but worth the effort.

**Live music** Musicians perform at a traditional Irish pub

## Traditional Music

Western Europe's most vibrant folk music is kept alive by musicians who ply their craft (and are plied with drink) in impromptu and organised sessions in pubs and music houses throughout the country; even the 'strictly for tourists' stuff will feature excellent performances.

**16 Dingle Peninsula**
Forget yourself in one of Dingle's music pubs.

**23 Musical Landscapes**
The best of the west's pubs, venues and music festivals.

**29 The North in a Nutshell** Visit the home of Enya, Clannad and a whole musical movement.

## Good Food

Throughout Ireland, there is abundant evidence of the foodie revolution as local chefs and producers combine international experience with the kind of meals that have always been taken for granted on well-run Irish farms.

**12 Wexford & Waterford**
Parts of west Waterford are a gourmet heaven.

**18 Southwestern Pantry** County Cork is the flag bearer of the foodie revolution.

**19 West Cork Villages**
Virtually every village in West Cork boasts a good restaurant.

**22 Best of the West** From Sligo to Kerry, there's great grub to be had.

## An Adrenalin Rush

Ireland has myriad ways for you to work up a sweat, from chasing chickens around a farmyard to paragliding off the edge of a mountain. There are plenty of family-friendly activities throughout the country, from heritage museums to ziplines across a forest canopy.

**14 Family Fun** From working farms to adventure centres – fun for the whole family.

**16 Dingle Peninsula**
Scuba diving and surfing in the beautiful southwest.

**32 Northwest on Adrenalin** Get breathless in the sea and up a mountain.

# NEED TO KNOW

## CURRENCY
Republic of Ireland: Euro (€);
Northern Ireland: pound
sterling (£)

## LANGUAGES
English, Irish

## VISAS
Generally not required by
citizens of Europe, Australia,
New Zealand, USA and
Canada; see p385 for details.

## FUEL
Petrol (gas) stations are
everywhere, but are limited
on motorways. Expect
to pay €1.30 per litre of
unleaded (€1.20 for diesel)
in the Republic and £1.15
for unleaded and diesel in
Northern Ireland.

## RENTAL CARS
Avis (www.avis.ie)
Europcar (www.europcar.ie)
Hertz (www.hertz.ie)
Thrifty (www.thrifty.ie)

## IMPORTANT NUMBERS
Country code (☏ 353
Republic of Ireland,
☏ 44 Northern Ireland)
Emergencies (☏ 999)
Roadside Assistance
(☏ 1800 667 788 Republic
of Ireland, ☏ 0800 887 766
Northern Ireland)

## Climate

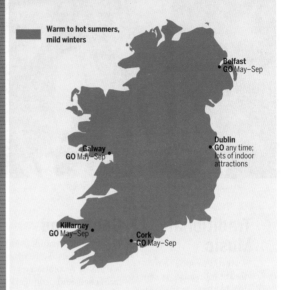

Warm to hot summers,
mild winters

Belfast
GO May–Sep

Dublin
GO any time;
lots of indoor
attractions

Galway
GO May–Sep

Killarney
GO May–Sep

Cork
GO May–Sep

- - - - - - - - - - - - - - - - - - - - - - - - - - - - - - -

## When to Go

### High Season (Jun–mid-Sep)
» Weather at its best

» Accommodation rates at their highest (especially in August)

» Tourist peak in Dublin, Kerry, southern and western coasts

### Shoulder Season (Easter to May, mid-Sep to Oct)
» Weather often good; sun and rain in May, 'Indian summers' and often warm in September

» Summer crowds and accommodation rates drop off

### Low Season (Nov–Feb)
» Reduced opening hours from October to Easter; some destinations close

» Cold and wet weather throughout the country; fog can reduce visibility

» Big-city attractions operate as normal

## Daily Costs

### Budget: Less than €60
» Dorm bed: €12–20
» Cheap meal in cafe or pub: €6–12
» Pint: €4.50–5 (more expensive in cities)

### Midrange: €60–120
» Double room in hotel or B&B: €80–180 (more expensive in Dublin)
» Main course in midrange restaurant: €12–25
» Car rental (per day): from €25–45

### Top End: More than €120
» Four-star hotel stay: from €150
» Three-course meal in good restaurant: around €50
» Top round of golf (midweek): from €90

## Eating

**Restaurants** From cheap cafes to Michelin-starred feasts, covering all kinds of cuisines.

**Cafes** For all-day breakfasts, sandwiches and basic dishes.

**Pubs** Pub grub ranges from toasted sandwiches to carefully crafted dishes.

**Hotels** All hotel restaurants take non-guests. They're a popular option in the countryside.

Eating price indicators represent the cost of a main dish:

| Republic/Northern Ireland | |
| --- | --- |
| €/£ | <€12/£12 |
| €€/££ | €12–25/ £12–20 |
| €€€/£££ | >€25/£20 |

## Sleeping

**Hotels** From chain hotels to Norman castles – with prices to match.

**B&Bs** Standards vary, but the B&B is the bedrock of Irish accommodation.

**Hostels** Feature clean dorms and wi-fi. Some have laundry and kitchen facilities.

Sleeping price indicators represent the cost of a double room in high season:

| Republic/ Northern Ireland | |
| --- | --- |
| €/£ | <€80/£50 |
| €€/££ | €80–180/ £50–120 |
| €€€/£££ | >€180/£120 |

## Arriving in Ireland

### Dublin Airport

**Rental cars** The main rental agencies have offices at the airport.

**Taxis** Taxis to the city take 30 to 45 minutes and cost €20 to €25.

**Buses** Run every 10 to 15 minutes to the city centre (€7).

### Cork Airport

**Rental cars** There are car-hire desks for the main companies.

**Taxis** A taxi to/from town costs €20 to €25.

**Buses** Run every half hour between 6am and 10pm to the train station (€7.40).

### Dun Laoghaire Ferry Port

**DART** (Suburban rail); 25 minutes to the centre of Dublin.

**Buses** Take around 45 minutes to the centre of Dublin.

## Mobile Phones

Phones from most other countries work in Ireland but attract roaming charges. Local SIM cards cost from €10; SIM and basic handsets around €40.

## Internet Access

Most hotels, B&Bs, hostels, bars and restaurants offer free wi-fi access. Internet cafes charge up to €6/£5 per hour.

## Money

ATMs are widely available. Credit and debit cards can be used in most places, but check first.

## Tipping

Not obligatory, but 10% to 15% in restaurants; €1/£1 per bag for hotel porters.

## Useful Websites

**Entertainment Ireland** (www.entertainment.ie) Countrywide listings for every kind of entertainment.

**Failte Ireland** (www. discoverireland.ie) Official tourist board website – practical info and a huge accommodation database.

**Lonely Planet** (www. lonelyplanet.com/ireland) Destination information, hotel bookings, traveller forums and more.

**Northern Ireland Tourist Board** (www.nitb.com) Official tourist site.

For more, see Road Trip Essentials (p372).

# CITY GUIDE

## DUBLIN

Ireland's largest city by far is also its buzzing capital, with superb restaurants, world-class museums and more nightlife than you could ever use, from theatre to its 1000-plus pubs. Still an essential part of the city's social life, these watering holes are the best place to take Dublin's pulse.

**Dublin** Trinity College

## Getting Around

The one-way system makes driving in Dublin tricky; the traffic can make it a test of patience. You can walk pretty much anywhere in the compact city centre.

## Parking

Street parking is scarce and costly, except on Sundays, when you can park on single-yellow lines. Sheltered car parks (around €5 per hour) are your best bet if your hotel doesn't have a car park.

## Discover the Taste of Dublin

Temple Bar has the biggest concentration of restaurants, mostly mid-priced and often bland; the best options are on the streets on either side of Grafton St. Top-end spots are around Merrion Sq and Fitzwilliam Sq.

## Live Like a Local

Base yourself in a suburb immediately south of the city centre, such as Ballsbridge, Donnybrook or Ranelagh, to experience the best of the city's B&B culture. The boutiques immediately west of Grafton St are the best for browsing.

## Useful Websites

**Dublin Tourism** (www.visitdublin.com) Sights, accommodation bookings and discounts.

**Entertainment.ie** (www.entertainment.ie) Comprehensive listings of events and gigs.

**Lonely Planet** (www.lonelyplanet.com/ireland/dublin) Travel tips, accommodation and a travellers' forum.

## Trips Through Dublin 1 2 5 14

**For more, check out our city and country guides. www.lonelyplanet.com**

# TOP EXPERIENCES

**➡ Stroll the Elizabethan Cobbles of Trinity College**
Ireland's most famous university is also Dublin's most atmospheric bit of city-centre real estate; it's home to the *Book of Kells*.

**➡ Discover Ireland's Treasures**
The National Museum of Ireland is where you'll find the country's most complete collection of medieval gold work, Celtic design and iconic treasures dating back 2500 years.

**➡ Indulge Your Thespian Side**
From classic plays to experimental new works, the city's theatres have something for everyone.

**➡ Saunter Through Georgian Squares**
The Georgian gems of St Stephen's Green and Merrion Sq are the best spots to catch a bit of urban R&R.

**➡ Get to Grips with Irish History**
The tour of Kilmainham Gaol is a hard-hitting exploration of the country's troubled past.

**➡ Tap into Your Inner Victorian Botanist**
Opened by Dr David Livingstone, the Natural History Museum, aka the 'dead zoo', has preserved its 19th-century spirit – as well as some two million stuffed animals.

**➡ Grab a Pint in a Traditional Pub**
There's nowhere better to sample a pint of Guinness – the 'black stuff' or 'liquid gold' – than in one of the city's many traditional pubs.

**CITY GUIDE**

Galway Shoppers at Galway Market

# GALWAY

Ireland's most bohemian burg has long celebrated difference, which accounts for its vibrant arts scene, easygoing pace and outstanding nightlife. Old-fashioned pubs with traditional sessions, theatres hosting experimental works, designated music venues in thrall to the heartfelt outpourings of the singer-songwriter... It's just another night in Galway.

## Getting Around

Traffic in and out of the city centre is a major issue during peak hours. The one-way system and network of pedestrianised streets can make getting around a little tricky.

## Parking

Parking throughout Galway's streets is metered. There are several multistorey and pay-and-display car parks around town.

## Discover the Taste of Galway

Seafood is Galway's speciality, be it fish and chips, ocean-fresh chowder or salmon cooked to perfection. Galway Bay oysters star on many menus. Pedestrianised Quay St is lined with restaurants aimed at the tourist throngs.

## Live Like a Local

Base yourself in the city centre so you can take full advantage of the city's tightly packed attractions. The west side, on the far side of the River Corrib, is where you'll find the best concentration of eateries, classic pubs and music venues.

## Useful Websites

**Discover Ireland** (www. discoverireland.ie) Sights, accommodation bookings and discounts.

**Galway Pub Guide** (www. galwaycitypubguide.com) Comprehensive guide to the heaving scene.

**Galway Tourism** (www. galwaytourism.ie) Local tourist information.

## Trips Through Galway

**Belfast** Inside a traditional pub

# BELFAST

Vibrant, confident and fascinating – not words that immediately jump to mind when imagining Belfast. But Northern Ireland's largest city has worked hard to get rid of its reputation as a violence-scarred protagonist of the news, and now offers great museums, fine dining and a wealth of shopping to go with its rich history.

## Getting Around

Belfast is easy enough to drive in, with a good road network and signposting enabling you to get where you want to go.

## Parking

For on-street parking between 8am and 6pm Monday to Saturday, you'll need to buy a ticket from a machine. For longer periods, head for one of the many multistorey car parks that are dotted around the city centre.

## Discover the Taste of Belfast

In the evening, the liveliest part of the city centre stretches south of Donegall Sq to Shaftesbury Sq. During the day, many pubs, cafes and restaurants do a roaring trade. South Belfast is also where you'll find some terrific restaurants.

## Live Like a Local

Most of Belfast's budget and midrange accommodation is south of the centre, in the university district around Botanic Ave, University Rd and Malone Rd. This area is also crammed with good-value restaurants and pubs, and is mostly within a 20-minute walk of City Hall.

## Useful Websites

**Belfast City Council** (www. belfastcity.gov.uk/events) Information on a wide range of organised events.

**Belfast Music** (www. belfastmusic.org) Online gig listings.

**Belfast Welcome Centre** (www.gotobelfast.com) Sights, accommodation bookings and discounts.

**Great Belfast Food** (www. greatbelfastfood.com) Stay up-to-date with Belfast's foodie scene.

## Trips Through Belfast

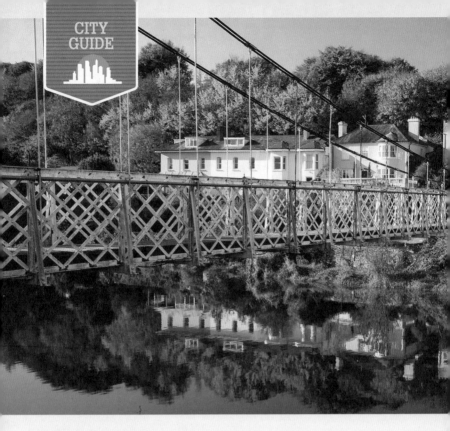

# CORK

Ireland's second city is second only in size; in every other respect it considers itself equal to Dublin (or even better). Great restaurants, top-class galleries and a vibrant pub scene lend credence to its claim, while the people are as friendly and welcoming as you'll find anywhere.

## Getting Around

Cork's compact centre and easy-to-follow one-way system makes driving a relatively hassle-free experience.

## Parking

Streetside parking requires scratch-card parking discs (€2 per hour), obtained from the tourist office and some newsagencies. There are several signposted car parks around the central area, with charges of €2 per hour and €12 overnight.

**Cork** Daly's Bridge over the River Lee

## TOP EXPERIENCES

### ➡ Look Upon Cork
Wander up through Shandon and explore the galleries, antique shops and cafes of the city's prettiest neighbourhood, perched on a hill on the northern side of town.

### ➡ Eyeball the Best of Irish Art
The Crawford Municipal Art Gallery is small, but it's packed with great art by such top Irish names as Jack B Yeats, Nathaniel Hone, Sir John Lavery and Mainie Jellett.

### ➡ Indulge Your Tastebuds
Cork's foodie scene is made famous by its collection of terrific restaurants, but don't forget the splendid Victorian English Market.

### ➡ Have a Night on the Town
Atmospheric old pubs, buzzing music venues and a well-respected theatre scene make for a memorable night out.

## Discover the Taste of Cork
The narrow pedestrianised streets north of St Patrick's St are packed with cafes and restaurants, and the place hops day and night. The English Market is *the* place for great produce and outstanding daytime eats.

## Live Like a Local
Base yourself in town, as close to St Patrick's St and the South Mall as possible. Once you've exhausted the warren of streets between these two locations, venture west across the Lee and wander up to Shandon, where Corkonians regularly take refuge from the city below.

## Useful Websites
**Cork City Tourism** (www.cometocork.com) Sights, accommodation bookings and discounts.

**People's Republic of Cork** (www.peoplesrepublicofcork.com) Indie guide to what's on in Cork.

**WhazOn?** (www.whazon.com) Comprehensive entertainment listings.

## Trips Through Cork 2 17 18 22

# IRELAND
## BY REGION

Framed by rugged coastlines and peppered with breathtaking scenery, Ireland's compact driving circuit could keep you busy for months. Here's your guide to each region and road trips for the best experiences.

## Galway & the West of Ireland (p245)

Connemara has a lyrical beauty that drives artists wild, while County Clare is the spiritual home of traditional Irish music. Between them are the Aran Islands, the very definition of windswept and remote. And don't forget Galway City, Ireland's colourful bohemian capital.

**Get musical on Trip**  23

**Go wild in Connemara on Trip**  24

## Cork & Southwest Ireland (p173)

The Ireland of the postcard and tourist brochures, the southwest's abundance of stunning drives and iconic scenery will leave you spoilt for choice. From the country's most popular drives to untrodden back roads meandering through the region's gourmet heartland, *this* is the scenic Ireland you came to see.

**See the best of Cork on Trip**  15

**Taste gourmet goodness on Trip**  18

## Belfast & the North of Ireland (p313)

Beyond the best-known driving routes along the Antrim Coast with its cluster of world-class attractions, the north of Ireland is as delightful as it is surprising, whether you're snaking up a meandering mountain pass in Donegal or exploring the fascinating cities of Belfast and Derry/Londonderry.

**Go mountain wild on Trip**  30

**Take giant footsteps on Trip** 34

## Dublin & Eastern Ireland (p77)

A capital city with all the attractions deserving of the title, Dublin can be explored on foot before you set off to experience its surrounding counties. Within an hour's drive of Dublin there are eye-catching Palladian mansions, remote mountain passes cutting through gorgeous glacial valleys, and prehistoric monuments of world renown.

**Explore ancient Ireland on Trip**  7

**Get mountain fever on Trip**  9

# IRELAND
## Classic Trips

CARL BRUEMMER/DESIGN PICS/GETTY IMAGES ©

23

GEORGE MUNDAY/GETTY IMAGES ©

15

## What is a Classic Trip?

All the trips in this book show you the best of Ireland, but we've chosen eight as our all-time favourites. These are our Classic Trips – the ones that lead you to the best of the iconic sights, the top activities and the unique Irish experiences. Turn the page to see our cross-regional Classic Trips, and look out for more Classic Trips on the following pages:

**1** Iconic
Ireland ................ 7 Days   34

**2** The Long
Way Round ......... 14 Days   48

**3** Tip to
Toe .................... 10 Days   62

**15** Ring of
Kerry .................... 4 Days   176

**17** Southwest
Blitz ..................... 4 Days   198

**22** Best of
the West .............. 6 Days   248

**23** Musical
Landscapes ......... 5 Days   260

**29** The North
in a Nutshell ....... 10 Days   316

Above: Music session in a traditional pub
Left: Ross Castle

# Classic Trip

# Iconic Ireland

**1**

*This trip gives you a glimpse of the very best Ireland has to offer, including the country's most famous attractions, most spectacular countryside, and most popular towns and villages.*

## TRIP HIGHLIGHTS

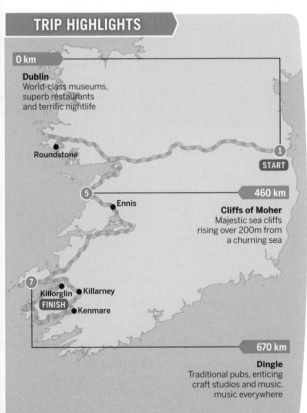

**0 km**

**Dublin**
World-class museums, superb restaurants and terrific nightlife

**Roundstone**

**START** ①

**5**

**Ennis**

**460 km**

**Cliffs of Moher**
Majestic sea cliffs rising over 200m from a churning sea

**7**
**Killorglin** • **Killarney**
**FINISH**
• **Kenmare**

**670 km**

**Dingle**
Traditional pubs, enticing craft studios and music, music everywhere

**7 DAYS**
**959KM / 596 MILES**

### GREAT FOR...

### BEST TIME TO GO

April to September, for the long days and best weather.

### 📷 ESSENTIAL PHOTO

The Lakes of Killarney from Ladies' View on the Ring of Kerry.

### ✓ BEST TWO DAYS

The Connemara peninsula and the Ring of Kerry.

**Dingle Peninsula** Minard Beach

35

## Classic Trip

# 1 Iconic Ireland

Every time-worn truth about Ireland will be found on this trip: the breathtaking scenery of stone-walled fields and wave-dashed cliffs; the picture-postcard villages and bustling towns; the ancient ruins that have stood since before history was written. The trip begins in Ireland's storied, fascinating capital and transports you to the wild west of Galway and Connemara before taking you south to the even wilder folds of County Kerry.

**Clifden** 4

p38 R341 3

**Roundstone**

Aran Islands

*ATLANTIC OCEAN*

Donegal Point

Loop Head

*Mouth of the Shannon*

*Tralee Bay* Tralee

**Slea Head** 8 **Dingle** 7 N86 R561

**Portmagee & Valentia Island** Kells N70 **Killorglin** FINISH

**Kenmare** 12 Sneem N70

p44 Skellig Michael **Caherdaniel** 11

*Bantry Bay* 19

---

**TRIP HIGHLIGHT**

### 1 Dublin

World-class museums, superb restaurants and the best collection of entertainment in the country – there are plenty of good reasons why the capital is the ideal place to start your trip. Get some sightseeing in on a walking tour (p170) before 'exploring' at least one of the city's storied – if not historic – pubs.

Your top stop should be the grounds of **Trinity College** (☎01-896 1000; www.tcd.ie; ⊘ 8am-10pm), home to the gloriously illuminated Book of Kells. It's kept in the Old Library's stunning 65m **Long Room** (www.tcd.ie/ visitors/book-of-kells; East Pavilion, Library Colonnades, Trinity College; adult/student/ child €10/9/free; ⊘9.30am-5pm Mon-Sat, 9.30am-4.30pm Sun May-Sep, 9.30am-5pm Mon-Sat, noon-4.30pm Sun Oct-Apr; 🚇 all city centre).

✗ 🛏 p46, p60, p95, p167

**The Drive »** It's a 208km trip to Galway city across the country along the M6 motorway, which has little in terms of visual highlights beyond green fields, which get greener and a little more wild the further west you go. Twenty-four kilometres south of Athlone (about halfway) is a worthwhile detour to Clonmacnoise.

---

### 2 Galway City

The best way to appreciate Galway is to amble –

36

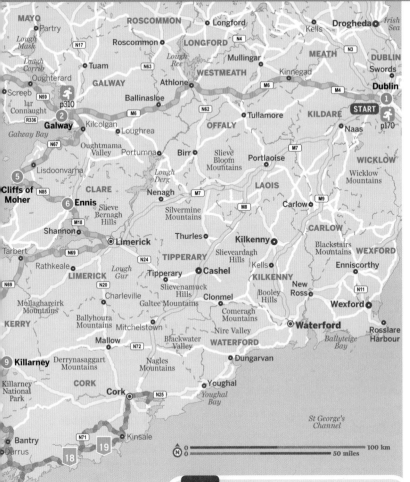

around Eyre Sq and
down Shop St towards
the Spanish Arch and the
River Corrib, stopping off
for a little liquid suste-
nance in one of the city's
classic old pubs. Top of
our list is **Tig Cóilí** (Mainguard St; ☺10.30am-midnight
Mon-Thu, to 12.30am Fri & Sat,
to 11pm Sun), a fire-engine-
red pub that draws

**LINK
YOUR
TRIP**

**18** **Southwestern
Pantry**

From Kenmare, it's a
42km drive south to
Durrus and the start of
the Southwestern Pantry
trip.

**19** **West Cork
Villages**

You can explore the
gorgeous villages of
West Cork from the
picturesque town of
Kinsale.

*Classic Trip*

them in with its two live *céilidh* (traditional music and dancing sessions) each day. A close second is the cornflower blue **Tigh Neachtain** (www.tigh neachtain.com; 17 Upper Cross St; ⏰10.30am-11.30pm Mon-Thu & Sun, 10.30am-12.30am Fri & Sat), known simply as Neachtain's (*nock*-tans) or Naughtons – stop and join the locals for a pint.

 p46, p74, p277

**The Drive** » The most direct route to Roundstone is to cut through Connemara along the N59, turning left on the Clifden Rd – a total of 76km. Alternatively, the 103km coastal route, via the R336 and R340, winds its way around small bays, coves and lovely seaside hamlets.

- - - - - - - - - - - -

### ❸ Roundstone

Huddled on a boat-filled harbour, Roundstone (Cloch na Rón) is one of Connemara's gems.

Colourful terrace houses and inviting pubs overlook the dark recess of Bertraghboy Bay, which is home to lobster trawlers and traditional *currachs* with tarred canvas bottoms stretched over wicker frames.

Just south of the village, in the remains of an old Franciscan monastery, is Malachy Kearns'. Kearns is Ireland's only full-time maker of traditional bodhráns (hand-held goatskin drums). Watch him work and buy a tin whistle, harp or booklet filled with Irish ballads; there's also a small free folk museum and a cafe.

**The Drive** » The 22km inland route from Roundstone to Clifden is a little longer, but the road is better (especially the N59) and the brown, barren beauty of Connemara is yours to behold. The 18km coastal route along the R341 brings you through more speckled landscape; to the south you'll have glimpses of the ocean.

 p277

- - - - - - - - - - - -

### ❹ Clifden

Connemara's 'capital', Clifden (An Clochán) is an appealing Victorian-era country town with an amoeba-shaped oval of streets offering evocative strolls. It presides over the head of the narrow bay where the River Owenglin tumbles into the sea. The surrounding countryside beckons you to walk through woods and above the shoreline.

❌ 🛏 p46

**The Drive** » It's 154km to the Cliffs of Moher; you'll have to backtrack through Galway city (take the N59) before turning south along the N67. This will take you through the unique striated landscape of the Burren, a moody, rocky and at times fearsome space accented with ancient burial chambers and medieval ruins.

- - - - - - - - - - - -

TRIP HIGHLIGHT

### ❺ Cliffs of Moher

Star of a million tourist brochures, the Cliffs of Moher (Aillte an Mothair, or Ailltreacha Mothair) are one of the most popular sights in Ireland.

The entirely vertical cliffs rise to a height of 203m, their edge falling away abruptly into the constantly churning sea. A series of heads, the dark limestone seems to march in a rigid formation that amazes, no matter how many times you look.

## DETOUR:
## THE SKY ROAD

**Start: ❹ Clifden**

If you head directly west from Clifden's Market Sq you'll come onto the Sky Road, a 12km route tracing a spectacular loop out to the township of Kingston and back to Clifden, taking in some rugged, stunningly beautiful coastal scenery en route. It's a cinch to drive, but you can also easily walk or cycle it.

**Skellig Michael** View to Little Skellig

# Classic Trip

## WHY THIS IS A CLASSIC TRIP
### FIONN DAVENPORT, WRITER

The loop from Dublin west to Galway and then south through Kerry into Cork explores all of Ireland's scenic heavy hitters. It's the kind of trip I'd make if I was introducing visiting friends to the very best Ireland has to offer, the kind of appealing appetiser that should entice them to come back and visit the country in greater depth.

Top: Staigue Fort
Left: Clifden
Right: The road between Kenmare and Killarney

PETE SEAWARD/LONELY PLANET ©

Such appeal comes at a price: crowds. This is check-off tourism big time and bus-loads come and go constantly in summer. A vast **visitor centre** (www.cliffsofmoher. ie; ⊙9am-9pm Jul & Aug, to 7.30pm June, to 7pm May & Sep, to 6.30pm Apr, to 6pm Mar & Oct, to 5pm Nov-Feb; admission to site adult/child €6/free) handles the hordes.

Like so many over-popular natural wonders, there's relief and joy if you're willing to walk for 10 minutes. Past the end of the 'Moher Wall' south, there's a trail along the cliffs to Hag's Head – few venture this far.

**The Drive »** The 39km drive to Ennis goes inland at Lahinch (famous for its world-class golf links); it's then 24km to your destination, through flat south Clare. Dotted with stone walls and fields, it's the classic Irish landscape.

ROBERT MCGRATH/GETTY IMAGES ©

### ⑥ Ennis

As the capital of a renowned music county, Ennis (Inis) is filled with pubs featuring trad music. In fact, this is the best reason to stay here. Where's best changes often; stroll the streets pub-hopping to find what's on any given night.

If you want to buy an authentic, well-made Irish instrument, pop into **Custy's Music Shop** (☎065-682 1727; www.custys music.com; Cook's Lane, off O'Connell St; ⊙10am-6pm Mon-Sat), which sells

fiddles and other musical items as well as giving general info about the local scene.

 p46, p269

**The Drive »** It's 186km to Dingle if you go via Limerick city, but only 142km if you go via the N68 to Killimer for the ferry across the Shannon estuary to Tarbert. The views get fabulous when you're beyond Tralee on the N86, especially if you take the 456m Connor Pass, Ireland's highest.

- - - - - - - - - - - - -

**TRIP HIGHLIGHT**

### ❼ Dingle Town

In summer, Dingle's hilly streets can be clogged with visitors, there's just no way around it; in other seasons, its authentic charms are all yours to savour. Many of Dingle's pubs double as shops, so you can enjoy Guinness and a singalong among such items as screws and nails, wellies and horseshoes.

 p47, p197, p259

**The Drive »** It's only 17km to Slea Head along the R559. The views – of the mountains to the north and the wild ocean to the south and west – are a big chunk of the reason you came to Ireland in the first place.

- - - - - - - - - - - - -

### ❽ Slea Head

Overlooking the mouth of Dingle Bay, Mt Eagle and the Blasket Islands, Slea Head has fine beaches, good walks and superbly preserved structures from Dingle's ancient past, including **beehive huts**, forts, inscribed stones and church sites. Dunmore Head is the westernmost point on the Irish mainland and the site of the wreckage in 1588 of two Spanish Armada ships.

The Iron Age **Dunbeg Fort** is a dramatic example of a promontory fortification, perched atop a sheer sea cliff about 7km southwest of Ventry on the road to Slea Head. The fort has four outer walls of stone. Inside are the remains of a house and a beehive hut, as well as an underground passage.

**The Drive »** The 88km to Killarney will take you through Annascaul (home to a pub once owned by Antarctic explorer Tom Crean) and Inch (whose beach is seen in *Ryan's Daughter*). At Castlemaine, turn south towards Miltown then take the R563 to Killarney.

## LOCAL KNOWLEDGE: ENNIS' BEST TRAD SESSION PUBS

**Cíaran's Bar** (1 Francis St; ⊙10.30am-11.30pm Mon-Thu, to 12.30am Fri & Sat, 12.30-11pm Sun) Slip into this small place by day and you can be just another geezer pondering a pint. At night there's usually trad music. Bet you wish you had a copy of the Guinness mural out front!

**Brogan's** (24 O'Connell St; ⊙10.30am-11.30pm Mon-Thu, to 12.30am Fri & Sat, 12.30-11pm Sun) On the corner of Cooke's Lane, Brogan's sees a fine bunch of musicians rattling even the stone floors from about 9pm Monday to Thursday, plus even more nights in summer.

**Cruise's Pub** (Abbey St; ⊙noon-2am) There are trad music sessions most nights from 9.30pm.

**Poet's Corner Bar** (Old Ground Hotel, O'Connell St; ⊙11am-11.30pm Mon-Thu, 11-12.30am Fri & Sat, noon-11pm Sun) This old pub often has massive trad sessions on Fridays.

**O'Dea's** (66 O'Connell St; ⊙10.30am-11.30pm Mon-Thu, to 12.30am Fri & Sat, 12.30-11pm Sun) Unchanged since at least the 1950s, this plain-tile-fronted pub is a hideout for local musicians serious about their trad sessions. Gets some of Clare's best.

**Dingle Peninsula** Sheep pasture

### 9 Killarney

Beyond its proximity to lakes, waterfalls, woodland and moors dwarfed by 1000m-plus peaks, Killarney has many charms of its own as well as being the gateway to the Ring of Kerry, perhaps *the* outstanding highlight of many a visit to Ireland.

Besides the breathtaking views of the mountains and glacial lakes, highlights of the 10,236-hectare Killarney National Park include Ireland's only wild herd of native red deer, the country's largest area of ancient oak woods and 19th-century Muckross House.

✕ ⊨ p47, p187, p197

The Drive ❯❯ It's 27km along the N71 to Kenmare, much of it through Killarney National Park with its magnificent views – especially Ladies' View (at 10km; much loved by Queen Victoria's ladies-in-waiting) and, 5km further on, Moll's Gap, a popular stop for photos and food.

### 10 Kenmare

Picturesque Kenmare carries its romantic reputation more stylishly

than does Killarney, and there is an elegance about its handsome central square and attractive buildings. It still gets very busy in summer, all the same. The town stands where the delightfully named Finnihy, Roughty and Sheen Rivers empty into Kenmare River. Kenmare makes a pleasant alternative to Killarney as a base for visiting the Ring of Kerry and the Beara Peninsula.

✕ 🛏 p47, p187, p209

**The Drive »** The 47km to Caherdaniel along the southern stretch of the Ring of Kerry duck in and out of view of Bantry Bay, with the marvellous Beara Peninsula to the south. Just before you reach Caherdaniel, a 4km detour north takes you to the rarely visited Staigue Fort, which dates from the 3rd or 4th century.

## ⑪ Caherdaniel

The big attraction here is **Derrynane National Historic Park** (☎ 066-947 5113; www.heritageireland. ie; ⏱10.30am-6pm Apr-Sep, 10am-5pm Wed-Sun mid-Mar–end Mar & Oct, 10am-4pm Sat & Sun Nov; adult/child €4/2), the family home

## DETOUR:
### SKELLIG MICHAEL

**Start: ⑫ Portmagee & Valentia Island**

The jagged, 217m-high rock of **Skellig Michael** (www.heritageireland.ie; ⏱mid-May–Sep) (Archangel Michael's Rock; like St Michael's Mount in Cornwall and Mont Saint Michel in Normandy) is the larger of the two Skellig Islands and a Unesco World Heritage Site. It looks like the last place on earth where anyone would try to land – let alone establish a community – yet early Christian monks survived here from the 6th until the 12th or 13th century. Influenced by the Coptic Church (founded by St Anthony in the deserts of Egypt and Libya), their determined quest for ultimate solitude led them to this remote, wind-blown edge of Europe.

In 2015, Skellig Michael featured as Luke Skywalker's secret retreat in *Star Wars: The Force Awakens* (and will feature in subsequent episodes of the third trilogy), attracting a whole new audience to the island's dramatic beauty.

It's a tough place to get to, and requires care to visit, but is worth every effort. You'll need to do your best grizzly sea-dog impression ('Argh!') on the 12km crossing, which can be rough. There are no toilets or shelter, so bring something to eat and drink, and wear stout shoes and weatherproof clothing. Due to the steep (and often slippery) terrain and sudden wind gusts, it's not suitable for young children or people with limited mobility.

Be aware that the island's fragility requires limits on the number of daily visitors. The 15 boats are licensed to carry no more than 12 passengers each, for a maximum of 180 people at any one time. It's wise to book ahead in July and August, bearing in mind that if the weather's bad the boats may not sail (about two days out of seven). Trips usually run from Easter until September, depending, again, on the weather.

Boats leave Portmagee, Ballinskelligs and Derrynane at around 10am and return at 3pm, and cost about €45 per person. Boat owners generally restrict you to two hours on the island, which is the bare minimum to see the monastery, look at the birds and have a picnic. The crossing takes about 1½ hours from Portmagee, 35 minutes to one hour from Ballinskelligs and 1¾ hours from Derrynane.

of Daniel O'Connell, the campaigner for Catholic emancipation. His ancestors bought the house and surrounding parkland, having grown rich on smuggling with France and Spain. It's largely furnished with O'Connell memorabilia, including the restored triumphal chariot in which he lapped Dublin after his release from prison in 1844.

**The Drive** ≫ Follow the N70 for about 18km and then turn left onto the R567, cutting through some of the wildest and most beautiful scenery on the peninsula, with the ragged outline of Skellig Michael never far from view. Turn left onto the R565; the whole drive is 35km long.

**Derrynane Estuary** Horseriding near Caherdaniel

## ⑫ Portmagee & Valentia Island

Portmagee's single street is a rainbow of colourful houses, and is much photographed. On summer mornings, the small pier comes to life with boats embarking on the choppy crossing to the Skellig Islands.

A bridge links Portmagee to 11km-long **Valentia Island** (Oileán Dairbhre), an altogether homier isle than the brooding Skelligs to the southwest. Like the Skellig Ring it leads to, Valentia is an essential, coach-free detour from the Ring of Kerry. Some lonely ruins are worth exploring.

Valentia was chosen as the site for the first transatlantic telegraph cable. When the connection was made in 1858, it put Caherciveen in direct contact with New York. The link worked for 27 days before failing, but went back into action years later.

The island makes an ideal driving loop. From April to October, there's a frequent, quick ferry trip at one end, as well as the bridge to Portmagee on the mainland at the other end.

**The Drive** ≫ On the 55km drive between Portmagee and Killorglin, keep the mountains to your right (south) and the sea – when you're near it – to your left (north). Twenty-four kilometres along is the unusual Glenbeigh Strand, a tendril of sand protruding into Dingle Bay with views of Inch Point and the Dingle Peninsula.

## ⑬ Killorglin

Killorglin (Cill Orglan) is a quiet enough town, but that all changes in mid-August, when the town erupts in celebration for Puck Fair, Ireland's best-known extant pagan festival.

First recorded in 1603, with hazy origins, this lively (read: boozy) festival is based around the custom of installing a billy goat (a poc, or puck), the symbol of mountainous Kerry, on a pedestal in the town, its horns festooned with ribbons. Other entertainment ranges from a horse fair and bonny baby competition to street theatre, concerts and fireworks; the pubs stay open until 3am.

Author Blake Morrison documents his mother's childhood here in *Things My Mother Never Told Me*.

# Eating & Sleeping

## Dublin

### ✕ 101 Talbot    Modern Irish €€

(www.101talbot.ie; 100-102 Talbot St; mains €17-24; ◷noon-3pm & 5-11pm Tue-Sat; ▢all city centre) This Dublin classic has expertly resisted every trendy wave and has been a stalwart of good Irish cooking since opening more than two decades ago. Its speciality is traditional meat-and-two-veg dinners, but with vague Mediterranean and even Middle Eastern influences: roast Wicklow venison with sweet potato, lentil and bacon cassoulet and a sensational Morccocan-style lamb tagine. Superb.

### 🛏 Number 31    Guesthouse €€€

(☎01-676 5011; www.number31.ie; 31 Leeson Close; s/d incl breakfast €200/240; P🤶; ▢all city centre) The city's most distinctive property is the former home of modernist architect Sam Stephenson, who successfully fused '60s style with 18th-century grace. Its 21 bedrooms are split between the retro coach house, with its coolly modern rooms, and the more elegant Georgian house, where rooms are individually furnished with tasteful French antiques and big comfortable beds. Gourmet breakfasts with kippers, homemade breads and granola are served in the conservatory.

## Galway City ➋

### ✕ Quays    Irish €€

(Quay St; mains lunch €11-14, dinner €17-22; ◷11am-10pm) This sprawling pub does a roaring business downstairs in its restaurant, which has hearty carvery lunches and more ambitious mains at night. The cold seafood platter stars the bounty from Galway Bay. Students on dates and out celebrating get rowdier as the pints and hours pass.

### 🛏 House Hotel    Hotel €€€

(☎091-538 900; www.thehousehotel.ie; Spanish Pde; r €140-220; P🤶) There's a hip and cool array of colour in the lobby at this smart and stylish boutique hotel. Public spaces contrast modern art with trad details and bold accents. Cat motifs abound. The 40 rooms are small but plush, with bright colour schemes and quality fabrics. Bathrooms ooze comfort.

## Clifden ➍

### ✕ Mitchell's    Seafood €€

(☎095-21867; www.mitchellsrestaurantclifden. com; Market St; lunch mains €7-15, dinner mains €17-28; ◷noon-10pm Mar-Oct) Seafood takes centre stage at this elegant spot. From a velvety chowder right through a long list of ever-changing and inventive specials, the produce of the surrounding waters is honoured. The wine list does the food justice. Lunch includes sandwiches and casual fare. Book for dinner.

### 🛏 Dolphin Beach    B&B €€

(☎095-21204; www.dolphinbeachhouse.com; Lower Sky Rd; s from €90, d €130-180, dinner €40; P🤶) This exquisite B&B, set amid some of Connemara's best coastal scenery, does everything right. The emphasis is on style, tranquillity, relaxation and gorgeous views, a formula that can be hard to tear yourself away from. It's 5km west of Clifden, tucked away off the Lower Sky Road.

## Ennis ➏

### ✕ Rowan Tree Cafe Bar    Mediterranean €€

(www.rowantreecafebar.ie; Harmony Row; mains €11-23; ◷10.30am-11pm; 🤶) There's nothing low rent about the excellent Med-accented fare served at this cafe-bar on the ground floor of the namesake hostel. The gorgeous main dining room has high ceilings and a wondrous old wooden floor from the 18th century; tables outside have river views. Ingredients are locally and organically sourced.

### 🛏 Old Ground Hotel                  Hotel €€

(☎065-682 8127; www.flynnhotels.com; O'Connell St; s/d from €120/150; P @ 🛜) A seasoned, charming and congenial space of polished floorboards, cornice-work, antiques and open fires, the lobby is always a scene: old friends sinking into sofas, deals cut at the tables, and ladies from the neighbouring church's altar society exchanging gossip over tea. Parts of this smart and rambling landmark date back to the 1800s. The 83 rooms vary greatly in size and decor – ask to inspect a few. On balmy days, retire to tables on the lawn.

## Dingle ⑦

### ✗ Idás                              Irish €€€

(☎066-915 0885; John St; mains €27-31; ⊙5.30-9.30pm Tue-Sun) Chef Kevin Murphy is dedicated to promoting the finest of Irish produce, much of it from Kerry, taking lamb and seafood and foraged herbs from the Dingle peninsula and creating delicately flavoured concoctions such as braised John Dory fillet with fennel dashi cream, pickled cucumber, wild garlic and salad burnet. An early-bird menu offers two/three courses for €24.50/28.50.

### ✗ Out of the Blue                Seafood €€€

(☎066-915 0811; www.outoftheblue.ie; The Wood; mains lunch €12.50-20, dinner €21-37; ⊙5-9.30pm Mon-Sat, 12.30-3pm & 5-9.30pm Sun) 'No chips', reads the menu of this funky blue-and-yellow, fishing-shack-style restaurant on the waterfront. Despite its rustic surrounds, this is one of Dingle's best restaurants, with an intense devotion to fresh local seafood (and only seafood); if they don't like the catch, they don't open. With seafood this good, who needs chips?

### 🛏 Pax House                         B&B €€

(☎066-915 1518; www.pax-house.com; Upper John St; d from €120; ⊙Mar-Nov; P @ 🛜) From its highly individual decor (including contemporary paintings) to the outstanding views over the estuary from room balconies and terrace, Pax House is a treat. Choose from less expensive hill-facing accommodation.

rooms that overlook the estuary, and two-room family suites opening onto the terrace. It's 1km southeast of the town centre.

## Killarney ⑨

### ✗ Brícin                              Irish €€

(www.bricin.com; 26 High St; mains €19-26; ⊙6-9pm Tue-Sat) Decorated with fittings from a convent, an orphanage and a school, this Celtic deco restaurant doubles as the town museum, with Jonathan Fisher's 18th-century views of the national park taking pride of place. Try the house speciality, boxty (traditional potato pancake). Two-/three-course dinner for €22/25 before 6.45pm.

### 🛏 Crystal Springs                    B&B €€

(☎064-663 3272; www.crystalspringsbb.com; Ballycasheen Cross, Woodlawn Rd; s/d €70/95; P 🛜) The timber deck of this wonderfully relaxing B&B overhangs the River Flesk, where trout anglers can fish for free. Rooms are richly furnished with patterned wallpapers and walnut timber; private bathrooms (most with spa baths) are huge. The glass-enclosed breakfast room also overlooks the rushing river. It's about a 15-minute stroll into town.

## Kenmare ⑩

### ✗ Horseshoe                      Pub Food €€

(☎064-664 1553; www.thehorseshoekenmare. com; 3 Main St; mains €14-26; ⊙kitchen 5-10pm Thu-Mon) Flower baskets brighten the entrance to this popular gastropub, which has a short but excellent menu that runs from Kenmare Bay mussels in creamy apple cider sauce to braised Kerry lamb on mustard mash.

### 🛏 Parknasilla Resort & Spa      Hotel €€€

(☎064-667 5600; www.parknasillaresort. com; Parknasilla; d/f/ste from €139/179/229; P @ 🛜 ⛱) This hotel has been wowing guests (including George Bernard Shaw) since 1895 with its pristine resort on the tree-fringed shores of the Kenmare River with views to the Beara Peninsula. From the modern, luxuriously appointed bedrooms to the top-grade spa, private 12-hole golf course and elegant restaurant, everything here is done just right. It's 3km southeast of Sneem.

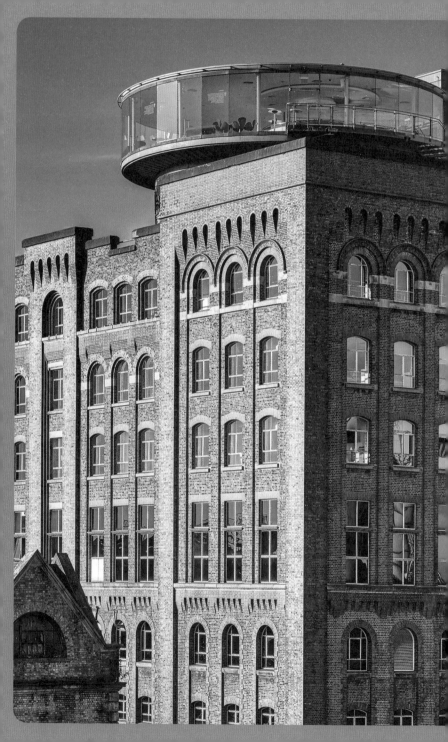

## Classic Trip

# The Long Way Round

**2**

*Why go in a straight line when you can perambulate at leisure?
This trip explores Ireland's jagged, scenic and spectacular edges;
a captivating loop that takes in the whole island.*

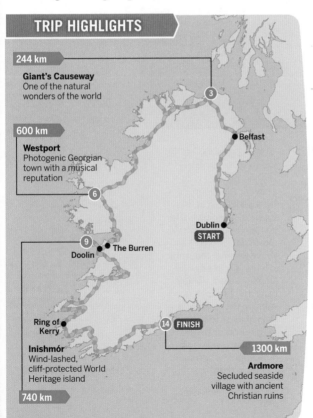

## TRIP HIGHLIGHTS

**244 km**

**Giant's Causeway**
One of the natural
wonders of the world

**600 km**

**Westport**
Photogenic Georgian
town with a musical
reputation

**Ring of Kerry**

**Inishmór**
Wind-lashed,
cliff-protected World
Heritage island

**740 km**

**Doolin**

**The Burren**

**Belfast**

**Dublin**
**START**

**FINISH**

**Ardmore**
Secluded seaside
village with ancient
Christian ruins

**1300 km**

**14 DAYS
1300KM /
807 MILES**

**GREAT FOR...**

**BEST TIME TO GO**

You'll have the best
weather (and crowds)
in June and August,
but September is ideal.

**ESSENTIAL
PHOTO**

Killahoey Beach from
the top of Horn Head.

**BEST TWO
DAYS**

Stops 7 to 9 allow you
to experience the very
best of the wild west,
including a day trip to
the Aran Islands.

# Classic Trip

## 2 The Long Way Round

There's a strong case to be made that the very best Ireland has to offer is closest to its jagged, dramatic coastlines: the splendid scenery, the best mountain ranges (geographically, Ireland is akin to a bowl, with raised edges) and most of its major towns and cities – Dublin, Belfast, Galway, Sligo and Cork. The western edge – between Donegal and Cork – corresponds to the Wild Atlantic Way driving route.

### 1 Dublin

From its music, art and literature to the legendary nightlife that has inspired those same musicians, artists and writers, Dublin has always known how to have fun and does it with deadly seriousness.

Should you tire of the city's more highbrow offerings, the **Guinness Storehouse** (www.guinness-storehouse.com; St James's Gate, South Market St; adult/student/child €18/16/6.50, connoisseur experience €48; ⏰9.30am-5pm Sep-Jun, to 7pm Jul & Aug; 🚌21A, 51B,

78, 78A, 123 from Fleet St, 🚃James's) is the most popular place to visit in town; a beer-lover's Disneyland and multi-media bells-and-whistles homage to the country's most famous export and the city's most enduring symbol. The old grain storehouse is a suitable cathedral in which to worship the black gold; shaped like a giant pint of Guinness, it rises seven impressive storeys high around a stunning central atrium.

🍴 🛏 p46, p60, p95, p167

SCOTLAND

Campbeltown

Giant's
Causeway ③

Ballycastle

North
Channel

**Dunfanaghy** ④
Rosses Bay
p53 N56
Letterkenny N13 N56

Buncrana
Coleraine
p52

Larne

**Derry** A2 A37 A26
Ballymena
A2

Strabane
Antrim

Donegal A5
Donegal Bay
Omagh

**Belfast** ②
Lisburn
Dromore

N15
Bundoran
Armagh
Banbridge
A1

**Sligo** ⑤
Enniskillen
Monaghan
Newry

Ballysadare
N17

Charlestown
N4
Longford
Dundalk
Dundalk Bay

Roscommon
N55
Mullingar
Drogheda
Irish Sea

Tuam
M6
Athlone
M6
M1

Ballinasloe
M6
Tullamore
Swords

N65
Birr
M7
Naas
**Dublin** ① START
Bray

Nenagh
M7
Portlaoise
Greystones

Thurles
Carlow
Wicklow

**Limerick**
③
**Kilkenny**
Arklow

Cashel
M9
M11

Tipperary
Enniscorthy

Clonmel
New Ross
**Wexford**

**Waterford** ◎
Rosslare Harbour

Mallow
M8
N25
13
Dungarvan
St George's Channel

Youghal
**Cork** 13 N25
14 **Ardmore**
Cobh
FINISH

ATLANTIC OCEAN

Ⓝ 0 ————————— 100 km
0 ————————— 50 miles

---

**The Drive ≫** It's 165km of motorway to Belfast – M1 in the Republic, A1 in Northern Ireland – but remember that the speed limit changes from kilometres to miles as you cross into the North.

- - - - - - - - - - -

## ② Belfast

Belfast is in many ways a brand-new city. Once lumped with Beirut, Baghdad and Bosnia as one of the four 'Bs' for travellers to avoid, in recent years it has pulled off a remarkable transformation from bombs-and-bullets pariah to a hip-hotels-and-hedonism party town.

The old shipyards on the Lagan continue to give way to the luxury apartments of the Titanic Quarter, whose centrepiece, the stunning, star-shaped edifice housing the **Titanic Belfast** (www.titanicbelfast.com; Queen's

## LINK YOUR TRIP

**③ Tip to Toe**

Kilmore Quay is 134km east of Ardmore, where you can pick up the toe part of this trip and do it in reverse.

**13 Blackwater Valley Drive**

From Ardmore, it's only 5km to Youghal, where you can explore the gorgeous valley of the Blackwater River.

Classic Trip

Rd; adult/child £17.50/7.25; ⏰9am-7pm Jun-Aug, to 6pm Apr, May & Sep, 10am-5pm Oct-Mar) centre, covering the ill-fated liner's construction here, has become the city's number-one tourist draw.

New venues keep popping up – already this decade historic **Crumlin Road Gaol** (📞028-9074 1501; www.crumlinroadgaol. com; 53-55 Crumlin Rd; day tour adult/child £8.50/6.50, evening tour £7.50/5.50; ⏰10am-5.30pm, last tour 4.30pm, evening tour 6pm) and **SS Nomadic** opened

to the public, and WWI warship **HMS Caroline** became a floating museum in 2016. They all add to a list of attractions that includes beautifully restored Victorian architecture, a glittering waterfront lined with modern art, a fantastic foodie scene and music-filled pubs.

If you're keen on learning more about the city's troubled history, take a walking tour of West Belfast.

🍴 🛏 p60, p359

**The Drive »** The *fastest* way to the causeway is to take the A26 north, through Ballymena, before turning off at Ballymoney – a total of 100km – but the longer (by 16km), more scenic route is

to take the A8 to Larne and follow the coast through handsome Cushendall and popular Ballycastle.

- - - - - - - - - - - -

TRIP HIGHLIGHT

### ❸ Giant's Causeway

When you first see it you'll understand why the ancients believed the causeway was not a natural feature. The vast expanse of regular, closely packed, hexagonal stone columns dipping gently beneath the waves looks for all the world like the handiwork of giants.

This spectacular rock formation – a national nature reserve and Northern Ireland's only Unesco World Heritage Site – is one of Ireland's

## DETOUR:
### GIANT'S CAUSEWAY TO BALLYCASTLE

**Start: ❸ Giant's Causeway**

Between the Giant's Causeway and Ballycastle lies the most scenic stretch of the Causeway Coast, with sea cliffs of contrasting black basalt and white chalk, rocky islands, picturesque little harbours and broad sweeps of sandy beach. It's best enjoyed on foot, following the 16.5km of waymarked **Causeway Coast Way** (www. walkni.com) between the Carrick-a-Rede car park and the Giant's Causeway, although the main attractions can also be reached by car or bus.

About 8km east of the Giant's Causeway is the meagre ruin of 16th-century **Dunseverick Castle**, spectacularly sited on a grassy bluff. Another 1.5km on is the tiny seaside hamlet of **Portbradden**, with half a dozen harbourside houses and the tiny, blue-and-white **St Gobban's Church**, said to be the smallest in Ireland. Visible from Portbradden and accessible via the next junction off the A2 is the spectacular **White Park Bay**, with its wide, sweeping sandy beach.

The main attraction on this stretch of coast is the famous (or notorious, depending on your head for heights) **Carrick-a-Rede Rope Bridge** (www.nationaltrust. org.uk; Ballintoy; adult/child £5.90/3; ⏰9.30am-7pm Apr-Aug, to 6pm Mar, Sep & Oct, to 3.30pm Nov-Feb). The 20m-long, 1m-wide bridge of wire rope spans the chasm between the sea cliffs and the little island of Carrick-a-Rede, swaying gently 30m above the rock-strewn water.

# DETOUR:
## HORN HEAD

**Start: ❹ Dunfanaghy**

Horn Head has some of Donegal's most spectacular coastal scenery and plenty of birdlife. Its dramatic quartzite cliffs, covered with bog and heather, rear over 180m high, and the view from their tops is heart-pounding.

The road circles the headland; the best approach by car is in a clockwise direction from the Falcarragh end of Dunfanaghy. On a fine day, you'll encounter tremendous views of Tory, Inishbofin, Inishdooey and tiny Inishbeg islands to the west; Sheep Haven Bay and the Rosguill Peninsula to the east; Malin Head to the northeast; and the coast of Scotland beyond. Take care in bad weather as the route can be perilous.

most impressive and atmospheric landscape features, but it can get very crowded. If you can, try to visit midweek or out of season to experience it at its most evocative. Sunset in spring and autumn is the best time for photographs.

Visiting the Giant's Causeway itself is free of charge but you pay to use the car park on a combined ticket with the **Giant's Causeway Visitor Experience** (☎028-2073 1855; www.nationaltrust.org. uk; adult/child with parking £9/4.50, without parking £7/3.25; ⊙9am-7pm Apr-Sep, to 6pm Feb, Mar & Oct, to 5pm Nov-Jan); parking-only tickets aren't available.

✗ p60

**The Drive »** Follow the A29 and A37 as far as Derry/Londonderry, then cross the invisible border into the Republic and take the N13 to Letterkenny before turning northwest along the N56 to Dunfanaghy. It's a total of 136km.

## ❹ Dunfanaghy

Huddled around the waterfront beneath the headland of Horn Head, Dunfanaghy's small, attractive town centre has a surprisingly wide range of accommodation and some of the finest dining options in the county's northwest. Glistening beaches, dramatic coastal cliffs, mountain trails and forests are all within a few kilometres.

✗ ⏸ p60, p327, p335

**The Drive »** The 145km south to Sligo town will take you back through Letterkenny (this stretch is the most scenic), after which you'll follow the N13 as far as Ballyshannon and then, as you cross into County Sligo, the N13 to Sligo town.

## ❺ Sligo Town

It's 100km to Westport, across the western edge of County Clare – as you follow the N17 (and the N5 once you pass Charlestown), the landscape is flat, the road flanked by fields, hedge rows and clusters of farmhouses. Castlebar, 15km before Westport, is a busy county town.

✗ ⏸ p60, p293, p301

**The Drive »** It's 100km to Westport, across the western edge of County Clare – as you follow the N17 (and the N5 once you pass Charlestown), the landscape is flat, the road flanked by fields, hedge rows and clusters of farmhouses. Castlebar, 15km before Westport, is a busy county town.

**TRIP HIGHLIGHT**

## ❻ Westport

There's a lot to be said for town planning, especially if 18th-century architect James Wyatt was the brains behind the job. Westport (Cathair na Mairt), positioned on the River Carrowbeg and the shores of Clew Bay, is easily Mayo's most beautiful town and a major tourist destination for visitors to this part of the country.

*Classic Trip*

## WHY THIS IS A CLASSIC TRIP
FIONN DAVENPORT, WRITER

Not only are you covering the spectacular landscapes of mountains and jagged coastlines of the Wild Atlantic Way, but you can also explore the modern incarnation of the country's earliest settlements, taking you from prehistoric monuments to bustling cities.

Top: Thatched cottage, Doolin
Left: Donkey, Inishmór
Right: Cliffs of Moher

JOHN ELK/GETTY IMAGES ©

It's a Georgian classic, its octagonal square and tidy streets lined with trees and handsome buildings, most of which date from the late 18th century.

✕ ⊨ p258, p293

**The Drive ››** Follow the N84 as far as the outskirts of Galway city – a trip of about 100km. Take the N18 south into County Clare. At Kilcolgan, turn onto the N67 and into the heart of the Burren.

## ❼ The Burren

The karst landscape of the Burren is not the green Ireland of postcards. But there are wildflowers in spring, giving the 560-sq-km Burren brilliant, if ephemeral, colour amid its austere beauty. Soil may be scarce, but the small amount that gathers in the cracks and faults is well drained and nutrient-rich. This, together with the mild Atlantic climate, supports an extraordinary mix of Mediterranean, Arctic and alpine plants. Of Ireland's native wildflowers, 75% are found here, including 24 species of beautiful orchids, the creamy-white burnet rose, the little starry flowers of mossy saxifrage and the magenta-coloured bloody cranesbill.

**The Drive ››** It's 36km southwest to Doolin along the R460 and R476 roads, which

**Classic Trip**

cut through more familiar Irish landscapes of green fields. The real pleasures along here are the villages – the likes of Kilfenora and Lisdoonvarna are great for a pit stop and even a session of traditional music.

## 8 Doolin

Doolin is renowned as a centre of Irish traditional music, but it's also known for its setting – 6km north of the Cliffs of Moher – and down near the ever-unsettled sea, the land is windblown, with huge rocks exposed by the long-vanished topsoil.

Many musicians live in the area, and they have a symbiotic relationship with the tourists: each desires the other and each year things grow a little larger. But given the heavy concentration of visitors, it's inevitable that standards don't always hold up to those in some of the less-trampled villages in Clare.

🛏 p95, p269

**The Drive »** Ferries from Doolin to Inishmór take about 90 minutes to make the crossing.

---

**TRIP HIGHLIGHT**

## 9 Inishmór

A step (and boat- or plane-ride) beyond the desolate beauty of Connemara are the Aran Islands. Most visitors are satisfied to explore only Inishmór (Árainn) and its main attraction, **Dún Aengus** (Dún Aonghasa; www.heritageireland.ie/en/west/dunaonghasa/; adult/child €4/2; ☻9.30am-6pm Apr-Oct, 9.30am-4pm Nov-Mar, closed Mon & Tue Jan & Feb), the stunning stone fort perched perilously on the island's towering cliffs.

Powerful swells pound the 60m-high cliff face. A complete lack of rails or other modern additions that would spoil this amazing ancient site means that you can not only go right up to the cliff's edge but also potentially fall to your doom below quite easily. When it's uncrowded, you can't help but feel the extraordinary energy that must have been harnessed to build this vast site.

The arid landscape west of Kilronan (Cill Rónáin), Inishmór's main settlement, is dominated by stone walls, boulders, scattered buildings and the odd patch of deep-green grass and potato plants.

🛏 p61, p269

**The Drive »** Once you're back on terra firma at Doolin, it's 223km to Dingle via the N85 through Ennis as far as Limerick City. The N69 will take you into County Kerry as far as Tralee, beyond which it's 50km on the N86 to Dingle.

---

## DOOLIN'S MUSIC PUBS

Doolin's three main music pubs (others are recent interlopers) are, in order of importance to the music scene:

» **McGann's** (www.mcgannspubdoolin.com; Roadford; ☻10am-12.30am, kitchen 10am-9.30pm) McGann's has all the classic touches of a full-on Irish music pub; the action often spills out onto the street. The food here is the best of the trio.

» **Gus O'Connor's Pub** (www.gusoconnorspubdoolin.net; Fisherstreet; ☻9am-midnight) Right on the water, this sprawling favourite packs them in and has a rollicking atmosphere when the music and drinking are in full swing.

» **MacDiarmada's** (Roadford; ☻bar 11am-midnight, kitchen 9am-9.30pm) Also known as McDermott's, this simple red-and-white old pub can be the rowdy favourite of locals. When the fiddles get going, it can seem like a scene out of a John Ford movie.

## 🔟 Dingle

Unlike the Ring of Kerry, where the cliffs tend to dominate the ocean, it's the ocean that dominates the smaller Dingle Peninsula. The opal-blue waters surrounding the promontory's multihued landscape of green hills and golden sands give rise to aquatic adventures and to fishing fleets that haul in fresh seafood that appears on the menus of some of the county's finest restaurants.

Centred on charming Dingle town, there's an alternative way of life here, lived by artisans and idiosyncratic characters and found at trad sessions and folkloric festivals across Dingle's tiny settlements.

The classic loop drive around Slea Head from Dingle town is 50km, but allow a day to take it all in – longer if you have time to stay overnight in Dingle town.

🍴 🛏 p47, p61, p197, p259

**The Drive »** Take the N86 as far as Annascaul and then the coastal R561 as far as Castlemaine. Then head southwest on the N70 to Killorglin and the Ring of Kerry. From Dingle, it's 53km.

## 1️⃣1️⃣ Ring of Kerry

The Ring of Kerry is the longest and the most diverse of Ireland's big circle drives, combining jaw-dropping coastal scenery with emerald pastures and villages.

The 179km circuit usually begins in Killarney and winds past pristine beaches, the island-dotted Atlantic, medieval ruins, mountains and loughs (lakes). The coastline is at its most rugged between Waterville and Caherdaniel in the southwest of the peninsula. It can get crowded in summer, but even then the remote Skellig Ring can be uncrowded and serene – and starkly beautiful.

The Ring of Kerry can easily be done as a day trip, but if you want to stretch it out, places to stay are scattered along the route. Killorglin and Kenmare have the best dining options, with some excellent restaurants; elsewhere, basic (sometimes very basic) pub fare is the norm.

The Ring's most popular diversion is the Gap of Dunloe, an awe-inspiring mountain pass at the western edge of Killarney National Park. It's signposted off the N72 between Killarney to Killorglin. The incredibly popular 19th-century Kate Kearney's Cottage is a pub where most visitors park their cars before walking up to the gap.

## 1️⃣2️⃣ Kenmare

If you've done the Ring in an anticlockwise fashion (or cut through the Gap of Dunloe), you'll end up in handsome Kenmare, a largely 18th-century town and the ideal alternative to Killarney as a place to stay overnight.

🍴 🛏 p47, p187, p209

**The Drive »** Picturesque villages, a fine stone circle and calming coastal scenery mark the less-taken, 143km route

---

## AN ANCIENT FORT

For a look at a well-preserved *caher* (walled fort) of the late Iron Age to early Christian period, stop at **Caherconnell Fort** (www.burrenforts.ie; R480; adult/child €7/4, with sheepdog demo €9.60/5.60; ⏰10am-6pm Jul & Aug, 10am-5pm Mar-Apr & Oct, 10am-5.30pm May, June & Sept), a privately run heritage attraction that's more serious than sideshow. Exhibits detail how the evolution of these defensive settlements may have reflected territorialism and competition for land among a growing, settling population. The drystone walling of the fort is in excellent condition. The top-notch visitor centre also has information on many other monuments in the area. It's about 1km south of Poulnabrone Dolmen on the R480.

PETER UNGER/GETTY IMAGES ©

*Classic Trip*

from Kenmare to Cork city. When you get to Leap, turn right onto the R597 and go as far as Rosscarbery; or, even better, take twice as long (even though it's only 24km more) and freelance your way along narrow roads near the water the entire way.

## ⑬ Cork City

Ireland's second city is first in every important respect, at least according to the locals, who cheerfully refer to it as the 'real capital of Ireland'. The compact city centre is surrounded by interesting waterways and is chock full of great restaurants fed by arguably the best foodie scene in the country.

🍴 🛏 p61, 209, p217, p259

**The Drive »** It's only 60km to Ardmore, but stop off in Midleton, 24km east of Cork

along the N25, and visit the whiskey museum. Just beyond Youghal, turn right onto the R671 for Ardmore.

**TRIP HIGHLIGHT**

## ⑭ Ardmore

Because it's off the main drag, Ardmore is a sleepy seaside village and one of the southeast's loveliest spots – the ideal destination for those looking for a little waterside R&R.

St Declan reputedly set up shop here sometime between AD 350 and 420, which would make Ardmore the first Christian bastion in Ireland – long before St Patrick landed. The village's 12th-century **round tower**, one of the best examples of these structures in Ireland, is the town's most distinctive architectural feature, but you should also check out the ruins of St Declan's church and well, on a bluff above the village.

🛏 p151

## LOCAL KNOWLEDGE:
### THE HEALY PASS

Instead of going directly into County Cork along the N71 from Kenmare, veer west onto the R571 and drive for 16km along the northern edge of the Beara Peninsula. At Lauragh, turn onto the R574 and take the breathtaking Healy Pass Road, which cuts through the peninsula and brings you from County Kerry into County Cork. At Adrigole, turn left onto the R572 and rejoin the N71 at Glengarriff, 17km east.

**Carrick-a-Rede Rope Bridge** Tourists cross the 30m-high bridge

# Eating & Sleeping

## Dublin ❶

### ✕ Fade Street Social — Modern Irish €€

(☎01-604 0066; www.fadestreetsocial.com; 4-6 Fade St; mains €19-32, tapas €5-12; ⊙12.30-10.30pm Mon-Fri, 5-10.30pm Sat & Sun; 🛜; ▢ all city centre) Two eateries in one, courtesy of renowned chef Dylan McGrath: at the front, the buzzy tapas bar, which serves up gourmet bites from a beautiful open kitchen. At the back, the more muted restaurant specialises in Irish cuts of meat – from veal to rabbit – served with home grown, organic vegetables. There's a bar upstairs too. Reservations suggested.

### ⊨ Westbury Hotel — Hotel €€€

(☎01-679 1122; www.doylecollection.com; Grafton St; r/ste from €240/360; ℗@🛜; ▢ all city centre) Tucked away just off Grafton St is one of the most elegant hotels in town, although you'll need to upgrade to a suite to really feel the luxury. The standard rooms are perfectly comfortable but not really of the same theme as the luxurious public space – the upstairs lobby is a great spot for afternoon tea or a drink.

## Belfast ❷

### ✕ Ginger — Bistro €€

(☎028-9024 4421; www.gingerbistro.com; 6-8 Hope St; mains lunch £10-12.50, dinner £16-24; ⊙5-9pm Mon, noon-3pm & 5-9.30pm Tue-Thu, noon-3pm & 5-10pm Fri & Sat; 🍴) Ginger is cosy and informal, but its food is anything but ordinary – the flame-haired owner/chef (hence the name) really knows what he's doing, sourcing top-quality Irish produce and creating exquisite dishes such as tea-smoked duck breast with ginger and sweet-potato puree.

### ⊨ Merchant Hotel — Hotel £££

(☎028-9023 4888; www.themerchanthotel. com; 16 Skipper St; d/ste from £200/300;

℗@🛜) Belfast's most flamboyant Victorian building (the old Ulster Bank head office) has been converted into the city's most flamboyant boutique hotel, a fabulous fusion of contemporary styling and old-fashioned elegance, with individually decorated rooms. Luxe leisure facilities at its gymnasium and spa include an eight-person rooftop hot tub. Its restaurant, **Great Room** (mains £19.50-28.50; ⊙7am-11pm), is magnificent.

## Giant's Causeway ❸

### ✕ 55 Degrees North — International ££

(☎028-7082 2811; www.55-north.com; 1 Causeway St; mains £10-19; ⊙12.30-2.30pm & 5-8.30pm Mon-Fri, to 9pm Sat, noon-8.30pm Sun; 🔆) Floor-to-ceiling windows allow you to soak up a spectacular panorama of sand and sea from this stylish restaurant. The food concentrates on clean, simple flavours.

## Dunfanaghy ❹

### ✕ Cove — Modern Irish €€

(☎074-913 6300; www.thecoverestaurant donegal.com; off N56, Rockhill, Port-na-Blagh; dinner mains €17-25; ⊙1-4pm Sun, 6.30-9pm Tue-Sun Jul & Aug, shorter hours rest of year, closed Jan–mid-Mar) Owners Siobhan Sweeney and Peter Byrne are perfectionists who tend to every detail in Cove's art-filled dining room, and on your plate. The cuisine is fresh and inventive. Seafood specials are deceptively simple with subtle Asian influences. After dinner, enjoy the elegant lounge upstairs. Book ahead.

## Sligo Town ❺

### ✕ Lyons Cafe — Modern European €

(☎071-914 2969; www.lyonscafe.com; Quay St; mains €7-15; ⊙9am-6pm Mon-Sat) Sligo's flagship department store, Lyons, opened in 1878 – with original leadlight windows and squeaky timber floors – and has been going strong since 1923. At its airy 1st-floor cafe, acclaimed chef (and cookbook author) Gary Stafford offers a fresh and seasonal menu.

## 🛏 Pearse Lodge     B&B €€

(☎071-916 1090; www.pearselodge.com; Pearse Rd; s/d from €50/80; @ 🛜) Welcoming owners Mary and Kieron have four stylish guest rooms with hardwood floors. The breakfast menu includes smoked salmon and French toast with bananas. A sunny sitting room opens to a garden. It's 700m southwest of the centre.

## Inishmór ⑦

### 🛏 Kilmurvey House     B&B €€

(☎099-61218; www.kilmurveyhouse.com; Kilmurvey; s/d from €50/90; ☺mid-Apr–mid-Oct) On the path leading to Dún Aengus is this grand 18th-century stone mansion. It's a beautiful setting and the 12 rooms are well maintained. Hearty meals (dinner €30) incorporate vegetables from the garden, and local fish and meats. You can swim at a pretty beach that's a short walk from the house.

## Dingle ⑩

### 🍴 Idás     Irish €€€

(☎066-915 0885; John St; mains €27-31; ☺5.30-9.30pm Tue-Sun) Chef Kevin Murphy is dedicated to promoting the finest of Irish produce, much of it from Kerry, taking lamb and seafood and foraged herbs from the Dingle peninsula and creating delicately flavoured concoctions such as braised John Dory fillet with fennel dashi cream, pickled cucumber, wild garlic and salad burnet. An early-bird menu offers two/three courses for €24.50/28.50.

### 🛏 Pax House     B&B €€

(☎066-915 1518; www.pax-house.com; Upper John St; d from €120; ☺Mar-Nov; P @ 🛜) From its highly individual decor to the outstanding views over the estuary from room balconies and terrace, Pax House is a treat. Choose from less expensive hill-facing accommodation, rooms that overlook the estuary, and two-room family suites opening onto the terrace. It's 1km southeast of the town centre.

## Kenmare ⑫

### 🍴 Tom Crean Fish & Wine     Irish €€

(☎064-664 1589; http://tomcrean.ie; Main St; 2-/3-course menus €25/29, mains €16.50; ☺5-9.30pm Thu-Sun late-Mar–Dec; 🛜) Named for Kerry's pioneering Antarctic explorer, and run by his granddaughter, this venerable restaurant uses only the best of local organic produce, cheeses and fresh seafood, all served in modern, low-key surrounds. The oysters *au naturel* capture the scent of the sea; the homemade ravioli of prawn mousse, and sesame seed-crusted Atlantic salmon with lime and coriander are divine.

### 🛏 Virginia's Guesthouse     B&B €€

(☎064-664 1021; www.virginias-kenmare.com; Henry St; s/d from €40/75; 🛜) You can't get more central than this award-winning B&B, whose creative breakfasts celebrate organic local produce (rhubarb and blueberries in season, for example, as well as fresh-squeezed OJ and porridge with whiskey). Its eight rooms are super-comfy without being fussy.

## Cork City ⑬

### 🍴 Market Lane     Irish, International €€

(☎021-427 4710; www.marketlane.ie; 5 Oliver Plunkett St; mains €10-25; ☺noon-10pm Mon-Thu, noon-10.30pm Fri & Sat, 1-9pm Sun; 🛜🍴) It's always hopping at this bright corner bistro. The menu is broad and hearty, changing to reflect what's fresh at the English Market: perhaps braised ox cheek in ale, or smoked haddock with bacon and cabbage? No reservations for fewer than six diners; sip a drink at the bar till a table is free.

### 🛏 Imperial Hotel     Hotel €€

(☎021-427 4040; www.flynnhotels.com; South Mall; d €130-200; P @ 🛜) Having recently celebrated its bicentenary – Thackeray, Dickens and Sir Walter Scott have all stayed here – the Imperial knows how to age gracefully. Public spaces resonate with period detail, while the 130 bedrooms feature writing desks, understated decor and modern touches including a luxurious spa and a digital music library. Irish Free State commander-in-chief Michael Collins spent his last night alive here; you can ask to check into his room.

# *Classic Trip*

# Tip to Toe

**3**

*If this trip were a film it would be a road epic. Sweep from mountain passes down cliffside roads past sandy shores to discover charismatic cities, big-name sights and hidden beaches.*

## TRIP HIGHLIGHTS

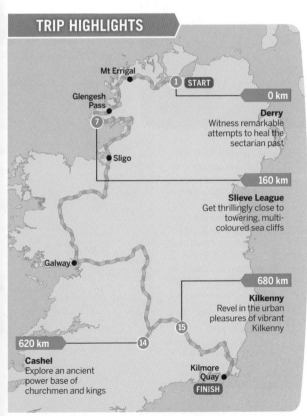

**10 DAYS**
**950KM / 590 MILES**

**GREAT FOR...**

**BEST TIME TO GO**

Spring and autumn are ideal; you'll miss the summer crowds.

**ESSENTIAL PHOTO**

Mountainous Glengesh Pass delivers a great 'did I really drive that?' snap.

**BEST THREE DAYS**

Stops 11 to 15 for party-town Galway, elegant Birr and iconic Rock of Cashel.

**Derry**
Witness remarkable attempts to heal the sectarian past

**Slieve League**
Get thrillingly close to towering, multi-coloured sea cliffs

**Kilkenny**
Revel in the urban pleasures of vibrant Kilkenny

**Cashel**
Explore an ancient power base of churchmen and kings

**Sligo** W. B. Yeats statue, by Rowan Gillespie www.rowangillespie.com

# Classic Trip

# 3 Tip to Toe

This 10-day trip takes in so much. You'll bob on a boat beneath 600m-high cliffs, clamber over castle ruins and marvel at massive seabird colonies. Scenery-rich routes link sites telling tales of rebellion, the Troubles, famine and faith. Memorable days connect experiences rich in Irish culture, from lyrical poetry to pubs alive with traditional music. On this trip you'll really discover Ireland – tip to toe, head to heart.

TRIP HIGHLIGHT

## ❶ Derry

Derry comes as a pleasant surprise to many visitors: a vibrant, riverside city, encircled by impressive, 17th-century fortifications. Like Belfast it has a past of bitter sectarian divisions, but here too a remarkable healing is under way. Get a true taste of both the scale of the problems and the progress by walking around the city (p370), strolling atop the city walls, passing Unionist strongholds and absorbing the powerful murals of the Republican Bogside district. Be sure to visit the **Tower Museum** (www.derrycity.gov.uk/museums; Union Hall Pl; adult/child £4/2; ☻10am-5.30pm), where audiovisual exhibits bring the city's rich and complex past to life.

✗ ⍾ p327, p359

The Drive >> As the A2/N13 heads west out of Derry towards Letterkenny, road signs switch from mph to km/h: you've just entered the Irish Republic. At Bridgend follow signs left up to

Grianán of Aileách (12km), a dizzying ascent.

- - - - - - - - - - -

## ❷ Grianán of Aileách

This fort encircles Grianán Hill like a halo. Duck in through its cave-like entrance and clamber up its tiered battlements for eye-popping views of Lough Swilly, with Inch Island plumb in the centre; Counties Donegal, Derry and Tyrone stretch out all the way around.

It's thought the site was in use in pre-Celtic times as a temple to the god Dagda, becoming the seat of the O'Neills between the 5th and 12th centuries. It was demolished by Murtogh O'Brien, king of Munster, and most of these remains are a 19th-century reconstruction.

**The Drive ››** The N13 cruises west to traffic-choked

## LINK YOUR TRIP

### 12 Wexford & Waterford

Scenic shorelines, birdlife and fishing villages. Start where this trips stops: Kilmore Quay.

### 24 Mountains & Moors

Drive deep into romantic Connemara. Pick it up from, and return to, Galway city on this trip's route.

Letterkenny (with some handy accommodation options). There, climb north gradually on the N56 towards Dunfanaghy, with the distant Glendowan Mountains sliding into view. Once up in the high hills, take the R255 left to Glenveagh National Park (50km) and Glenveagh Castle.

---

### ❸ Glenveagh National Park

Lakes shimmer like dew in mountainous **Glenveagh National Park** (Páirc Náisiúnta Ghleann Bheatha; www.glenveaghnational park.ie), where knuckles of rock alternate with green-gold bogs and oak and birch forest. In delightfully showy **Glenveagh Castle** (www.

glenveaghnationalpark.ie; off R251; 30min tour adult/child €5/2, bus from visitor centre adult/child $3/2; ⊙9am-6pm Apr-Oct, to 5pm Nov-Mar, last tours 45min before closing), rooms combine stuffed stags with flamboyant furnishings, with highlights being the tartan-and-antler-covered music room and the pink, candy-striped room (formerly Greta Garbo's).

The exotic gardens are spectacular too, with their terraces and Italianate style a marked contrast to the wildly beautiful landscape. A shuttle bus runs to the castle from the visitor centre, but the 3.6km walk is a better way to soak up the scenery.

**The Drive »** Head west on the R251, an exhilarating, bouncing drive through cinematic scenery: the Derryveagh Mountains tower to your left,

and the fast-approaching peak of Mt Errigal fills your windscreen ahead. At the hamlet of Dunlewey (Dún Lúiche; 16km), turn left to the lake.

---

### ❹ Dunlewey

Simply stepping out of your car in this mountain hamlet provides an insight into the isolated way of life this high in the hills. It's underlined at the **Dunlewey Centre** (Ionad Cois Locha; ☎074-953 1699; www.dunleweycentre. com; combined ticket adult/child €10.30/7.50; ⊙10.30am-5.30pm Easter-Sep, to 4.45pm Oct; 🚻), where the 30-minute tour of a thatched weaver's cottage reveals a huge loom, spartan bedroom (complete with chamber pot under the iron bedstead) and snug lounge warmed by a peat fire.

🛏 p74

**The Drive »** The R251, then the N56, begin a slow descent south, bumping past crags and sudden loughs and bogs. Shortly after heritage-town Ardara turn right, following brown signs to Glengesh Pass. It's an ear-popping ascent up hairpin bends and past wayside shrines. Near the top, 60km from Dunlewey, turn right into the walled parking bay.

---

### ↱ DETOUR: LOUGHREA PENINSULA

#### Start: ❹ Dunlewey

This leg's scenery is beautiful enough, but if you fancy some sandy shores with your mountains, try this detour. Around 20km south of Dungloe, at Maas, instead of swinging left on the N56 to Glenties, peel right onto the coastal R261, which winds deep into beautiful Loughrea Peninsula. Next, take a minor road right to **Narin**, following signs to the **beach** (trá), a 4km-long, spectacular, dune-backed, sandy stretch, where you can walk out to tiny **Iniskeel Island** at low tide.

Post-stroll, continue on the shoreside road, past Portnoo and Rossbeg, rejoining the R261, then the N56 at Ardara.

---

### ❺ Glengesh Pass

Glengesh Pass provides one of Donegal's most spectacular mountain views, and this parking spot is *the* place to take that holiday snap. A

V-shaped valley sweeps away far below, while the Derryveagh Mountains line up far behind. The road you've just driven up is a tiny ribbon, snaking off into the distance. There's a picnic area immediately below the parking spot, ensuring an al fresco meal with a truly memorable view.

**The Drive »** Edging over the pass, a cluster of wind turbines spin into view. Descend gradually, past unfenced grazing land (watch out for free-roaming sheep) and neat piles of drying peat. Suddenly, the sea around Glen Head appears. Head through Glencolumbcille (Gleann Cholm Cille; 16km) on the Malin Beg Rd; the folk village comes soon after.

- - - - - - - - - -

## 6 Glencolumbcille

Glencolumbcille may feel like the middle of nowhere, but the three-pub village offers scalloped beaches, a strong sense of Irish identity and an insight into a fast-disappearing way of life. **Father McDyer's Folk Village** (www.glenfolkvillage.com; Doonalt; adult/child €4.50/2.50; ☉10am-6pm Mon-Sat, noon-6pm Sun Easter-Sep) was set up in 1967 to freeze-frame traditional folk life for posterity. Its six thatched 18th- and 19th-century cottages are packed with everyday items, from beds and cooking pans to tools and open fires.

🛏 p74, p335

## DETOUR: DONEGAL CASTLE

**Start: 7 Slieve League**

Midway between Slieve League and Sligo, riverside **Donegal Castle** (☏074-972 2405; www.heritageireland.ie; Castle St; adult/child €4/2; ☉10am-6pm daily Easter–mid-Sep, 9.30am-4.30pm Thu-Mon mid-Sep–Easter) makes for a picturesque detour. The original 1474 castle was torched then rebuilt in 1623, along with a neighbouring Jacobean house. It's a deeply attractive spot: grassy lawns lead up to geometric battlements, and rooms are packed with fine furnishings and antiques.

The castle is in the centre of pretty Donegal town. Follow signs from the N56 and afterwards take the N15 to Sligo.

**The Drive »** The R263 snakes south and soon reveals the massive mountain of Slieve League. Edge past it to Carrick (An Charraig) then follow brown Slieve League signs south beside the inlet to tiny Teelin (Tieleann; 9km).

- - - - - - - - - -

**TRIP HIGHLIGHT**

## 7 Slieve League

The Cliffs of Moher may be more famous, but the ones at Slieve League are taller – the highest in Europe, in fact. This 600m-high, multicoloured rock face seems stark and otherworldly as it rears up from the Atlantic Ocean. A diminutive 12-seater boat, the **Nuala Star** (☏074-973 9365; www.sliabhleagueboattrips.com; Teelin Pier; tours per person €20-25; ☉hours vary Apr-Oct), sets off from Teelin to the foot of the cliffs. The trips are weather dependent and have to be booked. If the sea is too rough, you can drive or walk to the cliffs.

**The Drive »** The drive east from Carrick completes a gradual descent from wild, pitted hills to smoother urban life; remote homesteads give way to garden-fronted houses. The N56 skirts Donegal town, from where the N15 heads south to Sligo, 110km from Slieve League.

- - - - - - - - - -

## 8 Sligo Town

An appealing overnight base, vibrant Sligo combines lively pubs and futuristic buildings with old stone bridges and a historic abbey. It also shines a spotlight on William Butler Yeats (1865–1939), Sligo's greatest literary figure and one of Ireland's premier poets. The **Sligo County Museum** (☏071-911 1679; Stephen St; ☉9.30am-12.30pm Tue-Sat year-round,

# Classic Trip

### WHY THIS IS A CLASSIC TRIP
ISABEL ALBISTON, WRITER

It's not just about dizzying clifftops, the wild Atlantic roaring and spraying below and the only reminder of proximate civilisation drifting over in the scent of tangy peat smoke and the sound of bleating sheep; it's also about vibrant cities packed with culture and buzzing with nightlife. From the stark mountains in the north to the gentle lowlands of the south, this trip is one heck of a drive.

Top: County Donegal
Left: Guillemots, Kilmore Quay
Right: Galway City

MARK L STANLEY/GETTY IMAGES ©

68

MARK L STANLEY/GETTY IMAGES ©

2-4.50pm Tue-Sat May-Sep) showcases his manuscripts and letters, along with sepia photos, a copy of his 1923 Nobel Prize medal and a complete collection of his poetic works.

✗ ⮞ p74, p293, p301

**The Drive »** Take the N4 south then the N17 (signed Galway). Soon the R293 meanders left through Ballymote and a deeply agricultural landscape. Make for Gurteen (also spelt Gorteen), 32km from Sligo, following signs for the Coleman Irish Music Centre. It's the pink building right beside the main village crossroads.

## 9 Gurteen

You've just explored poetry, so now for another mainstay of Irish culture: music. The **Coleman Irish Music Centre** (☏071-918 2599; www.colemanirishmusic. com; ⊙10am-5pm Mon-Sat) champions melody and culture, south-Sligo style, with multimedia exhibits on musical history, instruments, famous musicians and Irish dancing. The centre also provides tuition and sheet-music sales and stages performances.

**The Drive »** Continue south on the R293, an undulating ribbon of a road that deposits you in bustling Ballaghaderreen. There pick up the N5 west (signed Westport) for an effortless cruise through lowlands that are grazed by

TRISH PUNCH/DESIGN PICS/GETTY IMAGES ©

cattle and dotted with rounded hills. Some 55km later, signs point right for the National Museum of Country Life.

- - - - - - - - - - - -

 **Castlebar**

Your discovery of Ireland's heritage continues, this time with a celebration of the ingenuity and self-sufficiency of the Irish people. The **National Museum of Country Life** (☎094-903 1755; www.museum.ie; off N5, Turlough Park; ☺10am-5pm Tue-Sat, 2-5pm Sun) explores everything from wickerwork to boat building, and herbal cures to traditional clothing. This historical one-stop shop is a comprehensive, absorbing depiction of rural traditions and skills between 1850 and 1950.

✗ p74

**The Drive »** From the outskirts of Castlebar, the N84 heads south (signed Galway), bouncing beside scattered settlements before dog-legging through appealing Ballinrobe. This hummocky landscape of fields and dry-stone walls is replaced by bogs edged with peat stacks as you near Galway city (80km).

- - - - - - - - - - - -

⑪ **Galway City**

The biggest reason to stop in Galway City is simply to revel in its hedonistic, culture-rich spirit. Narrow alleys lead from sight to sight beside strings of pubs overflowing with live music.

Start explorations at the quayside **Spanish Arch** (1584), thought to be an extension of Galway's medieval walls. Next walk a few paces to the **Galway City Museum** (www.galwaycitymuseum.ie; Spanish Pde; ☺10am-5pm Tue-Sat year-round, noon-5pm Sun Easter-Sep), where exhibits trace daily life in the city through history.

Highlights include the smelly medieval era and photos of President John F Kennedy's 1963 visit to Galway. Then stroll a few metres to the **Hall of the Red Earl** (www.galwaycivictrust.ie; Druid Lane; ☺9am-5pm Mon-Fri year-round, 10am-1pm Sat May-Sep), the artefact-rich archaeological remains of a 13th-century power base.

You can't leave Galway without experiencing a music session, so walk further up Quay St to nearby **Tig Cóilí** (Mainguard St; ☺10.30am-midnight Mon-Thu, to 12.30am Fri & Sat, to 11pm Sun), a gem of a fire-engine-red pub that stages two live *céilidh* (sessions of traditional music and dancing) a day.

🛏 p46, p74, p277

**The Drive »** Join the M6 towards Dublin for the hour-long, smooth motorway cruise to Athlone. Follow signs to Athlone West/Town Centre. Soon the River Shannon, bobbing with houseboats and pleasure cruisers, eases into view. Park by Athlone Castle (80km), which appears straight ahead.

- - - - - - - - - - - -

⑫ **Athlone**

The thriving riverside town of Athlone is an enchanting mix of stylish modern developments and ancient, twisting streets. **Viking Ship Cruises** (☎086 262 1136; www.vikingtoursireland.ie; The Quay; adult €12-16, child €6-8; ☺Easter-Oct; 🚶) runs

 **DETOUR: ATHENRY**

**Start:** ⑪ **Galway City**

Most people sweep past Athenry, but it actually boasts one of Ireland's most intact collections of medieval architecture. This amiable town features a restored, box-like Norman **castle** (www.heritageireland.ie; adult/child €4/2; ☺9.30am-6pm Easter-Sep), the medieval **Parish Church of St Mary's**, a 13th-century **Dominican Priory** (with superb masonry) and an original market cross.

Athenry sits beside the M6, and is signed off it.

trips from beside Athlone Castle, cruising the River Shannon aboard a replica Viking longship sailed by costumed crew. The best trip goes south to the stunning ruins at Clonmacnoise, allowing you a 90-minute wander there.

p74, p119

**The Drive »** Continue through Athlone, picking up the minor N62, which rises and dips past grazing livestock to Birr (45km). Soon a boggy landscape takes over; look for the swathes of exposed soil left by industrial-scale peat harvesting. At Birr follow signs to the imposing, crenellated gateway of Birr Castle.

## ⑬ Birr

Feel-good Birr is one of the Midlands' most attractive towns, with elegant pastel Georgian buildings and a spirited nightlife buzzing with live music. It also boasts **Birr Castle** (☎057-912 0336; www.birrcastle.com; off R439; gardens adult/child €9/5, gardens, exhibits & castle adult/child €18/10; ⊙9am-6pm mid-Mar–Oct, 10am-4pm Nov–mid-Mar; ℗ ♿), where magnificent, 1000-species-strong gardens frame a large artificial lake. Don't miss the romantic Hornbeam cloister and the 12m-high box hedge, planted in the 1780s and now one of the world's tallest.

p75, p119

### LOCAL KNOWLEDGE: PAY YOUR WAY

The M6 heading east out of Galway is a sleek, effortless drive. But like all shiny new things it has to be paid for: have your €1.90 ready for the toll booth 20km east of Athenry.

**The Drive »** The N62 loops south through Roscrea, with the Silvermine Mountains' dark tops creeping up on the right. Then come Templemore's wide streets, before the N62 wiggles onto the M8 (head towards Cork); the Rock of Cashel (74km) is signed 13km later.

**TRIP HIGHLIGHT**

## ⑭ Rock of Cashel

The iconic and much-photographed **Rock of Cashel** (www.heritageireland. ie; adult/child €7/3; ⊙9am-7pm early Jun–mid-Sep, to 5.30pm mid-Mar–early Jun & mid-Sep–mid-Oct, to 4.30pm mid-Oct–mid-Mar) is one of Ireland's highlights – Queen Elizabeth II included it on her historic 2011 visit. The 'rock' is a fortified hill, the defences of which shelter a clutch of historic religious monuments. The site has been a defensive one since the 4th century and its compelling features include the towering 13th-century Gothic cathedral, a 15th-century four-storey castle, an 11th-century round tower and a 12th-century Romanesque chapel.

The rock is a five-minute stroll along Bishop's Walk from the appealing market town of Cashel.

p111, p277

**The Drive »** As you head north up the M8 (signed Dublin) you'll notice rounded field-chequered hills, backed by a distant smudge of mountains. At Urlingford, take the R693 into central Kilkenny, 67km from Cashel.

**TRIP HIGHLIGHT**

## ⑮ Kilkenny

Kilkenny (Cill Chainnigh) is the Ireland of many people's imaginations, with its gracious medieval cathedral, tangle of 17th-century passageways, old-fashioned shopfronts and ancient live-music pubs. Make for **Kilkenny Castle** (www. kilkennycastle.ie; Castle Rd; adult/child €7/3; ⊙9.30am-5pm Mar-Sep, to 4.30pm Oct-Feb), a late-12th-century stone affair built by the son-in-law of Richard de Clare, the Anglo-Norman conqueror of Ireland (a man graced with the sobriquet 'Strongbow'). Forty-minute guided tours focus on the Long Gallery, an impressive hall with high ceilings,

*Classic Trip*

vividly painted Celtic and Pre-Raphaelite motifs and ranks of po-faced portraits.

🍴 🛏 p75, p143

**The Drive** » Pick up the R700 southeast to New Ross. Hills feature again here, both in the rise and fall of the twisting road and in the blue-black ridge of the Blackstairs Mountains far ahead. At New Ross (50km) make for the quay and the three-masted sailing vessel you can now see.

### 16 New Ross

In Ireland's Great Famine of 1845–51 a staggering three million people died or emigrated, especially to America and Australia. Many left in 'coffin ships', so called because of their appalling mortality rates. When you step aboard the replica **Dunbrody Famine Ship** (📞051-425 239; www.dunbrody.com; The Quay; adult/child €10/6; ⏰9am-6pm Apr-Sep, to 5pm Oct-Mar; 👶) you 'become' a migrant: you're allocated a living space and rations, while actors around you vividly re-create life on board. Expect cramped conditions, authentic sounds and smells and often-harrowing tales.

**The Drive** » Head onto the N30 to Enniscorthy (initially signed N23 to Rosslare), a gentle, rural leg punctuated by the frequent treat of roadside stalls selling sweet Wexford strawberries. As you head towards central Enniscorthy (32km), the National Rebellion Centre is a sharp left, up the hill.

- - - - - - - - - - -

### 17 Enniscorthy

Enniscorthy's warren of steep streets descends from Augustus Pugin's cathedral to a riverside Norman castle. But the town is most famous for some of the fiercest fighting of the 1798 uprising against British rule, when rebels captured the town. That story is told in the **National 1798 Rebellion Centre** (www.1798centre.ie; Parnell Rd; adult/child €7/3, incl Enniscorthy Castle €10/5; ⏰9.30am-5pm Mon-Fri, noon-5pm Sat Apr-Sep, 10am-4pm Mon-Fri, noon-5pm Sat Oct-Mar; 🅿 👶), where exhibits cover the French and American Revolutions that sparked Wexford's abortive revolt. It also chronicles what followed: the rebels' retreat and the massacre by English troops of hundreds of women and children.

🛏 p75

**The Drive** » Carry on through Enniscorthy, crossing the river to pick up the N11, south, to Wexford (19km). Then comes a long straight run, beside the River Slane and past more strawberry stalls, until the waters of Wexford Harbour glide into view.

PIERRE LECLERC/SHUTTERSTOCK ©

- - - - - - - - - - -

### 18 Wexford Town

The sleepy port town of Wexford is a pleasing place to stroll through heritage-rich streets beside a wide estuary. Guided tours (€5) set out at 11am from Monday to Saturday (March to October) from the **tourist office** (www.visitwexford.ie; Quay Front; ⏰9am-5.30pm Mon-Sat; 📶) on the main Custom House Quay; it also provides maps. Or explore by yourself: head up Harper's Lane to North Main St and the 18th-century **St Iberius' Church** (where Oscar

**Cashel** Rock of Cashel

Wilde's forebears were rectors). A left up George St leads to Abbey St and **Selskar Abbey** (Henry II did penance here after the murder of Thomas Becket); the 14th-century **Westgate** sits at the street's end.

🛏 p75

**The Drive ≫** The N25 to Rosslare runs along Wexford's boat-lined waterfront. After more fruit stalls, the R739 turns right through a gentle landscape of trees and rich pastures – it feels a world away from the harsh, high hills at your trip's start. Soon the thatched cottages of Kilmore Quay (20km) appear.

## 🔟 Kilmore Quay

This tiny, relaxed port is the perfect finish to your trans-Ireland trip. Seafood restaurants, fishermen's pubs and B&Bs cluster around a boat-packed harbour. Just offshore, the **Saltee Islands** (www.salteeislands. info; ⏰11.30am-4.30pm) overflow with gannets, guillemots, kittiwakes and puffins; **Declan Bates** (☎053-912 9684, 087 252 9736; Kilmore Quay Harbour; day trips €30) runs boat trips (booking required). If the weather scuppers that plan, stroll west from the quay to the

9km-long, wildlife-rich dunes of Ballyteigue Burrow, passing a memorial garden for those lost at sea, before reaching the Cull, a 4km-long sliver of land sheltering a slender inlet teeming with widgeons, oystercatchers, curlews and more.

🍴 🛏 p75

# Eating & Sleeping

## Letterkenny ②

### ✕ Lemon Tree — Modern Irish €€

(📞074-912 5788; www.thelemontreerestaurant. com; 39 Lower Main St; mains €15-22; ⏰5-9.30pm Mon-Thu, to 10pm Fri & Sat, 1-2.30pm & 5-9.30pm Sun; 🖉) White linen and dark-wood trim give this restaurant a contemporary atmosphere. The innovative menu offers fresh seafood, poultry and meat dishes sourced locally and prepared with French flair in the open kitchen.

### ⌁ Station House — Hotel €€

(📞074-912 3100; www.stationhouseletterkenny. com; Lower Main St; s/d €85/110; @🛜) Conveniently located in the centre of town, this large, modern hotel has 81 red-hued, wood-floored rooms with low lighting and glass-panelled bathrooms. Everything sparkles with good management.

## Dunlewey ④

### ⌁ Glen Heights B&B — B&B €€

(📞074-956 0844; www.glenheightsbb.com; Dunlewey; d €70; 🛜) Your breakfast may well go cold on the plate in front of you as you'll find it difficult to take your eyes off the breathtaking views of Dunlewey Lake and the Poisoned Glen from the conservatory. The three rooms are cosy and the Donegal charm is in full swing.

## Glencolumbcille ⑥

### ⌁ Glencolumbcille Lodge — Guesthouse €

(📞074-973 0302; www.ionadsuil.ie; s €20-35, d €35-50; 🛜) Overlooking sheep-filled paddocks near the village, this place calls itself the 'Hillwalkers Centre'. It has decent double and twin rooms with private bathrooms and an enormous self-catering kitchen. Given the weather, the clothes-drying room and peat fire are handy.

## Sligo Town ⑧

### ✕ Kate's Kitchen — Cafe €

(www.kateskitchen.ie; Castle St; mains from €6; ⏰8.30am-5.30pm Mon-Sat) Only the best local foodstuffs are sold at this lovely, contemporary shop. All the fixings for a prime picnic are combined with prepared foods. It also does a big lunchtime trade.

## Castlebar ⑩

### ✕ Rua Deli & Cafe — Modern Irish €€

(www.caferua.com; Spencer St; mains €9-14; ⏰8.30am-6pm Mon-Sat; 👶) This gourmet deli and cafe champions artisan, organic produce, Carrowholly cheese, Ballina smoked salmon and luscious prepared foods. Load up in the deli for a picnic in the nearby park. The cafe has artfully mismatched furniture and excellent fresh fare. Even the takeaway coffee is good. A second cafe location is on New Antrim St.

## Galway City ⑪

### ⌁ Skeffington Arms Hotel — Hotel €€

(📞091-563 173; www.skeffington.ie; Eyre Sq; r €85-190; @🛜) The 24 rooms at this well-managed hotel overlooking Eyre Sq are clean, modern and comfortable. Pass through the arched traditional entrance into a minimalist haven.

## Athlone ⑫

### ⌁ Bastion B&B — B&B €

(📞090-649 4954; www.thebastion.net; 2 Bastion St; s/d from €50/75; 🛜) You can't miss this brightly coloured facade near Athlone Castle. Inside, the white-on-white interiors are a canvas for eclectic artwork, cactus collections and Indian wall hangings. The seven rooms (five with private bathrooms) are crisp and clean, with dark wooden floors. Go for the spacious loft if you can. Breakfasts are fresh and healthy.

## Birr

### ⇌ Brendan House
B&B €€

(☎057-912 1818; www.tinjugstudio.com; Brendan St; s/d from €55/80; 🛜) Packed with knick-knacks, books, rugs, art and antiques, this Georgian town house is a bohemian delight. The three rooms share a bathroom (one of Birr's oldest, they claim). The four-poster beds, superb breakfast and artistic style are the real draws. The owners arrange mountain walks, castle and art tours, holistic treatments and art classes.

## Kilkenny 15

### ✕ Cafe Sol
Modern Irish €€

(☎056-776 4987; www.restaurantskilkenny. com; William St; mains lunch €9-14, dinner €16-25; ❂noon-4pm & 6-9pm Mon-Thu & Sun, to 10pm Fri & Sat; 🛜) Leisurely lunches stretch until 4pm at this much-loved restaurant. Local organic produce is featured in dishes that emphasise what's fresh each season. The flavours are frequently bold and have global influences. Service is excellent, albeit casual, and the whole place exudes a modern Med-bistro look.

### ⇌ Celtic House
B&B €€

(☎056-776 2249; www.celtic-house-bandb.com; 18 Michael St; r €60-80; P@🛜) Artist and author Angela Byrne extends one of Ireland's warmest welcomes at this spick-and-span B&B. Some of the bright rooms have views of the castle. Book ahead.

## Enniscorthy 17

### ⇌ Woodbrook House
Guesthouse €€€

(☎053-925 5114; www.woodbrookhouse.ie; Killanne; s/d from €100/160; ❂Easter-Jun & Aug-Sep; P🛜) Rebuilt after sustaining damage in the 1798 rebellion, this glorious Georgian country house has a superb setting beneath the Blackstairs Mountains. Green practices are used throughout and you can make arrangements for dinner (€50; organic, of course). It is 13km west of Enniscorthy.

## Wexford Town 18

### ✕ Greenacres
Bistro, Deli €€

(☎053-912 2975; www.greenacres.ie; 7 Selskar St; mains €9-24, 3-course set menus €33; ❂bistro 9am-10pm Mon-Sat; 🛜) Eating, shopping, culture...this place has it covered! Irish cheeses and local produce are beautifully displayed in the food hall, the wine selection is the best south of Dublin, and the gourmet bistro gets star rating for innovative ingredients such as wild pigeon, rock oysters and smoked rabbit. The upper floors house an excellent art gallery.

### ⇌ Cuasnog
B&B €€

(☎053-912 3637; www.cuasnog.com; St John's Rd; s €25-75, d €50-120; P🛜🐾) Hosts Caitríona and Theo not only extend a warm welcome – they also treat you to a pot of tea with smoked salmon and soda bread on arrival. The compact rooms have a comfortable feel with rustic furniture and fireplaces; breakfast includes homemade scones and local organic produce. Located a few minutes' walk from the centre on a sleepy residential street.

## Kilmore Quay 19

### ✕ Silver Fox
### Seafood Restaurant
Seafood €€€

(☎053-912 9888; www.thesilverfox.ie; Kilmore Quay; mains lunch €9-20, dinner €18-35; ❂noon-8pm Easter-Oct, shorter hours rest of year, closed Jan–mid-Feb; ♿) The Silver Fox's fresh-from-the-ocean offerings include locally landed plaice, langoustines, crab and mussels, plus daily specials depending on what arrives at the quay. The dining room exudes white table–clothed elegance; don't arrive in flip-flops. Bookings advised at weekends.

### ⇌ Mill Road Farm
B&B €

(☎053-912 9633; www.millroadfarm.com; R739; s/d €50/80; P🛜) About 2km northeast of Kilmore Quay this dairy farm has four daintily decorated guest rooms with lots of floral fabrics (three with sea views beyond the paddock); the owner breeds horses for racing. The sitting room has plenty of games and books for wet days. Breakfast includes homemade bread and free-range eggs.

# Dublin & Eastern Ireland

**A SPIDER'S WEB OF ROADS –** from motorways to tiny rural routes – lead you from Dublin's city centre to myriad delights.

Within an hour's drive from Dublin you can find yourself on a lonely mountain pass with only the odd sheep for company, or be transported back 3500 years in time to explore a passage grave built before the pyramids were a twinkle in a pharaoh's eye.

You're now in the heartland of Ireland's Ancient East, Failte Ireland's newest 'umbrella destination'. Our collection of itineraries that explore historic towns, castles, gardens and monastic monuments, which all serve to remind you of Ireland's breathtaking cultural heritage.

**Dublin** Temple Bar
YOHAN LB/500PX ©

# Dublin & Eastern Ireland

MONAGHAN

DOWN

Castleblayney

Carlingford Kilke

Butlersbridge

Dundalk

R173

Dundalk Bay

N2

CAVAN

Carrickmacross

LOUTH

M1

Iris Se

N55

Ardee

Dunleer

MEATH

Virginia

Clogherhead

Lough Sheelin

Oldcastle

Collon

Castletown

Slane

Drogheda

Crossakeel

N3

6

Laytown

N61

Lanesborough

Edgeworthstown

Duleek

Balbriggan

LONGFORD

N4

Crookedwood

Skyrne

Skerries

Roscommon

Corlea

Delvin

N3

M1

Rush

8

Lough Owel

N52

Trim

Ashbourne

Swords

Lecarrow

WESTMEATH

Mullingar

14

Howth

River Suck

Lough Ree

Lough Ennell

Kinnegad

Black Bull

N2

Athlone

M6

Moate

5

M6

Kilcock

Clonee

Aughrim

Kilbeggan

Bog of Allen

Edenderry

Celbridge

M4

DUBLIN

Sandyco

Shannonbridge

Clara Bog

Tullamore

KILDARE

Clondalkin

4

Rathcoole

Glencree

R759

9

Kilpedder

Cloghan

OFFALY

Kill

Blessington

Frankford

N62

Kinnitty

Monasterevin

Kilcullen

Hollywood

Sraghmore

Roundwood

Portumna

Birr

Slieve Bloom Mountains

LAOIS

Dunlavin

Laragh

Ashfore

Lough Derg

7

Roscrea

Clonenagh

Portlaoise

Ballitore

Drumgoff

Rathdrum

Greenane

Nenagh

Moneygall

Borris-in-Ossory

M8

Abbeyleix

N80

WICKLOW

M11

M7

Toomyvara

N62

Rathdowney

Durrow

N78

Carlow

N81

Arklow

R498

Templemore

Ballyragget

M9

Tullow

Silvermine Mountains

Urlingford

R693

10

Kildavin

R503

Thurles

Slieveardagh Hills

Kilkenny

Ferns

N11

Poulshone

TIPPERARY

Dundrum

M8

Ballingarry

Callan

Borris

Kiltealy

WEXFORD

N24

Cashel

R692

Stonyford

Glynn

Enniscorthy

Bansha

Fethard

11

Knocktopher

St Mullins

Clonroche

Blackwater

Newtown

Cappa

Dogstown

Booley Hills

M9

New Ross

N11

Cloheen

Cahir

Clonmel

Carrick-on-Suir

N24

Mullinavat

N25

Ferrycarrig

R639

Ballymacarbry

Waterford

Passage East

Wexford

Clashmore

WATERFORD

R733

Drinagh

Ballyduff

N72

Kilmacthomas

N25

12

Dunmore East

Rosslare Harbour

Tallowbridge

13

Boherawillin

Tramore

Bannow

Chour

M8

CORK

Aglish

Dungarvan

Annestown

Churchtown

Templetown

Kilmore Quay

Killeagh

Clashmore

Pulla

Curragh

St George's Channel

Midleton

Youghal

Cobh

N

0

0

40 km

25 miles

**4** **A Long Weekend Around Dublin 3 Days**
Seaside villages, monastic ruins and palatial Palladian mansions. (p81)

**5** **East to West 7 Days**
Cut across central Ireland from the cosmopolitan capital to the wilds of Connemara. (p89)

**6** **The Boyne Valley 2 Days**
A short trip that's long on history – from prehistoric monuments to bloody battlefields. (p97)

**7** **Ancient Ireland 4 Days**
A four-day marathon to explore 4000 years of Irish history, right back to the beginning. (p105)

**8** **Monasteries, Mountains & Mansions 3 Days**
A heritage trip that skirts on and off the beaten path. (p113)

**9** **Wicklow Mountains 3 Days**
Heritage and history along the spine of eastern Ireland's most scenic mountain range. (p121)

**10** **Carlow Back Roads 3 Days**
Uncover the hidden delights of Ireland's second-smallest county. (p129)

**11** **Kilkenny's Treasures 3 Days**
The best of a medieval city and its pleasant surroundings. (p137)

**12** **Wexford & Waterford 5 Days**
The sunny southeast revealed – from bustling harbour villages to moody monastic ruins. (p145)

**13** **Blackwater Valley Drive 2 Days**
Follow the river from the sea and discover one of the country's most charming backwaters. (p153)

**14** **Family Fun 3 Days**
Adventure, heritage and distractions for the whole family. (p161)

 **DON'T MISS**

**Brú na Bóinne**
Ireland's most important neolithic monument is a mesmerising experience. Let yourself be wowed on Trips

**Dublin**
Most visits to Ireland begin and end in the capital, so be a latter-day Dubliner on Trips 1 2 5 14

**Monasterboice**
Best experienced at sunset on a summer's day, when crowing ravens are your only company; contemplate the high crosses on Trip 6

**Clonegal**
An arched stone bridge over a river populated by swans and a banked by a multitude of flowers? Visit a real fairy-tale village on Trip 7

**Ballysaggartmore Towers**
A Gothic folly in the middle of a forest is testimony to love's foolish ambition. Let yourself dream on Trip 13

# A Long Weekend Around Dublin

**4**

*You don't have to venture far from the capital in any direction to find distractions, including cosy seaside towns, stunning monastic ruins and palatial 18th-century mansions.*

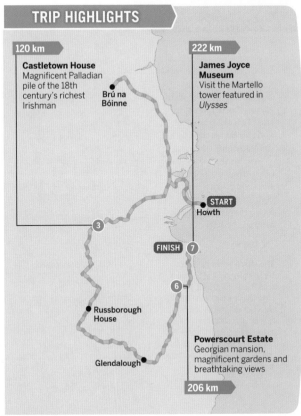

**120 km**

**Castletown House**
Magnificent Palladian pile of the 18th century's richest Irishman

Brú na Bóinne

**222 km**

**James Joyce Museum**
Visit the Martello tower featured in *Ulysses*

**START**
Howth

**3**

**FINISH** **7**

**6**

Russborough House

Glendalough

**Powerscourt Estate**
Georgian mansion, magnificent gardens and breathtaking views

**206 km**

**GREAT FOR...**

**BEST TIME TO GO**

April to September sees big crowds, but the sun also shines the most then.

**ESSENTIAL PHOTO**

Sugarloaf Mountain, from the entrance drive to Powerscourt Estate.

**BEST FOR CULTURE**

Russborough House, a Palladian pile with a top-notch art collection.

**Howth** A pretty port for yachting and fishing

81

## 4

# A Long Weekend Around Dublin

You can plunge into the very depths of Irish history, be awestruck by some of Ireland's most beautiful buildings and lose yourself in stunning countryside without ever being more than 50km from Dublin. This trip explores the very best of what the capital's environs have to offer – from coastal breaks to mountain retreats and a rip-roaring trip through 3500 years of history.

### 1 Howth

The pretty little port town of Howth is built on steep streets running down to its small but busy harbour, which has transformed itself from shipping port to yachting and fishing hub. Only 11km north of Dublin's city centre, it has long been a desirable residential suburb.

Howth is essentially a very large hill surrounded by cliffs, and the summit (171m) has excellent views across Dublin Bay right down to Wicklow. From the peak you can walk to the top of the Ben of Howth, which has a cairn said to mark a 2000-year-old Celtic royal grave. The 1814 Baily Lighthouse, at the south-eastern corner, is on the site of an old stone fort and can be reached by a dramatic cliff-top walk.

Besides the views, the other draw is the busy weekend market and the collection of good seafood restaurants huddled around the harbour.

✗ ⌂ p87

**The Drive »** For the 55km trip, take the right at Sutton onto Harbour Rd (R105) towards Baldoyle; with the Malahide estuary on your right and, on the spit of land beyond it, the famous Portmarnock Golf Links. Turn left onto Moyne Rd and take the M1 north, exiting at Junction 9 for Donore.

## ② Brú na Bóinne

Pharaoh hadn't even conceived of the pyramids when the neolithic pre-Celts built this vast necropolis on the banks of the River Boyne. Collectively known as Brú na Bóinne (the Boyne Palace), the passage tombs (and superb visitor centre; p99) are one of the most extraordinary sites in Europe and shouldn't be missed.

✕ ⌖ p103, p111

**The Drive »** Double-back onto the M1 and take the M50 *around* Dublin; take the exit at Junction 7 for the N4 and go west for 7km as far as Junction 5. Follow the R403 as far as Celbridge. The 71km trip should take about an hour.

TRIP HIGHLIGHT

## ③ Celbridge

The magnificent **Castletown House** (📞01-628 8252; www.castletown.ie;

## LINK YOUR TRIP

**1 Iconic Ireland**
Dublin is the starting point of this classic trip that delivers the country's five-star attractions.

**2 The Long Way Round**
From Dublin, take a couple of weeks to explore the country.

83

Celbridge; adult/child €7/3; ⊙10am-6pm mid-Mar–Oct) simply has no equal. It is Ireland's largest and most imposing Georgian estate, and a testament to the vast wealth enjoyed by the Anglo-Irish gentry during the 18th century.

Built between 1722 and 1732, the house was commissioned by Speaker of the Irish House of Commons William Conolly (1662–1729), who wanted a house suitable to his position as Ireland's richest man.

The original '16th-century Italian palazzo' design of the house was by the Italian architect Alessandro Galilei (1691–1737) in 1718. In 1724 the project was entrusted to Sir Edward Lovett Pearce (1699–1733).

The house is full of Palladian touches, including the terminating pavilions and the superb Long Gallery, full of family portraits and fancy stucco work by the Italian Francini brothers. Thomas Jefferson was such a fan of the style that much of Washington, DC is designed accordingly.

**The Drive »** The 30km drive will first take you south along the R405, through the western stretch of Dublin suburbia. Take the N82 for 2km. Turn left onto the N81 and travel uphill into the Wicklow Mountains. The huge Poulaphouca Reservoir, which delivers drinking water to the capital, is on your left just before you reach Blessington.

DAMIEN KELLY/500PX ©

## RUSSBOROUGH HOUSE: THE TERRORISTS, THE THIEVES & THE ART LOVERS

In 1974 the IRA decided to get into the art business by stealing 16 paintings from Russborough House. They were eventually all recovered, but 10 years later the notorious Dublin criminal Martin Cahill (aka the General) masterminded another robbery from the Russborough House collection, this time for Loyalist paramilitaries. On this occasion, however, only some of the works were recovered and of those, several were damaged beyond repair – a good thief does not a gentle curator make. In 1988 the owner, Sir Albert Beit, decided to hand over the most valuable of the paintings to the National Gallery; in return, the gallery agreed to lend other paintings to the collection as temporary exhibits. The sorry story didn't conclude there. In 2001 two thieves drove a jeep through the front doors, making off with two paintings worth nearly €4 million, including a Gainsborough that had been stolen, and recovered, twice before. To add abuse to the insult already added to injury, the house was broken into again in 2002, with the thieves taking five more paintings, including two by Rubens. Thankfully, all of the paintings were recovered after both attempts, but where a succession of thieves couldn't succeed, the cost of the upkeep did: in 2015 the owners announced they were going to auction off 10 of the paintings, a decision that caused much consternation as the family had always maintained that the collection was to be held in trust for the Irish people.

**Sandycove** Forty Foot promontory

### 4 Blessington

Dominating the one-street town of Blessington (pubs, shops, a handful of 17th- and 18th-century town houses) is magnificent **Russborough House** (☎045-865 239; www.russboroughhouse.ie; adult/child guided tours €12/9; ⏰10am-6pm mid-Mar–Dec), one of Ireland's finest stately homes, built for Joseph Leeson (1705–83), later the first Earl of Milltown and, later still, Lord Russborough. The Palladian pleasure palace was built between 1741 and 1751 to the design of Richard Cassels, who was at the height of his fame as an architect. Richard didn't live to see it finished, but the job was well executed by Francis Bindon.

The house remained in the Leeson family until 1931. In 1952 it was sold to Sir Alfred Beit, the nephew of the cofounder of the de Beers diamond-mining company. Uncle Alfred was an obsessive art collector, and when he died, his impressive haul – which includes works by Velázquez, Vermeer, Goya and Rubens – was passed on to his nephew, who brought it to Russborough House.

The admission price includes a 45-minute tour of the house, which is decorated in typical Georgian style.

🛏 p87

**The Drive »** Follow the N81 south and cut across the Wicklow Mountains on the R756 via the stunning Wicklow Gap. It's a 20km stretch to Laragh; Glendalough is only 3km further on.

### 5 Glendalough

Location, location, location. When St Kevin came to this spectacular glacial valley in the heart of the Wicklow Mountains in 498 to found a small monastic settlement, did he realise that the settlement would grow into one of Ireland's most important centres of learning and, 15 centuries later, one of the country's most popular tourist attractions? Probably not.

 p87, p127

**The Drive »** Overall distance 28km. Head northeast on the R755 for 16km, skirting the eastern edge of Wicklow Mountains National Park, then follow the road signs to Enniskerry.

**TRIP HIGHLIGHT**

### 6 Enniskerry

Backing onto the pretty village of Enniskerry is the expanse of **Powerscourt Estate** (www.powerscourt.ie; near Ennis-

kerry; admission to house free, gardens adult/child €8.50/5; ☺9.30am-5.30pm Mar-Oct, to dusk Nov-Feb), which gives contemporary observers a true insight into the style of the 18th-century super-rich. The main entrance is 500m south of the village square.

The estate has existed more or less since 1300, when the LePoer (later anglicised to Power) family built themselves a castle here. The property changed Anglo-Norman hands a few times before coming into the possession of Richard Wingfield, newly appointed Marshall of Ireland, in 1603. His descendants were to live here for the next 350 years.

Unfortunately, a fire in 1974 gutted most of the house, which remains largely off-limits, so

the biggest draw of the whole pile is the simply magnificent 20-hectare formal **gardens** and the breathtaking views that accompany them.

 p87, p127

**The Drive »** Continue onto the M11 north and take the exit for Dun Laoghaire. The Wyatville Rd becomes Church Rd; keep going north and follow the road signs for Sandycove. It's only 19km from Powerscourt to Sandycove.

**TRIP HIGHLIGHT**

### 7 Sandycove

The handsome seaside town of Sandycove is now just part of greater Dublin, but it is renowned for its excellent restaurants, pretty beach and a Martello tower – built by British forces to keep an eye out for a Napoleonic invasion – now housing the **James Joyce Museum** (☎01-280 9265; www.jamesjoycetower.com; Joyce Tower; ☺10am-4pm). This is where the action begins in James Joyce's epic novel *Ulysses*. The museum was opened in 1962 by Sylvia Beach, the Paris-based publisher who first dared to put *Ulysses* into print, and has photographs, letters, documents, various editions of Joyce's work and two death masks of Joyce on display.

 p87

## DETOUR: POWERSCOURT WATERFALL

### Start: 6 Enniskerry

Signposted from the Powerscourt Estate is the 130m **Powerscourt Waterfall** (near Enniskerry; adult/child €5.50/3.50; ☺9.30am-7pm May-Aug, 10.30am-5.30pm Mar-Apr, Sep & Oct, to 4.30pm Nov-Jan). It's the highest waterfall in Britain and Ireland, and is most impressive after heavy rain. A nature trail has been laid out around the base of the waterfall, taking you past giant redwoods, ancient oaks, beech, birch and rowan trees. There are plenty of birds in the vicinity, including the chaffinch, cuckoo, chiffchaff, raven and willow warbler. It's also a popular 7km walk to the waterfall.

# Eating & Sleeping

## Howth ❶

### 🍴 Aqua — Seafood €€€

(📞01-832 0690; www.aqua.ie; 1 West Pier; mains €29-32; ⏱lunch & dinner Tue-Sat; 🚌31, 31A from Beresford Pl, 🚊Howth) A contender for best seafood restaurant in Howth, Aqua serves top-quality fish dishes in its elegant dining room overlooking the harbour. The building was once home to the Howth Yacht Club.

### 🍴 House — Irish €€

(📞01-839 6388; www.thehouse-howth.ie; 4 Main St; mains €17-24; ⏱8.45am-4pm Mon, to 9.30pm Tue-Fri, 10am-10pm Sat & Sun; 🚌31, 31A from Beresford Pl, 🚊Howth) Wonderful spot on the main street leading away from the harbour where you can feast on dishes such as crunchy Bellingham blue-cheese polenta or wild Wicklow venison stew, as well as a fine selection of fish.

### 🛏 King Sitric — Boutique Hotel €€

(📞01-832 5235; www.kingsitric.ie; East Pier; r €150-205; 🚌31, 31A from Beresford Pl, 🚊Howth) This handsome boutique hotel above a long-established restaurant (two-course menu €30) has eight rooms with views of the port. The nautical theme is everywhere and each room is named after an Irish lighthouse.

## Blessington ❹

### 🛏 Rathsallagh House & Country Club — Hotel €€€

(📞045-403 112; www.rathsallagh.com; Dunlavin; r from €185) About 20km south of Blessington, this fabulous country manor, converted from Queen Anne stables in 1798, is more than just a fancy hotel. Luxury is par for the course here, from the splendidly appointed rooms to the exquisite country-house dining (mains €15 to €27) and the highly rated golf course that surrounds the estate.

## Glendalough ❺

### 🛏 Glendalough Hotel — Hotel €€

(📞0404-45135; www.glendaloughhotel.com; r from €65; 🅿@🛜) There's no mistaking Glendalough's best hotel, conveniently located next door to the visitor centre. There is also no shortage of takers for its 44 fairly luxurious bedrooms.

## Enniskerry ❻

### 🍴 Emilia's Ristorante — Italian €€

(📞01-276 1834; www.emilias.ie; Clock Tower, The Square; mains €17-23; ⏱5-10.45pm Mon-Sat, noon-9.30pm Sun) A lovely 1st-floor restaurant to satisfy even the most ardent craving for thin-crust pizzas. Emilia's does everything else just right too, from organic soups to perfect steaks, down to gorgeous meringue desserts.

### 🛏 Powerscourt Hotel & Spa — Hotel €€€

(📞01-274 8888; www.powerscourthotel.com; Powerscourt Estate; r from €170) Wicklow's most luxurious hotel is this 200-room stunner on the grounds of the Powerscourt Estate. Inside this Marriott-managed property all is OTT luxury, and the decor is a thoroughly contemporary version of the estate's Georgian style. The rooms are massive. Downstairs there's a decent restaurant and a superb spa.

## Sandycove ❼

### 🍴 Caviston's Seafood Restaurant — Seafood €€

(📞01-280 9245; www.cavistons.com; Glasthule Rd; mains €16-24; ⏱noon-5pm Tue-Thu, noon-midnight Fri & Sat; 🚊Sandycove) This is an excellent seafood restaurant with a long-standing reputation. From tuna loin to escalope of salmon, it's all fresh and beautifully presented. Menus change twice weekly in accordance with what the nets bring in. There's an adjoining produce shop, which is also wonderful.

# East to West

**5**

*Music, landscape and history are the keys to this trip, which transports you across Ireland's midriff from the bustling capital to the pastoral splendour of the west.*

## TRIP HIGHLIGHTS

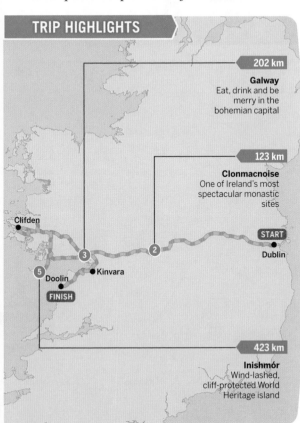

**202 km**

**Galway**
Eat, drink and be merry in the bohemian capital

**123 km**

**Clonmacnoise**
One of Ireland's most spectacular monastic sites

Clifden

③

②

START

Dublin

⑤ ● Kinvara
Doolin

FINISH

**423 km**

**Inishmór**
Wind-lashed, cliff-protected World Heritage island

**7 DAYS**
**435KM / 270 MILES**

**GREAT FOR...**

**BEST TIME TO GO**

The warmer months (April to September) are festival time in Galway.

**ESSENTIAL PHOTO**

Dún Aengus just before sunset.

**BEST TWO DAYS**

From the Aran Islands back to Connemara and down to County Clare and the Burren.

**Clonmacnoise** A monastic settlement on the banks of the River Shannon

89

# 5 | East to West

Go west! As you quit Dublin's suburban sprawl the landscape continues to soften and before you know it you're in Galway, gateway to beautiful, brooding Connemara, where the mountainous landscape is punctuated by brown bog and shimmering lakes. Explore one of the country's most magnificent spots before looping south into the Burren of County Clare, the spiritual home of Irish traditional music.

## ❶ Dublin

A day in the capital should give you enough time to take a walk around and check out the city's big-ticket items. Culture buffs should definitely take a stroll through the archaeology and history branch of the **National Museum of Ireland** (www.museum.ie; Kildare St; ⏰10am-5pm Tue-Sat, 2-5pm Sun; 🚌all city centre) – don't miss the Treasury's golden hoard of artefacts from the Bronze and Iron ages as well as its eerily

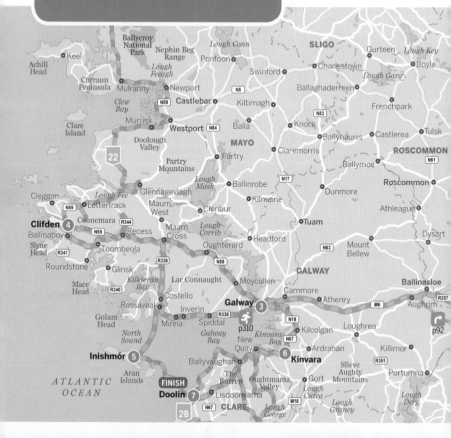

fascinating collection of preserved 'bog bodies'.

🍴 🛏 p46, p60, p95, p167

**The Drive »** The 130km drive to Clonmacnoise is largely uneventful, courtesy of the convenient M4/M6 tolled motorway, from which you see fields and little else. Take exit 7 towards Moate and get on the R444 – Clonmacnoise is signposted as you go.

- - - - - - - - - - - - - -

TRIP HIGHLIGHT

## ❷ Clonmacnoise

**Clonmacnoise** (www. heritageireland.ie; adult/child €7/3; ⏱9am-6.30pm Jun-Aug, 10am-6pm mid-Mar–May, Sep & Oct, 10am-5.30pm Nov–mid-Mar; **P**), straddling a hill overlooking a bend in the Shannon, is one of the main reasons Ireland got the moniker of 'land of saints and scholars.'

🛏 p95

## LINK YOUR TRIP

### 22 Best of the West

In Galway you can connect with this trip, which brings you from Sligo south to County Kerry.

### 28 County Clare

Explore the rest of lyrical County Clare by travelling the 40km from Doolin to Ennis.

**The Drive »** From Clonmacnoise, take the R357 for 22km towards Ballinasloe, Galway's county town and the first town you'll come to as you enter the county across the River Suck. Here you can rejoin the M6; it's 61km to Galway City.

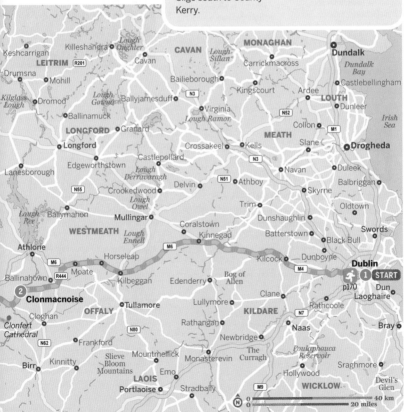

TRIP HIGHLIGHT

### ❸ Galway City

Galway City is the long-established, self-proclaimed and generally accepted capital of bohemian Ireland, with a long-standing tradition of attracting artists, musicians and other creative types to its pub- and cafe-lined streets.

 p46, p74, p95, p277

**The Drive »** The N59 cuts through the heart of the region – in the distance you'll see Connemara's mountain ranges, the Maumturks and the Twelve Bens. After about 58km, just before Recess, take a 5km detour north along the R344 and take in the majesty of the Lough Inagh Valley before rejoining the road and continuing towards Clifden, 28km further on.

### ❹ Clifden

Connemara's principal town is a genteel Victorian-era fishing port that makes a good stopover, especially during the summer months when it casts off its wintry covers and offers visitors a nice taster of what drew 19th-century tourists to it. You can amble about its narrow streets or stare at the sea from the head of the narrow bay into which falls the River Owenglin.

 p46, p95

**The Drive »** The R341 coast road goes to Roundstone, but cut through the Roundstone Bog from Ballinaboy for some fine scenery. Rejoin the R341 at Toombeola and turn left onto the N59 before turning right onto the R340 for the ferry to Inishmór from Rossaveal or a flight from Minna. From Clifden, it's 57km to Rossaveal, and 64km to Minna.

---

### DETOUR:
### THE MAN WHO REALLY FOUND AMERICA?

**Start: ❷ Clonmacnoise (p91)**

About 21km southeast of Ballinasloe along the R355 is the 12th-century **Clonfert Cathedral**, built on the site of a monastery said to have been founded in 563 by St Brendan 'the Navigator', who is believed to be buried here. Although the jury is out on whether St Brendan reached America's shores in a tiny *currach* rowing boat, there are Old Irish Ogham (the earliest form of writing in Ireland) carvings in West Virginia that date from as early as the 6th century, suggesting an Irish presence in America well before Columbus set foot there. The marvellous six-arch Romanesque doorway, adorned with surreal human heads, is reason enough to visit.

---

TRIP HIGHLIGHT

### ❺ Inishmór

Do not doubt that the effort you made to get here isn't worth it, for a visit to the largest of the Aran Islands (indeed, any of the three) is one of the more memorable things you'll do in Ireland. The big draw is the spectacular Stone Age fort of **Dún Aengus** (Dún Aonghasa; www.heritageireland.ie/en/ west/dunaonghasa/; adult/ child €4/2; ⏰9.30am-6pm Apr-Oct, 9.30am-4pm Nov-Mar, closed Mon & Tue Jan & Feb), but don't forget to explore some of the

**The Burren** A unique striated limestone landscape

island's other ruins, scattered about the place like so much historical detritus. There's also a lovely beach at **Kilmurvey** (west of Kilronan), while up to 50 grey seals sun themselves and feed in the shallows of **Port Chorrúch**.

🛏 p95, p269

**The Drive ≫** You'll have to go back to Minna or Rossaveal to pick up your car. On your way back along the R336 to Galway, stop off in Spiddal, in the heart of Connemara's *Gaelteacht* (Irish-speaking) heartland. Beyond Galway city, turn off the N18 and go 10km along the N67 to Kinvara.

### 6 Kinvara

The small stone harbour of Kinvara (sometimes spelt Kinvarra) sits snugly at the southeastern corner of Galway Bay, which accounts for its Irish name, Cinn Mhara (Head of the Sea). It's a posh little village, the kind of place where all the jeans have creases in them. It makes a good pit stop between Galway and Clare.

### THE BURREN

Stretching across northern Clare, from the Atlantic coast to Kinvara in County Galway, the Burren is a unique striated limestone landscape that was shaped beneath ancient seas, then forced high and dry by a great geological cataclysm. In the Burren, land and sea seem to merge into one vast, moody, rocky and at times fearsome space beneath huge skies, accented with ancient burial chambers and medieval ruins.

# CLARINBRIDGE OYSTER FESTIVAL

South of Galway, Clarinbridge (Droichead an Chláirin) and Kilcolgan (Cill Cholgáin) are at their busiest during the **Clarinbridge Oyster Festival** (www.clarinbridge.com; ☺mid-Sep), held during the second weekend of September. However, the oysters are actually at their best from May through the summer.

Oysters are celebrated year-round at **Paddy Burke's Oyster Inn** (www.paddyburkesgalway.com; off N18, Clarinbridge; mains €13-27; ☺10.30am-10pm Mon-Sat, from noon Sun), a thatched inn by the bridge dishing up heaped servings in a roadside location on the N18.

**Moran's Oyster Cottage** (www.moransoystercottage. com; The Weir, Kilcolgan; mains €15-27; ☺noon-9.30pm Sun-Thu, noon-10pm Fri & Sat) is a thatched pub and restaurant with a facade as plain as the inside of an oyster shell. Find a seat on the terrace overlooking Dunbulcaun Bay, where the oysters are reared before they arrive on your plate. It's a well-marked 2km west of the noxious N18, in a cove near Kilcolgan.

Dominating one end of the harbour is the chesspiece-style **Dunguaire Castle** (www.shannonheritage.com; off N67; adult/child €5/3; ☺10am-4pm Apr-early Oct), erected around 1520 by the O'Hynes clan and in excellent condition following extensive restoration. It is widely believed that the castle occupies the former site of the 6th-century royal palace of Guaire Aidhne, the king of Connaught.

Dunguaire's owners have included Oliver St John Gogarty (1878–1957) – poet, writer, surgeon and inspiration for James Joyce's fictional Buck Mulligan, one of the cast of *Ulysses*.

The least authentic way to visit the castle is to attend a **medieval banquet** (☎061-360 788; www.shannonheritage.com; adult/child €52/22; ☺5.30pm & 8.45pm Apr-Oct). Stage shows and shtick provide diversions while you plough through a big group meal.

**The Drive** » The N67 from Kinvara skirts along the western edge of the Burren; this particularly desolatelooking (but no less beautiful) landscape is in evidence beyond Ballyvaughan, about 20km on. Doolin is a further 23km away; just past Lisdoonvarna, take a right onto the R476.

- - - - - - - - - -

## ➐ Doolin

Only 6km north of the Cliffs of Moher, Doolin's rep as a terrific spot to spend a couple of days isn't just down to its proximity to one of the bone fide stars of the Irish tourist trail. It helps, sure, but Doolin's popularity is largely due to its pubs, or, rather, to the musicians that play in them: the area is full of talented players whose exquisite abilities can be enjoyed almost every night. There's lots of pubs to choose from, but if we had to pick one, it'd be **McGann's** (www. mcgannspubdoolin.com; Roadford; ☺10am-12.30am, kitchen 10am-9.30pm), complete with turf fires, dartboard and great grub.

🛏 p95

# Eating & Sleeping

## Dublin ①

### ✖ Green Hen — French €€

(📞01-670 7238; www.greenhen.ie; 33 Exchequer St; mains €18-27; ⏰noon-3pm daily, plus 5-11pm Sun-Thu, 5pm-1am Fri & Sat; 🖥all city centre) New York's SoHo meets Parisian brasserie at this stylish eatery, where elegance and economy live side-by-side. If you don't fancy gorging on oysters or tucking into a divine Irish Hereford rib-eye, you can opt for the *plat du jour* or avail yourself of the early-bird menus; watch out for its killer cocktails. Reservations recommended for dinner.

### 🛏 Number 31 — Guesthouse €€€

(📞01-676 5011; www.number31.ie; 31 Leeson Close; s/d incl breakfast €200/240; P🛜🖥all city centre) The city's most distinctive property is the former home of modernist architect Sam Stephenson, who successfully fused '60s style with 18th-century grace. Its 21 bedrooms are split between the retro coach house, with its coolly modern rooms, and the more elegant Georgian house, where rooms are individually furnished with tasteful French antiques and big comfortable beds. Breakfast included. Gourmet breakfasts with kippers, homemade breads and granola are served in the conservatory.

## Clonmacnoise ②

### 🛏 Kajon House — B&B €€

(📞090-967 4191; www.kajonhouse.ie; R444, Creevagh; s/d from €55/75; ⏰Mar-Oct; P🛜) If you want to stay near the ruins, this is your best option, just 1.5km southwest. It has cosy rooms, a spacious yard (complete with picnic table) and a warm welcome even by Irish standards. Delicious pancakes are available for breakfast; you may be able to arrange for dinner.

## Galway City ③

### 🛏 House Hotel — Hotel €€€

(📞091-538 900; www.thehousehotel.ie; Spanish Pde; r €140-220; P🛜) There's a hip and cool array of colour in the lobby at this smart and stylish boutique hotel. Public spaces contrast modern art with trad details and bold accents. The 40 rooms are small but plush, with bright colour schemes and quality fabrics.

## Clifden ④

### 🛏 Dolphin Beach — B&B €€

(📞095-21204; www.dolphinbeachhouse.com; Lower Sky Rd; s from €90, d €130-180, dinner €40; P🛜) This exquisite B&B, set amid some of Connemara's best coastal scenery, does everything right. The emphasis is on style, tranquillity, relaxation and gorgeous views, a formula that can be hard to tear yourself away from. It's 5km west of Clifden, tucked away off the Lower Sky Road.

## Inishmór ⑤

### 🛏 Kilmurvey House — B&B €€

(📞099-61218; www.kilmurveyhouse.com; Kilmurvey; s/d from €50/90; ⏰mid-Apr–mid-Oct) On the path leading to Dún Aengus is this grand 18th-century stone mansion. It's a beautiful setting and the 12 rooms are well maintained. Hearty meals (dinner €30) incorporate vegetables from the garden, and local fish and meats. You can swim at a pretty beach that's a short walk from the house.

## Doolin ⑦

### 🛏 Cullinan's Guesthouse — Inn €€

(📞065-707 4183; www.cullinansdoolin.com; d from €100; P🛜) Owned by well-known fiddle-player James Cullinan, the eight rooms at this smart place on the River Aille are very good-looking, with power showers and comfortable fittings.

# The Boyne Valley

**6**

*A trip through the cradle of Irish history, from prehistoric tombs to bloody battlefields, with monasteries and old castles thrown in for good measure.*

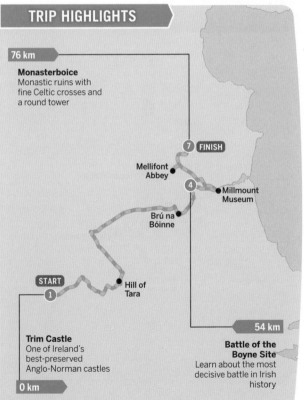

**76 km**

**Monasterboice**
Monastic ruins with fine Celtic crosses and a round tower

**7 FINISH**

**Mellifont Abbey**

**4**

**Millmount Museum**

**Brú na Bóinne**

**START**
**1**

**Hill of Tara**

**Trim Castle**
One of Ireland's best-preserved Anglo-Norman castles

**0 km**

**54 km**

**Battle of the Boyne Site**
Learn about the most decisive battle in Irish history

**2 DAYS**
**76KM / 47 MILES**

**GREAT FOR...**

### BEST TIME TO GO

The sun doesn't set until after 10pm between June and July, but September often gets the best weather.

### ESSENTIAL PHOTO

The round tower at Monasterboice at sunset.

### BEST FOR CULTURE

The magnificent neolithic passage tombs at Brú Na Bóinne.

**Brú Na Bóinne** Newgrange

# 6 The Boyne Valley

Only 112km long, the River Boyne isn't especially impressive, but its valley can lay claim to being Ireland's most significant historical stage. The breathtaking prehistoric passage tomb complex of Brú na Bóinne is the main highlight, but the remnants of Celtic forts, Norman castles and atmospheric monasteries are but the most obvious clues of the area's rich and longstanding legacy.

TRIP HIGHLIGHT

## 1 Trim

Remarkably preserved **Trim Castle** (King John's Castle; www.heritageireland. ie; adult/child incl tour €4/2; ☉10am-6pm mid-Mar–Oct, 9am-5pm Sat & Sun Nov– mid-Mar) was Ireland's largest Anglo-Norman fortification and is proof of Trim's medieval importance. Hugh de Lacy founded Trim Castle in 1173, but Rory O'Connor, said to have been the last high king of Ireland, destroyed this motte and

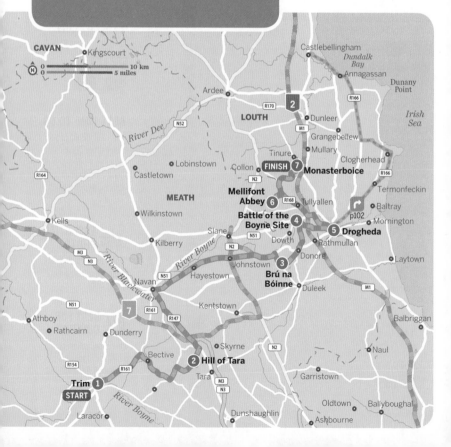

bailey within a year. The building you see today was begun around 1200 and has hardly been modified since, although it was badly damaged by Cromwellian forces when they took the town in 1649.

✕ ⇔ p103

**The Drive** ⟫ It's only 15km from Trim to Tara. Eight kilometres northeast of Trim, along the R161, is 12th-century Bective Abbey, built in the lush farmland still in evidence today on both sides of the road as you drive.

## ② Hill of Tara

The Hill of Tara is Ireland's most sacred stretch of turf, an entrance to the underworld, occupying a place at the heart of Irish history, legend and folklore. It was the home of the mystical druids, the

## LINK YOUR TRIP

### 2 The Long Way Round

From Monasterboice, head north on the M1 to Belfast and this hugely rewarding two-week trip.

### 7 Ancient Ireland

Connect to this trip from Brú na Bóinne and continue time travelling through Ireland's historic past.

priest-rulers of ancient Ireland, who practised their particular form of Celtic paganism under the watchful gaze of the all-powerful goddess Maeve (Medbh). Later it was the ceremonial capital of the high kings – 142 of them in all – who ruled until the arrival of Christianity in the 6th century. It is also one of the most important ancient sites in Europe, with a Stone Age passage tomb and prehistoric burial mounds that date back up to 5000 years. Although little remains other than humps and mounds of earth on the hill, its historic and folkloristic significance is immense.

The **Tara Visitor Centre** (☎046-902 5903; www.heritageireland.ie; adult/child €4/2; ☺visitor centre 10am-6pm mid-May–mid-Sep, site open 24hr year-round) is housed within a former Protestant church (with a window by artist Evie Hone) and screens a 20-minute audiovisual presentation about the site.

**The Drive** ⟫ From Tara, the 29km drive to Brú na Bóinne takes you through the county town of Navan, the crossroads of the busy Dublin road (M3/N3) and the Drogheda–Westmeath road (N51). If you stop here, Trimgate St is lined with restaurants and pubs. Two kilometres south of the centre is the relatively intact 16th-century Athlumney Castle.

‑ ‑ ‑ ‑ ‑ ‑ ‑ ‑ ‑

## ③ Brú na Bóinne

The vast neolithic necropolis known as Brú na Bóinne (the Boyne Palace) is one of the most extraordinary sites in Europe and shouldn't be missed. A thousand years older than Stonehenge, it's a powerful and evocative testament to the mind-boggling achievements of prehistoric humans.

The area consists of many different sites; the three principal ones are Newgrange, Knowth and Dowth, but only the first two are open to visitors, and then only as part of an organised tour which departs from the **Brú na Bóinne Visitor Centre** (☎041-988 0300; www.heritageireland.ie; Donore; adult/child visitor centre €3/2, visitor centre & Newgrange €6/3, visitor centre & Knowth €5/3, all 3 sites €11/6; ☺9am-6.30pm May-Sep, to 5pm Nov-Jan, 9.30am-5.30pm Feb-Apr & Oct), from where a bus will take you to the tombs. The centre houses an extraordinary series of interactive exhibits on prehistoric Ireland and its passage tombs, and has an excellent book and souvenir shop.

✕ ⇔ p103, p111

**The Drive** ⟫ The 7km drive from Brú na Bóinne is along a tiny rural road that takes you through the village of Donore. The battle site is 3km north of Donore, signposted off the N51.

TRIP HIGHLIGHT

## 4 Battle of the Boyne Site

More than 60,000 soldiers of the armies of King James II and King William III fought on this patch of farmland on the border of Counties Meath and Louth in 1690. In the end, William prevailed and James sailed off to France.

Today, the **battle site** (www.battleoftheboyne.ie; adult/child €4/2; ⏰10am-5pm May-Sep, 9.30am-4.30pm Mar & Apr, 9am-4pm Oct-Feb) is part of the Oldbridge Estate farm. At the visitor centre you can watch a short show about the battle, see original and replica weaponry of the time, and explore a laser battlefield model.

**The Drive »** It's only 6km to Drogheda; almost immediately you'll find yourself driving from fecund landscape into suburban sprawl as you approach Drogheda's outlying expanse.

## 5 Drogheda

Across the river from the main town of Drogheda is Millmount, which may have once been a prehistoric burial ground but is now home to a Martello Tower and army barracks.

Part of the barracks is now the **Millmount Museum** (☎041-983 3097; www.millmount.net; off Duleek St, Millmount; adult/child museum €3.50/2.50, tower €3/2, museum & tower €5.50/3; ⏰10am-5.30pm Mon-Sat, 2-5pm Sun), which has interesting displays about the town and its history. Exhibits include three wonderful late-18th-century guild banners, perhaps the last in the country. There's also a room devoted to Cromwell's brutal siege of Drogheda and the Battle of the Boyne. Across the courtyard, the **Governor's House** opens for temporary exhibitions.

✕ ⏢ p103, p167

**The Drive »** The rich pastureland that drew the early Irish here has largely disappeared beneath the suburban sprawl, but, after 2km, as you go left off the N1 onto the N51, you'll get a better sense of classic Irish farmland (even though you'll drive under the M1 motorway!). As you get to the Boyne, go right onto the Glen Rd until you get to Mellifont. The whole drive is 11km long.

## 6 Mellifont Abbey

In its Anglo-Norman prime, this **abbey** (☎041-982 6459; www.heritageireland.ie; Tullyallen; site admission free, visitor centre adult/student €4/2; ⏰site 24hr year-round, visitor centre 10am-6pm Jun-Aug) was the Cistercians' first and most magnificent centre in the country. Although the ruins are highly evocative and well worth exploring, they still don't

---

## CROMWELL'S DROGHEDA INVASION

Oliver Cromwell (1599–1658) may be lauded as England's first democrat and protector of the people, but he didn't have much love for the Irish, dismissing them as a dirty race of papists who had sided with Charles I during the Civil War. So when 'God's own Englishman' landed his 12,000 troops in Dublin in August 1649, he set out for Drogheda, determined to set a brutal example to any other town that might resist his armies.

Over a period of hours, an estimated 3000 people were massacred, mostly royalist soldiers but also priests, women and children. The defenders' leader, Englishman and royalist Sir Arthur Aston, was bludgeoned to death with his own (wooden) leg. Of the survivors, many were captured and sold into indentured servitude in the Caribbean.

Cromwell defended his action as God's righteous punishment of treacherous Catholics, and was quick to point out that he had never ordered the killing of non-combatants: it was the 17th century's version of 'collateral damage'.

**Clogherhead** Sunset on the shoreline

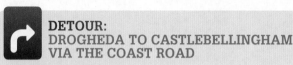

# DETOUR:
## DROGHEDA TO CASTLEBELLINGHAM VIA THE COAST ROAD

**Start: ⑤ Drogheda (p100)**

Most people just zip north along the M1 motorway, but if you want to meander along the coast and see a little of rural Ireland, opt for the R166 from Drogheda north along the coast.

The picturesque little village of **Termonfeckin** was, until 1656, the seat and castle of the primate of Armagh. The 15th-century **castle** (☎086 079 1484; key deposit €50; ⏰10am-6pm), or tower house, is tiny and worth a five-minute stop.

About 2km further north is the busy seaside and fishing centre of **Clogherhead**, with a good, shallow Blue Flag beach at Lurganboy. Squint to ignore the caravan parks and take in the lovely views of the Cooley and Mourne Mountains instead.

The 33km route comes to an end in **Castlebellingham**. The village grew up around an 18th-century crenellated mansion, and generations of mud farmers served the landlord within. From here you can come back on the M1; it's only 25km from Castlebellingham to Drogheda.

do real justice to the site's former splendour.

Mellifont's most recognisable building, and one of the finest pieces of Cistercian architecture in Ireland, is the lavabo, an octagonal washing house for the monks. It was built in the early 13th century and used lead pipes to bring water from the river. A number of other buildings would have surrounded this main part of the abbey.

The visitor centre describes monastic life in detail. The ruins themselves are always open and there's good picnicking next to the rushing stream. The abbey is about 1.5km off the main Drogheda–Collon road (R168).

**The Drive ≫** The easiest way to get to Monasterboice from Mellifont Abbey is to take the Old Mellifont Rd; after 1.5km turn left onto the R168 and then veer right onto The Gables. A further 3km on, turn left onto the N1 and, almost immediately, right onto the R132. It's only 12km in total.

- - - - - - - - - - - - -

**TRIP HIGHLIGHT**

## ⑦ Monasterboice

Crowing ravens lend an eerie atmosphere to **Monasterboice** (⏰sunrise-sunset), an intriguing monastic site containing a cemetery, two ancient church ruins, one of the finest and tallest round towers in Ireland, and two of the best high crosses.

The high crosses of Monasterboice are superb examples of Celtic art. The crosses had an important didactic use, bringing the gospels alive for the uneducated, and they were probably brightly painted originally, although all traces of colour have long disappeared.

Come early or late in the day to avoid the crowds.

# Eating & Sleeping

## Trim ①

### 🍴 StockHouse                    Steak €€

(📞046-943 7388; www.stockhouserestaurant.
ie; Finnegan's Way, Emmet House; mains €15-26;
⏰11.30am-3pm & 5-9pm Mon-Thu, to 10pm Fri,
5-10pm Sat, noon-8.30pm Sun) Cooked-to-order
dry-aged steaks from local abattoir/butcher
Coogan's are the stock-in-trade of this always-
packed restaurant, but noncarnivores can
choose from fish and vegetarian dishes such as
pastas. They also do a fine selection of fajitas.

### 🛏 Trim Castle Hotel            Hotel €€

(📞046-948 3000; www.trimcastlehotel.com;
Castle St; d/f from €85/135; 🅿 @ 🛜) Acres of
glossy marble in the foyer set the scene at this
contemporary hotel opposite Trim Castle. Some
of its stylish rooms come with balconies (try
for sprawling corner room 225). Its rooftop sun
terrace overlooks Trim Castle, and dining –
whether at breakfast, the bar's carvery,
or upmarket Jules Restaurant (Friday and
Saturday evenings only) – is top-notch.

## Brú na Bóinne ③

### 🍴 Brú na Bóinne
Visitor Centre Cafe              Cafe €

(dishes €4.50-12; ⏰breakfast & lunch; 🦽)
On the lower level of the Brú na Bóinne visitor
centre, this surprisingly good cafe's extensive
vegetarian options include nut and lentil loaf,
and eggplant and zucchini cake, plus plenty of
other treats like salmon and leek tart and beef
lasagne.

## Drogheda ⑤

### 🍴 Eastern Seaboard
Bar & Grill                       Irish €€

(www.easternseaboard.ie; Dublin Rd, 1
Bryanstown; mains €12-33; ⏰noon-10pm;
🛜🦽) Despite its unpromising location in
a business park near the train station, this
stylised, contemporary space is generally
packed. Adventurous food like pig's cheek
terrine with apple slaw, smoked mackerel pâté,
and coffee jelly and vanilla ice cream is served
continuously from lunchtime on – along with
frothy German beers on tap.

### 🛏 D Hotel                      Hotel €€

(📞041-987 7700; www.thedhotel.com; Scotch
Hall, Marsh Rd; d from €129; 🅿 @ 🛜) Slick,
hip and unexpected, this is Drogheda's top dog
when it comes to accommodation. Minimalist
rooms are bathed in light and decked out with
designer furniture and cool gadgets. There's
a stylish bar and restaurant, a mini-gym and
fantastic views of the city. The hotel is popular
for hen and stag parties: beware of pounding
music on weekends.

### 🛏 Scholars
Townhouse Hotel                  Hotel €€

(📞041-983 5410; www.scholarshotel.com; King
St; d from €75; 🅿 🛜) This former monastery
dates from 1867 and was recently revamped as
a family-owned hotel and restaurant. Despite
the 16 rooms being on the small side, there's
nothing monastic about the facilities, which
include power showers, an atmospheric bar and
a superb restaurant (bookings recommended).
The central location is ideal for exploring the
town.

# Ancient Ireland

**7**

*Go time travelling through middle Ireland's collection of ancient tombs, Celtic sites and monastic cities, and cover 3000 years in four days.*

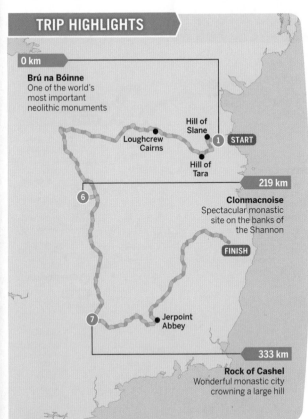

**0 km**

**Brú na Bóinne**
One of the world's most important neolithic monuments

Hill of Slane

Loughcrew Cairns

**1** START

Hill of Tara

**219 km**

**6**

**Clonmacnoise**
Spectacular monastic site on the banks of the Shannon

FINISH

**7**

Jerpoint Abbey

**333 km**

**Rock of Cashel**
Wonderful monastic city crowning a large hill

**4 DAYS**
**529KM /**
**329 MILES**

**GREAT FOR...**

**BEST TIME TO GO**

April to September, for the long days and the best weather.

**ESSENTIAL PHOTO**

The Rock of Cashel from the ruins of Hore Abbey.

**BEST FOR CULTURE**

The passage graves at Brú Na Bóinne.

**Jerpoint Abbey** One of Ireland's finest Cistercian ruins

105

# Ancient Ireland

This trip transports you from the neolithic era to the last days of the first millennium, via the signposts of Ireland's astonishing history: the prehistoric treasure trove of Cruachan Aí; the ancient passage graves of Brú Na Bóinne and Loughcrew; the ancient Celtic capital atop the Hill of Tara; and the rich monastic settlements of Clonmacnoise, Glendalough and Cashel – some of the most important early medieval universities in Europe.

TRIP HIGHLIGHT

### ❶ Brú na Bóinne

A thousand years older than Stonehenge, the extensive neolithic necropolis known as Brú na Bóinne (the Boyne Palace) is simply breathtaking, even if at first glance it just looks like a handful of raised mounds in the fecund fields of County Meath.

The largest artificial structures in Ireland until the construction of the Anglo-Norman castles 4000 years later,

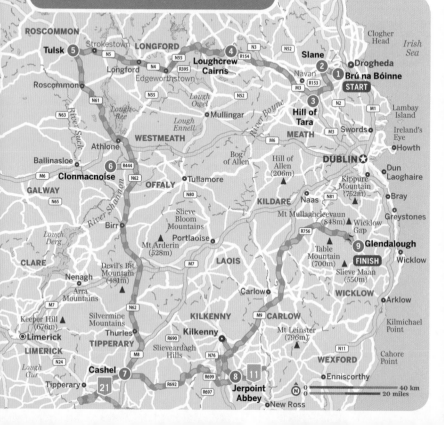

the necropolis was built to house VIP corpses.

Only two of the passage graves are open to visitors (Newgrange and Knowth) and they can only be visited as part of a carefully controlled organised tour departing from the **Brú na Bóinne Visitor Centre** (📞041-988 0300; www.heritageireland.ie; Donore; adult/child visitor centre €3/2, visitor centre & Newgrange €6/3, visitor centre & Knowth €5/3, all 3 sites €11/6; 🕐9am-6.30pm May-Sep, to 5pm Nov-Jan, 9.30am-5.30pm Feb-Apr & Oct).

✖️ 🏠 p103, p111

**The Drive »** Follow the signposts for Slane and the N2 as you wend your way across the Meath countryside for 8km or so; the Hill of Slane is 1km north of the village.

- - - - - - - - - - - -

## ② Slane

The fairly plain-looking **Hill of Slane** stands out

**LINK YOUR TRIP**

**11 Kilkenny's Treasures**

It's 20km from Jerpoint Abbey to Kilkenny, the first stop in the trip dedicated to the county.

**21 The Holy Glen**

In Cashel you can connect to this trip exploring the very best of County Tipperary.

only for its association with a thick slice of Celto-Christian mythology. According to legend, St Patrick lit a paschal (Easter) fire here in 433 to proclaim Christianity throughout the land.

It was also here that Patrick supposedly plucked a shamrock from the ground, using its three leaves to explain the paradox of the Holy Trinity – the union of the Father, the Son and the Holy Spirit in one.

**The Drive »** Go south on the N2 for 8km and turn right onto the R153. After 2km, take the left fork and keep going for 8km until you hit the R147. After 500m take a right and then, after 250m, the first left until you get to the Hill of Tara.

- - - - - - - - - - - -

## ③ Hill of Tara

The Hill of Tara (Teamhair) has occupied a special place in Irish legend and folklore for millennia, although it's not known exactly when people first settled on this gently sloping hill with its commanding views over the plains of Meath.

Tara's remains are not visually impressive. Only mounds and depressions in the grass mark where the Iron Age hill fort and surrounding ring forts once stood, but it remains an evocative, somewhat moving place, especially on a warm summer's

evening. To make sense of it all, stop by the **Tara Visitor Centre** (📞046-902 5903; www.heritage ireland.ie; adult/child €4/2; 🕐visitor centre 10am-6pm mid-May–mid-Sep, site open 24hr year-round).

**The Drive »** Head north and take the M3, which becomes the N3 after 13km. Keep going for 3km and at the roundabout take the first exit onto the R163. Follow it for 8km; it eventually morphs into the R154. The cairns are along here, just west of Oldcastle. The drive is 43km altogether.

- - - - - - - - - - - -

## ④ Loughcrew Cairns

There are 30-odd tombs here but they're hard to reach and relatively few people ever bother, which means you can enjoy this moody and evocative place in peace.

Like Brú na Bóinne, the graves were all built around 3000 BC, but unlike their better-known and better-excavated peers, the Loughcrew tombs were used at least until 750 BC. As at Newgrange, larger stones in some of the graves are decorated with spiral patterns. Some of the graves look like large piles of stones, while others are less obvious, their cairn having been removed.

Nearby is the new **Loughcrew Megalithic Centre** (📞049-854 1888; http://loughcrewmegalithic centre.com; 🕐11am-5pm), with a small but absorbing museum.

**The Drive »** The 87km between Loughcrew and Tulsk takes you through the heart of Middle Ireland, past small glacial lakes and low-lying hills. Follow the R395 to Edgeworthstown and take the N4 to Longford. Take the N5 as far as handsome Strokestown, where you should stop for an amble; Tulsk is 10km west along the same road.

## 5 Tulsk

Anyone with an interest in Celtic mythology will be enthralled by the area around the village of Tulsk in County Roscommon, which contains 60 ancient national monuments including standing stones, barrows, cairns and fortresses, making it the most important Celtic royal site in Europe.

The **Cruachan Aí Visitor Centre** (☎071-963 9268; www.rathcroghan.ie; N5; museum adult/child €5/3, site tour €7/3, combined museum & site tour €10/6; ☉visitor centre 9am-5pm Mon-Sat year-round, noon-4pm Sun May-Sep; ♿) has audiovisual displays and informative panels and maps that

explain the significance of the sites.

According to the legend of Táin Bó Cúailnge (Cattle Raid of Cooley), Queen Maeve (Medbh) had her palace at Cruachan. The Oweynagat Cave (Cave of the Cats), believed to be the entrance to the Celtic otherworld, is nearby.

**The Drive »** As you drive the 75km south to Clonmacnoise along the N61, you'll have Lough Ree on your left for much of the drive. Many of the lake's 50-plus islands were once inhabited by monks and their ecclesiastical treasures. These days, it's mostly anglers, sailors and birdwatchers who frequent it.

TRIP HIGHLIGHT

## 6 Clonmacnoise

Ancient Ireland is sometimes referred to as the 'land of saints and scholars', and one of the reasons why was the monastic city of **Clonmacnoise** (www.heritageireland.ie; adult/child €7/3; ☉9am-6.30pm Jun-Aug, 10am-6pm mid-Mar–May, Sep & Oct, 10am-5.30pm Nov–mid-Mar; ℗), one of Europe's most important centres of study between the 7th and 12th centuries. It was

a top university *before* Oxford was a glint in the scholar's eye.

Founded in 548 by St Ciarán, the monastery (whose name in Irish is *Cluain Mhic Nóis,* which means 'Meadow of the Sons of Nós') that became a bustling city is in remarkably good condition: enclosed within a walled field above a bend in the River Shannon is a superb collection of early churches, high crosses, round towers and graves, including those of the high kings of Ireland.

🛏 p111

## A NIGHT IN BIRR

Feel-good Birr, County Offaly, is one of the most attractive towns in the Midlands, with elegant pastel Georgian buildings lining its streets, a magnificent old castle (p116), an excellent choice of accommodation and spirited nightlife with great live music. Despite its appeal, Birr remains off the beaten track and you can enjoy its delights without jostling with the crowds.

**Brú na Bóinne** Newgrange passage grave

**The Drive »** It's 107km along the N62 to Cashel; overnighting in handsome Birr (which has great accommodation and nightlife, p111) is recommended.

------------

TRIP HIGHLIGHT

### 7 Cashel

Straddling a green hill above the town, the **Rock of Cashel** (www.heritage ireland.ie; adult/child €7/3; ⊙9am-7pm early Jun–mid-Sep, to 5.30pm mid-Mar–early Jun & mid-Sep–mid-Oct, to 4.30pm mid-Oct–mid-Mar) is one of Ireland's most important archaeological sites and one of the most evocative of all ancient monuments. An impor-

tant Celtic power base since the 4th century, most of what remains today dates from when it was gifted to the Church in 1101. Over the next 400 years, various bishops ordered the construction of the 13th-century **cathedral**, a wonderfully complete **round tower**, the finest **Romanesque chapel** (1127) in the country and the sturdy walls that surround it all. Although a collection of religious buildings, the rock was heavily fortified; the word 'cashel' is an Anglicisation of the Irish word *caiseal*, which means 'fortress'.

Scattered throughout are monuments, panels from 16th-century altar tombs and coats of arms. If you have binoculars, look for the numerous stone heads on capitals and corbels high above the ground.

✕ ⨭ p111, p277

**The Drive »** Tipperary and western Kilkenny are classic examples of good Irish farmland; as you wend your way east along the R692 and R690, you'll pass stud farms and cattle ranches. About 5km north of Cottrellstown, along the R697, is the 29m-high Kilree round tower and, next to it, a 9th-century high cross. The drive to Jerpoint Abbey from Cashel is 65km.

## LOCAL KNOWLEDGE: THE CASHEL SHOT

Cashel looks good from pretty much every angle, but the most atmospheric photo is from the ruins of **Hore Abbey**, set in flat farmland less than 1km west of Cashel.

## 8 Jerpoint Abbey

One of Ireland's finest Cistercian ruins, **Jerpoint Abbey** (☎056-772 4623; www.heritageireland.ie; Jerpoint, Thomastown; adult/child €4/2; ☺9am-5.30pm Mar-Sep, to 5pm Oct, to 4pm Nov, closed Dec-Feb) near Thomastown was established in the 12th century and has been partially restored. The tower and cloister are late 14th or early 15th century. The 45-minute tours are worth it, as the guides flesh out the abbey's fascinating history.

**The Drive »** As you come off the M9 and take the R756 east towards Laragh and Glendalough, you'll climb into the wildest parts of the Wicklow Mountains, eastern Ireland's most scenic spectacle. Just before Laragh you'll drive through the Wicklow Gap, between Mt Tonelagee (816m) to the north and Table Mountain (700m) to the southwest. Total distance to Glendalough: 117km.

## 9 Glendalough

Of all Ireland's monastic cities, none has the secluded beauty and isolated majesty of Glendalough, whose impressive ruins are more than rivalled by their setting: two dark glacial lakes at the foot of a forested valley that remain, despite the immense popularity of a visit, a profoundly peaceful and spiritual place.

In 498 the solitude-seeking St Kevin went to live in a Bronze Age tomb on the south side of the Upper Lake, but most of what you see dates from the 9th century onwards, when Kevin's settlement rivalled Clonmacnoise as one of Ireland's premier universities: huddled around the eastern end of the Lower Lake are Glendalough's most fascinating buildings, including a roofless cathedral, a couple of churches, a gatehouse and a round tower.

The **Glendalough Visitor Centre** (www.heritageireland.ie; adult/child €3/1; ☺9.30am-6pm mid-Mar–mid-Oct, to 5pm mid-Oct–mid-Mar) has a 17-minute audiovisual presentation called *Ireland of the Monasteries*.

✖ ⌷ p87, p127

# Eating & Sleeping

## Brú na Bóinne ❶

### 🛏 Newgrange Lodge — Hostel, Hotel €

(📞041-988 2478; www.newgrangelodge.com; camp site per tent €10, dm/d/f from €21/75/100; ⏰reception 8am-midnight; 🅿@🛜) Footsteps east of the Brú na Bóinne Visitor Centre, this converted farmhouse has good-value rooms ranging from dorms with four to 10 beds to hotel-standard doubles with private bathrooms. Superb facilities include a self-catering kitchen, two outdoor patios, a welcoming dining room/lounge with open fire, board games and books, plus free bikes. Rates include continental breakfast (with scrumptious homemade scones).

## Clonmacnoise ❷

### 🛏 Kajon House — B&B €€

(📞090-967 4191; www.kajonhouse.ie; R444, Creevagh; s/d from €55/75; ⏰Mar-Oct; 🅿🛜) If you want to stay near the ruins, this is your best option, just 1.5km southwest. It has cosy rooms, a spacious yard (complete with picnic table) and a warm welcome even by Irish standards. Delicious pancakes are available for breakfast; you may be able to arrange for dinner.

## Birr ❻

### 🛏 Brendan House — B&B €€

(📞057-912 1818; www.tinjugstudio.com; Brendan St; s/d from €55/80; 🛜) Packed with knick-knacks, books, rugs, art and antiques, this Georgian town house is a bohemian delight. The three rooms share a bathroom (one of Birr's oldest, they claim). The four-poster beds, period charm, superb breakfast and artistic style are the real draws. The owners arrange mountain walks, castle and art tours, holistic treatments and art classes.

## Cashel ❼

### 🍴 Cafe Hans — Cafe €€

(📞062-63660; Dominic St; mains €13-23; ⏰noon-5.30pm Tue-Sat; 🪑) Competition for the 32 seats is fierce at this gourmet cafe run by the same family as **Chez Hans** (📞062-61177; www.chezhans.net; Dominic St; mains €24-38, 2/3-course menus €28/33; ⏰6-10pm Tue-Sat) next door. There's a fantastic selection of salads, open sandwiches (including succulent prawns with tangy Marie Rose sauce) and filling fish, shellfish, lamb and vegetarian dishes, with a discerning wine selection and mouthwatering desserts. No credit cards. Enter via Moor Lane. Arrive before or after the lunchtime rush or plan on queuing.

### 🛏 Cashel Town B&B — B&B €

(📞062-62330; www.cashelbandb.com; 5 John St; s/d without bathroom €40/55, s/d/tr/q with private bathroom €5/65/90/120; 🅿🛜) Fresh produce from nearby farmers markets is cooked up for breakfast at this homey B&B. Within the 1808-built Georgian town house are seven comfortable rooms and a cosy guest lounge with a toasty open fire and a piano.

# Monasteries, Mountains & Mansions

## 8

*From mountains and monastic ruins to stately homes and historic whiskey distilleries, there's nothing fictional about this trip through middle Ireland.*

## TRIP HIGHLIGHTS

**278 km**

**Strokestown Park House & Famine Museum**
Beautiful Palladian house with thought-provoking museum

**7** **FINISH**

**150 km**

Corlea Trackway

**Clonmacnoise**
Spectacular monastic site on the banks of the Shannon

Belvedere House & Gardens

Celbridge
**START**

**4**

Tullamore

**3**

**116 km**

**Birr Castle Demesne**
A magnificent telescope, fabulous gardens and the world's tallest box hedges

**3 DAYS**
**278KM / 172 MILES**

**GREAT FOR...**

**BEST TIME TO GO**

Late spring and early autumn are ideal: smaller crowds and good weather.

**ESSENTIAL PHOTO**

Immortalise the gardens of Birr Castle Demesne.

**BEST FOR CULTURE**

Explore Ireland's history at Strokestown Park House & Famine Museum.

**Clonmacnoise** The Scripture Cross

113

# 8 Monasteries, Mountains & Mansions

This is a journey through Irish heritage, much of it overlapping with Ireland's Ancient East: handsome towns like Birr and Strokestown may not attract star billing but are all the better for it, while better-known attractions like Clonmacnoise and Castletown House are outstanding examples of monastic splendour and Georgian extravagance, respectively. And did we mention whiskey? How about a visit to the home of the smoothest Irish whiskey of all?

## ❶ Celbridge

Celbridge, County Kildare, is now a satellite town serving Dublin, only 20km to the east, but in the 18th century it was known as the location for Ireland's most magnificent Georgian pile, **Castletown House** (☏01-628 8252; www.castletown.ie; adult/child €7/3; ⊙10am–6pm mid-Mar–Oct), which simply has no peer.

The house was built between the years 1722 and 1732 for William Conolly (1662–1729), speaker of the Irish House of Commons and, at the time, Ireland's richest man.

The job of building a palace fit for a prince was entrusted to Sir Edward Lovett Pearce (1699–1733). Inspired by the work of Andrea Palladio, Pearce enlarged the original design of the house and added the colonnades and the terminating pavilions. Over in the United States, Thomas Jefferson became a Palladian acolyte and much of official Washington, DC is in this style.

A highlight of the opulent interior is the Long Gallery, replete with family portraits and exquisite stucco work by the Francini brothers.

**The Drive »** It's 74km to Tullamore from Celbridge, and most of the route is along the painless and featureless M4 and M6 motorways; at Junction 11 on the M4, be sure to take the left-hand fork onto the M6 towards Galway and Athlone. Exit the M6 at Junction 5; Tullamore is a further 9km along the N52.

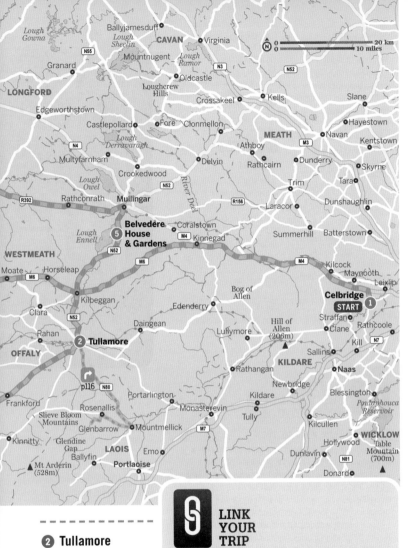

## ② Tullamore

Offaly's county town is a bustling but workaday place with a pleasant setting on the Grand Canal. It's best known for Tullamore Dew Whiskey, which was distilled in the town until 1954, when operations moved to

### LINK YOUR TRIP

**32** **Northwest on Adrenalin**

Explore the northwest's heart-racing activities with an easy 61km drive from Strokestown to Sligo.

**22** **Best of the West**

At trip's end, head west to Westport and pick up this western extravaganza.

Clonmel, County Tipperary.

In 2014 this all changed again, when the distillery opened a new factory on the edge of town. You can't visit it, but you can explore the town's distilling history in the refurbished **Tullamore Dew Heritage Centre** (☎057-932 5015; www.tullamoredew. com; Bury Quay; adult/student €12/9; ☺9.30am-6pm Mon-Sat, 11.30am-5pm Sun), located in a 19th-century canalside warehouse. At the end of the tour you'll get to sample some produce and, inevitably, be encouraged to buy it for friends and family.

✗ p119

## DETOUR: SLIEVE BLOOM MOUNTAINS

### Start: ❷ Tullamore (p115)

Although not as spectacular as some Irish ranges, the Slieve Bloom Mountains' sudden rise from a great plain and the absence of visitors make them highly attractive. You'll get a real sense of being away from it all as you tread the deserted blanket bogs, moorland, pine forests and isolated valleys.

For leisurely walking, **Glenbarrow**, southwest of Rosenallis, has an interesting trail by the cascading River Barrow. Other spots to check out are **Glendine Park**, near Glendine Gap, and **Cut mountain pass**.

For something more challenging, you could try the **Slieve Bloom Way**, a 77km signposted trail that does a complete circuit of the mountains, taking in most major points of interest. The recommended starting point is the car park at Glenbarrow, 5km from Rosenallis, from where the trail follows tracks, forest firebreaks and old roads around the mountains. The trail's highest point is at Glendine Gap (460m).

**The Drive** ❯❯ It's only 37km from Tullamore to Birr. As you drive the N52 south towards Birr, you'll skirt the northern edge of the Slieve Bloom Mountains, which rise suddenly from the great plain of middle Ireland.

- - - - - - - - - -

TRIP HIGHLIGHT

### ❸ Birr

The main reason to visit handsome Birr is to explore the attractions and gardens of **Birr Castle** (☎057-912 0336; www.birr castle.com; off R439; gardens adult/child €9/5, gardens, exhibits & castle adult/child €18/10; ☺9am-6pm mid-Mar–Oct, 10am-4pm Nov–mid-Mar; P ♿), built in 1620 by the Parsons family, who still own it to this day.

HC/ AXIOM/GETTY IMAGES ©

The Parsons were a remarkable family of pioneering Irish scientists, and their work is documented in the **historic science centre**. Exhibits include the massive telescope built by William Parsons in 1845, for 75 years the largest in the world. It was used to make innumerable discoveries, including the spiral galaxies, and to map the moon's surface. It is currently being restored.

Otherwise, the 50-hectare castle grounds are famous for their magnificent **gardens** set around a large artificial

lake. They hold over 1000 species of plants from all over the world; something always seems to be in bloom. Look for one of the world's tallest box hedges, planted in the 1780s and now standing 12m high, and the romantic Hornbeam cloister.

✕ 🛏 p119

**The Drive ❯❯** You'll see mostly fields of cows as you drive the 32km to Clonmacnoise along the N62; at Cloghan, turn left onto the slightly narrower and lonelier R357. You'll have the River Shannon on your left-hand side when you turn onto the R444 for the last 5km past Shannonbridge, which has a good restaurant (see p119).

- - - - - - - - - - -

TRIP HIGHLIGHT

### 4 Clonmacnoise

One of the most important monastic sites in Ireland, the marvellous monastic ruins of **Clonmacnoise** (www.heritageireland.ie; adult/child €7/3; ⌚9am-6.30pm Jun-Aug, 10am-6pm mid-Mar–May, Sep & Oct, 10am-5.30pm Nov–mid-Mar; P) are also one of the most popular tourist attractions in the country, so be prepared to share your visit with other awe-struck tourists and busloads of curious schoolkids.

🛏 p111

**The Drive ❯❯** Rejoin the M6 20km north of Clonmacnoise. At Junction 4, take the N52 north towards Mullingar; on your left, keep an eye out for Lough Ennell: the far side is home to Lilliput House, which was frequently used by Jonathan Swift and gave him the name he used in *Gulliver's Travels*. In total, the drive is 64km long – more if you detour to Athlone for a tasty Thai meal (see p119).

- - - - - - - - - - -

### 5 Belvedere House & Gardens

About 5.5km south of Mullingar, overlooking

## DETOUR:
## ONE OF IRELAND'S BEST TRADITIONAL PUBS

### Start: ❻ Corlea Trackway

About 10km east of Lanesborough is the tiny hamlet of Killashee, which is home to **Magan's**, a delightful old bar, grocery and hardware store that seems stuck in aspic, completely oblivious to the pull and push of modern life. It's well off the beaten track, and is rarely frequented by anyone other than locals, which makes it an even better destination for a pint.

Lough Ennell, is **Belvedere House** (☎044-934 9060; www.belvedere-house. ie; off N52; adult/child €8/4; ☺gardens 9.30am-8pm May-Aug, to 6pm Sep, Oct & Mar-Apr, to 4.30pm Nov-Feb; cafe & house to 5pm Mar-Oct, to 4pm Nov-Feb; ♿), an immense 18th-century hunting lodge set in 65 hectares of gardens. More than a few skeletons have come out of Belvedere's closets: the first earl, Lord Belfield, accused his wife and younger brother Arthur of adultery. She was placed under house arrest here for 30 years, and Arthur was jailed in London for the rest of his life. Meanwhile, the earl lived a life of decadence and debauchery. On his death, his wife emerged dressed in the fashion of three decades earlier, still protesting her innocence.

**The Drive »** Mullingar, just north, has a couple of good hotels and restaurants (see p119). From there drive northwest into County Longford, whose low hills have few tourist sights but the area is a haven for anglers who come for the superb

fishing around Lough Ree and Lanesborough. From Belvedere House, the drive to Corlea along the R392 is about 41km.

### ❻ Corlea Trackway

Longford's main attraction is the magnificent **Corlea Trackway** (☎043-332 2386; www.heritage ireland.ie; off R392, Keenagh; ☺10am-6pm May-Sep), an Iron Age bog road near Keenagh that was built in 148 BC. An 18m stretch of the historic track has now been preserved in a humidified hall at the visitor centre, where you can join a 45-minute tour that details the bog's unique flora and fauna, and fills you in on how the track was discovered and methods used to preserve it. Wear a wind-proof jacket as the bog land can be blowy.

**The Drive »** Strokestown is 27km northwest of Corlea along the R392 as far as Lanesborough, after which you'll cut through the green, lush countryside along the R371. After 10km, take a left onto the N5, which will take you right into Strokestown, 5km further on.

TRIP HIGHLIGHT

### ❼ Strokestown

Roscommon's most handsome town is, for nonresidents, all about **Strokestown Park House & Famine Museum** (☎071-963 3013; www. strokestownpark.ie; off N5; house, museum & gardens adult/child €14/6, 1 site only €9/6; ☺10.30am-5.30pm mid-Mar-Oct, to 4pm Nov-mid-Mar; tours noon, 2.30pm, 4.30pm mid-Mar-Oct, 2.30pm Nov-mid-Mar), the entrance to which is through the three Gothic arches at the end of Strokestown's main avenue.

Admission to this beautifully preserved Palladian house is by a 45-minute **guided tour**, taking in a galleried kitchen with state-of-the-art clockwork machinery, and a child's bedroom complete with 19th-century toys and fun-house mirrors.

In direct and deliberate contrast to the splendour of the house and its grounds is the harrowing **Strokestown Famine Museum**, which sheds light on the devastating 1840s potato blight. There's a huge amount of information to take in, but you'll emerge with an unblinking insight into the starvation of the poor, and the ignorance, callousness and cruelty of those who were in a position to help.

# Eating & Sleeping

## Tullamore ②

### ✕ Sirocco's      Italian €€

(☎057-935 2839; www.siroccos.net; Patrick St; mains €15-27; ⏰5-10pm Mon-Fri, 1-10pm Sat & Sun; 👶) Italian-Irish owned, this popular bistro caters to undecided taste buds and families with its wide selection of fresh pasta dishes and pizza, as well as meat, chicken and fish dishes. Reservations recommended.

## Birr ③

### ✕ Spinners on Castle St      Modern Irish €€

(☎057-912 3779; www.spinnersbirr.com; Castle St; bar mains €9-14, restaurant mains €19-36; ⏰restaurant 6-9pm Fri & Sat, bar 5-9pm Tue, 12.30-9pm Wed-Sun; 📶) This alluring restaurant is part of a complex that spans five restored Georgian houses. The bar is the perfect place to pause with a cheeseboard or burger. The restaurant has a seasonal menu that includes steaks and seafood. Service is excellent, as is the wine and drinks list. Stylish rooms upstairs are €80 to €140.

### 🛏 Brendan House      B&B €€

(☎057-912 1818; www.tinjugstudio.com; Brendan St; s/d from €55/80; 📶) Packed with knick-knacks, books, rugs, art and antiques, this Georgian town house is a bohemian delight. The three rooms share a bathroom (one of Birr's oldest, they claim). The four-poster beds, period charm, superb breakfast and artistic style are the real draws. The owners arrange mountain walks, castle and art tours, holistic treatments and art classes.

## Shannonbridge ③

### ✕ Parkers at The Old Fort      Modern Irish €€

(☎090-967 4973; www.theoldfortrestaurant. com; mains €12-15; ⏰12.30-9pm; P) Offers a sophisticated take on traditional cuisine in the suitably grand surroundings of a massive bridgehead.

## Athlone ④

### ✕ Kin Khao      Thai €€

(☎090-649 8805; www.kinkhaothai.ie; Abbey Lane; mains €15-19; ⏰12.30-2.30pm Wed-Fri, 5.30-10pm Mon-Sat, 1.30-10pm Sun) Renowned for its extensive menu of authentic Thai dishes, tables get booked early at this perfect antidote for yet another pub meal. Diners come from as far as Dublin; the chefs come from Thailand. There's also a take-away menu.

## Mullingar ⑤

### ✕ Miller & Cook      Cafe €

(☎044-934 0884; www.millerandcook.ie; 50 Pearse St; deli mains from €5, 2-/3-course dinner €22.95/26.95; ⏰deli 8.30am-4pm, restaurant 5-9pm Wed-Sat) Your one-stop shop for fine food and drink in Mullingar. The bakery and deli turn out beautiful goods, perfect for bagging up for a picnic. The cafe has excellent locally sourced fare. Sunday brunch is popular, as is the new upstairs restaurant.

### 🛏 Annebrook House Hotel      Hotel €€

(☎044-935 3300; www.annebrook.ie; Pearse St; s/d from €65/89; P 📶) Right in the town centre, the hub of this modern hotel is a lovely 19th-century house with strong connections to local author Maria Edgeworth. Accommodation is in an annexe, where modern rooms in neutral colours are very spacious. The River Brosna flows through the grounds.

# Wicklow Mountains

**9**

*Eastern Ireland's most forbidding mountain range is as magnificent as it is desolate, with narrow roads cutting through the gorse- and bracken-covered hilltops.*

## TRIP HIGHLIGHTS

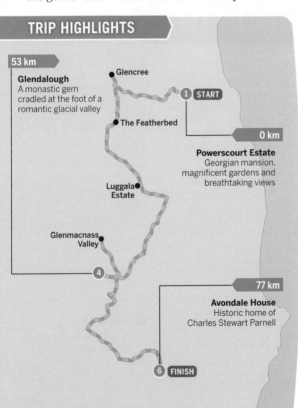

**53 km**

**Glendalough**
A monastic gem cradled at the foot of a romantic glacial valley

Glencree

**1** START

The Featherbed

**0 km**

**Powerscourt Estate**
Georgian mansion, magnificent gardens and breathtaking views

Luggala Estate

Glenmacnass Valley

**4**

**77 km**

**Avondale House**
Historic home of Charles Stewart Parnell

**6** FINISH

---

**3 DAYS**
**77KM / 47 MILES**

**GREAT FOR...**

**BEST TIME TO GO**

From late August to September, the crowds thin out and the heather is in bloom.

**ESSENTIAL PHOTO**

Looking down on Lough Tay and Luggala from the Sally Gap.

**BEST FOR CULTURE**

Glendalough: 1500 years of monastic history beautifully nestled in a glacial valley.

---

**Wicklow Mountains National Park** Glendalough round tower

121

# 9 Wicklow Mountains

This drive takes you down the spine of the Wicklow Mountains, whose dramatic scenery and weather-whipped bleakness make up for what they lack in height. Along the way you'll visit fine Palladian mansions and a beautiful monastic site nestled at the foot of a glacial valley – be prepared to pull over and gawp at the scenery that unfolds.

KILDARE

Blessington

Ballymore Eustace · **7**

Poulaphouce Reservoir

Valleymount

Hollywood

N81

Table Mountain (700m) ▲

Donard

Ballinclea · **WICKLOW**

Knockanarrigan

Glen of Imaal

Rathdangan

**TRIP HIGHLIGHT**

## ❶ Enniskerry

If you're coming from Dublin, Enniskerry is a handsome village at the top of the R117, aka the '21 Bends', but its pretty shops and cafes are merely a prelude to a visit to the superb 64-sq-km **Powerscourt Estate** (www.powerscourt.ie; near Enniskerry; admission to house free, gardens adult/child €8.50/5; ☺9.30am-5.30pm Mar-Oct, to dusk Nov-Feb), whose workers' domestic needs were the very reason Enniskerry was built in the first place.

Due to a fire, you can't visit the Palladian mansion save the ground-floor cafe and outlet of the popular Avoca handicrafts store, but it's the gardens that will have you in thrall. Laid out (mostly) in the 19th century, they are a magnificent blend of landscaped gardens, sweeping terraces, statuary, ornamental lakes, secret hollows, rambling walks and walled enclosures replete with more than 200 types of trees and shrubs, all beneath the stunning natural backdrop of the Great Sugarloaf Mountain to the southeast.

✗ ⌑ p87, p127

**The Drive »** The narrow, twisting L1011 cuts 11km through the northern edge of the mountains, with only a hint of what's to come further on. As you approach Glencree you'll pass through mostly forest.

## ❷ Glencree

Glencree is a leafy hamlet set into the side of the valley of the same name, which opens east to give a magnificent view down

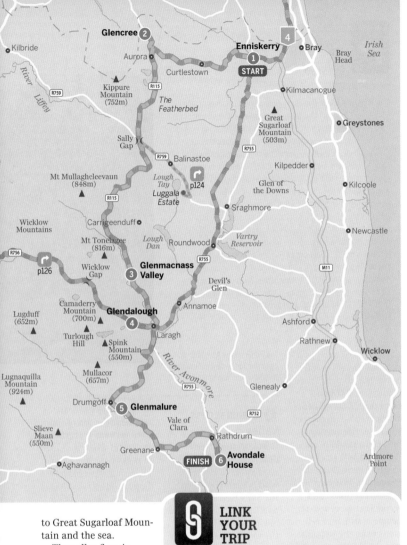

to Great Sugarloaf Mountain and the sea.

The valley floor is home to the Glencree Oak Project, an ambitious plan to reforest part of Glencree with the native oak vegetation that once covered most of the country, but now only covers 1% of Ireland's land mass.

## LINK YOUR TRIP

**4** **A Long Weekend Around Dublin**

From Enniskerry, hook up with this trip exploring the best of Dublin's surrounds.

**7** **Ancient Ireland**

At Glendalough you can start this trip through Ireland's ancient heritage...in reverse.

## DETOUR:
### LUGGALA

**Start: ➋ Glencree (p122)**

If you turn east at the Sally Gap crossroads onto the R759, you'll be on the Sally Gap, one of the two main east–west passes across the Wicklow Mountains and a stretch of road surrounded by some spectacular countryside. About 5km on, the narrow road passes above the dark and dramatic Lough Tay, whose scree slopes slide into Luggala (Fancy Mountain). This almost fairy-tale estate is owned by one Garech de Brún, member of the Guinness family and founder of Claddagh Records, a leading producer of Irish traditional and folk music. You can't visit the estate itself, but there's a popular looped walk that circles it from a height. The small River Cloghoge links Lough Tay with Lough Dan just to the south. You can continue on the R759 for another 3km or so, turning right onto the R755 for Roundwood, or double-back onto the Old Military Rd and make your way south via Glenmacnass.

The village, such as it is, has a tiny shop and a hostel but no pub. There's a poignant **German cemetery** (*Deutscher Soldatenfriedhof*) dedicated to 134 servicemen who died in Ireland during WWI and WWII. Just south of the village, the former military barracks is a retreat house and reconciliation centre for people of different religions from the Republic and the North.

**The Drive »** At Glencree you'll join Wicklow's loveliest, loneliest road, the Old Military Rd (R115), which cuts through a desolate valley of gorse and brown bog and gets more desolate as you go south. At about 11km you'll reach the Sally Gap crossroads; turn right onto the R759 for the gap itself or continue for another 15km to the Glenmacnass Valley.

- - - - - - - - - - - - -

### ➌ Glenmacnass Valley

Desolate and utterly deserted, the Glenmacnass Valley, a stretch of wild bogland between the Sally Gap crossroads and Laragh, is one of the most beautiful parts of the mountains, although the sense of isolation is quite dramatic.

The highest mountain to the west is Mt Mullaghcleevaun (848m), and the River Glenmacnass flows south and tumbles over the edge of the mountain plateau in a great foaming cascade. There's a car park near the top of the **Glenmacnass Waterfall**. Be careful when walking on rocks near the waterfall, as a few people have slipped to their deaths. There are fine walks up Mt Mullaghcleevaun or in the hills to the east of the car park.

**The Drive »** Beyond the Glenmacnass Valley, the Old Military Rd descends for 13km into Laragh, a busy crossroads village that serves as a supply point for nearby Glendalough. It's a good spot to stop and eat or buy provisions. Glendalough is 3km west of here.

**Enniskerry** Formal gardens at Powerscourt Estate

TRIP HIGHLIGHT

## ④ Glendalough

Wicklow's most visited attraction and one of the country's most important historic sites is the collection of ruined churches, buildings, shelters and round tower that make up the ancient monastic city of Glendalough, founded in 498 by St Kevin, who came to the (then) desolate valley looking for a spot of contemplative tranquillity. The ruins are certainly evocative, but it's their setting that makes them special: two dark and mysterious lakes tucked into a deep valley covered in forest.

You could spend a day exploring the ruins and taking in the local

### GLENDALOUGH VALLEY WALKS

There are nine marked walkways in the Glendalough Valley, the longest of which is about 10km, or about four hours' walking. Before you set off, drop by the **National Park Information Point** (☏0404-45425; www.wicklowmountainsnationalpark.ie; Miners' Rd, Bolger's Cottage, Upper Lake, Glendalough; ⊘10am-5.30pm May-Sep, to dusk Sat & Sun Oct-Apr) and pick up the relevant leaflet and trail map (all around €0.50). A word of warning: don't be fooled by the relative gentleness of the surrounding countryside or the fact that the Wicklow Mountains are really no taller than big hills. The weather can be merciless here, so be sure to take the usual precautions, have the right equipment and tell someone where you're going and when you should be back. For Mountain Rescue call ☏999.

# DETOUR:
## THE WICKLOW GAP

### Start: ❹ Glendalough (p125)

Between Mt Tonelagee (816m) to the north and Table Mountain (700m) to the southwest, the Wicklow Gap (R756) is the second major pass over the mountains. The eastern end of the road begins just to the north of Glendalough and climbs through some lovely scenery northwestwards up along the Glendassan Valley. It passes the remains of some old lead and zinc workings before meeting a side road that leads south and up Turlough Hill, the location of Ireland's only pumped-storage power station. You can walk up the hill for a look over the Upper Lake. The western end of the gap meets the N81, from which it's only a few kilometres north to Blessington and Russborough House.

scenery, but whatever you do, your exploration should start with a visit to the **Glendalough Visitor Centre** (www.heritageireland. ie; adult/child €3/1; ☺9.30am-6pm mid-Mar–mid-Oct, to 5pm mid-Oct–mid-Mar), which has a decent 17-minute audiovisual presentation called *Ireland of the Monasteries*.

✖️ 🛏️ p87, p127

**The Drive »** As you go deeper into the mountains southwest of Glendalough along the R755, near the southern end of the Military Rd, everything gets a bit wilder and more remote. It's an 11km drive to Glenmalure.

### ❺ Glenmalure

Beneath the western slopes of Wicklow's highest peak, Lugnaquilla (924m), is Glenmalure, a dark and sombre blind valley flanked by scree slopes of loose boulders. After coming over the mountains into Glenmalure, you turn northwest at the Drumgoff bridge. From there it's about 6km up the road beside the River Avonbeg to a car park where trails lead off in various directions.

🛏️ p127

**The Drive »** The tiny rural road to Rathdrum is called Riverside; it takes you down out of the mountains through some lush forest for 12km into Rathdrum for Avondale House.

TRIP HIGHLIGHT

### ❻ Avondale House

The quiet village of Rathdrum at the foot of the Vale of Clara comprises little more than a few old houses and shops, but it's not what's in the town that's of interest to visitors, however, but what's just outside it.

**Avondale House** (📞0404-46111; adult/student/child €7/6.50/4.50; ☺11am-6pm Easter-Oct) is a fine Palladian mansion surrounded by a marvellous 209-hectare estate, which was the birthplace and Irish home of the 'uncrowned king of Ireland', Charles Stewart Parnell (1846–91), the champion of the struggle for Home Rule and one of the key figures of the Irish independence movement. Designed by James Wyatt in 1779, the house's many highlights include a stunning vermilion-hued library and beautiful dining room.

Surrounding the house, running through the 200 hectares of forest and parkland (all managed by the Irish Forestry Service, Coillte), are many walking trails. You can visit the park during daylight hours year-round.

# Eating & Sleeping

## Enniskerry ❶

### ✗ Emilia's Ristorante     Italian €€

(☎01-276 1834; www.emilias.ie; Clock Tower, The Square; mains €17-23; ⊙5-10.45pm Mon-Sat, noon-9.30pm Sun) **A lovely 1st-floor restaurant to satisfy even the most ardent craving for thin-crust pizzas. Emilia's does everything else just right too, from organic soups to perfect steaks, down to gorgeous meringue desserts.**

### ⊨ Coolakay House     B&B €€

(☎01-286 2423; www.coolakayhouse.ie; Waterfall Rd, Coolakay; s/d from €55/75; P 🛜) **This modern working farm about 3km south of Enniskerry (it is signposted along the road) is a great option for walkers along the Wicklow Way. The bedrooms are all well-appointed and comfortable, the views are terrific and the breakfast sensational. March and April is lambing season and guests are encouraged to observe – and even name a newborn!**

## Glendalough ❹

### ✗ Wicklow Heather     International €€

(☎0404-45157; www.wicklowheather.ie; Glendalough Rd, Laragh; lunch mains €12-22, dinner mains €16-28, r from €75; ⊙noon-8.30pm) **This is the best place for anything substantial. The menu offers Wicklow lamb,** wild venison, Irish beef and fresh fish (the trout is excellent) – most of it sourced locally and all of it traceable from farm to fork. Next door is **Heather House** (www.heatherhouse.ie; Glendalough Rd, Laragh; r from €70), **the owners' B&B, where there are five well-appointed rooms, all with private bathroom.**

## Glenmalure ❺

### ⊨ Glenmalure Hostel     Hostel €

(☎01-830 4555; www.anoige.ie; Greenane; dm €15; ⊙daily Jun-Aug, Sat only Sep-May) **No telephone, no electricity (lighting is by gas), just a rustic two-storey former hunting lodge with 19 beds and running water. This place has a couple of heavyweight literary links: it was the setting for JM Synge's play *Shadow of a Gunman* – at the time it was owned by Maud Gonne, the unrequited love of WB Yeats. It's isolated, but is beautifully situated beneath Lugnaquilla.**

### ⊨ Glenmalure Log Cabin     Self-Catering €€

(☎01-269 6979; www.glenmalurepines.com; 11 Glenmalure Pines, Greenane; lodge 3/7 days €540/600; 🛜) **In the heart of Glenmalure, this modern, Scandinavian-style lodge has two rooms with private bathrooms, a fully equipped kitchen and a living room kitted out with all kinds of electronic amusements, including a DVD library. During the summer it's only available as a weekly rental.**

# Carlow Back Roads

# 10

*A jaunt through Ireland undisturbed by mass tourism, this trip reveals one of the country's most delightful, unexplored counties.*

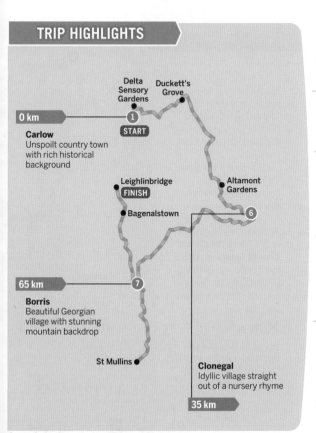

**Delta Sensory Gardens** **Duckett's Grove**

**0 km**

**1** START

**Carlow**
Unspoilt country town with rich historical background

**Leighlinbridge** FINISH

**Altamont Gardens**

**Bagenalstown**

**6**

**65 km**

**7**

**Borris**
Beautiful Georgian village with stunning mountain backdrop

**St Mullins**

**Clonegal**
Idyllic village straight out of a nursery rhyme

**35 km**

**3 DAYS**
**118KM / 73 MILES**

**GREAT FOR...**

**BEST TIME TO GO**
Carlow's flower festivals take place throughout July and September.

**ESSENTIAL PHOTO**
Immortalise the Black Castle from the banks of the Barrow.

**BEST FOR GARDENS**
The Altamont Gardens are the most spectacular of Carlow's beautiful gardens.

**County Carlow** Storm clouds gather over a field of wheat

# 10 Carlow Back Roads

Strings of quietly picturesque villages wind through Carlow, Ireland's second-smallest county. The scenic Blackstairs Mountains dominate the southeast, while the region's most dramatic chunk of history is Europe's biggest dolmen, just outside quiet Carlow town. A ruined Gothic mansion and a reputedly haunted castle form the backdrop to two of the county's best flower-filled gardens.

---

**TRIP HIGHLIGHT**

## ❶ Carlow Town

Carlow town's narrow streets and lanes are quiet these days, a far cry from 25 May 1789, when several hundred Irish insurgents were ambushed and executed by British troops during a ferocious battle in the middle of town. The dead were buried in gravel pits on the far side of the River Barrow, at Graiguecullen.

Built by William de Marshall on the site of an earlier Norman motte-and-bailey fort, the 13-century **castle** (Castle Hill; **P**) survived Cromwell's attentions

but was later converted into a lunatic asylum. The evocative portion that survives is a part of the keep flanked by two towers.

Other notable sights include the 19th-century **Cathedral of the Assumption** (www. carlowcathedral.ie; College St; ◷9am-5pm Mon-Sat, to 7pm Sun) and the **Carlow County Museum** (cnr College & Tullow Sts; ◷10am-5pm Mon-Sat, 2-4.30pm Sun Jun-Aug, 10am-4.30pm Mon-Sat Sep-May).

✕ ⏦ p135

**The Drive »** Take the Athy road (R417) north for about 1.5km; the Delta Sensory Gardens are on your left.

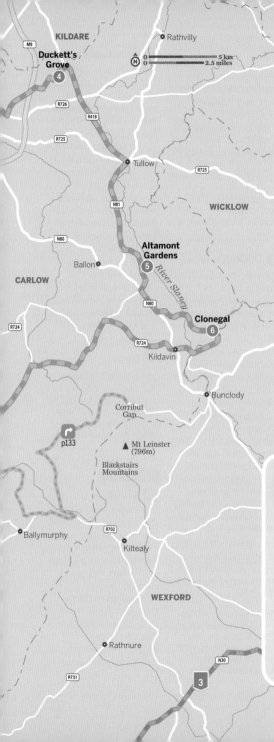

The map shows locations including KILDARE, Rathvilly, Duckett's Grove (4), Tullow, WICKLOW, Altamont Gardens (5), Ballon, CARLOW, Clonegal (6), Kildavin, River Slaney, Bunclody, Corribut Gap, p133, Mt Leinster (796m), Blackstairs Mountains, Ballymurphy, Kiltealy, WEXFORD, Rathnure, and route numbers M9, R726, R418, R725, N81, N80, R724, R702, R731, N30, as well as scale markers 0–5 km / 0–2.5 miles.

## ② **Delta Sensory Gardens**

Located in an incongruous industrial estate on the northern edge of Carlow town are these remarkable **gardens** (www.deltasensorygardens.com; Cannery Rd, Strawhall Industrial Estate; adult/child €5/free; ⊙9am-5.30pm Mon-Fri, from 11am Sat & Sun, closed weekends Nov, Jan & Feb; P ⛱). Some 16 interconnecting, themed gardens cover 1 hectare and span the five senses – from a sculpture garden to a formal rose garden, water and woodland garden, willow garden and a musical garden with mechanical fountains. Admission proceeds benefit the adjoining Delta Centre, which provides services and respite for adults with learning disabilities.

**The Drive ≫** Take the R726 and drive for 3km heading east

# LINK YOUR TRIP

### 3 **Tip to Toe**

Travel 14km from St Mullins south to New Ross, where you can join the north-to-south classic trip.

### 11 **Kilkenny's Treasures**

From Borris, it's only 10km to Graiguenamanagh, from where you can explore County Kilkenny.

131

## ARTISANAL GLASS

About 3km east of Kells, in the neighbouring county of Kilkenny, is the small village of Stonyford. The local highlight, the nationally renowned **Jerpoint Glass Studio** (www.jerpointglass.com; ⊙10am-6pm Mon-Sat, noon-5pm Sun), is housed in a rural stone-walled farm building 1km south of town, where you can watch workers craft molten glass into exquisite artistic and practical items.

from Carlow town. You'll have to park the car and walk 300m to the field.

### ❸ Browne's Hill Dolmen

Ireland's largest portal dolmen (tomb chamber) sits in a field and, from the road, doesn't look that impressive. But as you get closer you'll begin to appreciate the scale of this 5000-year-old monster. The entrance to the chamber is flanked by two large upright stones (known as orthostats or megaliths) topped by a granite capstone that alone weighs well over 100 tonnes.

It's unclear how the stones got here in the first place, but experts have narrowed it down to two possibilities: they were deposited here during the Ice Age, or Stone Age men ate a hell of a lot of spinach and figured out a way of carrying them to the field.

**The Drive »** Turn left onto Strawhall Ave (N80) and take the first exit at the Hacketstown Rd roundabout onto the R726. After 2km, take a left at the

signpost for Duckett's Grove; the house is 5km on, past the underpass for the M9 motorway.

### ❹ Duckett's Grove

Until the main building burnt in 1933, the Gothic fantasy that was **Duckett's Grove** (⊙gardens dawn-dusk, tea room noon-6pm Sat & Sun May-Aug, Sun only Sep & Oct; **P**) was Carlow's most impressive building, the centrepiece of an estate that once spread across five counties.

The house, which dates from the late 17th century, was transformed into a Gothic mansion in 1830 and was used as a training camp for the Irish Republican Army during the War of Independence. The ruins are still impressive, and surrounding them are the original high brick garden walls that frame two sprawling, interconnected formal gardens.

**The Drive »** Start the 18km drive by heading southwest on the R418 to Tullow before continuing south along the N81. After 6km, take a right for the Altamont Estate.

### ❺ Altamont Gardens

Generally considered to be the jewel in the Irish gardening crown, the 16-hectare **Altamont Estate** (www.heritageireland.ie; Kilbride, near Ballon; ⊙9am-6.30pm Apr-Sep, to 5pm Mar & Oct, to 4.30pm Feb & Nov, to 4pm Dec & Jan; **P**) is made up of informal and formal gardens, including a walled garden with carefully selected plantings arranged in naturalistic, idealised settings.

The estate's main avenue is lined with trees, including imported species like red oak and swamp cypresses, and it leads down to an artificial lake.

✕ ⊨ p135

**The Drive »** Take the N80 south for 2km and then the signposted left for Clonegal; the right turn takes you to Ballon, where there are a couple of good restaurants and hotels (see p135).

TRIP HIGHLIGHT

### ❻ Clonegal

The idyllic village of Clonegal has a tiny little centre out of a nursery rhyme with an arched stone bridge over a river that boasts swans and water flowers.

**Huntington Castle** (www.huntingtoncastle.com; Clonegal; house tours adult/child €9/4, gardens only €5/2.50; ⊙house noon-4pm daily Jun-Aug, Sat & Sun only May & Sep, gardens daily

10am-6pm May-Sep; P) is a spooky, dusty old keep built in 1625 by the Durdin-Robertson family, who still own it and live here today. The family conduct hour-long tours of the property, which, they claim, is haunted by two ghosts. The gardens combine the formal with rural fantasy.

**The Drive »** The R724 cuts across southern County Carlow; Borris is 29km away.

**Carlow Town** Boats on the River Barrow

TRIP HIGHLIGHT

## ➐ Borris

Handsome Borris is a seemingly untouched Georgian village, strung out like a string bean down the side of a hill, with a dramatic mountain backdrop. That's Mt Leinster, site of an excellent scenic drive.

🛏 p135

**The Drive »** It's 15km from Borris to St Mullins, mostly along the R729 with the Blackstairs Mountains to your left (east).

## DETOUR:
## MT LEINSTER
## SCENIC DRIVE

**Start:** ➐ **Borris**

The highest peak in the Blackstairs Mountains, Mt Leinster (796m) has magnificent views of Counties Waterford, Carlow, Kilkenny and Wicklow from the top.

From Borris, drive south along the R702 and almost immediately take the signposted left for Mt Leinster. Keep going and take the left for Bunclody at the T-junction. Continue around, keeping the mountain on your right; you'll arrive at the car park at **Corribut Gap**. The ground falls away steeply, offering stunning views of the Coolasnaghta valley to the north.

This is also the spot favoured by those taking advantage of Ireland's best hang-gliding spot – if you fancy taking off from the mountain, contact the **Irish Hang Gliding & Paragliding Association** (www.ihpa.ie) for further information.

## ➑ St Mullins

Tranquil little St Mullins sits 6km downstream from Graiguenamanagh, which is in County Kilkenny. The village is the maternal home of Michael Flatley of Riverdance fame. Sure enough, the river snakes through here in the shadow of Brandon Hill, as does the River Barrow towpath from Borris. From the river, a trail winds uphill to the ruined hulk of an old **monastery** surrounded by the graves of 1798 rebels. A 9th-century Celtic cross, badly worn down over the centuries, still stands beside the monastery. Nearby, **St Moling's Well** is a holy well that seems to attract spare change.

🛏 p135

133

## DETOUR:
### KILGRANEY HOUSE HERB GARDENS

**Start:** **7** Borris (p133)

There are herbs as you've never seen them grow in orderly profusion in **Kilgraney House Herb Gardens** (www.kilgraneyhouse.com; Bagenalstown; admission €3; ⏰2-5pm Thu-Sun May-Sep; P), which boasts a heady cocktail of medicinal and kitchen plants and also serves as a source of food for the inn and restaurant here. The re-created medieval monastic herb garden is a favourite. It's off the R705 halfway between Borris and Bagenalstown.

**The Drive »** It's 27km from St Mullins to Bagenalstown via Borris. The 12km stretch of the R705 from Borris to Bagenalstown follows the scenic River Barrow Valley, one of the nicest bits of road in all of Carlow.

### **9** Bagenalstown

About 12km north of Borris is Bagenalstown, which isn't quite as handsome, but is home to the **Carlow Brewing Company** (☎059-913 4356; www.carlowbrewing.com; Royal Oak Rd; tours €10.50; ⏰2pm Fri, by reservation only), a microbrewery that offers tours of its O'Hara's-brand beers. Its award-winning Irish stout bursts with flavour and certainly holds its own against that *other* Irish stout.

**The Drive »** Leighlinbridge is 4km on along the R705.

### **10** Leighlinbridge

Leighlinbridge would be just another Carlow town if it weren't for the ominous ruins of the **Black Castle** on the banks of Barrow. Built in 1181, this was one of the first Norman castles built in Ireland and was bequeathed to John de Claville by Henry II's lieutenant, Hugh de Lacy. The present castle was built by Sir Edward Bellingham in 1547 but was demolished by Cromwell's army in 1650. There's only half of a 14th-century round tower and a chunk of the bawn (defensive wall) left, but it is one of the most photogenic ruins in the whole county. You can access it from the river towpath.

## CARLOW IN BLOOM

County Carlow is renowned for its gardens, 16 of which form part of Ireland's first dedicated **garden trail** (www.carlowgardentrail.com). Most tourist offices will have a copy of the invaluable (and free) guide *Carlow Garden Trail*. Flower fans shouldn't miss County Carlow's summertime Garden Festival.

Our top five gardens:

**Delta Sensory Gardens** (p131) A multisensory, fountain-filled oasis.

**Huntington Gardens** (p132) Rambling, overgrown grounds in the shadow of a haunted castle.

**Duckett's Grove** (p132) Restored walled gardens behind a ruined Gothic mansion.

**Kilgraney House Herb Gardens** Aromatic gardens filled with medicinal and kitchen plants.

**Altamont Gardens** (p132) Heritage-listed Victorian splendour, hosting a weeklong Snowdrop Festival in February.

# Eating & Sleeping

## Carlow Town ①

### ✗ Lennons                    Modern Irish €€

(☎059-917 9245; www.lennons.ie; Visual Centre
for Contemporary Art, Old Dublin Rd; mains
lunch €8-12, dinner €17-25; ⊕10.30am-5pm
Mon-Sat, 6-9.30pm Thu-Sat, noon-4pm Sun;
ℙ🗑) Carlow's best dining is found amid
the arty surrounds of the Visual Centre for
Contemporary Art. It's a sleek and stylish space
with a patio bordering the grassy grounds of
St Patrick's College. Lunch features creative
sandwiches, salads and hot specials, while
dinner is more refined with a seasonal menu
that showcases local artisan produce. Book a
table at weekends.

### 🛏 Red Setter Guest House          B&B €€

(☎059-914 1848; www.redsetterguesthouse.
ie; 14 Dublin St; s/d/tr from €40/70/99; ℙ🗑)
Great attention to detail, simply furnished but
comfortable rooms, and extra touches such as
fresh flowers make this otherwise humble B&B
the town centre's winning choice.

## Ballon ⑤

### ✗ Forge Restaurant                Irish €

(www.theforgekilbride.ie; Kilbride Cross, near
Ballon; mains €5-10; ⊕9.30am-4.30pm
Mon-Sat, to 5pm Sun; ℙ🗑🚸) Mary Jordan
cooks up delicious healthy soups and hot lunch
specials using local produce at this former
blacksmith's forge near Altamont Gardens.
There are baked goods to take away plus deli
items and crafts for sale.

## 🛏 Sherwood Park
House                     Guesthouse €€

(☎059-915 9117; www.sherwoodparkhouse.ie;
Kilbride Cross, near Ballon; s/d from €65/100;
ℙ) This grey-stone Georgian manor dates from
1730. The five guest rooms are huge with period
niceties such as satin- and velvet-adorned four-
poster beds. You can make arrangements for
dinner (€40 per person); breakfast is included.
The house is on the minor road leading to
Altamont Gardens, which are just 600m away.

## Borris ⑦

### 🛏 Step House Hotel              Hotel €€€

(☎059-977 3209; www.stephousehotel.
ie; 66 Main St; s/d from €79/119; ℙ🗑) This
handsome hotel has elegant rooms decorated
in shades of pastel green and gold; the more
expensive bedrooms have balconies with views
of Mt Leinster. Tables in the Cellar Restaurant
are tucked in romantic corners beneath vaulted
ceilings, while the rustic-style bar is the perfect
place for a relaxing drink after a day's hiking or
sightseeing.

## St Mullins ⑧

### 🛏 Old Grainstore                Cottage €€

(☎051-424 440; www.oldgrainstorecottages.ie;
The Quay; cottages per week €550; ℙ) Martin
and Emer O'Brien have eschewed corporate life
to convert this former grain warehouse on the
River Barrow into three self-catering cottages
sleeping two to five people. The interiors are
stylish yet homely, with shelves of books
and wood-burning stoves. Shorter stays are
sometimes possible on request, and guests can
borrow bikes and kayaks free of charge.

# Kilkenny's Treasures

**11**

*Its namesake city is its marvellous centrepiece, but County Kilkenny's rolling hills, dotted with relics of Irish history, will soon have you running out of adjectives for green.*

## TRIP HIGHLIGHTS

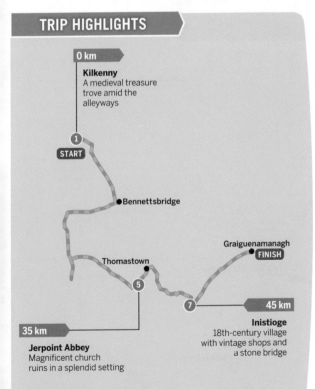

**0 km**

**Kilkenny**
A medieval treasure trove amid the alleyways

**1**
**START**

●Bennettsbridge

**Graiguenamanagh**
● **FINISH**

**Thomastown** ●
**5**

**7**
**45 km**

**35 km**

**Jerpoint Abbey**
Magnificent church ruins in a splendid setting

**Inistioge**
18th-century village with vintage shops and a stone bridge

**3 DAYS**
**58KM/36 MILES**

**GREAT FOR...**

**BEST TIME TO GO**

Spring and autumn are ideal: the weather's good but there are fewer visitors.

 **ESSENTIAL PHOTO**

Kells Priory at dusk.

✔ **BEST FOR TRADITIONAL CRAFTS**

The exquisitely made artisanal crafts at the Nicholas Mosse Irish Country Shop.

# 11 Kilkenny's Treasures

The enduring gift of the Normans, Kilkenny mesmerises visitors with its medieval alleys and castle, ruined abbeys and outstanding nightlife. Beyond the city limits, tiny roads navigate the beautiful valleys past the mementos of 800 years of Irish history, picture-postcard villages and a dynamic contemporary craft industry with a reputation that's admired countrywide.

TRIP HIGHLIGHT

## ❶ Kilkenny

Kilkenny (Cill Chainnigh) is the Ireland of many a visitor's imagination. Its majestic riverside castle, tangle of 17th-century passageways, rows of colourful, old-fashioned shopfronts and centuries-old pubs with traditional live music all have a timeless appeal, as does its splendid medieval cathedral.

Kilkenny's architectural charm owes a huge debt to the Middle Ages,

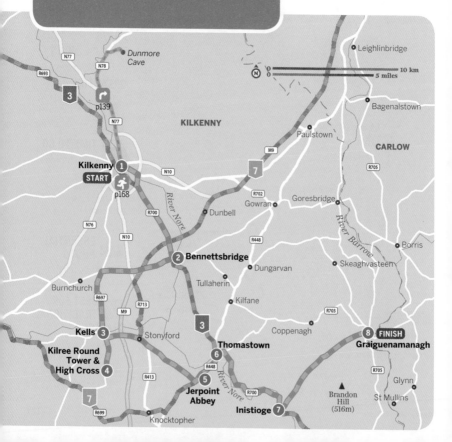

when the city was a seat of political power. It's also sometimes called the 'marble city' because of the local black limestone, used on floors and in decorative trim all over town.

You can cover pretty much everything on foot in half a day, but sampling its many delights will take much longer.

 p75, p143

**The Drive »** Drive southwest with the castle and the Nore on your immediate left until you reach the R700, aka the Bennettsbridge Rd. It's only a short 7km drive to Bennettsbridge.

## ② Bennettsbridge

Bennettsbridge is an arts-and-crafts treasure chest, although these treasures are scattered throughout the town,

## LINK YOUR TRIP

**3 Tip to Toe**
Kilkenny is one of the main stops on the classic Tip to Toe trip, which explores Ireland from north to south.

**7 Ancient Ireland**
From Kilree or Jerpoint Abbey you can connect to this trip that visits some of ancient Ireland's most important sites.

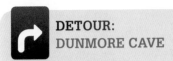

## DETOUR: DUNMORE CAVE

### Start: ① Kilkenny

Just 6km north of Kilkenny on the Castlecomer road (N78) are the striking calcite formations of **Dunmore Cave** (☏056-776 7726; www.heritageireland.ie; Ballyfoyle; adult/child €4/2; ☺9.30am-6.30pm mid Jun–mid Sep, shorter hrs rest of year; Ⓟ). In 928 marauding Vikings killed 1000 people at two ring forts near here. When survivors hid in the caverns, the Vikings tried to smoke them out by lighting fires at the entrance. It's thought that they then dragged off the men as slaves and left the women and children to suffocate. Excavations in 1973 uncovered the skeletons of at least 44 people, mostly women and children. They also found coins dating from the 10th century.

Admission to the cave is via a compulsory but highly worthwhile guided tour. Although well lit and spacious, it's damp and cold; bring warm clothes.

rather than within a concentrated area.

In a big mill by the river west of town, the **Nicholas Mosse Irish Country Shop** (www.nicholasmosse.com; ☺10am-6pm Mon-Sat, 1.30-5pm Sun) specialises in handmade spongeware – creamy-brown pottery decorated with sponged patterns. It also sells linen and other handmade craft items (although some hail from lands of cheap labour far from Ireland). Its cafe is the best choice locally for lunch, with a creative line-up of soups, sandwiches, hot dishes and its renowned scones.

On a small road above Nicholas Mosse, the **Nore View Folk Museum** (☏056-27749; Danesfort Rd, adult/child €5/2; ☺10am-

6pm) is the labour of love of Seamus Lawlor, a passionate chronicler of Irish life. The museum is full of fascinating facts about his private collection of local items, including farming tools, kitchen utensils and other wonderful old bric-a-brac.

**The Drive »** The 12km drive to Kells takes you across the flat, luscious green plain of central Kilkenny. Follow the Annamult Rd towards the N10, but turn left onto the R697.

## ③ Kells

Kells (not to be confused with Kells in County Meath) is a mere hamlet with a fine stone bridge on a tributary of the Nore. However, in **Kells Priory**, the village has one of Ireland's most impressive and romantic monastic sites. This is the best sort of ruin, where visitors can amble about whenever they like, with no tour guides, tours, set hours or fees. At dusk on a vaguely sunny day, the old priory is simply beautiful. Most days you stand a chance of exploring the site alone (apart from bleating and pooping sheep).

The ruins are 500m east of Kells on the Stonyford road.

**The Drive »** Kilree is only 3km south of Kells along a small country road.

## ④ Kilree Round Tower & High Cross

Standing in an overgrown graveyard is a 29m-high round tower that has lost its cap. It was built sometime between the 8th and 11th centuries, and served as a bell tower, although it was also a handy place of refuge for locals looking to escape the unwelcome attention of invaders.

Next to it, standing more than 2m tall, is a simple early high cross that was long believed to be the grave of a 9th-century Irish high king, Niall Caille, who drowned in the nearby river in 847 while attempting the rescue of a servant or soldier, even though experts now reckon the cross is older than

that. Still, Niall's resting place lies beyond the church grounds because he wasn't a Christian.

**The Drive »** The 17km drive will have you doubling back towards Kells, but then taking a right on the Stonyford road, past Kells Priory. You'll pass Mt Juliet on your left. Turn left on the R448, and Jerpoint Abbey is a further 1km on your right.

TRIP HIGHLIGHT

## ⑤ Jerpoint Abbey

Ireland has an abundance of church ruins, but few are quite as magnificent as those of **Jerpoint Abbey** (☎056-772 4623; www.heritageireland.ie; Jerpoint, Thomastown; adult/child €4/2; ⊗9am-5.30pm Mar-Sep, to 5pm Oct, to 4pm Nov, closed Dec-Feb), a fine exemplar of Cistercian power and church-building. The abbey was first established in the 12th century, with the tower and cloister added sometime in the late 14th or early 15th century. The excellent 45-minute tours happen throughout the day. Set yourself apart in the remains of the cloisters and see if you can hear the faint echo of a chant.

According to local legend, St Nicholas (or Santa Claus) is buried near the abbey. While retreating in the Crusades, the knights of Jerpoint removed his body from Myra in modern-day Turkey and reburied him in the **Church of St**

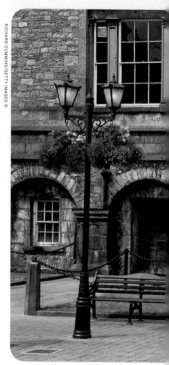

RICHARD CUMMINS/GETTY IMAGES ©

**Nicholas** to the west of the abbey. The grave is marked by a broken slab decorated with a carving of a monk.

**The Drive »** Thomastown is only a quick 2.5km northeast of Jerpoint on the R448.

## ⑥ Thomastown

Named after Welsh mercenary Thomas de Cantwell, Thomastown has some fragments of a medieval wall and the partly ruined 13th-century **Church of St Mary**. Down by the bridge, **Mullin's Castle** is the sole survivor of the 14 castles once here.

**Kilkenny** Flowers bloom outside the Old Jail and Courthouse

Like the rest of Kilkenny, the area has a vibrant craft scene. Look out for **Clay Creations** (📞087 257 0735; www.bridlyonsceramics. com; Low St; 🕙10am-5.30pm Wed-Sat, by appointment only Mon & Tue), displaying the quixotic ceramics and sculptures of local artist Brid Lyons.

✖ p143

**The Drive** » The 9km drive south to Inistioge along the R700 is a splendidly scenic one through the valley of the River Nore; keep an eye out for the views of the ruined 13th-century Grennan Castle on your right as you go.

---

TRIP HIGHLIGHT

## ❼ Inistioge

The little village of Inistioge (*in*-ish-teeg) is a picture. Its 18th-century, 10-arch **stone bridge** spans the River Nore and

vintage shops face its tranquil square.

About 500m south of the village is the heavily forested **Woodstock Gardens** (www.woodstock. ie; admission free, parking €4; 🕙9am-7pm Apr-Sep, 10am-4pm Oct-Mar), a beauty of

---

## TEEING OFF IN THOMASTOWN

Just 4km west of Thomastown, high-fliers tee off at the Jack Nicklaus–blessed **Mount Juliet** (📞056-777 3000; www.mountjuliet.ie; Mount Juliet Estate, Thomastown; green fees €59-95). Set over 600 wooded hectares, it also has its own equestrian centre, a gym and spa, two restaurants, wine master-classes, and posh rooms catering to every whim, right down to the pillow menu (accommodation from €120).

## TOWN OF BOOKS

Graiguenamanagh's narrow streets spill over with booksellers, authors and bibliophiles during the three-day **Town of Books Festival** (www.graiguenamanaghtownofbooks.com; ⊙late Aug). Plans are under way for Graiguenamanagh to become a year-round 'book town' in the same vein as Wales' Hay-on-Wye. Meanwhile, there are a couple of good used and antiquarian bookshops.

a park with expansive 19th-century gardens, picnic areas and trails. The panorama of the valley and village below is spectacular. Coming from town, follow the signs for Woodstock Estate and enter the large gates (despite appearances, it's a public road), then continue along the road for about 1km until you reach the car park (parking €4 in coins).

✕ ⨾ p143

**The Drive »** It's 11km from Inistioge to Graiguenamanagh on the Graigue road, aka the L4209, which is so narrow that you'll wonder if there's room for oncoming traffic (there is).

- - - - - - - - - - - - -

### ⑧ Graiguenamanagh

Graiguenamanagh (greg-*na*-muh-na; known locally simply as Graigue) is the kind of place where you could easily find yourself staying longer than planned. Spanning the Barrow, a six-arch stone bridge is illuminated at night and connects the village with the township of Tinnahinch on the County Carlow side of the river (look for the darker stones on the Carlow side – a legacy from being blown up during the 1798 rebellion).

The big attraction in town is the Cistercian **Duiske Abbey** (Main St; ⊙8am-6pm), once Ireland's largest and still very much a working parish (thanks to 800 years of changes and additions). To the right of the entrance look for the **Knight of Duiske**, a 14th-century, high-relief carving of a knight in chain mail who's reaching for his sword. On the floor nearby, a glass panel reveals some of the original 13th-century floor tiles, now 2m below the present floor level.

⨾ p143

# Eating & Sleeping

## Kilkenny ❶

### ✕ Campagne     Modern Irish €€€

(☎056-777 2858; www.campagne.ie;
5 Gashouse Lane; mains €29-32; ⊙12.30-
2.30pm Fri-Sun, 6-10pm Tue-Sat) Chef Garrett
Byrne was awarded a Michelin star for this bold,
stylish restaurant in his native Kilkenny. He's
passionate about supporting local and artisan
producers, and serves ever-changing, ever-
memorable meals, with a French accent to every
culinary creation. The three-course lunch and
early bird menu is €33.

### ⌸ Butler House     Boutique Hotel €€

(☎056-772 2828; www.butler.ie; 16 Patrick St;
s/d from €90/145; ⓟ @ ☎) You can't stay in
Kilkenny Castle, but this historic mansion is
the next best thing. Once the home of the earls
of Ormonde, today it houses a boutique hotel
with aristocratic trappings including sweeping
staircases, marble fireplaces, an art collection
and impeccable gardens. The generous rooms
are individually decorated and, to remind you
you're staying amid history, the floors creak.

## Thomastown ❻

### ✕ Blackberry Cafe     Cafe €

(www.theblackberrycafe.ie; Market St; mains
€5-9; ⊙9.30am-5.30pm Mon-Fri, 10am-5.30pm
Sat; ⚘) Superb thick-cut sandwiches, toasties,
quiche and warming soups are served with
pumpkin-seed-speckled soda bread here. Much
is organic, and the tarts and cakes are baked
daily. Between noon and 2pm, great-value hot
lunches see the place packed to bursting.

## Inistioge ❼

### ✕ Circle of Friends     Cafe €

(☎056-775 8800; High St; mains €6-14;
⊙11am-5pm Tue-Fri, to 6pm Sat & Sun, longer
hours Jun-Aug) With tables on the street, this
cheerful cafe has flavoured coffees (mint,
caramel and so on), all-day breakfasts, hot
dishes such as beer-battered cod and chips
and – the reason everyone's really here –
gargantuan servings of home-made desserts
such as pavlova.

### ⌸ Woodstock Arms     B&B €€

(☎056-775 8440; www.woodstockarms.ie;
The Square; s/d/tr from €40/70/90; ☎) This
picturesque pub has tables on the square and
seven basic bedrooms that are squeaky clean;
the triples are particularly spacious. Breakfast
is served in a pretty little room out the back with
wooden tables and traditional local china.

## Graiguenamanagh ❽

### ⌸ Waterside     Guesthouse €€

(☎059-972 4246; www.watersideguesthouse.
com; The Quay; s/d from €59/90; ⊙restaurant
6-10pm Mon-Sat, noon-3pm Sun Apr-Sep, Fri-Sun
only Oct-Mar; ☎) Overlooking the boats tied
up along the river, this inviting guesthouse and
restaurant occupies a converted 19th-century
grain store. Its 10 renovated bedrooms have
exposed timber beams, and the restaurant is
well regarded for its interesting modern Irish
menu (mains €18 to €26) and its regular 'After
Dinner Live' music acts featuring anything from
jazz to bluegrass.

# Wexford & Waterford

## 12

*Ireland's favourite beach destinations are dotted along the coastlines of Counties Wexford and Waterford, but there's far more to the region than just buckets and spades.*

## TRIP HIGHLIGHTS

**164 km**

**Dungarvan**
Bustling port of pastel-coloured houses and an excellent foodie scene

**75 km**

**Tintern Abbey**
Moody ruins of a once-powerful Cistercian abbey

START
● Enniscorthy

● Arthurstown  ③

②

⑥

● Ardmore
FINISH

**Kilmore Quay**
Fishing village straight out of a postcard

**43 km**

**5 DAYS
219KM / 136 MILES**

**GREAT FOR...**

**BEST TIME TO GO**

April to September, for the long days and best weather.

 **ESSENTIAL PHOTO**

Look down on Ardmore bay from St Declan's Church.

☑ **BEST FOR CULTURE**

Learn about bloody Irish history at the National 1798 Rebellion Centre.

**Tintern Abbey** 13th-century Cistercian abbey set in secluded woodlands

# 12 Wexford & Waterford

Collectively labelled the 'sunny southeast', Wexford and Waterford get less rainfall and more sunshine than anywhere else in Ireland, but the southeastern counties are about more than resort towns and pretty beaches. There's history aplenty round here, some stunning inland scenery and a vibrant foodie scene that mightn't be as well known as that in neighbouring Cork but is just as good.

**①** **Enniscorthy**

Busy Enniscorthy (Inis Coirthaidh) is an attractive hilly town on the banks of the Slaney in the heart of County Wexford, 20km north of Wexford town. For the Irish, its name is forever linked to some of the fiercest fighting of the 1798 Rising, when rebels captured the town and castle and set up camp nearby at **Vinegar Hill** (www.vinegarhill.ie).

Before climbing the hill (a 2km drive east of town), acquaint yourself with the

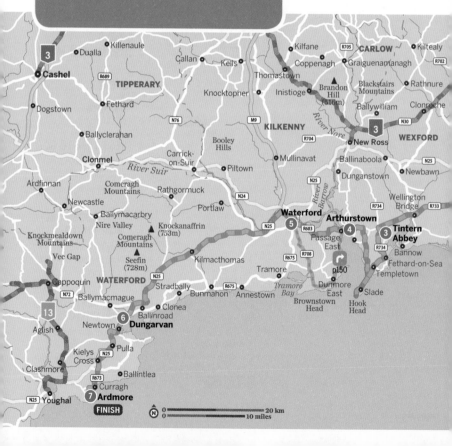

story of the rebellion with a visit to the **National 1798 Rebellion Centre** (www.1798centre.ie; Parnell Rd; adult/child €7/3; ☺9.30am-5pm Mon-Fri, noon-5pm Sat Apr-Sep, 10am-4pm Mon-Fri, noon-5pm Sat Oct-Mar; P 🛗), which tells the story of Wexford's abortive uprising against British rule in all its gory, fascinating detail. The rebels were inspired by the French and American Revolutions, but were beaten back by English troops, who then massacred hundreds of women and children as reprisal for the uprising.

Map showing route from Enniscorthy (START) via R741, Blackwater, Curracloe, Wexford Bay, Castlebridge, N11, Ferrycarrig, N25, Wexford, Drinagh, Murntown, Rosslare, Rosslare Harbour, R738, R739, Bridgetown, Tagoat, Kilrane, Kilmore, Chour, to Kilmore Quay. p148. Saltee Islands. *St George's Channel*

If you want to walk up Vinegar Hill, from Abbey Sq walk out of town along Mill Park Rd or south along the river.

🛏 p151

**The Drive »** It's 43km to Kilmore Quay. You'll skirt around Wexford Town on your way south along the N11; beyond the town, follow the directions for Rosslare and take the N25. Turn right onto the R739 to Kilmore Quay. The last stretch of road is the most scenic, as the countryside opens up in front of you.

- - - - - - - - - -

TRIP HIGHLIGHT

### ❷ Kilmore Quay

Straight out of a postcard, peaceful Kilmore Quay is a small village on the eastern side of Ballyteige Bay, noted for its lobsters and deep-sea fishing. Lining the attractive main street up from the harbour is a series of pretty whitewashed thatched cottages. The harbour is the jumping-off point for the Saltee Islands, home to Ireland's largest bird sanctuary, clearly visible out to sea.

The four-day **Seafood Festival** (www.kilmore quayseafoodfestival.com)

in the second week of July involves seafood tastings, music and dancing.

✕ 🛏 p151

**The Drive »** It's 29km from Kilmore Quay to the ruins of Tintern Abbey along the narrow R733. The promontory east of the Hook Peninsula, signposted as the Bannow Drive, is littered with Norman ruins, while Bannow Bay is a wildfowl sanctuary. As you cross Wellington Bridge onto the Hook Peninsula, keep an eye out for the remains of medieval Clonmines to the southwest.

- - - - - - - - - -

TRIP HIGHLIGHT

### ❸ Tintern Abbey

In better structural condition than its Welsh counterpart, from where its first monks hailed, Ireland's moody **Tintern Abbey** (www.heritageireland.ie; Saltmills; adult/child €4/2; ☺10am-5pm Apr-Oct; P) is secluded amid 40 hectares of woodland. William Marshal, Earl of Pembroke, founded the Cistercian abbey in the early 13th century after he nearly perished at sea and swore to establish a church if he made it ashore.

---

§ **LINK YOUR TRIP**

**3** **Tip to Toe**
You can hook up to this long country-length trip in Kilmore Quay.

**13** **Blackwater Valley Drive**
It's only 5km from Ardmore to Youghal and the start of the Blackwater Valley Drive.

The abbey is 1.5km from the town of Saltmills, amid wooded trails, lakes and idyllic streams. The grounds are always open, and a walk here is worth the trip at any time.

The Drive » The 9km route across the Hook Peninsula along the R753 is the quickest way to Arthurstown, but the most scenic route is the 35km circumference of the peninsula, passing villages like Slade, where the most activity is in the swirl of seagulls above the ruined castle and harbour. Beaches include the wonderfully secluded Dollar Bay and Booley Bay, just beyond Templetown. Don't forget to spot the world's oldest working lighthouse right at Hook Head.

## ❹ Arthurstown

Chef Kevin Dundon is a familiar face on Irish TV, and the author of cookbooks *Full On Irish*

and *Great Family Food*. His spa hotel **Dunbrody Country House** (☎051-389 600; www.dunbrodyhouse. com; s/d €145/255; P☎), in a period-decorated 1830s Georgian manor on 120-hectare grounds, is the stuff of foodies' fantasies, with a gourmet restaurant and cookery school (one-day courses from €175).

Beside the R733, some 6km north of Dundon's pile, the ruined **Dunbrody Abbey** (www.dunbrodyabbey. com; Campile; adult/child €3/1; ⊙11am-6pm mid-May–mid-Sep) is a remarkably intact Cistercian abbey founded by Strongbow in 1170 and completed in 1220. A combined ticket (adult/child €4/2) includes a **museum** with a huge doll's house, **minigolf**, and a very fun yew-hedge **maze** made up of over 1500 trees.

The Drive » Instead of going the long way around, cut out a long detour around Waterford Harbour and the River Barrow by taking the five-minute car ferry between Ballyhack in County Wexford and Passage East in County Waterford. Then follow the R683 to Waterford City. This way is only 15km long.

## ❺ Waterford City

Inhabited since AD 914, Waterford (Port Láirge) is Ireland's oldest city, and much of the centre's street plan has retained its medieval feel.

Waterford's 1000-year history is told in wonderful fashion in a trio of museums collectively known as the **Waterford Museum of Treasures** (www.waterfordtreasures.com) and include **Reginald's Tower** (The Quay; adult/child €4/2; ⊙9.30am-5.30pm late Mar–Dec, to 5pm Jan–late Mar, closed 24 Dec–6 Jan), the

---

## DETOUR:
### SALTEE ISLANDS

**Start: ❷ Kilmore Quay (p147)**

Just 4km offshore and accessible from Kilmore Quay via local boat (depending on the weather), the **Saltee Islands** (www.salteeislands.info; ⊙11.30am-4.30pm) constitute one of Europe's most important bird sanctuaries, home to over 375 recorded species, principally the gannet, guillemot, cormorant, kittiwake, puffin and Manx shearwater. It's a noisier but more peaceful existence than its past as the favoured haunt of privateers and smugglers. The islands are also where you'll find some of the oldest rocks in Europe, dating back 2000 million years or more; findings also suggest that the islands were inhabited by the pre-Celts as long ago as 3500 to 2000 BC. The best time to visit is the spring and early-summer nesting season; once the chicks can fly, the birds leave. By early August it's eerily quiet.

To get here, try **Declan Bates** (☎053-912 9684, 087 252 9736; Kilmore Quay Harbour; day trips €30) but be sure to book in advance. You can park the car in the town.

**Saltee Islands** Puffin

# DETOUR:
## PASSAGE COAST ROAD

### Start: ❹ Arthurstown (p148)

A little-travelled 11km-long coast road wiggles south between Passage East and Dunmore East to the south. At times single-vehicle-width and steep, it offers mesmerising views of the ocean and undulating fields that you won't see from the main thoroughfares. Follow the R708 north to Waterford city.

oldest complete building in Ireland; the **Bishop's Palace** (The Mall; adult/child €7/free, incl Medieval Museum €10/free; ⊙9.15am-6pm Mon-Fri, 9.30am-6pm Sat, 11am-5pm Sun Jun-Aug, to 5pm Sep-May), home to a great interactive museum; and the superb **Medieval Museum** (Greyfriars St; adult/child €7/free, incl Bishop's Palace €10/free; ⊙9.15am-5pm Mon-Fri, 10am-5pm Sat, 11am-5pm Sun, longer hours Jun-Aug), which tells the story of Waterford life before 1700.

Since 1783 the city has been famous for its production of high-quality crystal, but the factory closed in 2009 and all that's left is the **House of Waterford Crystal** (www. waterfordvisitorcentre.com; The Mall; adult/student €13/5; ⊙9am-6pm Mon-Sat, 9.30am-6pm Sun Apr-Oct, shorter hours Nov-Mar), a flashy showroom where you can see some pieces of crystal being blown.Most of the stuff for sale in the shop is made in Eastern Europe.

🛏 p151

**The Drive »** Follow the southern bank of the River Suir and take the N25 to get to Dungarvan, 41km away. Or travel south and take the R675 coastal route along the stunning Copper Coast, where you'll see azure waters and ebony cliff faces along the way.

- - - - - - - - - - - - - - - -

**TRIP HIGHLIGHT**

## ❻ Dungarvan

It isn't enough that Dungarvan has the looks: pastel-coloured houses huddled around a boat-filled port at the mouth of the River Colligan make it one of the southeast's prettiest towns. It now also has the charm, in the form of a fantastic foodie reputation.

At the heart of the town is the Norman **castle** (☎058-48144; www. heritageireland.ie; Castle St; ⊙10am-6pm late May-late Sep), which is slowly being restored to its once impregnable glory. But the real draws are culinary: Paul Flynn's **Tannery Cookery School** (☎058-45420; www.tannery.ie; 6 Church St; courses from €75), adjoining a fruit, vegie

and herb garden, is one of Ireland's best. The annual **Waterford Festival of Food** (www.waterfordfestivaloffood.com; ⊙mid-Apr) celebrates the area's abundant fresh produce.

🍴 🛏 p151

**The Drive »** It's an easy 25km drive along the N25 to the turn-off for Ardmore, which then becomes the very rural R673 as you move south to the coast. This is bucolic Ireland at its most pristine, with farmhouses the only interruption to a stretch of undulating fields and stone walls.

- - - - - - - - - - - - - - - -

## ❼ Ardmore

This enticing seaside village may look quiet these days, but it's claimed that St Declan set up shop here between 350 and 420. This brought Christianity to southeast Ireland long before St Patrick arrived from Britain.

In a striking position on a hill above town, the ruins of **St Declan's Church** stand on the site of St Declan's original monastery alongside an impressive cone-roofed, 29m-high, 12th-century **round tower**, one of the best examples of these structures in Ireland.

If you're looking for a bit of beautiful seclusion, you'll find it on **Ballyquin beach**, home to tide pools, fascinating rocks and sheltered sand. It's 1km off the R673, 4km northeast of Ardmore. Look for the small sign.

🛏 p151

# Eating & Sleeping

## Enniscorthy

### 🛏 Woodbrook House    Guesthouse €€€
(📞053-925 5114; www.woodbrookhouse.ie;
Killanne; s/d from €100/160; ⊙Easter-Jun
& Aug-Sep; P 🛜) Rebuilt after sustaining
damage in the 1798 rebellion, this glorious
Georgian country house has a superb setting
beneath the Blackstairs Mountains. The lobby
features a gravity-defying spiral staircase that
amazes now just as it did over 200 years ago.
Green practices are used throughout and you
can make arrangements for dinner. It is 13km
west of Enniscorthy.

## Kilmore Quay ②

### ✕ Silver Fox
### Seafood Restaurant    Seafood €€€
(📞053-912 9888; www.thesilverfox.ie; mains
lunch €9-20, dinner €18-35; ⊙noon-8pm
Easter-Oct, shorter hours rest of year, closed
Jan–mid-Feb; 🪑) The Silver Fox's fresh-from-
the-ocean offerings include locally landed
plaice, langoustines, crab and mussels, plus
daily specials depending on what arrives at
the quay. The dining room exudes white table–
clothed elegance; don't arrive in flip-flops.
Bookings advised at weekends.

### 🛏 Mill Road Farm    B&B €
(📞053-912 9633; www.millroadfarm.com; R739;
s/d €50/80; P 🛜) About 2km northeast of
Kilmore Quay this dairy farm has four daintily
decorated guest rooms with lots of floral
fabrics; the owner breeds horses for racing. The
sitting room has plenty of games and books for
wet days. Breakfast includes homemade bread
and free-range eggs.

## Waterford City ⑤

### 🛏 Waterford Castle    Heritage Hotel €€€
(📞051-878 203; www.waterfordcastleresort.
com; The Island, Ballinakill; r from €139, cottages
from €109; P @ 🛜) Getting away from it all is
an understatement at this turreted mid-19th-

century castle set on its own private island (a
free car ferry provides round-the-clock access).
All 19 castle rooms have claw-foot baths, and
some have four-poster beds. There are also 48
contemporary self-catering cottages on the
island. Both guests and nonguests can dine on
organic fare in chef Michael Quinn's sublime
oak-panelled restaurant, or play a round of golf
on the hotel's own course.

## Dungarvan ⑥

### ✕ Tannery    Modern Irish €€€
(📞058-45420; www.tannery.ie; 10 Quay St;
mains €28-29; ⊙12.30-2.30pm Fri, to 3.30pm
Sun, 5.30-9.30pm Tue-Sat) An old tannery
building houses this innovative and much-
lauded restaurant, where Paul Flynn creates
seasonally changing dishes that focus on just
a few flavours and celebrates them through
preparations that are at once comforting yet
surprising. Service is excellent. Book ahead.

### 🛏 Cairbre House    B&B €€
(📞058-42338; www.cairbrehouse.com;
Strandside North; s/d €45/86; ⊙closed mid-
Dec–mid-Jan; P 🛜) Blazing with colourful
flowers in summer, this four-room B&B is set on
a half-hectare of riverside gardens. The gardens
come into their own at breakfast, providing
many of the ingredients including fragrant
herbs; a small terrace and conservatory
overlook the water. It's 1km north of the town
centre, on the east side of the river.

## Ardmore ⑦

### 🛏 Cliff House Hotel    Luxury Hotel €€€
(📞024-87800; www.thecliffhousehotel.com;
Cliff Rd; r €200-425, ste €325-550; P 🛜 🏊)
All bedrooms at this cutting-edge hotel, built
into the hillside, overlook Ardmore Bay. Some
suites even have two-person floor-to-ceiling
glass showers so you don't miss those sea
views. There are more sea views from the indoor
swimming pool, the outdoor Jacuzzi and spa,
the bar and the modern Irish restaurant, which
has a Michelin star to its name.

# Blackwater Valley Drive

**13**

*Great things come in short drives: the Blackwater Valley trip is only 64km long, but packed with history, culture, stunning views and great places to stay – all off the beaten track.*

## TRIP HIGHLIGHTS

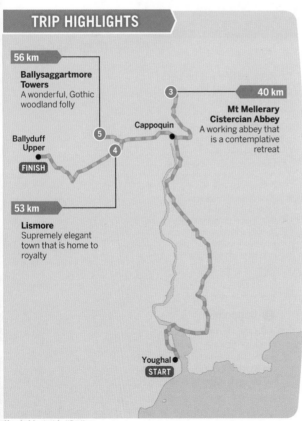

**56 km**

**Ballysaggartmore Towers**
A wonderful, Gothic woodland folly

**3** **40 km**

**Mt Mellerary Cistercian Abbey**
A working abbey that is a contemplative retreat

Cappoquin

**Ballyduff Upper**
FINISH

**5**

**4**

**53 km**

**Lismore**
Supremely elegant town that is home to royalty

Youghal
START

**2 DAYS**
**65KM / 40 MILES**

**GREAT FOR...**

**BEST TIME TO GO**
July and August, for traditional music.

 **ESSENTIAL PHOTO**

The architectural folly at Ballysaggartmore Towers.

 **BEST FOR FOODIES**

Aherne's Seafood Bar & Restaurant in Youghal.

**Youghal** Ancient fortifications

153

# 13 Blackwater Valley Drive

This short drive takes you through one of the most scenic and historic stretches of southern Ireland. From the mouth of the River Blackwater in Youghal (where you can take to the river by boat), explore the river valley northwards as far as historic Lismore before turning west with the river to find traditional villages, beautiful mountain passes and one of the country's best centres for traditional music and dancing.

## ❶ Youghal

The ancient seaport of Youghal (Eochaill; pronounced yawl), at the mouth of the River Blackwater, was a hotbed of rebellion against the English in the 16th century. Youghal was granted to Sir Walter Raleigh during the Elizabethan Plantation of Munster, and he spent brief spells living here in his house, Myrtle Grove. Oliver Cromwell spent the winter here in 1649.

Youghal has two Blue Flag beaches, ideal for building sandcastles modelled after the Clock Gate. **Claycastle** (2km) and **Front Strand** (1km) are both within walking distance of town, off the N25. Claycastle has summer lifeguards.

✖ 🛏 p159

**The Drive ››** Start the 33km drive by taking the N25 east towards Dungarvan and then go north along the R671 (direction Clonmel). Take the turn for Villierstown and follow the route to Cappoquin through the tree-lined of Dromana Woods. At the bridge over the River Finisk is a remarkable Hindu-Gothic gate, inspired by the Brighton Pavilion in England and unique to Ireland.

## ❷ Cappoquin

With the picturesque Blackwater Valley to the west, the small market town of Cappoquin sits neatly on a steep hillside

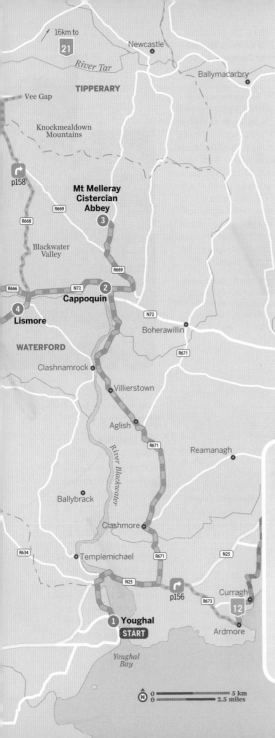

at the foot of the rounded, heathery Knockmealdown Mountains.

**Cappoquin House and Gardens** (www.cappoquin houseandgardens.com; garden €5, house & garden €10; ⊘ garden 10am-4pm Mon-Sat; P) is a magnificent 1779-built Georgian mansion and 2 hectares of formal gardens overlooking the River Blackwater. The entrance to the house is just north of the centre of Cappoquin; look for a set of huge black iron gates.

Cappoquin is also a good spot for anglers, as the town is right at the head of the Blackwater estuary, where there's some of the best game and coarse fishing in the country. The fishing season runs from the beginning of February to 30 September; in order to fish for salmon you'll have to purchase a

**LINK YOUR TRIP**

**12** **Wexford & Waterford**

Ardmore is only 5km from Youghal, from which you can explore the sunny southeast.

**21** **The Holy Glen**
Head 42km north from Lismore to Clonmel and explore some of Ireland's most important monastic sites.

state licence (one day/21 days €20/40) and a day permit (€20 to €50); you can buy both at the **Titelines Tackle & Gift Shop** (☎058-54152; Main St; ⏰9am-1pm & 2-5.30pm Mon-Sat).

p159

**The Drive »** It's only 6.5km to Mt Melleray. Just right off the R669 to Mt Melleray is a signpost for Glenshelane Park, which has lovely forest walks and picnic spots that are popular with locals.

TRIP HIGHLIGHT

## ❸ Mt Melleray Cistercian Abbey

A fully functioning monastery that is home to two dozen Trappist

monks, the beautiful 19th-century **Mt Melleray Cistercian Abbey** (www.mountmellerayabbey.org; ⏰7am-7pm; P) in the Knockmealdown foothills welcomes visitors wishing 'to take time for quiet contemplation'. In 1954 six of the monks departed for New Zealand, where they founded the Abbey of Our Lady of the Southern Star in a remote location near Takapau, on the North Island. There are tearooms (closed Monday) and a heritage centre.

**The Drive »** You'll have to double-back to Cappoquin (6.5km) and then take the N72 west for 6km to Lismore. The Blackwater River will be on your left as you go.

PETE SEAWARD/GETTY IMAGES ©

---

## ↱ DETOUR: ARDMORE

### Start: ❶ Youghal (p154)

Just 5km east of Youghal, and south off the N25 is the beautifully isolated seaside village of Ardmore, whose setting and heritage are unmatched – St Declan brought Christianity here a good century before St Patrick showed up. The ruins of **St Declan's Church** (Tower Hill; ⏰24hr) stand on the site of St Declan's original monastery, next to one of Ireland's best examples of a 12th-century round tower.

Ardmore is also home to one of the country's best hotels, the **Cliff House** (☎024-87800; www.thecliffhousehotel.com; Cliff Rd; r €200-425, ste €325-550; P🛜🍽), which has a Michelin-starred restaurant (menu from €65). From the hotel, there's a lovely, 5km circular **walk** that takes you past St Declan's Well, Ireland's oldest Christian ruin; the wreck of a crane ship that blew ashore in 1987; and a WWII lookout post.

TRIP HIGHLIGHT

## ❹ Lismore

Over the centuries, statesmen and luminaries have streamed through quiet, elegant Lismore, the location of a great monastic university founded by St Carthage in the 7th century. King Alfred of Wessex attended the university, Henry II visited the papal legate Bishop Christian O'Conarchy here in 1171, and even Fred Astaire dropped by when his sister Adele

**Lismore** Lismore Castle overlooks Blackwater River

married into the Cavendish family, who own the huge, 19th-century **castle** (www.lismorecastlegardens.com; gardens adult/child €8/5; ⏱10.30am-5.30pm Apr-Sep, last entry 4.30pm; ♿). You can't go inside (unless you rent it for an event), but you can visit the 3 hectares of ornate and manicured **gardens**. Thought to be the oldest in Ireland, there's a splendid yew walk where Edmund Spenser is said to have written *The Faerie Queen*.

Otherwise, pop into **St Carthage's Cathedral**

(1679), deemed by William Thackeray to be 'one of the neatest and prettiest edifices I have seen', and that was *before* the addition of the gorgeous Pre-Raphaelite Edward Burne-Jones stained-glass window.

✕ ⛏ p159

**The Drive »** Take the R666 Lismore to Fermoy road, signposted left over the bridge past Lismore Castle. The scenic drive overlooks the Blackwater; the 'towers' are signposted right about 3km out of Lismore.

## BLACKWATER CRUISE

If you want to explore the Blackwater River from the water, the jetty in Youghal is where you'll find the *Maeve*, which does 90-minute **tours** (☎087 988 9076; www.blackwatercruises.com; adult/child €20/10; ⏱Apr-Nov) of the river north to the remains of Templemichael Castle, about 8km north of Youghal. Captain Tony Gallagher is one of Youghal's best-known characters, as is his first mate, a dog called Pharaoh.

## DETOUR:
## THE VEE GAP

### Start: ④ Lismore (p156)

The R668 north of Lismore cuts through the Knockmealdown Mountains and crosses the border into southern Tipperary. The road rises sharply through lush wooded countryside for about 10km before emerging onto a beautiful upland plateau. A further 6km on, to your left, is Bay Lough, which makes for a nice amble. Beyond it is the Vee Gap, which cuts through the highest point of the mountains and offers superb views over three counties: Tipperary, Waterford and Limerick. Beyond the gap is the village of Clogheen, from where you can keep going to Clonmel.

**TRIP HIGHLIGHT**

### ⑤ Ballysaggartmore Towers

One of the more breathtaking bits of architectural folly in southern Ireland are just off the R666 road to Fermoy, in the heart of a woodland that was once the demesne of Arthur Keily-Ussher, an Anglo-Irish landlord with a reputation for harshness, ordering evictions of famine-stricken tenants for nonpayment of rent.

But he had a soft spot for his wife, who in 1834 demanded that he build her an estate to match that of her sister-in-law, so he ordered the construction of two Gothic-style gate **lodges** (one which serves as a bridge) as a prelude to a huge mansion. But Keily-Ussher ran out of money and the house was never built, a bit of hubris that, given his treatment of his tenants, left locals to delight in his misfortune.

The lodges are free to visit at any time.

**The Drive »** Head west on the N72 and after 6km turn right onto the smaller rural road for Ballyduff Upper, which is 3km further on.

### ⑥ Ballyduff Upper

This rural village (not to be confused with another Ballyduff in County Waterford) is a slice of traditional heaven: beautifully positioned on the Blackwater (the views are stunning), it goes about its business largely unperturbed by the demands of modern tourism.

During the summer, the big draw is the **Booley House** (☎058-60456; www.thebooleyhouse. com; adult/child €15/10; ⏲8.30pm Wed Jul & Aug), which since 1991 has been showcasing traditional Irish music, dancing and storytelling in its weekly show. The **Lismore Heritage Centre** (www.discoverlismore.com; Main St; adult/child €5/3.50; ⏲9.30am-5.30pm Mon-Fri year-round, 10am-5pm Sat & noon-5pm Sun Apr-Nov; ⊕) has details of upcoming shows.

The village's artistic tradition extends to amateur drama: companies from all over the country descend on St Michael's Hall for the annual **West Waterford Drama Festival** (www.adci.ie), which runs for 10 days in March.

# Eating & Sleeping

## Youghal ①

### ✕ Aherne's Seafood
### Bar & Restaurant                    Seafood €€

(☎024-92424; 163 North Main St; bar food
€10-18, dinner mains €24-33; ☺bar food noon-
10pm, dinner 6.30-9.30pm) Three generations
of the same family have run the award-winning
Aherne's. Seafood is the star, but there are also
plenty of meat and poultry dishes. Besides the
upmarket restaurant there's a stylish, cosy bar
and a much larger one popular with locals.

### 🛏 Avonmore House                   B&B €€

(☎024-92617; www.avonmoreyoughal.com;
South Abbey; d €64-90; P ✈) This grand
Georgian house near the clock tower was
built in 1752 on the site of a Franciscan abbey
destroyed by Cromwellian troops. Avonmore
belonged to the earls of Cork before passing
into private hands in 1826. Rooms are basic and
multicoloured.

## Cappoquin ②

### ✕ Barron's Bakery                   Bakery €

(www.barronsbakery.ie; The Square; mains
€4-9; ☺8.30am-5.30pm Mon-Sat) This famous
local bakery has used the same Scotch brick
ovens since 1887. Sandwiches, light meals
and a mouth-watering selection of cakes and
buns baked on the premises are available in
the cafe, while its handmade breads are famed
throughout the area.

### 🛏 Richmond House            Guesthouse €€

(☎058-54278; www.richmondhouse.net;
Carigeen; s/d from €70/120; ☺restaurant

6-9pm; P ✈) Dating from 1704 Richmond
House is set in 6 hectares of parkland. All the
same, its nine guest rooms – furnished with
countrified plaids, prints and mahogany – are
cosy rather than imposing, and service is
genuinely friendly. Nonguests are welcome at
its restaurant (per person €55; serving 6pm
to 9pm), where local produce includes West
Waterford lamb and Helvick harbour monkfish.

## Lismore ④

### ✕ Lismore Farmers Market           Market €

(Castle Ave; ☺10am-4pm Sun) The upscale
surrounds on the approach to the castle attract
a fab collection of vendors to this market,
including Naked Lunch – from Dungarvan's
**Nude Food** (www.nudefood.ie; 86 O'Connell
St; mains €10-17; ☺9.15am-6pm Mon-Thu, to
9.30pm Fri & Sat; 🍴 🐾) deli – whose tasty
sandwiches you can enjoy in the park or at
tables set up on the gravel path.

### ✕ Foley's                            Irish €€

(www.foleysonthemall.ie; Main St; lunch mains
€8-13, dinner €12-28; ☺12.30-5pm & 5-10pm)
This inviting Victorian pub, complete with
decorative wallpaper, leather-backed benches,
an open fire, and a beer garden out the back,
serves good steaks, fish and chips, and bangers
and mash.

### 🛏 Lismore House Hotel              Hotel €€

(☎058-72966; www.lismorehousehotel.com;
Main St; s/d from €59/99; P ✈) Ireland's
oldest purpose-built hotel was built in 1797 by
the Duke of Devonshire. He'd still recognise
the exterior, but the rooms within have had a
contemporary makeover with sleek dark-timber
furniture and cream-and-gold fabrics.

# Family Fun

*Want to keep everybody in the car happy, distracted and entertained? From pet farms to adventure centres, this trip is one for the whole family.*

## TRIP HIGHLIGHTS

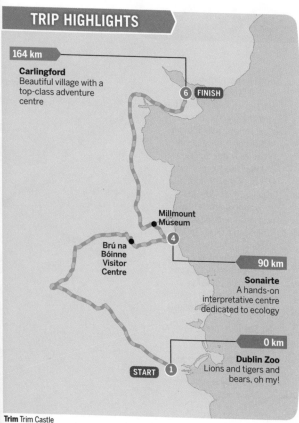

**164 km**

**Carlingford**
Beautiful village with a top-class adventure centre

**6 FINISH**

**Millmount Museum**

**4**

**Brú na Bóinne Visitor Centre**

**90 km**

**Sonairte**
A hands-on interpretative centre dedicated to ecology

**0 km**

**START** **1**

**Dublin Zoo**
Lions and tigers and bears, oh my!

**3 DAYS**
**164KM / 101 MILES**

**GREAT FOR...**

**BEST TIME TO GO**
April to September, for the long days and best weather.

**ESSENTIAL PHOTO**
Medieval Trim Castle is both memorable and impressive.

**BEST FOR FAMILIES**
The revamped Dublin Zoo has something for everyone.

**Trim** Trim Castle

# 14 Family Fun

Within an hour's drive of Dublin is a wealth of child-friendly activities and distractions. The big draws are the interactive exhibits of Brú na Bóinne and the superb adventure centre in Carlingford, but there's plenty more in between, including a popular pet farm where kids get to play with the animals and an ecological centre where they can learn about bee-keeping.

---

TRIP HIGHLIGHT

## ❶ Dublin

A bit of useless, interesting trivia: the original lion that roars at the beginning of all MGM films was Slats, born in the 12-hectare **Dublin Zoo** (www.dublinzoo.ie; Phoenix Park; adult/child/family €17/12/48; ⏰9.30am-6pm Mar-Sep, to dusk Oct-Feb; 🚌10 from O'Connell St, 25 & 26 from Middle Abbey St) in 1919. The zoo's other claim to fame is that it's one of the world's oldest, established in 1844. The lion-breeding program, established in 1857, is another highlight, and you can see these tough cats – from a distance – on the recently established 'African Plains', part of an expansion that saw the zoo double in size; other areas include 'World of Primates' and 'Fringes of the Arctic'.

Meet the Keeper is a big hit with kids, especially as they get a chance to feed the animals and participate in other activities. The City Farm is also excellent: it brings you within touching distance of chickens, cows, goats and pigs. There's also a zoo train and a nursery for infants.

🍴 🛏 p46, p60, p95, p167

**The Drive ≫** The 44km drive to Trim will take you through the 337-hectare Phoenix Park on your way north towards the

Map labels:

60km to 29

Newry

DOWN

ARMAGH

Mullaghbane • Meigh • N1

A29

Kilbroney Forest Park

Atticall

Warrenpoint

Flagstaff Viewpoint
Rostrevor

• Forkhill

p166

A2

Slieve Foye (587m)

Carlingford Lough

Carlingford 6
FINISH

Greencastle
Cranfield Point

A53

M1

• Dundalk

R173

Cooley Peninsula

Ballagan Point

R132

Dundalk Bay

• Tallanstown

LOUTH

• Castlebellingham

Ardee •
N33

R166

• Annagassan

Dunany Point

Dunleer •

N2

M1

• Grangebellew

Tinure •
• Mullary

• Clogherhead

R166

Collon •

• Termonfeckin

Tullyallen •
• Baltray

Irish Sea

Drogheda 5
R132

Slane •
Newgrange
• Mornington

• Rathmullan

Brú na Bóinne 7
Donore
R152

Johnstown •
3

4 • Laytown
Sonairte

R150

Kentstown •
Duleek

• Balbriggan

M1

• Skyrne
N2

• Naul

• Skerries

• Tara

Garristown •

M3

R129

R108

Dunshaughlin •
Oldtown • Ballyboughal

• Lusk
• Rush

Ashbourne •

• Portrane

Ratoath •

Broad Meadow Water

• Donabate

Batterstown •
• Black Bull

Swords •

• Malahide
Portmarnock

M3

Ireland's Eye

Dunboyne •

M1

• Clonee

Howth •
North Bull Island

Maynooth •

River Liffey

N3

p170

Howth Summit (171m)

M4

• Leixlip

M50

Phoenix Park

START
1 Dublin

Dublin Bay

• Celbridge

Straffan • Clondalkin •

N11

---

M1 motorway, passing Áras an Uachtaráin (the residence of the president) and the American ambassador's residence along the way. Stay on the M3 and get off at the first exit after the toll: Trim is 15km further on along the R154.

- - - - - - - - - - -

## ② Trim

If you've watched *Braveheart*, Mel Gibson's 1996 epic about Scots rebel William Wallace, then you may recognise the remarkably preserved **Trim Castle** (King John's Castle; www.heritageireland. ie; adult/child incl tour €4/2; ⊙10am–6pm mid-Mar–Oct, 9am–5pm Sat & Sun Nov–mid-Mar), which made a very acceptable stand-in for the castle at York.

Founded in 1173 by Hugh de Lacy, this was Ireland's largest Anglo-Norman fortification, but the original was destroyed by Rory O'Connor, Ireland's last high king, within a

DUBLIN & EASTERN IRELAND **14** FAMILY FUN

# LINK YOUR TRIP

**7** **Ancient Ireland**
You can connect to this trip through time at Brú na Bóinne.

**29** **The North in a Nutshell**
From Carlingford, it's only 80km along the A1 to Belfast and the beginning of this trip.

year of its construction: what you see here is the reconstruction, dating from 1200, and it's hardly changed since (even though it was given one hell of a shellacking by Cromwellian forces in 1649).

🍴 🛏 p103, p167

**The Drive »** Halfway along the 33km drive to Brú na Bóinne you'll hit the county town of Navan, which is pretty unremarkable except for the traffic – expect delays. Past Navan, the R147 is a classic rural road, with nothing but fields on either side and private houses.

### ❸ Brú na Bóinne Visitor Centre

Bringing the neolithic period to life and putting the extraordinary accomplishments of Brú na Bóinne's constructors in remarkable and fascinating context is this excellent **visitor centre** (📞041-988 0300; www.heri tageireland.ie; Donore; adult/child visitor centre €3/2, visitor centre & Newgrange €6/3, visi-

tor centre & Knowth €5/3, all 3 sites €11/6; ⏰9am-6.30pm May-Sep, to 5pm Nov-Jan, 9.30am-5.30pm Feb-Apr & Oct). It explains in brilliant, interactive detail exactly how people lived 3500 years ago and how they managed to garner the mathematical genius to construct a passage tomb that allows for the precise alignment of the sun during the winter solstice.

A bus will bring you from the visitor centre to the passage tomb itself, where a guide explains how it all came about. The tour finishes with a re-creation of the winter solstice illumination: even with artificial light it's a pretty cool moment.

🍴 🛏 p103, p111

**The Drive »** The quickest way to go is the 16km via the small village of Donore, passing the site of the Battle of the Boyne (1690). Take the R152 for 3km and then turn left onto the R150. After 6km, take a left then the first right (still the R150) and keep going until you reach

Sonairte, on your right about 1km shy of Laytown.

TRIP HIGHLIGHT

### ❹ Sonairte

Just outside the seaside village of Laytown, on the road to Julianstown, is **Sonairte** (📞041-982 7572; www.sonairte.ie; the Ninch; garden free, individual activities adult/child €3/1; ⏰10.30am-4.30pm Tue-Sun Feb-Dec; 👶), the National Ecology Centre. Dedicated to promoting ecological awareness, the centre is a wonderful place for kids to learn about sustainable living and organic horticulture. You

---

## NEWGRANGE WINTER SOLSTICE

From the Brú na Bóinne Visitor Centre take the bus to **Newgrange** where there lies the finest Stone Age passage tomb in Ireland. From here, at 8.20am on the winter solstice (between 18 and 23 December), the rising sun's rays shine through the roof box above the entrance, creep slowly down the long passage and illuminate the tomb chamber for 17 minutes. This is one of the country's most memorable, even mystical, experiences. There's a simulated winter sunrise for every group taken into the mound.

**Dublin** Chimpanzees at Dublin Zoo

can take a guided tour of the organic gardens and 200-year-old orchard, follow the nature trail or river walk, or take a course in anything from bee-keeping to foraging for wild food and organic gardening. There's a shop and organic cafe on-site, and a **farmers market** from 10.30am to 4pm.

Laytown itself is best known for the **Laytown Races** (www.meath.ie), the only official beach-run horse race in Europe, which has been run here in late August or early September since 1876.

**The Drive »** Head west on the R150 for 2km and turn right (north) onto the R132 for Drogheda, 6km further on. Keep left so as not to cross the river: Millmount will be on your left as you proceed down John St.

### NEWGRANGE FARM

One for the kids. A few hundred metres down the hill to the west of Newgrange tomb is a 135-hectare **working farm** (☏041-982 4119; www.newgrangefarm.com; Newgrange; adult/family €10/15.42; ☺10am-6pm mid-Mar–Aug). This hands-on, family-run farm allows visitors to feed ducks and lambs, and tour exotic bird aviaries. Charming Farmer Bill keeps things interesting, and demonstrations of threshing, sheepdog work and shoeing a horse are absorbing. Sunday at 3pm is a special time when the 'sheep derby' is run. Finding jockeys small enough wasn't easy, so teddy bears are tied to the animals' backs. Visiting children are made owners of their own sheep for the race. There are good family rates (two/four/six people €15/28/42).

## DETOUR:
## FLAGSTAFF VIEWPOINT

### Start: ❻ Carlingford

Travelling along the Cooley Peninsula from Carlingford to Newry in Northern Ireland, a quick 3km detour rewards you with sweeping views of Carlingford Lough, framed by rugged, forested mountains, green fields and glittering blue Irish Sea beyond.

Flagstaff Viewpoint lies *just* over the border in County Armagh. Heading northwest along the coast road (the R173), follow the signs to your left onto Ferryhill Rd, then turn right up to the viewpoint's car park. The quickest way to reach Newry from here is to retrace your steps and rejoin the R173.

### ❺ Drogheda

If the younger kids can stomach a little more history, the **Millmount Museum** (☎041-983 3097; www.millmount.net; off Duleek St, Millmount; adult/child museum €3.50/2.50, tower €3/2, museum & tower €5.50/3; ⏰10am-5.30pm Mon-Sat, 2-5pm Sun), across the river from the main town of Drogheda, has 9000 years of it to tell. But it does so in an engaging, interactive way: the various collections touch on all aspects of the area's past, from geology to Cromwell's brutal siege of the town.

The cobbled basement is full of gadgets and utensils from bygone times, including a cast-iron pressure cooker and an early model of a sofa bed. A series of craft studios allow you to see the work of craftspeople working in a variety of mediums, from ceramics to silk.

✗ 🛏 p103, p167

**The Drive »** Carlingford is 60km north of Drogheda along the M1 and, for the last 14km, the R173. Alternatively, you can take the longer, but much more scenic, coastal R166, which wends its way through the lovely villages of Termonfeckin and Clogherhead before rejoining the main road at Castlebellingham.

**TRIP HIGHLIGHT**

### ❻ Carlingford

Amid the medieval ruins and whitewashed houses, this vibrant little village buzzes with great pubs, chic restaurants, upmarket boutiques, spirited festivals and gorgeous views of the mountains and across Carlingford Lough to Northern Ireland.

Besides the medieval ruins, attractions include a pretty interesting **heritage centre** (☎042-937 3454; www.carlingfordheritagecentre.com; Churchyard Lane; adult/concession €3/1.50; ⏰10am-12.30pm & 2-4pm Mon-Fri) on the town's history, and the beginning of the 40km **Táin Trail**, which makes a circuit of the Cooley Peninsula through the Cooley Mountains. The route is a mixture of surfaced roads, forest tracks and green paths.

We recommend you check out the **Carlingford Adventure Centre** (☎042-937 3100; www.carlingfordadventure.com; Tholsel St), which runs a wide range of activities including sailing, kayaking, windsurfing, rock climbing and archery.

If you're here in mid-August, the **Carlingford Oyster Festival** (www.carlingford.ie) celebrates Carlingford's famous oysters with an oyster treasure hunt, fishing competition, music, food markets and a regatta on Carlingford Lough.

🛏 p167

# Eating & Sleeping

## Dublin ❶

### 🛏 Trinity Lodge
Guesthouse €€

(📞01-617 0900; www.trinitylodge.com; 12 S
Frederick St; r from €150; 📶; 🖥 all city centre,
🚉St Stephen's Green) Martin Sheen's grin
greets you upon entering this award-winning
guesthouse, which he declared his favourite
spot for an Irish stay. Marty's not the only one:
this place is so popular they've added a second
town house across the road, which has also
been kitted out to the highest standards. Room
2 of the original house has a lovely bay window.

## Trim ❷

### 🍴 StockHouse
Steak €€

(📞046-943 7388; www.stockhouserestaurant.
ie; Finnegan's Way, Emmet House; mains €15-26;
🕙11.30am-3pm & 5-9pm Mon-Thu, to 10pm Fri,
5-10pm Sat, noon-8.30pm Sun) Cooked-to-order
dry-aged steaks from local abattoir/butcher
Coogan's are the stock-in-trade of this always-
packed restaurant, but noncarnivores can
choose from fish and vegetarian dishes such as
pastas. They also do a fine selection of fajitas.

## Drogheda ❺

### 🍴 Kitchen
Mediterranean €€

(📞041-983 4630; 2 South Quay; mains €17-28;
🕙11am-9pm Wed, 11am-10pm Thu-Sat, noon-
9pm Sun; 📶👶) Sage-green on the outside

and cranberry-coloured inside, Drogheda's
best restaurant is aptly named for its shiny
open kitchen. Organic local produce is used
along with worldly ingredients such as Cypriot
haloumi and Spanish Serrano ham. Breads are
made on-site and there's an excellent choice of
wine by the glass. Don't miss the salted-caramel
baked Alaska for dessert.

### 🍴 Eastern Seaboard
### Bar & Grill
Irish €€

(www.easternseaboard.ie; Dublin Rd, 1
Bryanstown; mains €12-33; 🕙noon-10pm;
📶👶) Despite its unpromising location in
a business park near the train station, this
stylised, contemporary space is generally
packed. Adventurous food like pig's cheek
terrine with apple slaw, smoked mackerel pâté,
and coffee jelly and vanilla ice cream is served
continuously from lunchtime on – along with
frothy German beers on tap.

## Carlingford ❻

### 🛏 Carlingford House
B&B €€

(📞042-937 3118; http://carlingfordhouse.
com; Dundalk St; d from €85; 📶) In the village
centre, but set back from the road in manicured
grounds, this stately 1844 manor house (once
the local doctor's house) is especially stunning
in warmer months when it's enveloped by
vines. Inside, the welcoming hosts achieve
the perfect balance of old-world character
and contemporary flair, and serve exceptional
breakfasts.

# STRETCH YOUR LEGS
# KILKENNY

**Start/Finish** Kilkenny Castle

**Distance** 2.5km

**Duration** 2 hours

Kilkenny's medieval centre is conveniently compact, with most of the major sights collected between the castle to the south and the cathedral to the north.

Take this walk on Trips

## Kilkenny Castle

Rising above the Nore, **Kilkenny Castle** (www.kilkennycastle.ie; Castle Rd; adult/child €7/3; ⊙9.30am-5pm Mar-Sep, to 4.30pm Oct-Feb) is one of Ireland's most visited heritage sites. Regular 40-minute guided tours focus on the **Long Gallery**, in the wing of the castle nearest the river. The gallery, which showcases stuffy portraits of the Butler family members over the centuries, is an impressive hall with high ceilings vividly painted with Celtic and Pre-Raphaelite motifs.

The Walk » Cross Castle Rd; the design centre is adjacent to the castle.

## National Craft Gallery & Design Centre

Contemporary Irish crafts are showcased at this imaginative **gallery** (www.nationalcraftgallery.ie; Castle Yard; ⊙10am-5.30pm Tue-Sat, 11am-5.30pm Sun; 🖼) in the former castle stables that also house the shops of the Kilkenny Design Centre. Ceramics dominate, but exhibits often feature furniture, jewellery and weaving from the members of the Crafts Council of Ireland.

The Walk » Turn left and walk north onto High St until you reach the Tholsel on your right.

## Tholsel

The Tholsel (City Hall) on High St was built in 1761 on the spot where Dame Alice Kyteler's maid Petronella was burned at the stake in 1324 for witchcraft (even if it was actually Dame Alice who was most likely the guilty party).

The Walk » The Butter Slip is a narrow alley just right after the Tholsel.

## Butter Slip

With its arched entry and stone steps, Butter Slip, a narrow and dark walkway connecting High St with St Kieran's St (previously called Low Lane), is the most picturesque of Kilkenny's many narrow medieval corridors. It was built in 1616 and was once lined with the stalls of butter vendors.

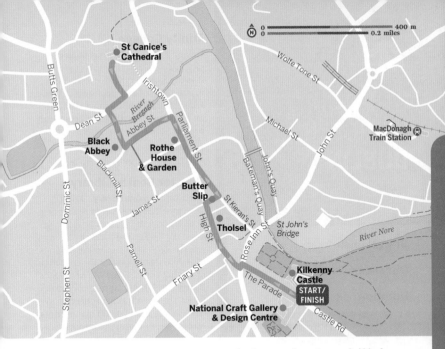

The Walk ≫ Turn left on St Kieran's St and rejoin High St; Rothe House is on your left.

## Rothe House & Garden

Ireland's best surviving example of a 16th-century merchant's house is the Tudor Rothe House. Built around a series of courtyards, it now houses a **museum** (www.rothehouse.com; Parliament St; adult/child €5.50/4.50; ☺10.30am-5pm Mon-Sat, 3-5pm Sun Apr-Oct, 10.30am-4.30pm Mon-Sat Nov-Mar) with local artefacts including a well-used Viking sword found nearby and a grinning head sculpted by a Celtic artist. Recent changes include new exhibits about the Rothe family and ongoing restorations of the urban gardens out the back.

The Walk ≫ Continue on Parliament St and after 200m take a left on Abbey St.

## Black Abbey

This Dominican **abbey** (Abbey St; ☺7.30am-7pm Mon-Sat & 9am-7pm Sun Apr-Sep, 7.30am-5.30pm Mon-Sat, from 9am Sun Oct-Mar) was founded in 1225 by William Marshall and takes its name from the monks' black habits. In 1543, six years after Henry VIII's dissolution of the monasteries, it was turned into a courthouse. Much of what survives dates from the 18th and 19th centuries, but remnants of more ancient archways are evident within the newer stonework. Look for the 13th-century coffins near the entrance.

The Walk ≫ Walk north through the lane and take a right on Dean St, then a left onto Coach St into the cathedral grounds.

## St Canice's Cathedral

Soaring over the north end of the centre is Ireland's second-largest medieval **cathedral** (www.stcanicescathedral.ie; St Canice's Pl; cathedral €4, round tower €3, combined €6; ☺9am-6pm Mon-Sat, 1-6pm Sun, shorter hours Sep-May) after St Patrick's in Dublin. Legend has it that the first monastery was built here in the 6th century by St Canice, Kilkenny's patron saint.

The Walk ≫ Go back down Parliament St to the castle, stopping in a pub or two along the way.

# STRETCH YOUR LEGS
# DUBLIN

**Start/Finish** Trinity College

**Distance** 4.9km

**Duration** 3 hours

Dublin's most important attractions are concentrated on the south side of the Liffey, split between the older medieval town dominated by the castle and the two cathedrals, and the handsome 18th-century city that is a showcase of exquisite Georgian aesthetics.

Take this walk on Trips

## Trinity College

Ireland's most prestigious **university** (☎01-896 1000; www.tcd.ie; College Green; ⏰8am-10pm; 🚌all city centre) is a masterpiece of architecture and land-scaping, and Dublin's most attractive bit of historical real estate, beautifully preserved in Georgian aspic.

**The Walk »** From Trinity College, walk west along Dame St and turn into Dublin Castle.

## Chester Beatty Library

The world-famous **library** (☎01-407 0750; www.cbl.ie; Dublin Castle; ⏰10am-5pm Mon-Fri, 11am-5pm Sat, 1-5pm Sun year-round, closed Mon Nov-Feb, free tours 1pm Wed, 3pm & 4pm Sun; 🚌all city centre), in the grounds of Dublin Castle, houses the collection of mining engineer Sir Alfred Chester Beatty (1875–1968). Spread over two floors, the breathtaking collection in-cludes more than 20,000 manuscripts, rare books, miniature paintings, clay tablets, costumes and other objects of historical and aesthetic importance.

**The Walk »** Exit the castle and walk west; you'll see Christ Church Cathedral directly in front of you.

## Christ Church Cathedral

Its hilltop location and eye-catching flying buttresses make this the most photogenic by far of Dublin's three **cathedrals** (Church of the Holy Trinity; www.christchurchcathedral.ie; Christ Church Pl; adult/student/child €6/4.50/2; ⏰9am-5pm Mon-Sat, 12.30-2.30pm Sun year-round, longer hours Jun-Aug; 🚌50, 50A, 56A from Aston Quay, 54, 54A from Burgh Quay) as well as one of the capital's most recognisable sym-bols. It was founded in 1030 on what was then the southern edge of Dublin's Viking settlement. The Normans re-built the lot in stone from 1172.

**The Walk »** Go south along Nicholas St (which becomes New St); St Patrick's is 400m along.

## St Patrick's Cathedral

Reputedly, it was at this **cathedral** (www.stpatrickscathedral.ie; St Patrick's Close;

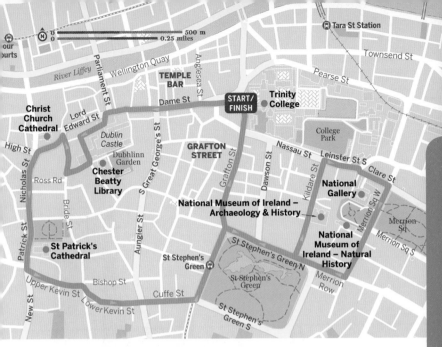

adult/student/child €6/5/free; ☉9.30am-5pm Mon-Fri, 9am-6pm Sat, 9-10.30am & 12.30-2.30pm Sun; 🚌50, 50A, 56A from Aston Quay, 54, 54A from Burgh Quay) that St Paddy himself dunked the Irish heathens into the waters of a well. Although there's been a church here since the 5th century, the present building dates from 1190 or 1225 (opinions differ).

**The Walk ≫** Just south of St Patrick's, turn left onto Kevin St and keep going until you reach St Stephen's Green; cross it and then turn onto Kildare St.

## National Museum of Ireland – Archaeology & History

The star attraction of this branch of the **National Museum of Ireland** (www. museum.ie; Kildare St; ☉10am-5pm Tue-Sat, 2-5pm Sun; 🚌all city centre) is the Treasury, home to the finest collection of Bronze Age and Iron Age gold artefacts in the world, and the world's most complete collection of medieval Celtic metalwork.

**The Walk ≫** Walk north on Kildare St and turn right on Nassau St, then stay right on Clare St.

## National Museum of Ireland – Natural History

Dusty, weird and utterly compelling, and a window into Victorian times, this **museum** (Upper Merrion St; ☉10am-5pm Tue-Sat, 2-5pm Sun; 🚌7, 44 from city centre) has barely changed since Scottish explorer Dr David Livingstone opened it in 1857 – before disappearing into the African jungle for a meeting with Henry Stanley.

**The Walk ≫** Turn right onto Merrion Row, skirt St Stephen's Green and go right into Grafton St to head back to Trinity College.

# Cork & Southwest Ireland

**THE SOUTHWEST CONTAINS SOME OF IRELAND'S MOST ICONIC SCENERY:** crenellated coastlines, green fields criss-crossed by tumbledown stone walls, and mist-shrouded mountain peaks and bogs.

This idyllic area claims the country's top three peninsula drives – the Ring of Kerry, Dingle Peninsula and Ring of Beara – as well as a shoal of charming fishing towns and villages that have helped establish the southwest as a gourmet heartland, fanning out from the country's spirited second-largest city, Cork.

The region's exquisite beauty makes it one of Ireland's most popular tourist destinations, but there's always an isolated cove or untrodden trail to discover along its roads.

**Cobh** St Colman's Cathedral
CONNIE COLEMAN/GETTY IMAGES ©

# Cork & Southwest Ireland

Ballymoe

Lough Mask

**MAYO**

Dunmore

Roscommon

Cong

Athleague

Ballymahon

Maam Cross

**Tuam**

N61

**ROSCOMMON**

Lough Ree

Mount Bellew

N17

**Athlone**

Lough Corrib

**GALWAY**

**Ballinasloe**

M6

Aughrim

Shannonbridge

N62

**Galway**

M6

Laurencetown

Cloghan

Galway Bay

N18

Killimor

Banagher

**OFFALY**

New Quay

Portumna

**Birr**

Inishmór
Inishmaan

Carron

Gort

N52

Borrisokane

Aran Islands

Inisheer

Corofin

Lough Derg

Whitegate

Roscrea

Liscannor

M18

**CLARE**

**Nenagh**

Inagh

Ballina

N62

**Ennis**

M7

Templemore

R473

**TIPPERARY**

Kilkee

Doonbeg

N68

**Shannon**

Bunratty

20

**Thurles**

Kilrush

Labasheeda

**Limerick**

M8

Carrigaholt

R487

Tarbert

Foynes

N69

Kilbaha

Glin

Rathkeale

Adare

N21

**LIMERICK**

**Cashel**

Mouth of the Shannon

Ballybunion

N24

21

Bansha

Newtown

Fethard

Listowel

Abbeyfeale

Kilmallock

N20

Cahir

N24

Maharees Islands

Banna

**KERRY**

N21

Charleville

M8

**Clonmel**

Tralee Bay

**Tralee**

Castleisland

Newmarket

Buttevant

Castletownroche

**WATERFORD**

Cloghane

Castlemaine

Farranfore

Kanturk

N73

Fermoy

Dunquin

16

Dingle Peninsula

R563

Killorglin

N72

**Mallow**

N72

Tallowbridge

Great Blasket

Dingle

N70

**Killarney**

Millstreet

N20

Rathcormack

Kells

Moll's Gap

Killarney National Park

R582

M8

Youghal

Cahersiveen

**CORK**

Midleton

N25

Youghal Bay

Valentia Island

N71

**Kenmare**

N22

Macroom

**Cork**

N70

Sneem

N70

Glengarriff

R585

17

N22

Cobh

Cloyne

Waterville

15

Lauragh

R754

Dunmanway

Bandon

Kinsale

Caherdaniel

R572

**Bantry**

N71

Scariff

Eyeries

Adrigole

Drimoleague

Timoleague

Allihies

19

Durrus

N71

Clonakilty

Dursey Island

Beara Peninsula

Sheep's Head Peninsula

Ballydehob

18

Rosscarbery

Goleen

Skibbereen

Mizen Head Peninsula

Baltimore

Cape Clear Island

*ATLANTIC OCEAN*

0 ——— 50 km
0 ——— 25 miles

Ilnacullin (Garinish Island) An Italianate garden off the shore of Glengariff

**Ring of Kerry 4 Days**
15 Weave your way past jaw-dropping scenery as you circumnavigate the Iveragh Peninsula. (p177)

16 **Dingle Peninsula 3–4 Days**
Dingle's ancient landscape is ringed by quaint fishing villages and spectacular beaches. (p189)

**Southwest Blitz 4 Days**
17 Blitz the best of southwest Ireland's coast, countryside and cosmopolitan city life. (p199)

18 **Southwestern Pantry 5 Days**
Sample some of the country's finest seafood, artisan produce and sociable markets. (p211)

19 **West Cork Villages 7 Days**
Colourful villages burst with life in West Cork, including its picturesque peninsulas. (p219)

20 **Shannon River Route 4 Days**
Meander alongside Ireland's mightiest river and get out on the water too. (p227)

21 **The Holy Glen 2–3 Days**
Awe-inspiring mountain vistas and sacred sites including the extraordinary Rock of Cashel. (p235)

 DON'T MISS

**Hunt Museum**
Limerick's true treasure hunt: open drawers and poke around its collections on Trip 20

**Garinish (Ilnacullin) Island**
Sail from Glengarriff past islands and seal colonies to Garinish's subtropical gardens on Trip 19

**Killarney Jaunting Cars**
Clip-clop in a traditional horse-drawn jaunting car on Trips 15 16 17

**Cork City Gaol**
Models of suffering prisoners bring home the harshness of the 19th-century penal system on Trip 17

**Rough Point Diving**
Dive crystal-clear waters and spot whales and dolphins on Trip 16

**Durrus Farmhouse Cheese**
Taste Durrus' famous cheese at its farm on Trip 18

*Classic Trip*

# Ring of Kerry

**15**

*Circumnavigating the Iveragh Peninsula, the Ring of Kerry is the longest and most diverse of Ireland's prized peninsula drives, combining jaw-dropping cliffs with soaring mountains.*

## TRIP HIGHLIGHTS

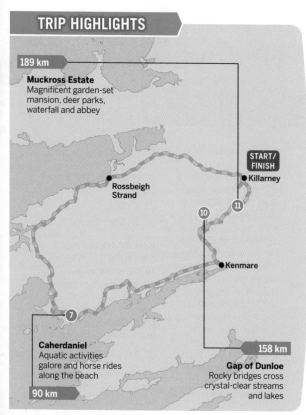

**189 km**

**Muckross Estate**
Magnificent garden-set mansion, deer parks, waterfall and abbey

**START/ FINISH**
● Killarney

● **Rossbeigh Strand**

⑩ ⑪

● Kenmare

⑦

**Caherdaniel**
Aquatic activities galore and horse rides along the beach

**90 km**

**158 km**

**Gap of Dunloe**
Rocky bridges cross crystal-clear streams and lakes

**4 DAYS**
**202KM / 125 MILES**

### GREAT FOR...

### BEST TIME TO GO

Late spring and early autumn for temperate weather free of summer crowds.

### ESSENTIAL PHOTO

Ross Castle as you row a boat to Inisfallen.

### BEST FOR WILDLIFE

Killarney National Park, home to Ireland's only wild herd of native red deer.

**Waterville County** Coastal scenery

## Classic Trip

## 15 Ring of Kerry

You can drive the Ring of Kerry in a day, but the longer you spend, the more you'll enjoy it. The circuit winds past pristine beaches, the island-dotted Atlantic, medieval ruins, mountains and loughs, with the coastline at its most rugged between Waterville and Caherdaniel in the peninsula's southwest. You'll also find plenty of opportunities for serene, starkly beautiful detours, such as the Skellig Ring and the Cromane Peninsula.

*Map labels:*
R560
Dingle
N86
Ventry
Dingle Bay
Knocknadobar (688m)
Killelan Mountain (275m)
**Cahersiveen** 5
Knightstown
Valentia Island
p181
Portmagee
N70
R565
**Waterville** 6
Ballinskelligs
Ballinskelligs Bay
Bolus Head
Derrynane Bay
Scariff

### 1 Killarney

A town that's been practising the tourism game for more than 250 years, Killarney is a well-oiled machine driven by the sublime scenery of its namesake national park, and competition keeps standards high. Killarney nights are lively and most pubs put on live music.

Killarney and its surrounds have been inhabited probably since the Neolithic period and were certainly the site of some important Bronze Age settlements, based on the copper ore mined on Ross Island. Killarney changed hands between warring tribes, the most notable of which were the Fir Bolg ('Bag Men'), expert stonemasons who built forts and devised Ogham script. It wasn't until the 17th century that Viscount Kenmare developed the town as an Irish version of England's Lake District. Among its notable 19th-century tourists were Queen Victoria and Romantic poet Percy Bysshe Shelley, who began *Queen Mab* here.

The town can easily be explored on foot in an hour or two, or you can get around by taking a horse-drawn jaunting car.

 p47, p187, p197

**The Drive** » From Killarney, head 22km west to Killorglin

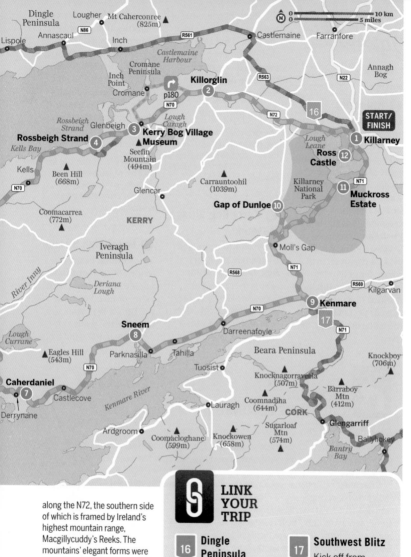

along the N72, the southern side of which is framed by Ireland's highest mountain range, Macgillycuddy's Reeks. The mountains' elegant forms were carved by glaciers, with summits buttressed by ridges of purplish rock. The name derives from the ancient Mac Gilla Muchudas clan; reek means 'pointed hill'. In Irish, they're known as Na Crucha Dubha (the Black Tops).

## LINK YOUR TRIP

**Dingle Peninsula**

Another of Ireland's iconic peninsula drives, the picturesque Dingle Peninsula, is on Killarney's doorstep.

**Southwest Blitz**

Kick off from Killarney along the Ring of Kerry's coastline and continue into captivating County Cork.

## ② Killorglin

Killorglin (Cill Orglan) is quieter than the waters of the River Laune that lap against its 1885-built eight-arched bridge – except in mid-August, when there's an explosion of time-honoured ceremonies at the famous **Puck Fair** (Aonach an Phuic; ☎066-976 2366; www.puck fair.ie), a pagan festival whose first recorded mention was in 1603. A statue of King Puck (a goat) peers out from the Killarney side of the river.

Killorglin has some of the finest eateries along the Ring. That said, there's not much competition along much of the route until you reach Kenmare.

🍴 🛏 p187, p209

**The Drive »** Killorglin sits at the crossroads of the N72 and the N70; continue 13km along the N70 to the Kerry Bog Village Museum.

## ③ Kerry Bog Village Museum

Between Killorglin and Glenbeigh, the **Kerry Bog Village Museum** (www.kerrybogvillage.ie; Ballincleave, Glenbeigh; adult/child €6.50/4.50; ◷8.30am–6pm; Ⓟ⛟) re-creates a 19th-century bog village, typical of the small communities that carved out a precarious living in the harsh environment of Ireland's ubiquitous peat bogs. You'll see the thatched homes of the turf cutter, blacksmith, thatcher and labourer, as well as a dairy, and meet rare Kerry Bog ponies.

**The Drive »** It's less than 1km from the museum to the village of Glenbeigh; turn off here and drive 2km west to unique Rossbeigh Strand.

## ④ Rossbeigh Strand

This unusual beach is a tendril of sand protruding into Dingle Bay, with views of Inch Point and the Dingle Peninsula. On one side, the sea is ruffled by Atlantic winds; on

---

## DETOUR:
## CROMANE PENINSULA

**Start: ② Killorglin**

Open fields give way to spectacular water vistas and multihued sunsets on the Cromane Peninsula, with its tiny namesake village sitting at the base of a narrow shingle spit.

Cromane's exceptional restaurant, **Jack's Coastguard Restaurant** (☎066-976 9102; http://jackscromane.com; 2-/3-course menus €33/39, dinner mains €16.50-32.50; ◷6-9pm Wed-Sat, 1-3.30pm & 6-9pm Sun, hrs may vary; Ⓟ⛟), is a local secret and justifies the trip. Entering this 1866-built coastguard station feels like arriving at a low-key village pub, but a narrow doorway at the back of the bar leads to a striking, whitewashed contemporary space where lights glitter from midnight-blue ceiling panels, and there are stained glass and metallic fish sculptures, a pianist and huge picture windows overlooking the water. Seafood is the standout, but there's also steak, roast lamb and a veggie dish of the day.

Cromane is 9km from Killorglin. Heading southwest from Killorglin along the N70, take the second right and continue straight ahead until you get to the crossroads. Turn right; Jack's Coastguard Restaurant is on your left.

For more info on the area, visit www.cromane.net.

## DETOUR:
## VALENTIA ISLAND & THE SKELLIG RING

**Start: ⑤ Cahersiveen**

If you're here between April and October, and you're detouring via Valentia Island and the Skellig Ring, a **ferry service** (☎087 241 8973; one way/return car €7/10, cyclist €2/3, pedestrian €1.50/2; ⏱7.45am-10pm Mon-Sat, 9am-10pm Sun Jul & Aug, 7.45am-9.30pm Mon-Sat, 9am-9.30pm Sun Apr-Jun, Sep & Oct) from Reenard Point, 5km southwest of Cahersiveen, provides a handy shortcut to Knightstown on Valentia Island. The five-minute crossing departs every 10 minutes. Alternatively, there's a bridge from Portmagee to Valentia Island.

Crowned by Geokaun Mountain, 11km-long Valentia Island (Oileán Dairbhre) makes an ideal driving loop, with some lonely ruins that are worth exploring. Knightstown, the only town, has pubs, food and walks.

The **Skellig Experience** (☎066-947 6306; www.skelligexperience.com; adult/child €5/3, incl cruise €30/17.50; ⏱10am-7pm Jul & Aug, to 6pm May, Jun & Sep, to 5pm Tue-Sat Mar, Apr, Oct & Nov; P) heritage centre, in a distinctive building with turf-covered barrel roofs, has informative exhibits on the Skellig Islands offshore. From April to September, it also runs two-hour cruises around the Skelligs. If the weather's bad, there's often the option of a 90-minute mini-cruise (€22/11, including museum entry) in the harbour and channel.

Immediately across the bridge on the mainland, Portmagee's single street is a rainbow of colourful houses. On summer mornings the small pier comes to life with boats embarking on the choppy crossing to the Skellig Islands. Portmagee holds **set-dancing workshops** (www.moorings.ie) over the May bank holiday weekend, with plenty of stomping practice sessions in the town's **Bridge Bar** (⏱food noon-9pm), a friendly local gathering point that's also good for impromptu music year-round and more formal sessions in summer.

The wild and beautiful, 18km-long Skellig Ring road links Portmagee and Waterville via a Gaeltacht (Irish-speaking) area centred on Ballinskelligs (Baile an Sceilg), with the ragged outline of Skellig Michael never far from view.

the other, it's sheltered and calm.

**The Drive »** Rejoin the N70 and continue 25km south to Cahersiveen.

- - - - - - - - - - - -

## ⑤ Cahersiveen

Cahersiveen's population – over 30,000 in 1841 – was decimated by the Great Famine and emigration to the New World. A sleepy outpost remains, overshadowed by the 688m peak of **Knocknadobar**. It looks rather dour compared with the peninsula's other settlements, but the atmospheric remains of 16th-century **Ballycarbery Castle**, 2.4km along the road to White Strand Beach from the town centre, are well worth a visit.

Along the same road are two stone ring forts. The larger, **Cahergall**, dates from the 10th century and has stairways on the inside walls, a *clochán* (circular stone building shaped like an old-fashioned beehive) and the remains of a house. The smaller, 9th-century **Leacanabuile** has an entrance to an underground passage. Their inner walls and chambers give a strong sense of what life was like in a ring fort. Leave your car in the parking area next to a stone

## WHY THIS IS A CLASSIC TRIP
CATHERINE LE NEVEZ, WRITER

In a land criss-crossed with classic drives, the Ring of Kerry is perhaps the most classic of all. Now a key stretch of the Wild Atlantic Way, the Ring showcases Ireland's most spectacular coastal scenery, its ancient and recent history, its low-ceilinged pubs with crackling turf fires and spontaneous, high-spirited trad-music sessions, and the Emerald Isle's most engaging asset: its welcoming, warm-hearted locals.

Above: Ross Castle, Killarney
Left: Killarney National Park
Right: Standing stones, Waterville

JORG GREUEL/GETTY IMAGES ©

wall and walk up the footpaths.

**The Drive** >> From Cahersiveen you can continue 17km along the classic Ring of Kerry on the N70 to Waterville, or take the ultrascenic route via Valentia Island and the Skellig Ring, and rejoin the N70 at Waterville.

### 6 Waterville

A line of colourful houses on the N70 between Lough Currane and Ballinskelligs Bay, Waterville is charm-challenged in the way of many mass-consumption beach resorts. A statue of its most famous guest, Charlie Chaplin, beams from the seafront. The **Charlie Chaplin Comedy Film Festival** (http://chaplinfilmfestival.com) is held in August.

Waterville is home to a world-renowned **links golf course**. At the north end of Lough Currane, **Church Island** has the ruins of a medieval church and beehive cell reputedly founded as a monastic settlement by St Finian in the 6th century.

🛏 p187

**The Drive** >> Squiggle your way for 14km along the Ring's most tortuous stretch, past plunging cliffs and soaring mountains, to Caherdaniel.

*Classic Trip*

TRIP HIGHLIGHT

### ❼ Caherdaniel

The scattered hamlet of Caherdaniel counts two of the Ring of Kerry's highlights: Derrynane National Historic Park, surrounded by subtropical gardens; and bar-restaurant **Scarriff Inn** (☎066-947 5132; http://scarriffinn.com; Caherdaniel; ⓧ9am-9pm, kitchen hrs vary), with its picture windows framing what it plausibly claims is 'Ireland's finest view' over rugged cliffs and islands.

Most activity here centres on the Blue Flag beach. **Derrynane Sea Sports** (☎087 908 1208; www.derrynaneseasports.com; Derrynane Beach) organises sailing, canoeing, surfing, windsurfing and water-skiing (from €40 per person), as well as

equipment hire (around €10 per hour). **Eagle Rock Equestrian Centre** (☎066-947 5145; www.eaglerockcentre.com; Ballycarnahan; per hr €35) offers beach, mountain and woodland horse treks for all levels.

**The Drive** ❯❯ Wind your way east along the N70 for 21km to Sneem.

### ❽ Sneem

Sneem's Irish name, An tSnaidhm, translates to 'the knot', which is thought to refer to the River Sneem that swirls, knot-like, into nearby Kenmare Bay.

Take a gander at the town's two cute squares, then pop into the **Blue Bull** (☎064-664 5382; South Sq; mains €17-29; ⓧfood noon-2pm & 6-9.30pm), a perfect little old stone pub, for a pint.

🛏 p187

**The Drive** ❯❯ Along the 27km drive to Kenmare, the N70 drifts away from the water to coast along under a canopy of trees.

### TOP TIP:
### AROUND (AND ACROSS) THE RING

Tour buses travel anticlockwise around the Ring, and authorities generally encourage visitors to drive in the same direction to avoid traffic congestion and accidents. If you travel clockwise, watch out on blind corners. There's little traffic on the Ballaghbeama Gap, which cuts across the peninsula's central highlands and has some spectacular views.

### ❾ Kenmare

The copper-covered limestone spire of Holy Cross Church, drawing the eye to the wooded hills above town, may make you forget for a split second that Kenmare is a seaside town. With rivers named Finnihy, Roughty and Sheen emptying into Kenmare Bay, you couldn't be anywhere other than southwest Ireland.

In the 18th century Kenmare was laid out to an X-shaped plan, with a triangular market square in the centre. Today the inverted V to the south is the focus. Kenmare Bay stretches out to the southwest, and there are glorious views of the mountains.

Signposted southwest of the square is an early Bronze Age **stone circle**, one of the biggest in southwest Ireland. Fifteen stones ring a boulder dolmen, a burial monument rarely found outside this part of the country.

🍴 🛏 p46, p187, p209

**The Drive** ❯❯ The coastal scenery might be finished, but, if anything, the next 23km are even more stunning as you head north from Kenmare to the Gap of Dunloe on the vista-crazy N71, winding between rock and lake, with plenty of lay-bys (shoulders) to stop and admire the views (and recover from the switchback bends).

# KILLARNEY NATIONAL PARK

Designated a Unesco Biosphere Reserve in 1982, **Killarney National Park** (www.killarneynationalpark.ie) is among the finest of Ireland's national parks. And while its proximity to one of the southwest's largest and liveliest urban centres (including pedestrian entrances right in Killarney's town centre) is an ongoing threat due to high visitor numbers, it's an important conservation area for many rare species. Within its 102 sq km is Ireland's only wild herd of native red deer, which has lived here continuously for 12,000 years, as well as the country's largest area of ancient oak woods and views of most of its major mountains.

The glacial Lough Leane (the Lower Lake or 'Lake of Learning'), Muckross Lake and the Upper Lake make up about a quarter of the park. Their peaty waters are as rich in wildlife as the surrounding land: cormorants skim across the surface, deer swim out to graze on islands, and salmon, trout and perch prosper in a pike-free environment. Lough Leane has vistas of reeds and swans.

With a bit of luck, you might see white-tailed sea eagles, with their 2.5m wingspan, soaring overhead. The eagles were reintroduced here in 2007 after more than 100 years of local extinction. There are now more than 50 in the park and they're starting to settle in Ireland's rivers, lakes and coastal regions. And like Killarney itself, the park is also home to plenty of summer visitors, including migratory cuckoos, swallows and swifts.

Keep your eyes peeled, too, for the park's smallest residents – its insects, including the northern emerald dragonfly, which isn't normally found this far south in Europe and is believed to have been marooned here after the last ice age.

TRIP HIGHLIGHT

## ⑩ Gap of Dunloe

Just west of Killarney National Park, the Gap of Dunloe is ruggedly beautiful. In the winter it's an awe-inspiring mountain pass, over-shadowed by Purple Mountain and Macgilly-cuddy's Reeks. In high summer it's a bottleneck for the tourist trade, with buses ferrying countless visitors here for horse-and-trap rides through the Gap.

On the southern side, surrounded by lush, green pastures, is **Lord Brandon's Cottage** (Gear-hameen, Beaufort; dishes €3-8; ⊗8am-3pm Apr-Oct), accessed by turning left at Moll's Gap on the R568, then taking the first right, another right at the bottom of the hill, then right again at the crossroads (about 13km from the N71 all up). A simple 19th-century hunting lodge, it has an open-air cafe and a dock for boats crossing Killarney National Park's Upper Lake. From here a (very) narrow road weaves up the hill to the Gap – theoretically you can drive this 8km route to the 19th-century pub **Kate Kearney's Cottage** (☎064-664 4146; www.katekearneyscottage.com; mains €11-23.50; ⊗food noon-8pm; P ♿) and back *but* only outside summer. Even then walkers and cyclists have right of way, and the precipitous hairpin bends are nerve-testing. It's worth walking or taking a jaunting car (or, if you're carrying two wheels, cycling) through the Gap, however: the scenery is a fantasy of rocky bridges over clear mountain streams and lakes. Alternatively, there are various options for exploring the Gap from Killarney.

The Drive » Continue on the N71 north through Killarney National Park to Muckross Estate (32km).

Classic Trip

---

TRIP HIGHLIGHT

## ⑪ Muckross Estate

The core of Killarney National Park is Muckross Estate, donated to the state by Arthur Bourn Vincent in 1932. **Muckross House** (☏064-667 0144; www.muckross-house. ie; adult/child €9/6, incl Muckross Traditional Farms €15/10.50; ⊘9am-7pm Jul & Aug, to 5.30pm Sep-Jun; P) is a 19th-century mansion, restored to its former glory and packed with period fittings. Entrance is by guided tour.

The beautiful **gardens** slope down, and a block behind the house contains a restaurant, craft shop and studios where you can see potters, weavers and bookbinders at work. Jaunting cars wait to run you through deer parks and woodland to **Torc Waterfall** and **Muckross Abbey** (about

€20 each, return; haggling can reap discounts). The visitor centre has an excellent cafe.

Adjacent to Muckross House are the **Muckross Traditional Farms** (☏064-663 0804; www.muckross-house.ie; adult/child €9/6, incl Muckross House €15/10.50; ⊘10am-6pm Jun-Aug, 1-6pm May & Sep, 1-6pm Sat & Sun Apr & Oct). These reproductions of 1930s Kerry farms, complete with chickens, pigs, cattle and horses, re-create farming and living conditions when people had to live off the land.

**The Drive** ⟩⟩ Continuing a further 2km north through the national park brings you to historic Ross Castle.

---

## ⑫ Ross Castle

Restored by Dúchas, **Ross Castle** (☏064-663 5851; www.heritageireland. ie; Ross Rd; adult/child €4/2; ⊘9.30am-5.45pm early Mar-Oct; P) dates back to the 15th century, when it was a residence of the O'Donoghues. It was the last place in Munster to

succumb to Cromwell's forces, thanks partly to its cunning spiral staircase, every step of which is a different height in order to break an attacker's stride. Access is by guided tour only.

You can hire boats (around €5) from Ross Castle to row out to **Inisfallen**, the largest of Killarney National Park's 26 islands. The first monastery on Inisfallen is said to have been founded by St Finian the Leper in the 7th century. The island's fame dates from the early 13th century when the Annals of Inisfallen were written here. Now in the Bodleian Library at Oxford, they remain a vital source of information on early Munster history. Inisfallen shelters the ruins of a 12th-century oratory with a carved Romanesque doorway and a monastery on the site of St Finian's original.

**The Drive** ⟩⟩ It's just 3km north from Ross Castle back to Killarney.

# Eating & Sleeping

## Killarney ❶

### 🛏 Aghadoe
### Heights Hotel    Luxury Hotel €€€

(☎064-663 1766; www.aghadoeheights.com;
Aghadoe; d/f/ste from €249/319/390, bar mains
€15-29.50; ⊙bar 11am-9.30pm; P @ 🛜 ⋈)
A huge, glassed-in swimming pool overlooking
the lakes is the centrepiece of this stunning
contemporary hotel, but you can also soak
up the views from the **bar** and **Lake Room
Restaurant** (mains €21-38; ⊙6.30-9.30pm;
🚼), both of which are open to nonguests, as
is the decadent spa, with 11 treatment rooms
and four-chamber thermal suite. Heavenly beds
have memory foam mattresses.

## Killorglin ❷

### ✕ Bianconi    Irish €€

(☎066-976 1146; www.bianconi.ie; Bridge St;
mains €14.50-25; ⊙8am-11.30pm Mon-Thu,
8am-12.30am Fri & Sat, 6-11pm Sun; 🛜🚼)
Bang in the centre of town, this Victorian-style
pub has a classy ambience and an equally
classy menu. Its spectacular salads, such as
Cashel blue cheese, apple, toasted almonds
and chorizo, are a meal in themselves. Upstairs,
newly refurbished guest rooms (doubles from
€110) have olive and truffle tones and luxurious
bathrooms (try for a roll-top tub).

### 🛏 Coffey's River's Edge    B&B €

(☎066-976 1750; www.coffeysriversedge.com;
Lower Bridge St; s/d €50/70; P 🛜) You can sit
out on the balcony overlooking the River Laune
at this contemporary B&B with spotless spring-
toned rooms and hardwood floors. Central
location next to the bridge.

## Waterville ❻

### 🛏 Brookhaven House    B&B €€

(☎066-947 4431; www.brookhavenhouse.
com; New Line Rd; d €80-120; P 🛜) The pick
of Waterville's B&Bs is the contemporary

Brookhaven House, run by a friendly family, with
spick-and-span rooms, comfy beds and a sunny
sea-view breakfast room.

## Sneem ❽

### 🛏 Parknasilla Resort & Spa    Hotel €€

(☎064-667 5600; www.parknasillaresort.
com; Parknasilla; d/f/ste from €139/179/229;
P @ 🛜 ⋈) This hotel has been wowing guests
(including George Bernard Shaw) since 1895
with its pristine resort on the tree-fringed
shores of the Kenmare River with views to the
Beara Peninsula. From the modern, luxuriously
appointed bedrooms to the top-grade spa,
private 12-hole golf course and elegant
restaurant, everything here is done just right.
It's 3km southeast of Sneem.

## Kenmare ❾

### ✕ Horseshoe    Pub Food €€

(☎064-664 1553; www.thehorseshoekenmare.
com; 3 Main St; mains €14-26; ⊙kitchen 5-10pm
Thu-Mon) Flower baskets brighten the entrance
to this popular gastropub, which has a short but
excellent menu that runs from Kenmare Bay
mussels in creamy apple cider sauce to braised
Kerry lamb on mustard mash.

### ✕ Tom Crean Fish & Wine    Irish €€

(☎064-664 1589; http://tomcrean.ie; Main
St; 2-/3-course menus €25/29, mains €16.50;
⊙5-9.30pm Thu-Sun late-Mar–Dec; 🛜) Named
for Kerry's pioneering Antarctic explorer,
and run by his granddaughter, this venerable
restaurant uses only the best of local organic
produce, cheeses and fresh seafood, all served
in modern, low-key surrounds.

### 🛏 Virginia's Guesthouse    B&B €€

(☎064-664 1021; www.virginias-kenmare.com;
Henry St; s/d from €40/75; 🛜) You can't get
more central than this award-winning B&B,
whose creative breakfasts celebrate organic
local produce (rhubarb and blueberries in
season, for example, as well as fresh-squeezed
OJ and porridge with whiskey).

# Dingle Peninsula

**16**

*Driving around this history-steeped peninsula, you'll encounter churches, castles, neolithic monuments, captivating scenery and artistic little Dingle, the peninsula's delightful 'capital'.*

## TRIP HIGHLIGHTS

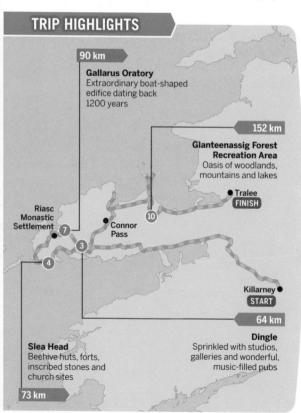

**90 km**

**Gallarus Oratory**
Extraordinary boat-shaped edifice dating back 1200 years

**152 km**

**Glanteenassig Forest Recreation Area**
Oasis of woodlands, mountains and lakes

● Tralee
FINISH

**Riasc Monastic Settlement** 7

● **Connor Pass** 10

3

4

Killarney ●
START

**64 km**

**Dingle**
Sprinkled with studios, galleries and wonderful, music-filled pubs

**Slea Head**
Beehive huts, forts, inscribed stones and church sites

**73 km**

---

**3–4 DAYS
185KM / 115 MILES**

**GREAT FOR...**

**BEST TIME TO GO**
June, July and August offer the best beach weather.

**ESSENTIAL PHOTO**
Snap a perfect peninsula panorama from atop Connor Pass.

**BEST FOR HISTORY**
Slea Head's astonishing concentration of ancient sites.

---

**Blasket Islands** Head to the Blasket Islands from Ventry Harbour

# 16 | Dingle Peninsula

As you twist and turn along this figure-of-eight drive, the coast is the star of the show. The opal-blue waters surrounding the Dingle Peninsula provide a wealth of aquatic adventures and impossibly fresh seafood, and you'll find that where the promontory meets the ocean – at wave-pounded rocks, secluded coves and wide, golden-sand beaches – Dingle's beauty is at its most unforgettable.

## ❶ Killarney

The lively tourist town of Killarney is an ideal place to kick off your trip, with a plethora of places to eat, drink and sleep. If you have time, the 102-sq-km Killarney National Park (p185), immediately to its south, and the Gap of Dunloe (p185), with its rocky terrain, babbling brooks and alpine lakes, are well worth exploring. On a tight schedule, however, you can still get a good overview of the area – and entertaining com-

mentary, too – aboard a horse-drawn jaunting car, also known as a trap, which comes with a driver called a jarvey. The pick-up point, nick-named 'the Ha Ha' or 'the Block', is on Kenmare Pl. Trips cost €30 to €80, depending on distance; traps officially carry four people.

✕ ⊨ p47, p187, p197

**The Drive »** The quickest route from Killarney to the peninsula passes through Castlemaine. Turn west here onto the R561; you'll soon meet the coast before coming to the seaside town of Inch (41km).

## ❷ Inch

Inch's 5km-long sand spit was a location for the movies *Ryan's Daughter* and *Playboy of the Western World*. Sarah Miles, the lead in the former film, described her stay here as 'brief but bonny'.

The dunes are certainly bonny, scattered with the remains of shipwrecks and Stone Age and Iron Age settlements. The west-facing beach is also a hot surfing spot; waves average 1m to 3m. You can learn to ride them with **Offshore Surf School** (☎087 294 6519; http://offshoresurfschool. ie; adult/child per 2hr from €25/20, board & wetsuit hire per 1/2hr €10/15; ⊗9am-6pm).

Cars are allowed on the beach, but don't end up providing others with laughs by getting stuck. **Sammy's** (☎066-915 8118; www.sammysinchbeach. com; mains €10-16; ⊗9.30am-10pm, reduced hrs in winter; 🛜♿), at the entrance to the beach, is the nerve centre of the village. In addition to its beach-facing bar-restaurant, there's a shop, tourist information and trad sessions during the summer.

**The Drive »** Shadowing the coast, about 7km west of Inch, Annascaul (Abhainn an Scáil; also spelled Anascaul) is home to a cracking pub, the South Pole Inn, run by Antarctic explorer Tom Crean in his retirement and now something

§ **LINK YOUR TRIP**

**15** **Ring of Kerry**
From Tralee it's a quick 22km zip along the N22 to pick up Ireland's most famous driving loop in Killarney.

**17** **Southwest Blitz**
Killarney is also the jumping-off point for another classic Irish road trip along the Ring of Kerry and a stunning swathe of County Cork.

of a Crean museum. Continuing 18km west of Annascaul brings you into Dingle town.

TRIP HIGHLIGHT

## ③ Dingle Town

Framed by its fishing port, the peninsula's charming little capital is quaint without even trying. Dingle is one of Ireland's largest Gaeltacht (Irish-speaking) towns (although locals have voted to retain the name Dingle rather than go by the officially sanctioned An Daingean) and has long drawn runaways from across the world, making it a surprisingly cosmopolitan, creative place.

This is one of those towns whose very fabric is its attraction. Wander the higgledy-piggledy streets, shop for hand-crafted jewellery, arts, crafts and artisan food and pop into old-school pubs. Two untouched examples are **Foxy John's** (Main St; ☺10am-11pm; ☎) and **Curran's** (Main St; ☺10am-11pm), which respectively have old stock of hardware and outdoor clothing lying about.

Dingle's most famous 'resident' is Fungie the dolphin. Boats leave Dingle's pier daily for one-hour **dolphin-spotting trips** (☎066-915 2626; www.dingledolphin.com; The Pier; adult/child €16/8). On land, the **Dingle Oceanworld** (☎066-915 2111; www.dingle-oceanworld.ie; The Wood;

adult/child €13.50/8.75; ☺10am-7pm Jul & Aug, to 5pm Sep-Jun; ☺) aquarium has a walk-through tunnel and a touch pool.

Don't leave Dingle without catching traditional live music at pubs such as the **Small Bridge Bar** (An Droichead Beag; Lower Main St; ☺1pm-late), where sessions kick off at 9.30pm nightly, and standout seafood at its restaurants.

🍴 🛏 p47, p197, p259

**The Drive »** West of Dingle, along the R559, the Slea Head drive runs around the tip of Dingle Peninsula. Driving clockwise offers the best views, and although it's a mere 50km in length, doing this stretch justice requires a full day, at least.

TRIP HIGHLIGHT

## ④ Slea Head

Overlooking the mouth of Dingle Bay, Mt Eagle and Europe's most westerly islands, the Blasket Islands, Slea Head has fine beaches and superbly preserved structures from Dingle's ancient past, including beehive huts, forts, inscribed stones and church sites.

The nearby village of **Ventry** (Ceann Trá), 6km west of Dingle town, is idyllically set next to a wide sandy bay. Full-day boat trips to the Blasket Islands with **Blasket Islands Eco Marine Tours** (☎086 335 3805; www.marine tours.ie; Ventry; per person €55) depart from Ventry

Harbour, with three hours ashore on Great Blasket; shorter trips are available. The **Celtic & Prehistoric Museum** (☎087 770 3280; Kilvicadownig, Ventry; admission €5; ☺10am-5.30pm mid-Mar–Oct; ℗), 4km southwest of the village, squeezes in an incredible collection of Celtic and prehistoric artefacts.

About 4km further west, the Iron Age **Dunbeg Fort** is a dramatic example of a promontory fortification, perched atop a sheer sea cliff. Inside the fort's four outer stone walls are the remains of a house and

**Slea Head** Dunbeg Fort

a beehive hut, as well as an underground passage. The **Fahan beehive huts**, including two fully intact huts, are 500m west of Dunbeg Fort on the inland side of the road. When the kiosks are open in summer, expect to be charged €3 for entrance to the sights.

**The Drive »** Continuing northwest from Slea Head for just over 2km brings you to Dunmore Head, the westernmost point on the Irish mainland and the site of the wreckage, from 1588, of two Spanish Armada ships. From here it's around 3km to Dunquin.

## 5 Dunquin

Yet another pause on a road of scenic pauses, Dunquin is a scattered village beneath Mt Eagle and Croaghmarhin.

The Blasket Islands are visible offshore. Dunquin's **Blasket Centre** (Ionad an Bhlascaoid Mhóir; ☎066-915 6444; www. heritageireland.ie; adult/ child €4/2; ☺10am-6pm Apr-Oct; **P**) is a wonderful interpretive centre with a floor-to-ceiling window overlooking the islands. Great Blasket Island's rich community of storytellers and musicians is profiled, along

with its literary visitors such as John Millington Synge, writer of *Playboy of the Western World*. Prosaic practicalities of island life are covered by exhibits on shipbuilding and fishing. There's a cafe with Blasket views and a bookshop.

**The Drive »** North from Dunquin is Clogher Head (a short walk takes you out to the head, with views down to a perfect little beach at Clogher – a prime resting spot for seals). Follow the road another 500m around to the crossroads, where a narrow paved track leads to the beach. Back on the loop road, head inland towards Ballyferriter (about 9km in all).

## DETOUR:
## DÚN AN ÓIR FORT

**Start: 5 Dunquin (p193)**

En route between Dunquin and Ballyferriter, turn north 1km east of Clogher, from where narrow roads run to the east of the Dingle Golf Links course to **Dún an Óir Fort** (Fort of Gold), the scene of a hideous massacre during the 1580 Irish rebellion against English rule. All that remains is a network of grassy ridges, but it's a pretty spot overlooking sheltered Smerwick Harbour.

The fort is about 6km from Clogher. Return on the same road to just south of the golf course and turn east to rejoin the R559 and continue to Ballyferriter.

boat, it has a doorway on the western side and a round-headed window on the east. Inside the doorway are two projecting stones with holes that once supported the door.

**The Drive »** Pass back through Dingle town before cutting across Connor Pass to reach the northern side of the peninsula. About 6km before you reach Kilcummin, a narrow road leads north to the quiet villages of Cloghane (23km) and Brandon, and finally to Brandon Point overlooking Brandon Bay.

### 6 Ballyferriter

Housed in the 19th-century schoolhouse in the tiny village of Ballyferriter (Baile an Fheirtearaigh), the **Dingle Peninsula Museum** (Músaem Chorca Dhuibhne; ☏066-915 6100; www.westkerrymuseum.com; admission €3.50; ☺10am-5pm Jun-Sep, by reservation rest of yr; P) has displays on the peninsula's archaeology and ecology. Across the street there's a lonely, lichen-covered church.

The remains of the 5th- or 6th-century **Riasc Monastic Settlement** are an impressive, haunting sight, particularly the pillar with beautiful Celtic designs. Excavations have also revealed the foundations of an oratory first built with wood and later stone, a kiln for drying corn and a cemetery. The ruins are signposted as 'Mainistir Riaisc'

along a narrow lane off the R559, about 2km east of Ballyferriter.

**The Drive »** The landscape around Ballyferriter is a rocky patchwork of varying shades of green, stitched by miles and miles of ancient stone walls. Wind your way along the R559 some 2km east of the Riasc Monastic Settlement turn-off to reach an amazing dry-stone oratory.

**TRIP HIGHLIGHT**

### 7 Gallarus Oratory

The dry-stone **Gallarus Oratory** (☏066-915 5333; www.gallarusoratory.ie; ☺10am-6pm Easter-Sep; P) is quite a sight, standing in its lonely spot beneath the brown hills as it has done for some 1200 years. It has withstood the elements perfectly, apart from a slight sagging in the roof. Traces of mortar suggest that the interior and exterior walls may have been plastered. Shaped like an upturned

### 8 Cloghane

Cloghane (An Clochán) is another little piece of peninsula beauty. The village's friendly pubs nestle between Mt Brandon and Brandon Bay, with views across the water to the Stradbally Mountains.

For many, the main goal is scaling 951m-high **Mt Brandon** (Cnoc Bhréanainn), Ireland's eighth-highest peak. If that sounds too energetic, there are plenty of coastal strolls.

The 5km drive from Cloghane out to **Brandon Point** follows ever-narrower single-track roads wandered by sheep, culminating in cliffs with fantastic views north and east.

On the last weekend in July, Cloghane celebrates the ancient Celtic harvest festival **Lughnasa** with events – especially bonfires – both in the village

**Killarney** Killarney National Park

and atop Mt Brandon. The **Brandon Regatta**, a traditional *currach* (rowing boat race), takes place in late August.

**The Drive »** Retrace your route to Cloghane and head east to Kilcummin (7km) and continue a further 7km east to Castlegregory, the Dingle Peninsula's water-sports playground.

- - - - - - - - - - - - -

**⑨ Castlegregory**

A highlight of the quiet village of Castlegregory (Caislean an Ghriare) is the vista to the often-snowy hills to the south (a lowlight is the sprawl of holiday homes).

However, things change when you drive up the sand-strewn road along the **Rough Point Peninsula**, the broad spit of land between Tralee Bay and Brandon Bay. Great underwater visibility makes this one

of Ireland's best diving areas, where you can glimpse pilot whales, orcas, sunfish and dolphins. Professional dive shop **Waterworld** (☎066-713 9292; www.waterworld.ie; Harbour House, Scraggane Pier) can help you out. **Jamie Knox Watersports** (☎066-713 9411; www.jamieknox.com; Maharees, Castlegregory)

offers surf, windsurf, kitesurf, canoe and pedalo hire and lessons.

✖ p197

**The Drive »** Follow the road signs 7km south of Castlegregory to one of the Dingle Peninsula's least-known gems, the Glanteenassig Forest Recreation Area.

---

## CONNOR PASS

At 456m, Connor (or Conor) Pass is Ireland's highest mountain pass. On a foggy day you'll see nothing but the road just in front of you, but in fine weather it offers phenomenal views of Dingle Harbour to the south and Mt Brandon to the north. The road is in good shape, despite being very narrow and *very* steep (large signs portend doom for buses and trucks).

The car park at the pass yields views down to two lakes in the rock-strewn valley below, plus the remains of walls and huts where people once lived impossibly hard lives. When visibility is good, the 10-minute climb to the summit is well worth it for the kind of vistas that inspire mountain climbers.

195

## ⑩ Glanteenassig Forest Recreation Area

Encompassing 450 hectares of woodland, mountains, lakes and bog, **Glanteenassig Forest Recreation Area** (www.coillteoutdoors.ie; ☺8am-10pm May-Aug, 9am-6pm Sep-Apr) is a magical, little-visited treasure. There are two **lakes**; you can drive right up to the higher lake, which is encircled by a plank boardwalk, though it's too narrow for wheelchairs or prams.

The Drive » From Glanteenassig Forest Recreation Area, follow the signs for 7km to the village of Aughacasla – home to the wonderful Seven Hogs inn – on the northern coast road (the R560), which links up with the N86 to Blennerville (27km in total).

## ⑪ Blennerville

Blennerville, just over 1km southwest of Tralee on the N86, used to be the city's chief port, though the harbour has long since silted in. A 19th-century flour **windmill** (☎066-712 1064; adult/child €5/3; ☺9am-6pm Jun-Aug, 9.30am-5.30pm Apr, May, Sep & Oct) here has

been restored and is the largest working mill in Ireland and Britain. Its modern visitor centre houses an exhibition on grain milling and on the thousands of emigrants who boarded 'coffin ships' from what was then Kerry's largest embarkation point. Admission includes a 30-minute guided windmill tour.

The Drive » Staying on the N86 brings you into the heart of Tralee.

## ⑫ Tralee

Although Tralee is Kerry's county town, it's more engaged with the business of everyday life than the tourist trade. Elegant Denny St and Day Pl are the oldest parts of town, with 18th-century buildings, while the Square, just south of the Mall, is a pleasant, open contemporary space hosting **farmers markets** (liveliest on Saturday).

A 15-minute nature-safari boat ride is the highlight of a visit to Tralee's **wetlands centre** (☎066-712 6700; www.tralee baywetlands.org; Ballyard Rd; adult/child €6/4; ☺10am-7pm Jul & Aug, to 5pm Sep, Oct & Mar-Jun, 11am-4pm Nov-Feb). You can also get a good overview of the reserve's 3000 hectares, encom-

passing saltwater and freshwater habitats, from the 20m-high viewing tower (accessible by lift/elevator), and spot wildlife from bird hides.

In Ireland and beyond, Tralee is synonymous with the **Rose of Tralee** (http://roseoftralee.ie) beauty pageant, open to Irish women and women of Irish descent from around the world (the 'roses'). It takes place amid five days of celebrations in August.

An absolute treat is the **Kerry County Museum** (☎066-712 7777; http://kerry museum.ie; Denny St; adult/child €5/free; ☺9.30am-5.30pm Jun-Aug, to 5pm Tue-Sat Sep-May), with excellent interpretive displays on Irish historical events and trends. The Medieval Experience re-creates life (smells and all) in Tralee in 1450.

Ingeniously converted from a terrace house, **Roundy's** (5 Broguemakers Ln; ☺6pm-11.30pm Thu & Sun, to 12.30am Fri & Sat) is Tralee's hippest little bar, spinning old-school funk, while **Baily's Corner** (30 Lower Castle St; ☺9am-11.30pm Mon-Thu, to 12.30am Fri & Sat, 4-11pm Sun; ☏) is deservedly popular for its traditional sessions.

🛏 p197

# Eating & Sleeping

## Killarney ❶

### ✗ Treyvaud's
Irish €€€

(☎064-663 3062; http://treyvaudsrestaurant.
com; 62 High St; mains lunch €7.50-14, dinner
€17-30; ⏱5-10pm Mon, noon-10pm Tue-Thu &
Sun, noon-10.30pm Fri & Sat) Michael Treyvaud's
modish restaurant has a strong reputation
for subtle dishes that merge trad Irish with
seductive European influences. The seafood
chowder at lunch is a velvet stew of mussels and
salmon; dinner mains include the best of local
lamb and a hearty bacon-and-cabbage platter.

### 🛏 Fairview
B&B €€

(☎064-663 4164; www.fairviewkillarney.com;
College St; d from €119; P @ 🛜) Done out in
beautiful timbers, the individually decorated
rooms (some with classical printed wallpaper,
some with contemporary sofas and glass) at this
boutique guesthouse offer more bang for your
buck than bigger, less personal places. A veritable
feast is laid on at breakfast, and the elegant in-
house restaurant is a winner come evening.

## Dingle Town ❸

### ✗ John Benny's
Pub Food €€

(☎066-915 1215; www.johnbennyspub.com;
Strand St; mains €13-22; ⏱kitchen noon-
9.30pm, bar noon-11pm) A toasty cast-iron
woodstove, stone slab floor, memorabilia on the
walls, great staff and no intrusive TV make this
one of Dingle's most enjoyable traditional pubs.
Glenbeigh oysters and Cromane mussels are
menu highlights. Local musicians pour in most
nights for rockin' trad sessions.

### ✗ Out of the Blue
Seafood €€€

(☎066-915 0811; www.outoftheblue.ie; The
Wood; mains lunch €12.50-20, dinner €21-37;
⏱5-9.30pm Mon-Sat, 12.30-3pm & 5-9.30pm
Sun) 'No chips', reads the menu of this funky
blue-and-yellow, fishing-shack-style restaurant on
the waterfront. Despite its rustic surrounds, this
is one of Dingle's best restaurants, with an intense
devotion to fresh local seafood (and only seafood);
if they don't like the catch, they don't open.

### 🛏 Harbour Nights
B&B €€

(☎066-915 2499; www.dinglebandb.com; The
Wood; d €70-90; P 🛜) Half the rooms at this
waterfront B&B have balconies with stunning
views over Dingle's harbour, as does the
upstairs sitting room, which opens to a terrace.

### 🛏 Pax House
B&B €€

(☎066-915 1518; www.pax-house.com; Upper
John St; d from €120; ⏱Mar-Nov; P @ 🛜)
From its highly individual decor (including
contemporary paintings) to the outstanding
views over the estuary from room balconies
and terrace, Pax House is a treat. Choose from
less expensive hill-facing accommodation,
rooms that overlook the estuary, and two-room
family suites opening onto the terrace. It's 1km
southeast of the town centre.

## Castlegregory ❾

### ✗ Harbour House
Seafood €€

(☎066-713 9292; www.maharees.ie; Scraggane
Pier; mains €6-15; ⏱dinner; P 🛜 ♿) This
family-run hotel with leisure centre, restaurant
and dive school – overlooking the Maharees
Islands – has its own fishing boat, bringing
catches 'from the tide to the table'. Meals also
include vegetables grown in the garden out the
back. Its 15 rooms (single/double from €40/80)
are comfortable and contemporary.

## Tralee ⓬

### 🛏 Meadowlands Hotel
Hotel €€

(☎066-718 0444; www.meadowlandshotel.
com; Oakpark Rd; s/d/f from €85/113/142;
P 🛜) Strolling distance from town but far
enough away to be quiet, Meadowlands is
an unexpectedly romantic four-star hotel.
Rooms are done out in autumnal hues and
service is spot-on; ask about discounted rates.
Its cavernous, beam-ceilinged bar, serving
top-notch seafood (the owners have their own
fishing fleet), is at least as popular with locals as
it is with visitors.

## Classic Trip

# Southwest Blitz

**17**

*Catch the very best of Ireland's southwest along this classic route as it curls from Killarney along the Ring of Kerry coast and across County Cork's lush countryside to charming Dungarvan.*

## TRIP HIGHLIGHTS

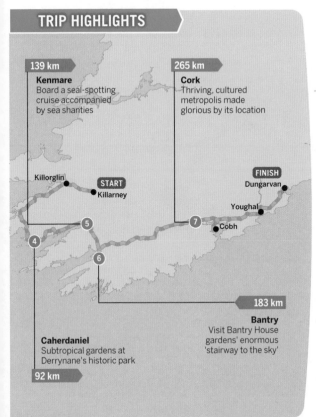

**139 km**
**Kenmare**
Board a seal-spotting cruise accompanied by sea shanties

**265 km**
**Cork**
Thriving, cultured metropolis made glorious by its location

Killorglin

**START**
Killarney

5

4

6

**FINISH**
Dungarvan

Youghal

7 Cobh

**183 km**
**Bantry**
Visit Bantry House gardens' enormous 'stairway to the sky'

**Caherdaniel**
Subtropical gardens at Derrynane's historic park

**92 km**

---

**4 DAYS**
**369KM /**
**229 MILES**

### GREAT FOR...

### BEST TIME TO GO

Late spring and early autumn for the best weather and manageable crowds.

### ESSENTIAL PHOTO

The Scarriff Inn's view across rocky coastline and scattered islands.

### BEST FOR FAMILIES

Ride the train or stroll around animal-filled Fota Wildlife Park.

---

**Bantry** Lobster pots stacked on the dock

# Classic Trip

## 17 Southwest Blitz

This drive around the country's stunning southwest conjures up iconic impressions of Ireland: soaring stone castles, dizzying sea cliffs, wide, sandy beaches, crystal-clear lakes, dense woodlands and boat-filled harbours. Villages you'll encounter en route spill over with brightly painted buildings, vibrant markets and cosy pubs with toe-tapping live music, perfectly poured pints and fantastic craic.

- - - - - - - - - - - - - - -

### ❶ Killarney

Killarney's biggest attraction, in every sense, is **Killarney National Park** (www.killarneynationalpark.ie), with magnificent Muckross Estate at its heart. If you're not doing the classic Ring of Kerry route that brings you through the park, you should definitely consider a detour here. Right in town, there are pedestrian entrances to the park opposite **St Mary's Cathedral** (www.killarneyparish.com; Cathedral Pl; ⏲8am-6.15pm Mon-Fri, to 7.30pm Sat, to 7pm Sun), a superb example of Gothic revival architecture, built between 1842 and 1855.

Also worth a visit in the town centre is the 1860s **Franciscan Friary** (www.franciscans.ie; Fair Hill; ⏲8am-7pm Mon-Sat, 8.30am-6pm Sun), with an ornate Flemish-style altarpiece, some impressive tilework and, most notably, stained-glass windows by Harry Clarke. The Dublin artist's organic style was influenced by

### LINK YOUR TRIP

**13 Blackwater Valley Drive**

Youghal is the starting point for a glorious drive through the Blackwater Valley.

**19 West Cork Villages**

From Cork city, it's a quick 27km trip south to Kinsale to wind your way around West Cork's picturesque peninsulas.

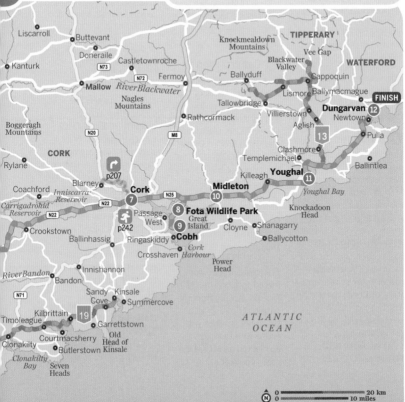

CORK & SOUTHWEST IRELAND **17** SOUTHWEST BLITZ

201

art nouveau, art deco and symbolism.

Plunkett and College Sts are lined with pubs; behind leaded-glass doors, tiny traditional **O'Connor's** (http://oconnors traditionalpub.com; 7 High St; ⏰10.30am-11pm Mon-Thu, to 12.30am Fri & Sat, 12.30-11pm Sun) is one of Killarney's most popular haunts, with live music every night.

✕ 🛏 p47, p187, p197

**The Drive ⟫** It's 22km west to Killorglin on the N72. To visit the too-gorgeous-for-words Gap of Dunloe, after 5km turn south onto Gap Rd and follow it for 3km to Kate Kearney's Cottage, where many drivers park in order to walk up to the Gap. You can also hire ponies and jaunting cars here (bring cash).

- - - - - - - - - - -

## ❷ Killorglin

Unless you're here during mid-August's ancient **Puck Fair** (Aonach an Phuic; 📞066-976 2366; www.puckfair.ie), the main reason to pause at the pretty riverside town of Killorglin (Cill Orglan) is its excellent selection of eateries. These become rather more scarce on the Ring of Kerry coast road until you get to Kenmare, so considering picking up picnic fare here, too.

At smokery **KRD Fisheries** (📞066-976 1106; www.krdfisheries.com; Tralee Rd; ⏰9am-1pm & 2-5pm Mon-Fri, 9am-1pm Sat, 9-11am Sun) you can buy salmon direct from the premises. Nearby, Jack Healy bakes amazing breads and also makes pâté and beautiful sandwiches at **Jack's Bakery** (Lower Bridge St; dishes €2-6.50; ⏰8am-6.45pm Mon-Fri, to 6pm Sat, 9am-2pm Sun).

✕ p107, p209

**The Drive ⟫** It's 40km from Killorglin to Cahersiveen. En route, you'll pass the turn-off to the little-known Cromane Peninsula, with a truly exceptional restaurant, as well as the quaint and insightful Kerry Bog Village Museum and the turn-off to Rossbeigh Strand, with dazzling views north to the Dingle Peninsula.

- - - - - - - - - - -

## ❸ Cahersiveen

The ruined cottage on the eastern bank of the Carhan River, on the left as you cross the bridge to Cahersiveen, is the humble birthplace of Daniel O'Connell (1775–1847). On the opposite bank there's a stolid bust statue of O'Connell. Known as 'the Great Liberator', O'Connell was elected to the British Parliament in 1828, but as a Catholic he couldn't take his seat. The government was forced to pass the 1829 Act of Catholic Emancipation, allowing some well-off Catholics voting rights and the right to be elected as MPs. Learn more about it at the

**Old Barracks Heritage Centre** (📞066-401 0430; www.oldbarrackscahersiveen. com; Bridge St; adult/child €4/2; ⏰10am-5.30pm Mon-Sat, 11am-5.30pm Sun; 🅿), housed in a tower of the former Royal Irish Constabulary (RIC). The barracks were burnt down in 1922 by anti-Treaty forces.

Ballycarbery Castle and ring forts are located here; Cahersiveen is also a jumping-off point for exploring Valentia Island and the Skellig Ring.

**The Drive ⟫** Continue from Cahersiveen for 17km along the N70 to Waterville. From Waterville the rugged, rocky coastline is at its most dramatic as the road twists, turns and twists again along the 12km stretch to Caherdaniel.

- - - - - - - - - - -

TRIP HIGHLIGHT

## ❹ Caherdaniel

Hiding between Derrynane Bay and the foothills of Eagles Hill, Caherdaniel barely qualifies as a tiny hamlet. Businesses are scattered about the undergrowth like smugglers, which is fitting since this was once a haven for the same.

There's a Blue Flag **beach**, plenty of activities, good hikes and pubs where you may be tempted to break into pirate talk.

Sublime **Derrynane National Historic Park** (📞066-947 5113; www. heritageireland.ie; Derrynane; adult/child €4/2; ⏰10.30am-

6pm Apr-Sep, 10am-5pm Wed-Sun mid-Mar–end Mar & Oct, 10am-4pm Sat & Sun Nov; **P** **⛊**) incorporates **Derrynane House**, the ancestral home of Daniel O'Connell, whose family made money smuggling from their base by the dunes. It's also home to astonishing **gardens**, warmed by the Gulf Stream, with palms, 4m-high tree ferns, gunnera ('giant rhubarb') and other South American species. A **walking track** through the gardens leads to wetlands, beaches and cliff tops.

At the **Scarriff Inn** (☑066-947 5132; http://scarriffinn.com; Caherdaniel; ⊙9am-9pm, kitchen hrs vary), wall-to-wall windows frame what the owners plausibly claim is 'Ireland's finest view', looking across the rocky coastline and scattered islands to Kenmare Bay and Bantry Bay. Drink it in over a snack, steak or seafood (call ahead to confirm seasonal kitchen hours) or just a pint. Or wake to the view from one of the six airy rooms with private bathrooms at the inn's neighbouring B&B (doubles from €70), which can also organise dive trips and fishing gear.

**The Drive »** The N70 zigzags for 21km east to the quaint, colourful little village of Sneem. This area is home to one of the finest castle hotels in the country, the Parknasilla Resort

and Spa. It's a further 27km drive along the N70 to Kenmare.

‑ ‑ ‑ ‑ ‑ ‑ ‑ ‑ ‑ ‑ ‑ ‑ ‑

TRIP HIGHLIGHT

## ⑤ Kenmare

Set around its triangular market square, the sophisticated town of Kenmare is stunningly situated by Kenmare Bay.

Reached through the tourist office, the **Kenmare Heritage Centre** (☑064-664 1233; The Square; ⊙9.30am-5.15pm Mon-Sat Apr-Oct, shorter hrs Nov-Mar) tells the history of the town, from its founding as Neidín by the swashbuckling Sir William Petty in 1670. The centre also relates the story of the Poor Clare Convent, founded in 1861, which is still standing behind Holy Cross Church.

Local women were taught needlepoint lace making at the convent, and their lacework catapulted Kenmare to international fame. Upstairs from the Heritage Centre, the **Kenmare Lace and Design Centre** (www.kenmarelace.ie; The Square; ⊙10.15am-5.30pm Mon-Sat Apr-Oct, shorter hrs Nov-Mar) has displays, including designs for 'the most important piece of lace ever made in Ireland' (in a 19th-century critic's opinion).

**Star Sailing** (☑064-664 1222; www.staroutdoors.ie; Dauros; **⛊**) offers activities such as sailing (from €65 per hour for up to six people; you'll need some

prior experience), sea kayaking (single/double per hour €20/36) and hill walking for all levels.

Warm yourself with tea, coffee, rum and the captain's sea shanties on an entertaining two-hour voyage with **Seafari** (☑064-664 2059; www.seafari.ie; Kenmare Pier; adult/child €25/12.50; ⊙Apr-Oct) to spot Ireland's biggest seal colony and other marine life. Binoculars (and lollipops!) are provided.

✕ 🛏 p47, p187, p209

**The Drive »** Leave the Ring of Kerry at Kenmare and take the N71 south for 44km to Bantry. For a scenic alternative, consider driving via the Ring of Beara, encircling the Beara Peninsula. If you don't have time to do the entire Ring, a shorter option is to cut across the Beara's spectacular Healy Pass Rd (R574).

‑ ‑ ‑ ‑ ‑ ‑ ‑ ‑ ‑ ‑ ‑ ‑ ‑

TRIP HIGHLIGHT

## ⑥ Bantry

Framed by the craggy Caha Mountains, sweeping Bantry Bay is an idyllic inlet famed for its oysters and mussels. On approach, 1km southwest of the town centre on the N71, is **Bantry House** (☑027-50047; www.bantryhouse.com; Bantry Bay; house & garden adult/child €11/3, garden only €5/3; ⊙10am-5pm Jun-Aug, 10am-5pm Tue-Sun Apr, May, Sep & Oct; **P**), the former home of Richard White, who earned his place in history when in 1798 he warned authorities of the

*Classic Trip*

### WHY THIS IS A CLASSIC TRIP
CATHERINE
LE NEVEZ, WRITER

Journeying from Killarney to Dungarvan, this trip not only incorporates all of Ireland's definitive elements but also plenty of unexpected ones, from the *Titanic*'s fateful final port to exotic animals roaming free in an island-set zoo to a spine-tingling former prison – as well as countless opportunities for serendipitous detours (because, of course, serendipity is what makes a road trip a true classic).

ROBERT MCGRATH/GETTY IMAGES ©

Top: St Fin Barre's Cathedral, Cork
Left: Bantry House
Right: Ring of Kerry, near Caherdaniel

imminent landing of patriot Wolfe Tone and his French fleet to join the countrywide rebellion of the United Irishmen. Storms prevented the fleet from landing, altering the course of Irish history. The house's **gardens** are its great glory, and it hosts the weeklong **West Cork Chamber Music Festival** (www.westcorkmusic. ie) in June/July, when it closes to the public (the garden, craft shop and tearoom remain open).

✖ p209, p225

**The Drive ›› ** Head north on the N71 to the crossroads at Ballylickey and take the R585, then the N22 through rugged terrain that softens to patchwork farmland along the 86km journey to Cork city.

- - - - - - - - - - - -

TRIP HIGHLIGHT

## ⑦ Cork City

Ireland's second city is first in every important respect – at least according to the locals, who cheerfully refer to it as the 'real capital of Ireland'.

A flurry of urban renewal has resulted in new buildings, bars and arts centres and tidied-up thoroughfares. The best of the city is still happily traditional, though – snug pubs with regular live-music sessions, excellent local produce in an ever-expanding list of restaurants and a genuinely proud welcome from the locals.

Cork swings during the **Guinness Jazz Festival** (www.corkjazzfestival.com), with an all-star line-up in venues across town in late October. An eclectic week-long program of international films screens in October/November during the **Cork Film Festival** (www.corkfilmfest.org).

About 2km west of the city centre, faint-hearted souls may find the imposing former prison, **Cork City Gaol** (☎021-430 5022; http://corkcitygaol.com; Convent Ave; adult/child €8/5; ⏰9.30am-5pm Apr-Sep, 10am-4pm Oct-Mar),

grim, but it's actually very moving, bringing home the harshness of the 19th-century penal system. An audio tour guides you around the restored cells, with models of suffering prisoners and sadistic-looking guards. The most common crime was simply poverty, with many of the inmates sentenced to hard labour for stealing loaves of bread. The prison closed in 1923, re-opening in 1927 as a radio station; the Governor's House has been converted into the Radio Museum Experience (€2).

✗ 🍴 p61, p209, p217, p259

**The Drive »** Head east of central Cork via the N8 and N25, and take the turn-off to Cobh to reach Fota Wildlife Park (18km).

### ❽ Fota Wildlife Park

Kangaroos bound, monkeys and gibbons leap and scream on wooded islands, and cheetahs run without a cage or fence in sight at the huge outdoor **Fota Wildlife Park** (☎021-481 2678; www.fotawildlife.ie; Carrigtwohill, Fota Island; adult/child €15.50/10; ⏰10am-6pm Mon-Sat, 10.30am-6pm Sun, last admission 4.30pm).

A **tour train** (one way/return €1/2) runs a circuit round the park every 15 minutes in high season, but the 2km **circular walk** offers a more close-up experience.

From the wildlife park, you can stroll to the Regency-style **Fota House** (☎021-481 5543; www.

---

## DETOUR:
## GOUGANE BARRA FOREST PARK

**Start: ❻ Bantry (p203)**

Almost alpine in feel, **Gougane Barra** (www.gouganebarra.com) is a truly magical part of inland County Cork, with spectacular vistas of craggy mountains, silver streams and pine forests sweeping down to a mountain lake that is the source of the River Lee. St Finbarre, the founder of Cork, established a monastery here in the 6th century. He had a hermitage on the island in Gougane Barra Lake (Lough an Ghugain), which is now approached by a short causeway. The small chapel on the island has fine stained-glass representations of obscure Celtic saints. A loop road runs through the park, with plenty of opportunities to walk the well-marked network of paths and nature trails through the forest.

The only place to air your hiking boots is the **Gougane Barra Hotel** (☎026-47069; www.gouganebarrahotel.com; d from €109; 🅿🛜). There's an on-site restaurant (lunch mains €13.50 to €15, two-/three-course dinner menus €23.70/30), a cafe and a pub next door. The hotel runs a summer theatre festival.

To reach the forest park, turn off the N71 onto the R584 about 6km north of Bantry and follow it north for 23km. Retrace your route to the N71 to continue back to Bantry and on to Cork City.

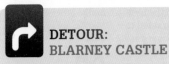

## DETOUR:
## BLARNEY CASTLE

**Start: ⑦ Cork City (p205)**

If you need proof of the power of a good yarn, join the queue to get into the 15th-century **Blarney Castle** (☏021-438 5252; www.blarneycastle.ie; adult/child €13/5; ☺9am-7pm Mon-Sat, to 6pm Sun Jun-Aug, shorter hrs Sep-May; P), one of Ireland's most inexplicably popular tourist attractions.

The clichéd **Blarney Stone** is perched at the top of a steep climb up slippery spiral staircases. On the battlements, you bend backwards over a long, long drop (with safety grill and attendant to prevent tragedy) to kiss the stone. Once you're upright, don't forget to admire the stunning views before descending. Queen Elizabeth I is said to have invented the term 'to talk blarney' out of exasperation with Lord Blarney's ability to talk endlessly without ever actually agreeing to her demands.

If the throngs get too much, vanish into the Rock Close, part of the beautiful and often ignored gardens.

Head out of central Cork via Merchant's Quay and the N20; Blarney is about 10km northwest of the city.

fotahouse.com; Carrigtwohill, Fota Island; house tours adult/child €8/3, house & gardens €11/4; ☺10am-5pm Mon-Sat, 11am-4pm Sun Apr-Sep). The mostly barren interior contains a fine kitchen and ornate plasterwork ceilings; interactive displays bring the rooms to life.

Attached to the house is the 150-year-old **arboretum**, which has a Victorian fernery, a magnolia walk and some beautiful trees, including giant redwoods and a Chinese ghost tree.

**The Drive »** From Fota Wildlife Park, head south for 5km to Cobh.

- - - - - - - - - -

### ⑨ Cobh

For many years Cobh (pronounced 'cove') was the port of Cork. During the Famine, some 2.5 million people left Ireland through the glistening estuary. In 1838 the *Sirius,* the first steamship to cross the Atlantic, sailed from Cobh, and the *Titanic* made its final stop here in 1912.

The original White Star Line offices, where 123 passengers embarked on the *Titanic,* now houses the unmissable **Titanic Experience Cobh** (☏021-481 4412; www.titanicexperiencecobh.ie; 20 Casement Sq; adult/child €9.50/5.50; ☺9am-6pm May-Sep, 10am-5.30pm Oct-Apr; ♿). Admission is by tour, which is partly guided and partly interactive, with holograms, audiovisual presentations and exhibits.

Standing dramatically above Cobh, the massive French Gothic **St Colman's Cathedral** (☏021-481 3222; www.cobhcathedralparish.ie; Cathedral Pl; admission by donation; ☺8am-6pm May-Oct, to 5pm Nov-Apr) is out of proportion to the town. Its 47-bell carillon, the largest in Ireland, weighs a stonking 3440kg.

In 1849 Cobh was renamed Queenstown after Queen Victoria paid a visit; the name lasted until Irish independence in 1921. Housed in the old train station, **Cobh, The Queenstown Story** (☏021-481 3591; www.cobhheritage.com; Lower Rd; adult/child €9.50/5; ☺9.30am-6pm Apr-Oct, to 5pm Nov-Mar, last admission 1hr before closing) has exhibits evoking the

*Classic Trip*

Famine tragedy, a genealogy centre and a cafe.

🛏 p209

**The Drive »** Travel north on the R624, then east on the N25 to Midleton (18km in total).

---

## ⑩ Midleton

The number-one attraction in Midleton is the former whiskey distillery now housing the **Jameson Experience** (📞021-461 3594; www.jamesonwhiskey.com; Old Distillery Walk; tours adult/child €16/8; ⏰shop 9am-6pm, tours 11am, 1pm, 2.45pm & 4.15pm). Attractive cafes and a great **farmers market** (www.midletonfarmersmarket.com; Main St; ⏰9am-2pm Sat) make it worth stopping for a while.

**The Drive »** Continue on the N25 for the 28km drive to Youghal.

---

## ⑪ Youghal

The ancient seaport of Youghal (Eochaill; pronounced 'yawl'), at the mouth of the River Blackwater, was a hotbed of rebellion against the English in the 16th century. Oliver Cromwell wintered here in 1649 as he sought to drum up support for his war in England and quell in-

surgence from the Irish. Youghal was granted to Sir Walter Raleigh during the Elizabethan Plantation of Munster.

The curious **Clock Gate** was built in 1777 and served as a clock tower and jail concurrently; several prisoners taken in the 1798 Rising were hanged from its windows.

Main St has an interesting curve that follows the original shore; many of the shopfronts are from the 19th century. Further up the street are six almshouses built by Englishman Richard Boyle, who bought Raleigh's Irish estates and became the first earl of Cork in 1616 in recognition of his work in creating 'a very excellent colony'. Across the road is the 15th-century tower house, **Tynte's Castle** (www.tyntescastle.com; North Main St), which originally had a defensive riverfront position before the River Blackwater silted up and changed course.

Built in 1220, **St Mary's Collegiate Church** incorporates elements of an earlier Danish church dating back to the 11th century. The churchyard is bounded by a fine stretch of the 13th-century town wall and one of the remaining turrets.

Beside the church, **Myrtle Grove** is the former home of Sir Walter Raleigh. His **gardens**,

on the other side of St Mary's, are open to the public.

🍴🛏 p159

**The Drive »** Rejoin the N25 and cross the River Blackwater. Continue following the N25 northeast for the final run to Dungarvan, a 31km trip in all.

---

## ⑫ Dungarvan

One of Ireland's most enchanting coastal towns, pastel-shaded Dungarvan is best known by its foodie reputation, but there are some intriguing sights, too. On the waterfront, **Dungarvan Castle** (📞058-48144; www.heritageireland.ie; Castle St; ⏰10am-6pm late May-late Sep) dates back to the 12th century. Admission is by (free) guided tour only.

Housed in a handsome building dating from the 17th century, the **Old Market House Arts Centre** (📞058-48944; Lower Main St; ⏰11am-1.30pm & 2.30-5pm Tue-Fri, 1-5pm Sat) showcases contemporary art by local artists.

The **Waterford County Museum** (www.waterfordcountymuseum.org; St Augustine St; ⏰10am-5pm Mon-Fri) covers maritime heritage (with relics from shipwrecks), Famine history, local personalities and various other titbits, all displayed in an 18th-century grain store.

🍴🛏 p151

# Eating & Sleeping

## Killorglin ❷

### ✕ Giovannelli — Italian €€

(☎087 123 1353; Lower Bridge St; mains €19-29; ⏱7-9pm Mon-Sat) **Northern Italian** native Daniele Giovannelli makes all of his pasta by hand at this simple but intimate little restaurant. Highlights of the blackboard menu might include seafood linguine with mussels in the shell, or beef ravioli in sage butter. Wonderful wines by the bottle and glass, too.

## Kenmare ❺

### 🛏 Sheen Falls Lodge — Heritage Hotel €€€

(☎064-664 1600; www.sheenfallslodge. ie; Knockduragh; d €180-235; ⏱Feb-Dec; P@🛜🏊) The Marquis of Landsdowne's former summer residence still feels like an aristocrats' playground, with a fine-dining French restaurant, a cocktail bar, a spa and 66 rooms with Italian marble bathrooms, all in a glorious setting beside a waterfall on the River Sheen with views across Kenmare Bay to Carrantuohil. Amenities are many – salmon fishing or clay-pigeon shooting, anyone?

## Bantry ❻

### ✕ Manning's Emporium — Cafe, Deli €

(☎027-50456; www.manningsemporium. ie; Ballylickey; mains €7.50-12.50; ⏱shop 10am-6pm, lunch noon-3pm Mon-Fri, brunch 10am-3pm Sat & Sun; P) This gourmet deli and cafe is an Aladdin's cave of West Cork's finest food. Tasting plates are the best way to sample the local artisan produce and farmhouse cheeses on offer. Foodie events take place regularly. It's on the N71 in Ballylickey (on the right approaching from Bantry).

## Cork City ❼

### ✕ Jacques Restaurant — Modern Irish €€

(☎021-427 7387; www.jacquesrestaurant.ie; 23 Oliver Plunkett St; mains lunch €8-13, dinner €22-26; ⏱10am-4pm Mon, to 10pm Tue-Sat) **Sisters** Jacqueline and Eithne Barry draw on a terrific network of local suppliers that they've built up over three decades to help them realise their culinary ambitions – the freshest Cork food cooked simply, without frills. The menu changes daily: smoked quail with celeriac remoulade, perhaps, or Castletownbere crab with spaghetti.

### 🛏 Auburn House — B&B €€

(☎021-450 8555; www.auburnguesthouse. com; 3 Garfield Tce, Wellington Rd; s/d/tr €58/80/106; P🛜) There's a warm family welcome at this neat B&B, which has smallish but well-kept rooms brightened by window boxes. Try to bag one of the back rooms, which are quieter and have sweeping views over the city. Breakfast includes vegetarian options; the location near the fun of MacCurtain St is a plus.

### 🛏 Imperial Hotel — Hotel €€

(☎021-427 4040; www.flynnhotels.com; South Mall; d €130-200; P@🛜) Having recently celebrated its bicentenary – Thackeray, Dickens and Sir Walter Scott have all stayed here – the Imperial knows how to age gracefully. Public spaces resonate with period detail – marble floors, elaborate floral bouquets and more – while the 130 bedrooms feature writing desks, understated decor and modern touches, including a luxurious spa and a digital music library.

## Cobh ❾

### 🛏 Commodore Hotel — Hotel €€

(☎021-481 1277; www.commodorehotel.ie; 4 Westbourne Pl; s/d €60/110; 🛜🏊) A classic seaside hotel with soaring chandeliered hallways and 42 well-appointed rooms (it's worth paying extra for one with a sea view). The pool is indoors, and a roof garden offers yet more views.

# Southwestern Pantry

## 18

*County Cork has earned itself a justifiable reputation as the gourmet capital of Ireland. Graze your way around the county on this foodie's fantasy while also feasting on its sumptuous scenery.*

## TRIP HIGHLIGHTS

**139 km**

**Belvelly**
Sublime smoked salmon at Ireland's oldest smokehouse

**126 km**

**Cork City**
Cork's 1788-established English Market showcases the county's fare

**START**
Durrus

**58 km**

**Clonakilty**
Home to the country's most famous black pudding

**FINISH**
Midleton

**Kinsale**
Sensational seafood, food festivals and gourmet purveyors galore

**100 km**

**5 DAYS**
**165KM / 103 MILES**

**GREAT FOR...**

**BEST TIME TO GO**
Produce is at its most abundant from spring onwards.

**ESSENTIAL PHOTO**
Kinsale's boat-filled harbour is a vision.

**BEST FOR FOODIES**
The English Market in Cork showcases the county's tantalising bounty.

**Cork** Fishing boats in the harbour

# 18 Southwestern Pantry

Farmers markets, fishing fleets hauling in fresh-as-it-gets seafood, the country's oldest smokehouse and its black pudding, as well as icons such as Cork's mouth-watering English Market, Jameson's old whiskey distillery, the wonderful Ballymaloe House and prestigious cookery school and some of the nation's finest eateries are among the treats awaiting in Ireland's southwestern pantry. *Bain taitneamh as do bhéil* (bon appétit)!

## ① Durrus

This little crossroads at the head of Dunmanus Bay has become something of a gourmet hotspot in recent years and earned an international reputation for its cheese, thanks to the likes of **Durrus Farmhouse** (✆027-61100; www.discoverfarm housecheese.ie; Coomkeen; ⊙11am-1pm Fri or by appointment). Its produce is sold here and as far afield as America. You can't visit the production area, but Jeffa Gill gives informal 10-minute presentations.

To reach the farm, drive 900m out of Durrus along the Ahakista road, turn right at St James' Church and continue for 3km until you see the sign for the farm.

**The Drive** ≫ From Durrus, zigzag 30km southeast on the N71 to Skibbereen.

- - - - - - - - - -

## ② Skibbereen

Try to time your journey through the busy market town of Skibbereen (Sciobairín) to catch the **farmers market** (www.skibbereenmarket.com; Old Market Sq; ⊙9.30am-1.30pm Sat).

If you're in town in mid-September, don't miss the **Taste of West Cork Food Festival** (www.atasteofwestcork.com), with a lively market and events at local restaurants.

Popular cooking courses at **Good Things Café** (☑028-51948; www.thegoodthingscafe.com; 68 Bridge St; mains €8-25; ⊙12.30-4pm Tue & Wed, 12.30-4pm & 6-9pm Thu-Sat; ℗) include A Dozen Quickies in a Day (a dozen dishes for your repertoire; €140) and a hands-on fish cooking course (€175) for those whose kitchen skills

extend no further than the microwave.

🛏 p225

**The Drive** ≫ It's 33km along the N71 from Skibbereen to Clonakilty; there are also slower but more scenic alternatives along the coast.

- - - - - - - - - -

TRIP HIGHLIGHT

## ③ Clonakilty

Clonakilty is legendary as the birthplace of Michael Collins, commander-in-chief of the army of the Irish Free State, which won independence from Britain in 1922. It's also home to the most famous black pudding in the country. The best place to buy the town's renowned blood sausage is **Edward Twomey** (☑023-883 4835; www.clonakiltyblackpudding.ie; 16 Pearse St; ⊙9am-6pm Mon-Sat), with different varieties based on the original 1880s recipe. Look out for it, too, at Clonakilty's weekly

**LINK YOUR TRIP**

**13** **Blackwater Valley Drive**

Head 26km east along the N25 for more glorious food over the border in County Waterford.

**19** **West Cork Villages**

Return to Kinsale to discover Cork's picturesque peninsulas.

**farmers market** (Pearse St; ◷9am-2pm Fri).

 p217

**The Drive** » Continue 42km east along the N71 through farming country interspersed with towns and villages to Kinsale (alternatively you can take the narrow R600 for 35km).

---------

## ④ Kinsale

Harbour-set Kinsale (Cionn tSáile) is revered for its foodie scene, thanks in large part to its busy fishing fleet.

A weekly **farmers market** (Short Quay; ◷9am-2pm Wed) takes place in front of Jim Edwards' restaurant on Market Quay. Handmade chocolates and pastel-shaded macarons are among the enticing wares at artisan chocolatier **Kinsale**

**Chocolate Boutique** (www.kinsalechocolate.ie; 6 Exchange Bldgs, Market Sq; ◷10am-6pm May-Aug, 11am-5pm Wed & Thu, 10am-6pm Fri & Sat, 2-6pm Sun Sep-Apr).

Kinsale's roots in the wine trade are on display at the early-16th-century **Desmond Castle** (📞021-477 4855; www.heritageireland. ie; Cork St; adult/child €4/2; ◷10am-6pm Tue-Sun Easter–mid-Sep), which houses a small **wine museum**.

Tastings, meals and harbour cruises take place during Kinsale's two-day **Gourmet Festival** (www.kinsale restaurants.com) in early October.

✕ 🛏 p217

**The Drive** » Head north for 27km on the R600 through patchwork farmland to Ireland's second-largest city.

------------

TRIP HIGHLIGHT

## ⑤ Cork City

Cork's food scene is reason enough to visit. Stretch your legs (and work off all that fine food) on a walk incorporating its **Butter Museum** (📞021-430 0600; www.corkbutter. museum; O'Connell Sq; adult/child €4/3; ◷10am-6pm Jul & Aug, to 5pm Mar-Jun, Sep & Oct, 11am-3pm Sat & Sun Nov-Feb).

Cork's **English Market** (www.englishmarket.ie; main entrance Princes St; ◷8am-6pm Mon-Sat) is a local – no, make that national – treasure. It could just as easily be called the Victorian Market for its ornate vaulted ceilings and columns. Scores of vendors sell some of the very best local produce, meats, cheeses and takeaway food

---

## ↪ DETOUR:
### BALTIMORE

**Start:** ② **Skibbereen (p213)**

Not only does Baltimore, 13km south of Skibbereen on the R595, have aquatic activities galore, but its seafood is sublime.

Over the last weekend of May, Baltimore's **Seafood Festival** (www.baltimore. ie) sees jazz bands perform, wooden boats parade and pubs bring out free mussels and prawns.

**The Lookout** (Chez Youen; 📞028-20600; www.waterfrontbaltimore.ie; The Quay; mains €16-40; ◷6.30-9.30pm daily Aug, Wed-Sat Jun, Jul & Sep, Fri & Sat May), upstairs at the Waterfront hotel, enjoys elevated sea views and serves luscious shellfish platters containing lobsters, prawns, brown crabs, velvet crabs, shrimps and oysters. Check opening times online.

The beautiful gardens at the **Glebe Gardens & Café** (📞028-20232; www. glebegardens.com; Skibbereen Rd; mains lunch €6-15, dinner €18-25; ◷10am-6pm Wed, Thu & Sun, to 10pm Fri & Sat Apr-Sep, 10am-6pm Wed-Sun Oct-Mar; P 🛜) are an attraction in themselves (admission is €5). If you're dining, lavender and herbs add fragrant aromas that waft over the tables inside and out. Food is simple and fresh, and is sourced from the gardens and a list of local purveyors.

**Cork** The English Market

in the region. Favourites include **On the Pig's Back** (☎021-427 0232; www.onthepigsback.ie; English Market; ⊙9am-5.30pm Mon-Sat), serving house-made sausages and incredible cheeses.

On a mezzanine overlooking part of the market is one of Cork's best eateries. **Farmgate Café** (☎021-427 8134; www.farmgate.ie; Princes St, English Market; mains €8-13;

⊙8.30am-5pm Mon-Sat) is an unmissable experience. Everything, from the rock oysters to the ingredients for Irish stew and raspberry crumble, is sourced from the market below. The best seats are at the balcony counter overlooking the passing parade of shoppers. On fine days, picnic in nearby **Bishop Lucey Park**.

The narrow, pedestrianised streets in Cork's **Huguenot Quarter** north of St Patrick's St throng with cafes and restaurants with outside tables; many serve till late.

Don't leave Cork without sampling Chocolatier's Hot Chocolate (€4) at **O'Connaill** (☎021-437 3407; 16b French Church St; ⊙10am-5.30pm Mon-Sat, noon-5pm Sun; 🛜) confectioners.

OLIVER STREWE/GETTY IMAGES ©

# DETOUR:
## BALLYMALOE HOUSE & COOKERY SCHOOL

**Start: ❼ Midleton**

Drawing up at wisteria-clad **Ballymaloe House** (☎021-465 2531; www.ballymaloe.ie; Shanagarry; s/d from €145/240; P 🛜 🐾 🐶), 12km southeast of Midleton on the R629, you know you've arrived somewhere special. Rooms are period-furnished and the beautiful grounds include a tennis court, swimming pool and shop. The menu at its celebrated restaurant is drawn up daily according to the produce available from Ballymaloe's extensive farms and other local sources. It also runs wine and gardening weekends.

Just over 3km further east (go through the village of Shanagarry and turn left opposite the church), TV personality Darina Allen runs the famous **Ballymaloe Cookery School** (☎021-464 6785; www.ballymaloecookeryschool.com; Shanagarry). Book lessons, which include half-day sessions (€75 to €145), well in advance. There are pretty cottages for overnight students around the 40-hectare organic farm.

✕ 🛏 p61, p209, p217, p259

**The Drive »** Some 19km east of Cork along the N25 is the feted Belvelly smokehouse.

**TRIP HIGHLIGHT**

## ❻ Belvelly

No trip to County Cork is complete without a visit to an artisan food producer, and the effervescent Frank Hederman is more than happy to show you around **Belvelly** (☎021-481 1089; www.frankhederman.com; Belvelly; free for individuals, charge for groups; ☺ by reservation 9am-5pm Mon-Fri), the oldest natural smokehouse in Ireland. Seafood and cheese are smoked here, but the speciality is fish – in particular, salmon. In a traditional process that takes 24 hours from start to finish, the fish is filleted and cured before being hung in the tiny smokehouse over beech woodchips. Phone or email Frank to arrange your visit.

**The Drive »** It's just 14km from Belvelly to Midleton.

## ❼ Midleton

Aficionados of fine Irish whiskey will know the main reason to linger in this bustling market town is to visit the restored 200-year-old building housing the **Jameson Experience** (☎021-461 3594; www.jamesonwhiskey.com; Old Distillery Walk; tours adult/child €16/8; ☺ shop 9am-6pm, tours 11am, 1pm, 2.45pm & 4.15pm) – and to purchase bottles of Jameson Whiskey, of course. Exhibits and tours explain the process of taking barley and creating whiskey (Jameson is today made in a modern factory in Cork).

Midleton's **farmers market** (www.midletonfarmersmarket.com; Main St; ☺ 9am-2pm Sat), behind the courthouse, is one of Cork's best markets, with bushels of local produce and producers who are happy to chat.

The original and sister establishment to Cork's Farmgate Café, **Farmgate Restaurant** (☎021-463 2771; www.farmgate.ie; Broderick St; mains lunch €11-18, dinner €15-26; ☺ restaurant 9am-5pm Tue & Wed, 9am-5pm & 6.30-9.30pm Thu-Sat, shop 9am-6pm Tue-Sat) also has a shop selling amazing baked goods and local, often organic, produce, cheeses and preserves.

# Eating & Sleeping

## Clonakilty ❸

### 🍴 An Súgán       Seafood €€

(☎023-883 3719; www.ansugan.com; 41 Wolfe
Tone St; mains lunch €11-17, dinner €13-27;
⏱noon-10pm) At this traditional bar with a
reputation for excellent seafood, you dine in a
room crammed with knick-knacks – jugs dangle
from the ceiling, business cards are stuffed
in the rafters, and lanterns dot the walls. But
there's nothing idiosyncratic about the food –
the seafood chowder and crab cakes are great,
and there's a choice of about 10 kinds of fish.

### 🛏 Emmet Hotel       Hotel €€

(☎023-883 3394; www.emmethotel.com;
Emmet Sq; s/d/f from €69/99/129; 🛜) This
lovely Georgian hotel on the elegant main
square successfully mixes period charm and Old
World service with the perks of a modern hotel.
The 20 rooms are large and plush; the on-site
restaurant, bistro and bar all serve up tasty Irish
food made from organic and local ingredients.

## Kinsale ❹

### 🍴 Finn's Table       Modern Irish €€€

(☎021-470 9636; www.finnstable.com; 6 Main
St; mains €22-32; ⏱6-10pm Mon, Tue & Thu-
Sat) Owning a gourmet restaurant in Kinsale
means plenty of competition, but John and Julie
Finn's venture is more than up to the challenge.
The restaurant is elegant but unstuffy, with
a warm welcome, and its menu of seasonal,
locally sourced produce rarely fails to please.
Seafood (including lobster when in season) is
from West Cork, while meat is from the Finn
family's butchers.

### 🍴 Fishy Fishy Cafe       Seafood €€€

(☎021-470 0415; www.fishyfishy.ie; Crowley's
Quay; mains €19-33; ⏱noon-9pm Mar-Oct,
shorter hours rest of year) One of the most
famous seafood restaurants in the country,
Fishy Fishy has a wonderful setting, with stark
white walls splashed with bright artwork and
steel fish sculptures, and a terrific decked
terrace at the front. All the fish is caught locally;

try the lobster thermidor or chilled seafood
platter served with homemade mayonnaise.

### 🍴 Jim Edwards       Seafood €€

(☎021-477 2541; www.jimedwardskinsale.com;
Market Quay; mains bar €14-19.50, restaurant
€15-29.50; ⏱bar food 12.30-10pm, restaurant
5.30-10pm) Bar food at this unassuming pub
is way above standard, and the restaurant is
exceptional. A very traditional ambience belies
the high quality of the menu, which doffs a cap
to meat-eaters but specialises in all kinds of
locally caught fish.

### 🛏 Pier House       B&B €€

(☎021-477 4169; www.pierhousekinsale.com;
Pier Rd; d €100-140; 🅿🛜) Set back from the
road in a sheltered garden, this is a lovely place
to rest your head. Pristine rooms, decorated
with shell-and-driftwood sculptures, have black-
granite bathrooms with power showers and
underfloor heating; four open to balconies.

## Cork City ❺

### 🍴 Cafe Paradiso       Vegetarian €€

(☎021-427 7939; www.cafeparadiso.ie; 16
Lancaster Quay; 2-/3-course menus €33/40;
⏱5.30-10pm Mon-Sat; 🌱) A contender for best
restaurant in town of any genre, Paradiso serves
contemporary vegetarian dishes, including
vegan fare: how about sweet chilli–glazed
pan-fried tofu with Asian greens in tamarind
and coconut broth? Reservations are essential.
The cafe also has funky rooms upstairs
(from €180/220 per single/double, including
breakfast and dinner).

### 🛏 Garnish House       B&B €€

(☎021-427 5111; www.garnish.ie; 18 Western Rd;
s/d/tr/f from €85/97/113/115; 🅿🛜) Attention
is lavished upon guests at this award-winning
B&B, where the legendary breakfast menu (30
choices) ranges from fresh fish to French toast.
Typical of the touches here is freshly cooked
porridge, served with creamed honey and
your choice of whiskey or Baileys; enjoy it out
on the garden terrace. The 14 rooms are very
comfortable; reception is open 24 hours.

# West Cork Villages

**19**

*West Cork claims some of Ireland's most scenic driving country, with three spectacular peninsulas and a cache of maritime villages filled with colourful shops and pubs alive with music.*

## TRIP HIGHLIGHTS

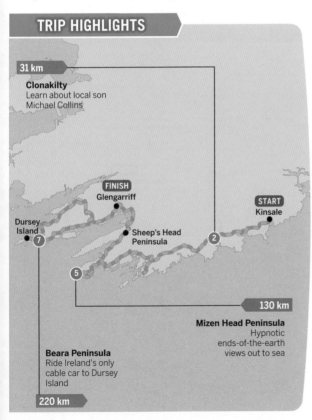

**31 km**

**Clonakilty**
Learn about local son Michael Collins

**FINISH**
**Glengarriff**

**START**
**Kinsale**

**Dursey Island**
7

**Sheep's Head Peninsula**

2

5

**130 km**

**Mizen Head Peninsula**
Hypnotic ends-of-the-earth views out to sea

**Beara Peninsula**
Ride Ireland's only cable car to Dursey Island

**220 km**

**7 DAYS**
**354KM /**
**220 MILES**

**GREAT FOR...**

**BEST TIME TO GO**

West Cork's villages are liveliest between April and October.

 **ESSENTIAL PHOTO**

Plumes of white water at the far-flung Mizen Head Signal Station.

 **BEST AERIAL VIEWS**

Take the cable car from the Beara Peninsula to tiny Dursey Island.

**Beara Peninsula** Houses dot the rocky landscape

# West Cork Villages

This trip contains one of Ireland's trinity of top peninsula drives: the spellbinding Beara Peninsula, straddling Counties Cork and Kerry. Beara's southern side, along Bantry Bay, harbours working fishing villages, while on the rugged northern side craggy roads cut in and out of nooks and crannies and tiny coves are like pearls in a sea of rocks.

## ❶ Kinsale

Narrow, winding streets lined with artsy shops and a harbour full of bobbing fishing boats and pleasure yachts make Kinsale (Cionn tSáile) one of Ireland's favourite midsize towns. Its superb food is a bonus.

The peninsula of Scilly is barely a 10-minute walk southeast, from where a lovely walking path continues 3km east to Summercove and the vast 17th-century, star-shaped **Charles Fort** (📞021-477 2263; www.heritageireland.ie;

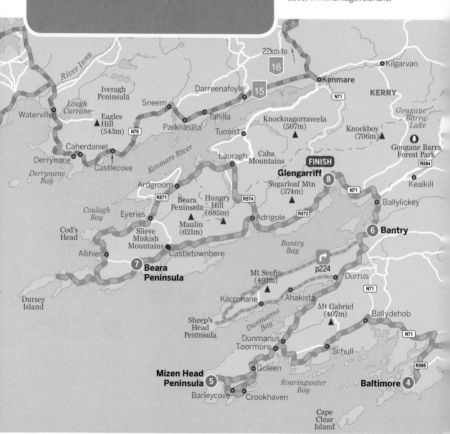

Summercove; adult/child €4/2; 🕙10am-6pm mid-Mar-Oct, to 5pm Nov–mid-Mar).

✕ 🛏 p217

**The Drive ❯❯** At times you'll meet the coast as you wind 35km west along the R600 to Clonakilty.

- - - - - - - - - - - -

TRIP HIGHLIGHT

## ➋ Clonakilty

Cheerful Clonakilty is a bustling market town coursed by little waterways. It serves as a hub for the scores of beguiling little coastal towns that surround it.

Superb miniature models of the main towns in West Cork star at the **West Cork Model Railway Village** (📞023-883 3224; www.modelvillage. ie; Inchydoney Rd; adult/child incl train ride €11/6.50; 🕙11am-5pm). A road train departs from the village on a 20-minute guided circuit of Clonakilty.

A visit to the **Michael Collins Centre** (📞023-884 6107; www.michaelcollins centre.com; Castleview; adult/child €5/3; 🕙10.30am-5pm Mon-Fri, 11am-2pm Sat mid-Jun–Sep), signposted off the R600 between

## LINK YOUR TRIP

**15** **Ring of Kerry**
Head 27km north from Glengarriff to pick up the Ring of Kerry in Kenmare.

**16** **Dingle Peninsula**
Killarney, 60km north of Glengarriff, is the gateway to the charming Dingle Peninsula.

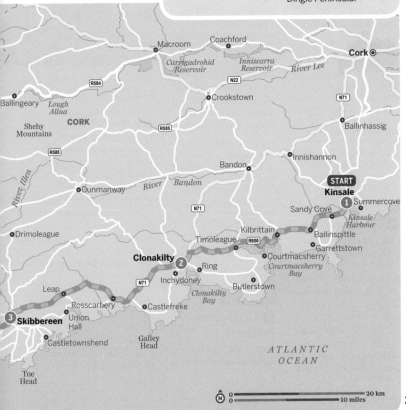

Timoleague and Clonakilty, is an excellent way to make sense of the life of Clonakilty's most famous son, Irish Free State commander-in-chief Michael Collins. The main negotiator of the 1921 Anglo-Irish Treaty, Collins was forced to make major concessions, including the partition of the country, famously declaring that he was signing his own death warrant. He was tragically correct, as Civil War broke out in the treaty's aftermath. A tour reveals photos, letters and a reconstruction of the 1920s country lane, complete with armoured vehicle, where Collins was killed.

✕ ⌂ p217

**The Drive »** It's 33km along the N71 from Clonakilty to Skibbereen, but it's possible to freelance along the coast the entire way. As a taster, at Rosscarbery, you can turn left onto the R597, which takes you past the pretty villages of Glandore (Cuan Dor) and Union Hall, and the turn-off to the Drombeg Stone Circle, and rejoin the N71 at Leap.

### ❸ Skibbereen

Weekending swells and yachties from Dublin descend on the busy market town of Skibbereen (Sciobairín), which is as close to glitzy as West Cork gets. It's a far cry from the Famine, when Skib was hit perhaps harder than any other town in Ireland, with huge num-

bers of the local population emigrating or dying of starvation or disease. The **Skibbereen Heritage Centre** (☏028-40900; www.skibbheritage.com; Upper Bridge St; adult/child €6/3; ◷10am-6pm Mon-Sat mid-May–late Sep, 10am-6pm Tue-Sat mid-Mar–mid-May & late Sep-Oct, closed Nov–mid-Mar) puts its history into harrowing perspective.

⌂ p225

**The Drive »** Islands are dotted offshore to the west as you drive 13km south on the R595 to Baltimore.

### ❹ Baltimore

Crusty old sea dog Baltimore has a busy little port full of fishing trawlers. There's excellent **diving** on the reefs around Fastnet Rock (the waters are warmed by the Gulf Stream and a number of shipwrecks lie nearby) and a variety of **cruises**.

**The Drive »** Retrace your route north to the N71, which rolls west through Ballydehob, the gateway to the Mizen, and then on to the pretty village of Schull (pronounced 'skull'). Travelling on into the undulating countryside along the coastal road takes you through ever-smaller settlements to the village of Goleen. Baltimore to Goleen is 48km.

TRIP HIGHLIGHT

### ❺ Mizen Head Peninsula

Even upon arriving at the welcoming village

STEPHEN SAKS/GETTY IMAGES ©

of Goleen, the Mizen Head Peninsula isn't over. Continue first to **Barleycove Beach**, with vast sand dunes hemmed in by two long bluffs dissolving into the surf. Then take the increasingly narrow roads to spectacular Mizen Head, Ireland's most southwesterly point. It's dominated by the **Mizen Head Signal Station** (☏028-35115; www.mizenhead.ie; Mizen Head; adult/child €6/4.50; ◷10am-6pm Jun-Aug, 10.30am-5pm mid-Mar–May, Sep & Oct, 11am-4pm Sat & Sun Nov–mid-Mar; ♿), completed in 1909 to warn ships

**Kinsale** Colourful buildings line cobbled streets

off rocks that appear in the water around here like crushed ice in cola. From the visitors centre, various pathways lead to the station, culminating in the crossing of a spectacular **arched bridge** that spans a vast gulf in the cliffs.

Pints in the sunshine are the reward for venturing on the crooked road to the outpost of **Crookhaven** (if it's raining, make that 'pints by the fireplace...'). In its heyday Crookhaven's natural harbour was an important anchorage, and mail from America was collected here.

Leaving Crookhaven, you'll spot a turn-off to the left, marked **Brow Head** – the Irish mainland's southernmost point. Park at the bottom of the hill – the track is very narrow and there's nowhere to pull over should you meet a tractor coming the other way. After 1km the road ends and a path continues to the head.

🛏 p225

**The Drive »** Bear north to join the scenic coast road that follows the edge of Dunmanus Bay for most of the way to Durrus. Continue north to Bantry, 60km north of Goleen.

- - - - - - - - - -

## ⑥ Bantry

Don't miss a visit to Bantry House (p203) and its glorious gardens, 1km southwest of the town centre on the N71.

🍴 🛏 p209, p225

**The Drive »** Continue north on the N71 to Glengarriff and the Beara Peninsula. The striations of the peninsula's underlying bedrock become evident as you drive west on the R572 towards Castletownbere, 50km from Bantry. On the highest hills – Sugarloaf Mountain and Hungry Hill – rock walls known as 'benches' snake backwards and forwards across the slopes.

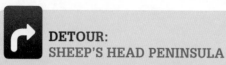

## DETOUR:
### SHEEP'S HEAD PENINSULA

**Start:** ❺ **Mizen Head Peninsula (p222)**

At Durrus, one road heads for Bantry; take the other, which turns west to circumnavigate Sheep's Head Peninsula.

The least visited of Cork's three peninsulas, Sheep's Head has a charm all its own – and plenty of sheep. There are good seascapes from along most of the loop road. The Goat's Path Rd has terrific views and runs between Gortnakilly and Kilcrohane (on the north and south coast, respectively) over the western flank of Mt Seefin.

**Ahakista** (Atha an Chiste) consists of a couple of pubs and a few houses stretched along the R591. An ancient **stone circle** is signposted at the southern end of Ahakista; access is via a short pathway. The peninsula's other village is **Kilcrohane**, 6km to the southwest, beside a fine beach. You can get pub food in both villages. Rejoin the N71 at Bantry.

For more information about the area, visit www.thesheepsheadway.ie.

---

**TRIP HIGHLIGHT**

### ❼ Beara Peninsula

Encircling the Beara Peninsula, the Ring of Beara is, along with the Ring of Kerry and Dingle, one of Ireland's podium peninsula drives.

In the fishing town of **Castletownbere** (Baile Chais Bhéara), you might recognise the front-cover photo of the late Pete McCarthy's bestseller, *McCarthy's Bar,* in three dimensions on Main St.

Tiny **Dursey Island**, at the end of the peninsula, is reached by Ireland's only **cable car** (☎028-21766; www.durseyisland.ie; adult/child return €8/4; ⏰9.30am-8pm Jul & Aug, less frequent trips Sep-Jun), which sways 30m above Dursey Sound.

It's 12km from the cable car to **Allihies** (Na hAilichí). From here the beautiful R575 coast road,

with hedges of fuchsias and rhododendrons, twists and turns for about 12km to **Eyeries**, a cluster of brightly coloured houses overlooking Coulagh Bay. From Eyeries you can forsake the R571 for the even smaller coast roads (lanes, really) to the north and east, with views north to the Ring of Kerry.

At the crossroads of **Ardgroom** (Ard Dhór), heading east towards Lauragh, look for signs pointing to the Bronze Age **stone circle**.

✕ 🛏 p225

**The Drive »** Cut across the spectacular Healy Pass Rd (R574) to Adrigole and return on the R572 to Glengarriff (32km). Alternatively, leaving Lauragh, you can skip Glengarriff a second time and take the R573, which hugs the coast, rejoining the more no-nonsense R571 at Tuoist for the 16km run east to Kenmare in County Kerry.

### ❽ Glengarriff

Offshore from the village of Glengarriff, subtropical plants flourish in the rich soil and warm climate of the magical Italianate garden on **Ilnacullin (Garinish Island)** (☎027-63040; www.heritageireland.ie/en/southwest/ilnacullin-garinishisland/; adult/child €4/2; ⏰9.30am-5.30pm Mon-Fri & Sun, to 6pm Sat Jul & Aug, shorter hrs Apr-Jun, Sep & Oct, closed Nov-Mar). Ferry companies, including **Blue Pool Ferry** (☎027-63333; www.bluepoolferry.com; adult/child return €10/5), leave every 30 minutes for the 15-minute boat trip past islands and seal colonies when the garden is open; fares don't include garden entry.

🛏 p225, p259

# Eating & Sleeping

## Skibbereen ❸

### 🛏 Bridge House · B&B €

(☎028-21273; www.bridgehouseskibbereen. com; 46 Bridge St; s/d €45/75; 🛜) Mona Best has turned her entire house into a work of art, filling the rooms with Victorian tableaux and period memorabilia. The whole place bursts at the seams with cherished clutter, dressed-up dummies and fragrant fresh flowers. Personalised service extends to Champagne breakfasts for guests celebrating a birthday – not bad for a B&B!

## Mizen Head Peninsula ❺

### 🛏 Heron's Cove · B&B €€

(☎028-35225; www.heronscove.com; Harbour Rd; s/d from €50/80; P 🛜) A delightful location on the shores of the tidal inlet of Goleen Harbour makes this fine restaurant and B&B a top choice. Rooms have been refurbished, and several have balconies overlooking the inlet. The small **restaurant** (three-course dinner €30, 7pm to 9.30pm May to August, by reservation September to April) has an excellent menu of organic and local food.

## Bantry ❻

### ✖ Fish Kitchen · Seafood €€

(☎027-56651; http://thefishkitchen.ie; New St; mains lunch €7.50-11, dinner €15-28; ⊘noon-9pm Tue-Sat) This outstanding little restaurant above a fish shop does seafood to perfection, from the live-tank local oysters (served with lemon and Tabasco sauce) to Bantry Bay mussels in white wine. If you don't fancy sea fare, it does a juicy steak, too.

### 🛏 Bantry House · Historic Hotel €€€

(☎027-50047; www.bantryhouse.com; Bantry Bay; d from €169; ⊘Apr-Oct; P 🛜) Guest rooms in this aristocratic mansion are decorated with antiques and contemporary furnishings – when you're not playing croquet, lawn tennis or billiards you can lounge in the library, once the doors of the historic house

have closed to the public (guests have free access to the house). If you just want to visit, and not stay overnight, see p203 for admission details.

### 🛏 Sea View House Hotel · Hotel €€€

(☎027-50073; www.seaviewhousehotel.com; Ballylickey; s/d/f from €100/150/165; P 🛜) You'll find everything you'd expect from a luxury hotel here: country-house ambience, tastefully decorated public rooms, expansive service and 25 cosy, smart bedrooms. The hotel is on the N71 in Ballylickey, 5km north of Bantry.

## Beara Peninsula ❼

### ✖ Olde Bakery · Modern Irish €€

(☎027-70869; Castletown House; mains €13-24; ⊘5.30-9.30pm daily, plus noon-4.30pm Sun Apr-Sep) One of the best restaurants in town, the Olde Bakery serves top regional seafood. The handful of tables out front are ideal on a summer evening.

### 🛏 Rodeen B&B · B&B €€

(☎027-70158; http://rodeencountryhouse. com; Ballard; s/d €50/80; ⊘Apr-Oct; P) A delightful, six-room haven, tucked away above the eastern approach to town. The musical instrument–filled house has stunning sea views and is surrounded by gardens full of crumbling Delphic columns. Flowers from the garden grace the breakfast table, and there are home-baked scones with honey from host Ellen's bees.

## Glengarriff ❽

### 🛏 Casey's Hotel · Hotel €€

(☎027-63010; www.caseyshotelglengarriff. ie; Main St; s €55-80, d €90-140; P @ 🛜) Old-fashioned Casey's has been welcoming guests since 1884 (Eamon de Valera stayed here). The 19 rooms have been modernised a bit but are still small. It's got stacks of atmosphere, and the vast terrace is a treat. The bar serves classics such as beef-and-Guinness pie; the restaurant ups the ante with posh seafood and steak dishes.

# Shannon River Route

## 20

*Follow the majestic River Shannon as it wends from Lough Derg to the broad estuary at vibrant Limerick city, and take in the stupendous views at Loop Head.*

## TRIP HIGHLIGHTS

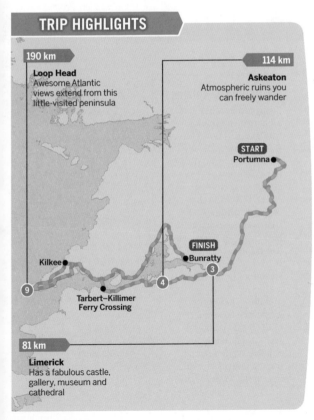

**190 km**

**Loop Head**
Awesome Atlantic views extend from this little-visited peninsula

**114 km**

**Askeaton**
Atmospheric ruins you can freely wander

**START**
Portumna •

**FINISH**
• Bunratty
③

Kilkee •

④

⑨

Tarbert–Killimer
Ferry Crossing

**81 km**

**Limerick**
Has a fabulous castle, gallery, museum and cathedral

---

**4 DAYS**
**296KM / 184 MILES**

### GREAT FOR...

### BEST TIME TO GO

Even in high summer there are plenty of crowd-free escapes.

### ESSENTIAL PHOTO

The soaring cliffs on the aptly named 'Scenic Loop' road west of Kilkee.

### BEST FOR DOLPHIN SPOTTING

Estuary-set Kilrush has a nature centre, dolphin trail and cruises.

---

**Bunratty** Bunratty Castle

# 20 Shannon River Route

Ireland's longest river provides a stunning backdrop to this route, but you'll also get out on the water. The car-ferry crossing from Tarbert in County Kerry to Killimer in County Clare takes just 20 minutes and, because the estuary is sheltered, you can usually look forward to smooth sailing.

## ❶ Portumna

In the far southeastern corner of County Galway, the lakeside town of Portumna is popular for boating and fishing.

Impressive **Portumna Castle & Gardens** (www.heritageireland.ie; Castle Ave; adult/child €4/2; ⏰9.30am–6pm Easter–mid-Oct) was built in the early 1600s by Richard de Burgo and boasts an elaborate, geometrical organic garden.

**The Drive »** From Portumna, cross the River Shannon – also the county border – into County Tipperary. Take the N65 south for 7km, then turn west onto the R493, winding through farmland. At Hogan's Pass, turn west on the R494, following it to Ballina (52km in all).

## ❷ Ballina & Killaloe

Facing each other across a narrow channel, Ballina and Killaloe (Cill Da Lúa) are really one destination, even if they have different personalities (and counties). A fine 1770 13-arch one-lane **bridge** spans the river, linking the pair. You can walk it in five minutes, or drive it in about 20 (a Byzantine system of lights controls traffic).

Ballina, in County Tipperary, has some of the better pubs and restaurants, while Killaloe typifies picturesque County Clare. It lies on the western banks of lower Loch Deirgeirt (the southern extension of Lough Derg), where it narrows at one of the principal crossings of the Shannon.

**The Drive »** Continue following the R494, then the M7 southwest to Limerick city (about 24km).

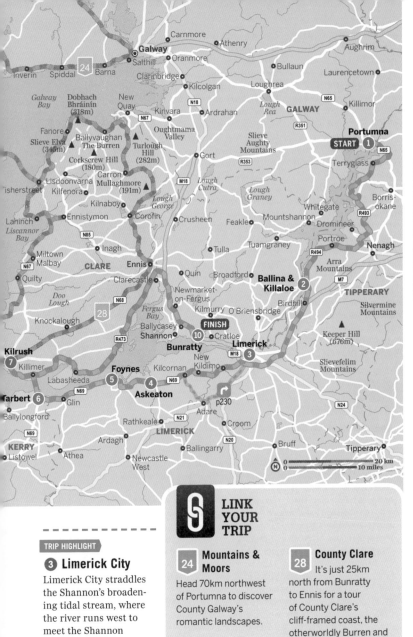

**LINK YOUR TRIP**

---

**TRIP HIGHLIGHT**

**❸ Limerick City**

Limerick City straddles the Shannon's broadening tidal stream, where the river runs west to meet the Shannon Estuary. Despite some unexpected glitz and gloss, it doesn't shy away

**24 Mountains & Moors**

Head 70km northwest of Portumna to discover County Galway's romantic landscapes.

**28 County Clare**

It's just 25km north from Bunratty to Ennis for a tour of County Clare's cliff-framed coast, the otherworldly Burren and music-filled pubs.

from its tough past, as portrayed in Frank McCourt's *Angela's Ashes*.

Limerick has an intriguing **castle** (www.shannonheritage.com; Nicholas St; adult/child €10/5.25; ⏱9.30am-7.30pm May-Sep, to 6pm Apr & Oct, to 5pm Nov & Dec, closed Jan-Mar), built by King John of England between 1200 and 1212 on King's Island; the ancient **St Mary's Cathedral** (☎061-310 293; www.cathedral.limerick.anglican.org; Bridge St; suggested donation €4; ⏱9am-5pm Mon-Fri, to 4pm Sat & Sun), founded in 1168 by Donal Mór O'Brien, king of Munster; and the fabulous **Hunt Museum** (www.huntmuseum.com; Custom House, Rutland St; adult/child €5/2.50; ⏱10am-5pm Mon-Sat, 2-5pm Sun; ), with the finest collection of Bronze Age, Iron Age and medieval treasures outside Dublin.

The dynamic **Limerick City Gallery of Art** (www.gallery.limerick.ie; Carnegie Bldg, Pery Sq; ⏱10am-5.30pm Mon-Wed, Fri & Sat, to 8pm Thu, noon-5.30pm Sun) is set in the city's Georgian area. Limerick also has a contemporary cafe culture, especially along its revitalised riverbanks, and renowned nightlife to go with its uncompromised pubs – as well as locals who go out of their way to welcome you.

✕ 🛏 p233

**The Drive »** The narrow, peaceful N69 follows the Shannon Estuary west from Limerick; it's 27km to Askeaton.

# DETOUR:
## ADARE

### Start: ❸ Limerick City (p229)

Frequently dubbed 'Ireland's prettiest village', Adare centres on its clutch of perfectly preserved thatched cottages built by the 19th-century English landlord, the Earl of Dunraven, for workers constructing Adare Manor (now a palatial hotel). Today the cottages house craft shops and some of the region's finest restaurants.

In the middle of the village, Adare's **heritage centre** (☎061-396 666; http://adareheritagecentre.ie; Main St; ⏱9am-6pm) has entertaining exhibits on the history and the medieval context of the village's buildings and can point you to a number of fascinating religious sites. It also books tours of **Adare Castle** (Desmond Castle; ☎tour bookings 061-396 666; www.heritageireland.ie/en/shannon-region/adarecastle; tours adult/child €8/6; ⏱tours hourly 11am-5pm Jun-Sep). Dating back to around 1200, this picturesque feudal ruin was wrecked by Cromwell's troops in 1657. Restoration work is ongoing; look for the ruined great hall, with its early-13th-century windows. You can view the castle from the main road, the riverside footpath, or the grounds of the Augustinian priory.

From Limerick city, the fastest way to reach Adare is to take the M20 and N21 16km southwest to the village on the banks of the River Maigue. From Adare it's 9km northwest to rejoin the N69 at Kilcornan. Or you can take the N69 from Limerick to Kilcornan and slip down to Adare. See p233 for Eating and Sleeping options.

**Loop Head** County Clare's southernmost point

TRIP HIGHLIGHT

## 4 Askeaton

Hidden just off the N69, evocative ruins in the pint-sized village of Askeaton include the mid-1300s **Desmond Castle** (☑ tourist office bookings 061-392 149; ⊙ weekends by appointment May-Oct), a 1389-built **Franciscan friary**, and **St Mary's Church of Ireland** and **Knights Templar Tower**, built around 1829, as well as the 1740 **Hellfire** gentlemen's club. Restoration of the ruins started in 2007 and is expected to finish in 2017. The town's **tourist office** (☑061-392 149; askeatontouristoffice@ gmail.com; The Square; ⊙9am-5pm Mon-Fri) has details of ruins that you can freely wander (depending on restoration works) and can arrange free **guided tours** lasting about one hour led by passionate local historians.

**The Drive »** Stunning vistas of the wide Shannon Estuary come into view as you drive 12km to Foynes.

## 5 Foynes

Foynes is an essential stop along the route to visit the fascinating **Foynes Flying Boat Museum** (www.flyingboat museum.com; adult/child €11/6; ⊙9.30am-6pm Jun-Aug, to 5pm mid-Mar–May & Sep–mid-Nov, closed mid-Nov– mid-Mar). From 1939 to 1945 this was the landing place for the flying boats that linked North America with the British Isles. Big Pan Am clippers – there's a replica here – would set down in the estuary and refuel.

**The Drive »** The most scenic stretch of the N69 is the 20km from Foynes to Tarbert in northern County Kerry, which hugs the estuary's edge.

### ⑥ Tarbert

The lively little harbour town of Tarbert is where you'll hop on the car ferry to Killimer, in County Clare, saving yourself 137km of driving.

Before you do so, though, it's worth visiting the renovated **Tarbert Bridewell Jail & Courthouse** (http://tarbertbridewell.com/museum.html; adult/child €5/2.50; ⏱10am-6pm Apr-Sep, to 4pm Mon-Fri Oct-Mar), which has exhibits on the rough social and political conditions of the 19th century. From the jail, the 6.1km **John F Leslie Woodland Walk** runs along Tarbert Bay towards the river mouth.

The ferry dock is clearly signposted 2.2km west of Tarbert. Services are operated by **Shannon Ferry Limited** (☎068-905 3124; www.shannonferries.com; cars €18, motorcyclists, cyclists & pedestrians €5; ⏱7.30am-9.30pm Mon-Sat, 9.30am-9.30pm Sun Jun-Aug, 7.30am-8.30pm Mon-Sat, 9.30am-8.30pm Sun Apr, May & Sep, 7.30am-7.30pm Mon-Sat, 9.30am-7.30pm Sun Oct-Mar; 🛜). Ferries depart hourly (every half-hour in high summer).

The Drive » The crossing from Tarbert to Killimer takes 20 minutes; from there it's an 8km drive west to Kilrush.

### ⑦ Kilrush

Opportunities for up-close encounters with the bottlenose dolphins living in the Shannon abound in the atmospheric town of Kilrush (Cill Rois), which also harbours the remarkable 'lost' **Vandeleur Walled Garden** (www.vandeleurwalledgarden.ie; Killimer Rd; ⏱10am-7pm daily Apr-Sep, 9.30am-5pm Mon-Sat Oct-Mar).

🍴 p309

The Drive » Continue 14km west along the N67 to the beach haven of Kilkee.

### ⑧ Kilkee

The centrepiece of Kilkee (Cill Chaoi) is its wide, sheltered, powdery white-sand beach. The sweeping semicircular bay has high cliffs on the north end and weathered rocks to the south. The waters are very tidal, with wide-open sandy expanses replaced by pounding waves in just a few hours.

Kilkee has plenty of guesthouses and B&Bs, though during high season, rates can soar and vacancies are scarce.

🍴 p233

The Drive » The 26.5km drive from Kilkee south to Loop Head ends in cliffs plunging into the Atlantic.

TRIP HIGHLIGHT

### ⑨ Loop Head

Capped by a working lighthouse, Loop Head (Ceann Léime) is County Clare's southernmost point. It has breathtaking views as well as cycling, fishing and snorkelling opportunities (including hire).

The Drive » On the R487, follow the 'Scenic Loop' (an understatement): you'll be struck by one stunning vista of soaring coastal cliffs after another. From Killimer continue north on the R473 to Kilbreckan, where you can hop on the M18 south to Bunratty (110km all up).

### ⑩ Bunratty

Bunratty (Bun Raite) draws more tourists than any other place in the region. The namesake **castle** (www.shannonheritage.com/BunrattyCastle AndFolkPark; castle & folk park adult/child €11/8.50; ⏱castle 9am-4pm, folk park 9am-5.50pm; ♿) has stood over the area for centuries. In recent decades it's been spiffed up and swamped by attractions and gift shops. A theme park re-creates a clichéd – and sanitised – Irish village of old.

With all the hoopla, it's easy to overlook the actual village, at the back of the theme park, which has numerous leafy spots to eat and sleep.

# Eating & Sleeping

## Limerick City ③

### ✕ Milk Market                          Market €

(www.milkmarketlimerick.ie; Cornmarket Row;
⏱10am-3pm Fri, 8am-3pm Sat, 11am-3pm Sun)
Pick from organic produce and local foods like
cheese at the traditional food market held in
Limerick's old market buildings, or browse its
produce and craft shops. Traditional live music
regularly takes place here.

### ✕ Chocolat                     International €€

(☎061-609 709; www.chocolatrestaurant.ie;
109 O'Connell St; mains €12.50-25, 3-course
lunch/dinner menus €15/23; ⏱noon-9.30pm
Mon-Sat, 1-9pm Sun) Bathed in dark-chocolate
hues, with soft ambient music, this international
restaurant is a smart choice. There's an eclectic
but down-to-earth menu, from Thai curry to
burgers, fajitas, yan pang chicken, pasta and
surf-and-turf. Cocktails are inventive and
generous. Worth booking ahead.

### ⛏ George Boutique Hotel          Hotel €€

(☎061-460 400; www.georgelimerick.com;
Shannon St; s/d/tr/f from €70/79/99/109;
P 🛜) The lobby is rather tacky, but rooms – in
blond wood, caramels and browns, some with
shower, others with bath – are congenially
neutral and comfortable at this brisk and
frequently booked-out hotel.

### ⛏ The Boutique Hotel              Hotel €€

(☎061-315 320; www.theboutique.ie; Denmark
St; s/d from €69/79; @🛜) Rotating works of
original art by Limerick artist Claire De Lacy,
a fish tank in the lobby, a glassed-in breakfast
room on the first-floor balcony and red-and-
white-striped decor set this groovy little

hotel apart from the pack. Its location near
pedestrianised laneways minimises traffic, but
it can still get noisy on weekends and during
events, when the city's hopping.

## Adare ③

### ⛏ Berkeley Lodge                    B&B €€

(☎061-396 857; www.adare.org; Station Rd;
s/d/f €50/80/100; P 🛜) This detached
house around 400m north of the Adare
Heritage Centre has six cutesy and rather floral
rooms – each in a different colour – with great
breakfasts. It's a three-minute walk to the
centre and is kid-friendly.

### ⛏ Dunraven Arms                      Inn €€

(☎061-605 900; www.dunravenhotel.com; Main
St; s/d from €100/120; 🛜🏊) This jewel of an
inn, built in 1792, has 86 smart rooms, with
antiques, high thread-count linens and –
for the choosy – four-poster beds, plus a great
**restaurant** (restaurant mains €16-26, bar
menu mains €13-18; ⏱noon-2.15pm & 7.30-
9.30pm) and bar.

## Kilkee ⑧

### ✕ Diamond Rocks Cafe               Cafe €

(☎086 372 1063; http://diamondrockscafe.
com; West End; mains €5-12; ⏱9.30am-7pm
Jun-Aug, 10am-5.30pm Sat & Sun Sep-May)
This modern cafe (with a huge terrace) serves
food far above the norm for the types of places
usually found in such a stunning spot, with fresh
salads, chowders, sandwiches, breakfasts and a
plethora of daily specials.

# The Holy Glen

## 21

This hallowed patch of County Tipperary shelters the Glen of Aherlow and the Rock of Cashel, crowned by historic buildings that seem like an ethereal extension of the landscape itself.

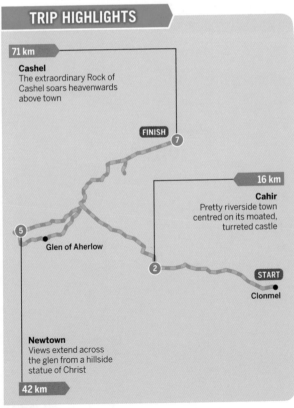

## TRIP HIGHLIGHTS

**71 km**

**Cashel**
The extraordinary Rock of Cashel soars heavenwards above town

**FINISH** ⑦

**16 km**

**Cahir**
Pretty riverside town centred on its moated, turreted castle

⑤

● **Glen of Aherlow**

②

**START**

● **Clonmel**

**Newtown**
Views extend across the glen from a hillside statue of Christ

**42 km**

### 2–3 DAYS
### 71KM / 45 MILES

### GREAT FOR...

### BEST TIME TO GO
Autumnal colours are glorious and herald a walking festival.

### 📷 ESSENTIAL PHOTO

The awe-inspiring Rock of Cashel from inside the Hore Abbey ruins.

### ☑ BEST CASTLE
Cahir Castle, like the quintessential beach sandcastle, with towers and moat.

**Cahir** Cahir Castle

# 21 | The Holy Glen

The landscapes viewed from your car windows are sublime, and it's easy to get out and about among them. The Glen of Aherlow is renowned for its walking. You will encounter varying terrain, from lush riverbanks on the Aherlow to pine forests in the hills and windswept, rocky grasslands that seem to stretch on forever.

---

## ❶ Clonmel

County Tipperary's largest and busiest town, Clonmel (Cluain Meala; 'Meadows of Honey') sits on the northern bank of the River Suir. Its historical buildings include the beautifully restored **Main Guard** (📞052-612 7484; www.heritageireland.ie; Sarsfield St; ⏰9am-5pm Tue-Sun Easter-Sep, hrs may vary), a Butler courthouse dating from 1675; the 1802-built **County Courthouse** (Nelson St), where the Young Irelanders of 1848 were tried and sentenced

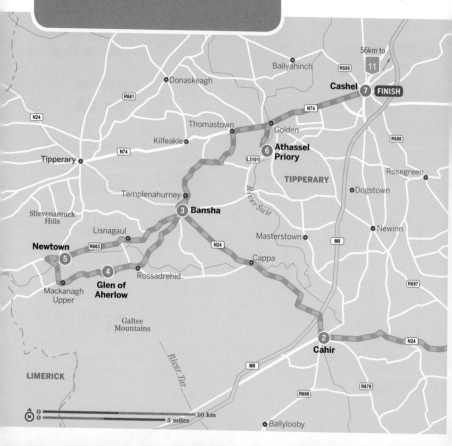

to transportation to Australia; and the **Franciscan Friary** (www.franciscans.ie; Mitchell St; ⊙8am-6pm). Inside the friary, near the door, a 1533 Butler tomb depicts a knight and his lady. There's some fine modern stained glass, especially in St Anthony's Chapel.

Informative displays on County Tipperary's history, from Neolithic times to the present, are covered at the well-put-together **South Tipperary County Museum** (www.tipperarycoco.ie; Mick Delahunty Sq; ⊙10am-4.45pm Tue-Sat), which also hosts changing exhibitions.

✕ ⛱ p241

**The Drive ⟫** It's a quick 17km trip along the N24 west to Cahir.

- - - - - - - - - - - -

TRIP HIGHLIGHT

### ② Cahir

At the eastern tip of the Galtee Mountains, the compact town of Cahir (An Cathair; pronounced 'care') encircles the moated **Cahir Castle** (☎052-744 1011; www.heritageireland.ie; Castle St; adult/child €4/2; ⊙9am-6.30pm mid-Jun–Aug, 9.30am-5.30pm Mar–mid-Jun & Sep–mid-Oct, 9.30am-4.30pm mid-Oct–Feb), a feudal fantasy of rocky foundations, massive walls, turrets and towers, defences and dungeons. Founded by Conor O'Brien in 1142, it passed to the Butler family in 1375. In 1599 the Earl of Essex used cannons to shatter its walls, and it was surrendered to Cromwell in 1650. Its future usefulness may have discouraged the typical Cromwellian 'deconstruc-

tion', and it remains one of Ireland's largest and most intact medieval castles.

Walking paths follow the banks of the **River Suir** – a pretty path from behind the town car park meanders 2km south to the thatched **Swiss Cottage** (☎052-744 1144; www.heritageireland.ie; Cahir Park; adult/child €4/2; ⊙10am-6pm Easter-Oct), surrounded by roses, lavender and honeysuckle. A lavish example of Regency Picturesque, it's more a sizeable house. The compulsory 30-minute guided tours are thoroughly enjoyable.

**The Drive ⟫** Drive northwest for 14km through farmland along the N24 (which, despite being a national road, is narrow and twisting) to the village of Bansha, the jumping-off point for the Glen of Aherlow.

- - - - - - - - - - - -

### ③ Bansha

The tiny village of Bansha (An Bháinseach, meaning 'a grassy place') sits at the eastern end of the Glen of Aherlow.

**LINK YOUR TRIP**

 **Kilkenny's Treasures**

Head 60km northeast of Cashel along the M8 and R693 to discover the medieval treasures of County Kilkenny.

 **Blackwater Valley Drive**

Travel 87km south from Cashel to Youghal (County Cork), via Lismore, for the beautiful Blackwater Valley.

Although Bansha itself has just a handful of facilities, it makes a good pit stop before embarking on the prettiest stretch of this trip.

**The Drive »** From Bansha the 11km drive west takes in the best of County Tipperary's verdant, mountainous landscapes. Leave Bansha on the R663 and, after 500m, take the left fork (repeat: *left* fork) in the road. Keep your eyes peeled for walkers and cyclists as you drive.

### ④ Glen of Aherlow

Cradled by the Slievenamuck Hills and the Galtee Mountains, this gorgeous valley is a scenic drive within a scenic drive. From Bansha you'll travel through a scattering of hamlets, including Booleen, Rossadrehid and Mackanagh Upper, with majestic mountain views.

**The Drive »** At Mackanagh Upper, turn north to connect with the R663, following it east (4.2km in total) to reach the glen's tourism hub, Newtown.

**TRIP HIGHLIGHT**

### ⑤ Newtown

The R663 from Bansha and the R664 south from Tipperary town converge at Newtown.

Hidden around the back of the pub, the enthusiastically staffed Glen of Aherlow **tourist office** (☎062-56331; http://aherlow.com; Coach Rd; ☺9.30am-5pm Mon-Fri year-round, plus 10am-4pm Sat Jun-Aug) is an excellent source of local information, including details about **walking festivals**.

For views of biblical proportions, head 1.6km north of Newtown on the R664 to its lofty **viewing point** and **Christ the King statue**, on the side of the Slievenamuck Hills facing the Galtee Mountains. The statue's raised hand is believed to bless those who pass by it and live beneath it. Initially erected in 1950, the original statue was damaged in 1975, but replaced soon after with an identical sculpture.

There's a good range of rural accommodation, including some bucolic campgrounds.

🛏 p241

**Glen of Aherlow** Looking towards the Galtee Mountains

**The Drive »** Continue along the scenic R663 to Bansha and head northeast on Barrack St (the N24) towards Thomastown to connect with the N74 east to the village of Golden. From Golden, head 2km south along the narrow road signposted 'Athassel Priory' (23.5km total).

## 6 Athassel Priory

The atmospheric – and, at dusk, delightfully creepy – ruins of Athassel Priory sit in the shallow and verdant River Suir valley. The original buildings date from 1205, and Athassel was once one of the richest and most important monasteries in Ireland. What survives is substantial: the gatehouse and portcullis gateway, the cloister and stretches of walled enclosure, as well as some medieval tomb effigies.

Roadside parking is limited and very tight. The priory is reached across often-muddy fields.

**The Drive »** Return to Golden and continue east along the N74 for 7km to the grand finale of the trip, Cashel, resplendently crowned by the Rock of Cashel.

# THE GALTEE MOUNTAINS

Extending west from Cahir for 23km, the Galtees stand slightly aloof from the other mountain groups in Ireland's south. They rise comparatively gradually from the sprawling 'Tipperary Plain' and much more steeply from beautiful Glen of Aherlow to the north. The range's highest peak is Galtymore Mountain (919m), which towers over at least 12 other distinct summits. A prominent landmark far and wide, it stands proud of the rest of the range by almost 100m and is one of Ireland's 12 Munros (peaks or summits over 3000 feet). Valleys bite deep into the main ridge, composed of old red sandstone, so that the Galtees (pronounced with a short 'a' as in 'fact') are characterised by long spurs reaching out from the relatively narrow main ridge. Tors, created by frost-shattering during the last ice age, are scattered along the ridge, notably forming a heap of conglomerate boulders known as O'Loughnan's Castle. The north face of the range is punctuated by corries – relics of the ice age that hide Lough Muskry and Bohreen Lough, impounded by massed moraine. A third small lake, Lough Curra, is a hollow predating glaciation and later blocked off by moraine. The uplands of the range are largely covered with blanket bog, and conifer plantations are widespread across the lower slopes. The Glen of Aherlow tourist office in Newtown has information on walking in the area.

- - - - - - - - - - - - - - -

**TRIP HIGHLIGHT**

## 7 Cashel

Rising from a grassy plain on the edge of the town, the **Rock of Cashel** (www.heritageireland.ie; adult/child €7/3; ⊙9am-7pm early Jun–mid-Sep, to 5.30pm mid-Mar–early Jun & mid-Sep–mid-Oct, to 4.30pm mid-Oct–mid-Mar) is one of Ireland's most spectacular archaeological sites. The 'Rock' is a prominent green hill, banded with limestone outcrops, which bristles with ancient fortifications – the word 'cashel' is an Anglicised version of the Irish word *caiseal*, meaning 'fortress'. Sturdy walls circle an enclosure that contains a complete round tower, a 13th-century Gothic cathedral and the finest 12th-century Roman-

esque chapel in Ireland. For more than 1000 years the Rock of Cashel was a symbol of power and the seat of kings and churchmen who ruled over the region. It's a five-minute stroll from the town centre to the Rock; pretty paths include the **Bishop's Walk**. There are a couple of parking spaces for visitors with disabilities at the top of the approach road to the ticket office.

Just under 1km from the Rock, in flat farmland, is the formidable ruin of 13th-century **Hore Abbey**. Originally Benedictine and settled by monks from Glastonbury in England at the end of the 12th century, it later became a Cistercian house.

Next to the car park below the Rock, heritage

centre **Brú Ború** (☎062-61122; www.bruboru.ie; The Kiln; centre admission free, exhibitions adult/child €5/3; ⊙centre 9am-5pm Mon, to 11pm Tue-Sat mid-Jun–Aug, 9am-5pm Mon-Fri Sep–mid-Jun, exhibitions 9am-5pm Mon-Fri) offers an absorbing insight into Irish traditional music, dance and song.

Town museums include the engaging **Cashel Folk Village** (☎062-63601; www.cashelfolkvillage.ie; St Dominic St; adult/child €5/3.50; ⊙9am-7.30pm mid-Jun–mid-Sep, 9.30am-5.30pm mid-Mar–mid-Jun & mid-Sep–mid-Oct, 9.30am-4.30pm mid-Oct–mid-Mar), exhibiting old buildings, shopfronts and memorabilia from around Cashel.

✕ ⊨ p241, p277

# Eating & Sleeping

## Clonmel ❶

### ✗ Befani's
Mediterranean €€

(📞052-617 7893; www.befani.com; 6 Sarsfield St; mains €15-28; ⏱restaurant 9-11am, 12.30-2.30pm & 5.30-9.30pm Mon-Sat, 12.30-3.30pm & 5.30-9.30pm Sun; 🛜) Between the Main Guard and the Suir, Befani's brings the Mediterranean to Clonmel. At lunchtime, there's a mouthwatering tapas menu; mains include balsamic-braised Irish lamb shoulder and a rich bouillabaisse in lobster broth. Its nine guestrooms (single/double €40/70), of varying sizes, are presentable but rather dull.

### 🛏 Hotel Minella
Hotel €€€

(📞052-612 2388; http://hotelminella.com; Coleville Rd; s €125-140, d €130-155, f €150-180, ste €180-350; 🅿🛜♨) This family-run luxury hotel sits amid extensive grounds on the south bank of the River Suir, 2km east of the centre. Its 90 rooms are divided between an 1863 mansion and a new wing. The latter has almost every kind of convenience, including two suites with outdoor hot tubs on private terraces overlooking the river. Rates include breakfast.

## Newtown ❺

### 🛏 Aherlow House Hotel
Hotel €

(📞062-56153; www.aherlowhouse.ie; Newtown; s/d/lodge from €65/85/149, mains €20-32; ⏱restaurant 6-10pm Mon-Sat, 12.30-3.30pm Sun; 🅿🛜) Up a pine-forested track from the R663, this 1928 hunting lodge has been turned into a luxurious woodland retreat with 29 rooms with king-size beds and 15 contemporary self-catering lodges (minimum two-night stay). There's a flowing bar, a fine restaurant, and glorious mountain views from the terrace.

### 🛏 Ballinacourty House Camping Park & B&B
Campground, B&B €

(📞062-56000; www.ballinacourtyhse.com; Glen of Aherlow; camp sites €10, s/d €52/70, 2-/3-/4-course menus €22/25/30; ⏱restaurant 6-8.30pm Mon-Sat, 12.30-2.30pm Sun; 🅿) Set against a great backdrop of the Galtees, this attractive site is 10km west from Bansha, and past Newtown. It has excellent facilities, as well as a fine garden, a much-loved restaurant serving classic Irish fare, a wine bar and a tennis court. An old stone house has been renovated and now offers B&B accommodation.

### 🛏 Homeleigh Farmhouse
B&B €€

(📞062-56228; www.homeleighfarmhouse. com; Newtown; s/d €50/80, 4-course dinner menu €28; 🅿🛜) Just west of Newtown and the Coach Road Inn on the R663, this working bungalow farm rents out simple rooms with views onto fields and the garden, in a modern home. Furnishings are traditional and you can arrange for dinner. This is really ground zero for local hiking.

## Cashel ❼

### ✗ Cafe Hans
Cafe €€

(📞062-63660; Dominic St; mains €13-23; ⏱noon-5.30pm Tue-Sat; 🚶) Competition for the 32 seats is fierce at this gourmet cafe run by the same family as **Chez Hans** (📞062-61177; www.chezhans.net; Dominic St; mains €24-38, 2-/3-course menus €28/33; ⏱6-10pm Tue-Sat) next door. There's a fantastic selection of salads, open sandwiches (including succulent prawns with tangy Marie Rose sauce) and filling fish, shellfish, lamb and vegetarian dishes, with a discerning wine selection and mouthwatering desserts. No credit cards. Enter via Moor Lane. Arrive before or after the lunchtime rush or plan on queuing.

### 🛏 Cashel Town B&B
B&B €

(📞062-62330; www.cashelbandb.com; 5 John St; s/d without bathroom €40/55, s/d/tr/q with private bathroom €55/65/90/120; 🅿🛜) Fresh produce from nearby farmers markets is cooked up for breakfast at this homey B&B. Within the 1808-built Georgian town house are seven comfortable rooms and a cosy guest lounge with a toasty open fire and a piano.

# STRETCH YOUR LEGS
## CORK CITY

**Start/Finish:** Lewis Glucksman Gallery

**Distance:** 4.7km

**Duration:** 3 hours

The River Lee flows around Cork's central island of grand Georgian parades, 17th-century alleys and modern masterpieces. As you criss-cross it between galleries and architectural attractions, you'll discover that the single-best sight is the city itself.

Take this walk on Trips

## Lewis Glucksman Gallery

Situated on the leafy campus of prestigious University College Cork (UCC), the award-winning limestone, steel and timber **Lewis Glucksman Gallery** (☎021-490 1844; www.glucksman.org; University College Cork, Western Rd; suggested donation €5; ◷10am-5pm Tue-Sat, 2-5pm Sun; ♿) displays the best in national and international contemporary art and installation.

The Walk ≫ From UCC, you can take a shortcut through the car park en route to St Fin Barre's Cathedral.

## St Fin Barre's Cathedral

Spires, gargoyles and sculpture adorn Cork's Protestant **St Fin Barre's Cathedral** (☎021-496 3387; http://corkcathedral.webs. com; Bishop St; adult/child €5/3; ◷9.30am-5.30pm Mon-Sat, 1.30-2.30pm & 4.30-6pm Sun Apr-Nov, reduced hrs Dec-Mar). Local legend says the golden angel on the eastern side will blow its horn when the Apocalypse is due to start... The grandeur continues inside, with marble floor mosaics, a huge pulpit and a bishop's throne.

The Walk ≫ Turn east on Bishop St and follow the riverside quays. Cross the bridge north at Mary St to reach the English Market.

## English Market

Cork's ornate **English Market** (www. englishmarket.ie; main entrance Princes St; ◷8am-6pm Mon-Sat) is a must-see, but you're also spoiled for dining options.

The Walk ≫ Princes St meets St Patrick's St, the main shopping and commercial area. Turn left onto Academy St and right on Emmet Pl to the city's premier gallery.

## Crawford Municipal Art Gallery

Highlights of the permanent collection at Cork's public gallery, **Crawford Municipal Art Gallery** (☎021-480 5042; www.crawford artgallery.ie; Emmet Pl; ◷10am-5pm Mon-Wed, Fri & Sat, to 8pm Thu), covering the 17th century to today, include works by Sir John Lavery, Jack B Yeats, Nathaniel Hone and a room devoted to Irish women artists,

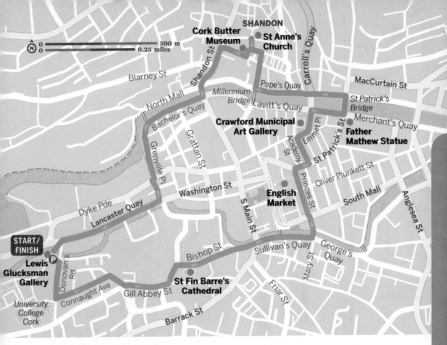

including Mainie Jellet and Evie Hone. The Sculpture Galleries contain plaster casts of Roman and Greek statues, given to King George IV by the pope in 1822.

*The Walk* » Continue on Emmet Pl, passing Cork Opera House before turning right on Lavitt's Quay and rejoining St Patrick's St.

## Father Mathew Statue

The imposing statue on St Patrick's St, just south of the River Lee North Channel, is of Father Theobald Mathew, who crusaded against the ills of alcohol in the 1830s and 1840s with such success that 250,000 people took the 'pledge' and whiskey production was cut in half.

*The Walk* » Head north over St Patrick's Bridge turning west to the hillside neighbourhood of Shandon, with galleries, antique shops and cafes along its lanes and squares lined with old row houses.

## St Anne's Church

Shandon is dominated by the 1722 **St Anne's Church** (☎021-450 5906; www.shandonbells.ie; John Redmond St, Shandon; tower incl bells adult/child €5/4; ☻10am-5pm

Mon-Sat, 11.30am-4.30pm Sun Jun-Sep, shorter hrs Oct-May), aka the 'Four-Faced Liar', so called as each of the tower's four clocks used to tell a different time. Ring the **bells** on the 1st floor and continue the 132 steps to the top for 360-degree views of the city.

*The Walk* » It's a short walk south on Exchange St and right on John Redmond St to the Cork Butter Museum.

## Cork Butter Museum

Cork's long tradition of butter manufacturing is related through displays and dioramas in the **Cork Butter Museum** (☎021-430 0600; www.corkbutter.museum; O'Connell Sq; adult/child €4/3; ☻10am-6pm Jul & Aug, to 5pm Mar-Jun, Sep & Oct, 11am-3pm Sat & Sun Nov-Feb). The square in front features the round **Firkin Crane** (☎021-450 7487; http://firkincrane.ie; O'Connell Sq, Shandon) building, central to the old butter market and now housing a dance centre.

*The Walk* » Head across the island along the 1.5km walk back to UCC and the Lewis Glucksman Gallery.

# Galway & the West of Ireland

**LITTLE WONDER THE WEST OF IRELAND IS TOP OF MOST MUST-SEE LISTS –** apart from the weather, it has it all. Mayo offers wild, romantic beauty, but without the crowds. Timeless Connemara, with its bogs, lonely valleys, white beaches and intriguing villages, is one of Europe's most stunning corners. For fun and frolic, Westport and Galway deliver, though you may never leave the cosy bars of County Clare or the mesmerising landscapes of The Burren and Aran Islands. Counties Kerry and Cork feature Ireland's iconic scenery: crenellated coastlines, green fields criss-crossed by stone walls, ancient sites and mist-shrouded peaks. A plethora of fine eateries, pubs and entertainment adds to the rewards.

**Galway** The banks of the River Corrib
JOHN ELK/GETTY IMAGES ©

# Galway &
# the West of
# Ireland

ATLANTIC
OCEAN

**Connor Pass** Mt Brandon

 **Best of the West 6 Days**
**22** The ultimate tour of Ireland's best westerly sights. (p249)

 **Musical Landscapes 5 Days**
**23** A ride round County Clare's hottest trad music spots. (p261)

 **Mountains & Moors 6 Days**
**24** Connemara's wilderness and cultivated villages. (p271)

 **Loughs of the West 3–4 Days**
**25** The best of County Galway and Mayo's lake and riverside routes. (p279)

**North Mayo & Sligo 4 Days**
**26** A windswept trip along the region's rugged coastline. (p287)

 **Sligo Surrounds 5 Days**
**27** A historic tour of poet WB Yeats' backyard. (p295)

 **County Clare 7 Days**
**28** The beautiful Burren and the heritage town of Clare. (p303)

**DON'T MISS**

**Céide Fields**
One of the world's major prehistoric sites still feels as undiscovered as it was 50 years ago. Unearth it on Trip **22**

**Inisheer**
A trip to the smallest of the Aran Islands will take you far from 21st-century living. Sail there on Trips **23** **28**

**Ennistymon**
This authentic market town in County Clare gives a genuine taste of country living. Savour its fine bars on Trips **23** **28**

**Dingle Town**
A colourful fishing village at the end of the earth (well, the Connor Pass) provides delightful eateries and dolphin- and people-watching. Dive in on Trip **22**

**Galway**
You may find it hard to leave the City of Tribes. Go for its culture, conviviality and craic on Trips **22** **23** **24** **25**

## Classic Trip

# Best of the West

**22**

*This is a rewarding foray through the west's ultimate stops, taking in mysterious megalithic remains, historic national parks and lively market towns, all in an epic coastal landscape.*

## TRIP HIGHLIGHTS

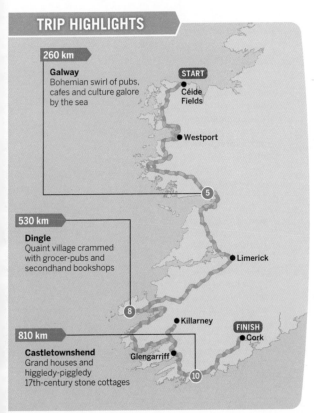

**260 km**

**Galway**
Bohemian swirl of pubs, cafes and culture galore by the sea

**START**
Céide Fields

Westport

**5**

**530 km**

**Dingle**
Quaint village crammed with grocer-pubs and secondhand bookshops

Limerick

**8**

**810 km**

**Castletownshend**
Grand houses and higgledy-piggledy 17th-century stone cottages

Killarney

Glengarriff

**FINISH**
Cork

**10**

**6 DAYS**
**890KM / 553 MILES**

### GREAT FOR...

### BEST TIME TO GO
July, for the best selection of summer festivals.

### ESSENTIAL PHOTO
Clew Bay's many islands from the foot of Croagh Patrick.

### BEST FOR DOLPHIN-WATCHING
Fungie the dolphin in Dingle Bay delivers thrills to young and old.

**Galway** Fishing in the harbour

# Classic Trip

## 22 Best of the West

The most westerly fringe of Europe is the wild, rugged and incredibly beautiful west of Ireland. Its quintessential landscapes are the reason Irish tourism created the Wild Atlantic Way as its signature driving route. Here you'll discover the best beaches in Europe, the epic landscapes of Connemara, culture-packed Galway and Clare, and the kingdom of Kerry right round to West Cork's wonderful fishing villages.

### ① Céide Fields

A famous wit once described archaeology as being all about 'a series of small walls'. The most exciting of these walls may be at Céide Fields, 8km northwest of Ballycastle. During the 1930s, local man Patrick Caulfield was digging in the bog when he noticed piled-up stones buried beneath it. About 40 years later, his son Seamus, who had become an archaeologist on the basis of his father's discovery, uncovered the world's most extensive Stone Age monument, consisting of stone-walled fields, houses and megalithic tombs; as early as five millennia ago a thriving farming community had lived here. The award-winning **Interpretive Centre** (☏096-43325; www.heritageireland.ie; off R314; adult/child €4/2; ✪ visitor centre 10am-6pm Jun-Sep, to 5pm Easter-May & Oct, last tour 1hr before closing) gives a fascinating glimpse into these times. However, it's a good idea to take a guided tour of the site itself, or it may seem nothing more than, well, a series of small walls.

**The Drive »** Head south to the hillside village of Mulranny, overlooking a wide Blue Flag beach and a prime vantage point for counting the 365 or so islands that grace Clew Bay.

ATLANTIC OCEAN

Annascal
**Dingle** ⑧
Dingle Bay    Kells
Caherciveen ○
Waterville ○
Derrynane ○
Dursey Island

Ⓝ 0 ⎯⎯⎯⎯ 40 km
　 0 ⎯⎯⎯⎯ 20 miles

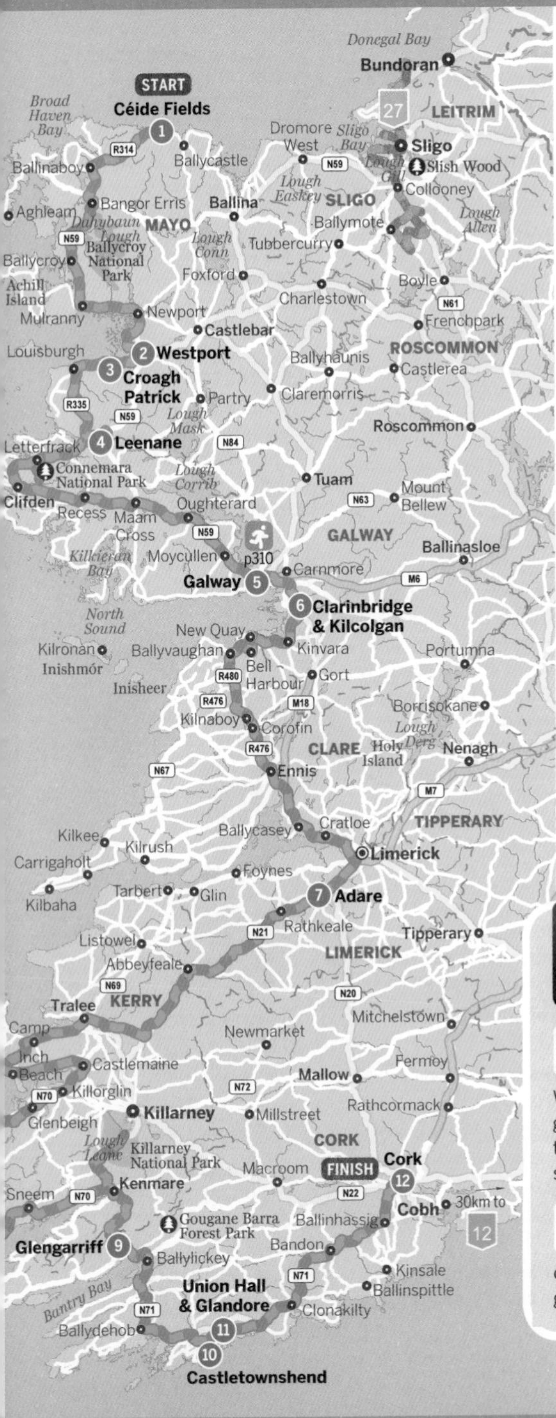


En route to the picturesque 11th-century village of Newport look for signs for 15th-century Rockfleet Castle. After a wiggling 12km drive south you'll reach the atmospheric, pub-packed, heritage town of Westport.

## 2 Westport

Bright and vibrant even in the depths of winter, Westport is a photogenic Georgian town with tree-lined streets, a riverside mall and a great vibe. A couple of kilometres west on Clew Bay, the town's harbour, Westport Quay, is a picturesque spot for a sundowner. Matt Malloy, the fife player from the Chieftains, opened **Matt Molloy's** (☎098-27663; wwwmattmolloy.ie; Bridge St; ⏲12.30-11.30pm), an old-school pub, years ago – and the good times haven't let up. Head to the back room around 9pm and you'll catch live *céilidh* (traditional

### LINK YOUR TRIP

**12 Wexford & Waterford**

When you hit Cork, keep going east through Ardmore to experience Ireland's sunny southeast.

**27 Sligo Surrounds**

From Céide Fields continue northeast for a glimpse of Sligo's wild side.

Classic Trip

music and dancing). Or perhaps an old man will simply slide into a chair and croon a few classics. **Westport House** (☎098-27766; www.westporthouse.ie; Quay Rd; house only adult/child €13/6.50, house & pirate adventure park €21/16.50; ☺10am-6pm Jun-Aug, 10am-4pm Mar-May & Sep-Nov, hrs vary Dec, closed Jan & Feb; 🚻) is a charming Georgian mansion, gardens and adventure playground that makes a terrific day's outing for all ages.

 p258

**The Drive >>** Just 8km southwest of town is Croagh Patrick, one of Ireland's most famous pilgrimage sites.

## ❸ Croagh Patrick

St Patrick couldn't have picked a better spot for a pilgrimage than this conical mountain (also known as 'the Reek'). On a clear day the tough two-hour climb rewards with stunning views over Clew Bay and its sandy islets. It was on Croagh Patrick that Ireland's patron saint fasted for 40 days and nights, and where he reputedly banished venomous snakes. Climbing the 765m holy mountain is an act of penance for thousands of pilgrims on the last Sunday of July (Reek Sunday). The truly contrite (or more fit) take the original 40km route from Ballintubber Abbey, Tóchar Phádraig (Patrick's Causeway), and ascend the mountain barefoot. A less strenuous trail begins in the village of Murrisk.

**The Drive >>** This scenic route heads along Dooagh Valley on the R335 to Leenane. The side roads to the north and west of the valley lead to glorious beaches, but it's not all pretty here; the route is the site of a tragic Famine walk of 1849, when in icy weather 400 people died as they walked from Louisburgh to Delphi and back, in vain search of aid from a landlord.

## ❹ Leenane

The small village of Leenane (also spelled Leenaun) rests on the shore of dramatic **Killary Harbour**. Dotted with mussel rafts, the long, narrow harbour is Ireland's only fjord – maybe. Slicing 16km inland and more than 45m deep in the centre, it certainly looks like a fjord, although some scientific studies suggest it may not actually have been glaciated. **Mt Mweelrea** (819m) towers to its north.

---

## FESTIVALS OF FUN

Galway's packed calendar of festivals turns the city and surrounding communities into what feels like one nonstop party; streets overflow with revellers, and pubs and restaurants often extend their opening hours. The following are highlights:

**Cúirt International Festival of Literature** (www.cuirt.ie) Top-name authors converge on Galway in April for one of Ireland's premier literary festivals.

**Galway International Arts Festival** (www.giaf.ie) A two-week extravaganza of theatre, music and comedy in mid-July.

**Galway Film Fleadh** (www.galwayfilmfleadh.com) One of Ireland's biggest film festivals, held in July.

**Galway Race Week** (www.galwayraces.com) Horse races in Ballybrit, 3km east of the city, are the centrepiece each August of Galway's biggest, most boisterous festival of all.

**Galway International Oyster and Seafood Festival** (www.galwayoysterfest.com) Oysters are washed down with plenty of pints in the last week in September.

Leenane boasts both stage and screen connections. It was the location for *The Field* (1989), a movie with Richard Harris based on John B Keane's play about a tenant farmer's ill-fated plans to pass on a rented piece of land to his son.

🛏 p258

The Drive >> From Leenane, an ultrascenic loop of Connemara via the N59 crosses the beauty spots of Kylemore Abbey and Connemara National Park and then on through the lively town of Clifden, where you continue east through Maam Cross into Galway City, all in under two hours.

- - - - - - - - - - - - -

TRIP HIGHLIGHT

### ⑤ Galway City

Galway City is a swirl of enticing old pubs that hum with trad music sessions throughout the year. More importantly, it has an overlaying vibe of fun and frolic that's addictive. Soak it up on a walk through the city's medieval centre. Galway is often referred to as the 'most Irish' of Ireland's cities (and it's the only one where you're likely to hear Irish spoken in the streets, shops and pubs).

**Tigh Neachtain** (www. tighneachtain.com; 17 Upper Cross St; ⏰10.30am-11.30pm Mon-Thu & Sun, 10.30am-12.30am Fri & Sat), a 19th-century pub – known simply as Neachtain's (*nock*-tans) or Naughtons and painted a bright cornflower blue – has a wraparound string

of tables outside, many shaded by a large tree. It's a must-stop place where a polyglot mix of locals plop down and let the world pass them by. The long-established and award-winning **Druid Theatre** (☎091-568 660; www.druid.ie; Druid Lane) is famed for staging experimental works by young Irish playwrights, as well as new adaptations of classics.

🍽 🛏 p46, p74, p258, p277

The Drive >> Take time to smell the oysters on the busy seaside route between Galway city and County Clare. If you're a sucker for oysters, you're in for a welcome pit stop at Clarinbridge and Kilcolgan.

- - - - - - - - - - - - -

### ⑥ Clarinbridge & Kilcolgan

Some 16km south of Galway, Clarinbridge (Droichead an Chláirin) and Kilcolgan (Cill Cholgáin) are at their busiest during the **Clarinbridge Oyster Festival** (www.

clarenbridge.com), held during the second weekend of September. However, the oysters are actually at their best from May through the summer. Oysters are celebrated year-round at **Paddy Burke's Oyster Inn** (www.paddyburkesgalway. com; off N18, Clarinbridge; mains €13-27; ⏰10.30am-10pm Mon-Sat, from noon Sun), a thatched inn by the bridge dishing up heaped servings in a roadside location on the N18.

**Moran's Oyster Cottage** (www.moransoystercottage. com; The Weir, Kilcolgan; mains €15-27; ⏰noon-9.30pm Sun-Thu, noon-10pm Fri & Sat) is a thatched pub and restaurant with a facade as plain as the inside of an oyster shell. Find a seat on the terrace overlooking Dunbulcaun Bay, where the oysters are reared before they arrive on your plate, and you'll think the world's your, well, oyster. It's a well-marked 2km west of the busy N18, in a quiet cove near Kilcolgan.

### WHY THIS IS A CLASSIC TRIP
FIONN DAVENPORT, WRITER

For many visitors, the best of the west is synonymous with the best of Ireland – the wild, rugged scenery is reason enough to do it, and that's before you meet the people, visit the pubs and eat the food. Six days is just about right to enjoy the experience, but you're just as likely to find a spot where you'll want to stay and grow old.

Above: Irish seafood chowder
Left: Irish dancers, Galway
Right: Waterfall, Connor Pass

HAOLIANG/GETTY IMAGES ©

NEIL SETCHFIELD/GETTY IMAGES ©

RICHARD CUMMINS/GETTY IMAGES ©

**The Drive** »» From the N67, it's just a short jaunt down to the sleepy stone harbour village of Kinvara. From Ballyvaughan the scenery along the R480 is inspiring, highlighting the barren Burren at its best. Amazing prehistoric stone structures can be found throughout this area. Pass through Corofin and Ennis to the impossibly pretty Adare. It's just over two hours of driving in all.

## ❼ Adare

Often dubbed 'Ireland's prettiest village', Adare centres on its clutch of perfectly preserved thatched cottages built by the 19th-century English landlord, the earl of Dunraven, for workers constructing Adare Manor. Today, the cottages house craft shops and some of the county's finest restaurants, with prestigious golf courses nearby. Unsurprisingly, tourists are drawn to the postcard-perfect village, on the River Maigue, by the busload. Dating back to around 1200, **Desmond Castle** (🎧tour bookings 061-396 666; www. heritageireland.ie/en/shannon-region/adarecastle; tours adult/child €8/6; ⊙tours hourly 11am-5pm Jun-Sep), a picturesque feudal ruin, saw rough usage until it was finally wrecked for good by Cromwell's troops in 1657.

✗ 🛏 p233, p258

**The Drive** »» It's about two hours' drive southwest to Dingle (128km). The scenery ramps

Classic Trip

up several notches as you head from Tralee onto the peninsula – where the roads are pretty twisty – and over the famously picturesque Connor Pass.

---

TRIP HIGHLIGHT

## 8 Dingle Town

If you've arrived via the dramatic mountaintop Connor Pass, the fishing town of Dingle can feel like an oasis at the end of the earth...and maybe that's just what it is. Chocolate-box quaint, though grounded by a typical Kerry earthiness, its streets are crammed with brightly painted grocer-pubs and great restaurants, secondhand bookshops and, in summer, coachloads of visitors. Announced by stars in the pavement bearing the names of its celebrity customers, **Dick Mack's** (Green St; ☺3pm-12.30am Mon-Sat, to 11.30pm Sun) has an irrepressible sense of self. Ancient wood and ancient snugs dominate the interior, which is lit like the inside of a whiskey bottle.

Dingle Bay's most famous resident (maybe the most famous resident in the whole area) is Fungie, a bottlenose dolphin that's been a friendly presence since 1983. There are regular boat tours to go out on the water and say 'hi'.

✕ 🛏 p47, p197, p259

**The Drive »** Dragging yourself away from Dingle, take the peninsula's lower road (R561) back, passing the windswept 5km stretch of dune-backed Inch Beach. Veer south at Castlemaine round the jewel of the southwest, the Ring of Kerry, through Kenmare to the magnificent Killarney National Park. The scenery becomes a lot wilder at Glengarriff on the awe-inspiring Beara Peninsula.

---

## 9 Glengarriff

Hidden deep in the Bantry Bay area, Glengarriff (Gleann Garbh) is an attractive village that snares plenty of passers-by. In the second half of the 19th century, Glengarriff became a popular retreat for prosperous Victorians, who sailed from England. The tropical Italianate garden on **Ilnacullin** (**Garinish Island**) (☎027-63040; www.heritageireland.ie/en/south-west/ilnacullin-garinishisland/; adult/child €4/2; ☺9.30am-5.30pm Mon-Fri & Sun, to 6pm Sat Jul & Aug, shorter hrs Apr-Jun, Sep & Oct, closed Nov-Mar) is the top sight in Glengarriff. Subtropical plants flourish in the rich soil and warm climate. The camellias, magnolias and rhododendrons especially provide a seasonal blaze of colour. This little miracle of a place was created in the early 20th century, when the island's owner commissioned the English architect Harold Peto to design him a garden on the then-barren outcrop.

🛏 p225, p259

**The Drive »** Wend your way down the N71 through Ballydehob and on to pretty Skibbereen, where you access the R596 to Castletownshend. Glengarriff to Castletownshend is 57km.

---

TRIP HIGHLIGHT

## 10 Castletownshend

Castletownshend is one of Ireland's most intriguing villages, its grand houses and ancient stone cottages tumbling down the precipitously steep main street. At the bottom of the hill is a small quayside and the castle (really a crenellated mansion), after which the village is named, and en route, a chapel with fine stained-glass windows designed by renowned Irish artist Harry Clarke. The **castle** (☎028-36100; www.castle-townshend.com; d from €70, self-catering apartments & cottages per week from €150), sitting imposingly on the waterfront, is a rocky fantasy. Huge mullioned windows obviate any authenticity of the decorative defensive touches. The seven guest rooms range from one with an old four-poster, where you can play 'royal and consort' games, to small but bright rooms.

**The Drive** » Back at the N71, it's less than 10km to the dual villages of Union Hall and Glandore at Glandore Harbour.

## ⑪ Union Hall & Glandore

The pretty waterside villages of Union Hall and Glandore (Cuan Dor) burst into life in summer, when fleets of yachts tack into the shelter of the Glandore Harbour inlet. A tangle of back roads meander across the area; you should, too. Accessible from Glandore via a long, narrow causeway over the estuary, Union Hall was named after the 1800 Act of Union, which abolished the separate Irish parliament. There's an ATM, a post office and a general store here.

**The Drive** » From here you can glide into Cork, 70km away, in about 1½ hours. Along the way, you'll drive through Clonakilty, where you can buy Ireland's most famous black (blood) pudding. Rather than follow the main N71 all the way, explore the minor roads to the south – the picturesque R597 and R598.

## TOP TIP: THAT'S A GAS

A word of caution for visitors driving the wilds of Connemara: they're not called wilds for nothin'. There are long distances between filling stations on those gorgeous swaths of uninhabited valley and sheep-dotted mountainside. What's more, those few stations are often closed by early evening, so make sure you have enough fuel to keep you going for at least 80km. Find stations at Recess, Clifden and Kylemore.

## ⑫ Cork City

Competing fiercely with Dublin for recognition, the south's largest city has arguably every bit as much to offer as the capital, yet on a smaller and even friendlier scale. The River Lee flows around the centre, an island packed with grand Georgian parades, cramped 17th-century alleys and modern masterpieces such as the opera house. Dotted around the compact centre are a host of historic buildings, cosmopolitan restaurants, local markets and cosy traditional bars. The award-winning **Lewis Glucksman Gallery** (☎021-490 1844; www.glucksman.org; University College Cork, Western Rd; suggested donation €5; ⊙10am-5pm Tue-Sat, 2-5pm Sun; 🚲), in the grounds of University College Cork (UCC), is a startling limestone, steel and timber construction that displays the best in both national and international contemporary art and installation. It's always buzzing with people attending lectures, viewing the artwork or procrastinating in the cafe.

✖ 🛏 p61, p209, p217, p259

# Eating & Sleeping

## Westport ②

### ✕ An Port Mór     Modern Irish €€

(☎098-26730; www.anportmor.com; 1 Brewery Pl; mains €15-28; ◷5-9.30pm Tue-Sat) **Hidden down a lane off Bridge St, proprietor-chef Frankie Mallon's little restaurant packs quite a punch. It's an intimate place with a series of long narrow rooms and a menu that features excellent meats and much-lauded seafood (try the Clew Bay scallops). Most everything is procured from the region.**

### 🛏 St Anthony's Riverside B&B     B&B €€

(☎087-630 1550; www.st-anthonys.com; Distillery Rd; r from €80; 🛜) This genteel B&B sits under cover of a large hedge and thick, twisted vines inhabited by birds. The 11 rooms have clean lines and restful, light colours. Bathrooms feature Jacuzzis or power showers. Breakfast is excellent.

## Leenane ④

### 🛏 Delphi Lodge     Lodge €€€

(☎095-42222; www.delphilodge.ie; off R335; s/d/ste from €140/230/280, dinner €60; P @ 🛜) Set among stunning mountain and lake vistas, this isolated 1830s country house has 13 smart bedrooms and a bevy of common areas including a library and billiards room. Cooking is modern Irish, sourced locally, with meals at a vast communal table. Outside is all walks, fishing and shooting. It's 13km northwest of Leenane. Rates include breakfast.

There are also five cottages for rent on the estate.

## Galway City ⑤

### ✕ Aniar     Modern Irish €€€

(☎091-535 947; www.aniarrestaurant.ie; 53 Lower Dominick St; menus €90-120, with wine pairings €140-190; ◷6-10pm Tue-Thu, 5.30-10pm Fri & Sat) Deeply committed to the flavours and food producers of Galway and West Ireland, Aniar wears its Michelin star with pride. There's no fuss, however. The casual spring-green dining area is a relaxed place to taste from the nightly, daily-changing menu. The wine list favours small producers. Reserve.

### 🛏 Heron's Rest     B&B €€

(☎091-539 574; www.theheronsrest.com; 16a Longwalk; s/d from €80/140; 🛜) Ideally located in a lovely row of houses on the banks of the Corrib, the thoughtful hosts here give you deck chairs so you can sit outside and enjoy the scene. Other touches include holiday-friendly breakfast times (8am to 11am), decanters of port (enough for a glass or two) and more. Rooms, with double-glazed windows and water views, are small and cute.

## Adare ⑦

### ✕ Restaurant 1826 Adare     Modern Irish €€

(☎061-396 004; www.1826adare.ie; Main St; mains €20-27; ◷5.30-9pm Wed-Fri, 6-930pm Sat, 3-8pm Sun; 🚸) One of Ireland's most pedigreed chefs, Wade Murphy is wowing diners at this art-lined 1826 thatched cottage. His passion for local seasonal produce is apparent in such dishes as pan-seared Atlantic cod with wilted baby spinach, dry-aged rib-eye steak and citrus crème fraîche brûlée.

### 🛏 Adare Manor    Hotel €€€

(📞061-605 200; www.adaremanor.com; Main
St; d from €380; 🅿 @ 🛜 🎿) Hopefully by the
time you visit, this magnificent castle hotel
will have reopened following a massive refurb
that began in early 2016. A new bedroom
wing and a huge ballroom are just some of the
additions to an elegant property dripping in
antique furniture and class. The manor's superb
Oakroom **restaurant** (mains €24-36; ⏱6.30-
10pm) and lavish **high tea** (€28.50; ⏱2-5pm)
are also open to nonguests.

## Dingle Town ⑧

### ✖ Out of the Blue    Seafood €€€

(📞066-915 0811; www.outoftheblue.ie; The
Wood; mains lunch €12.50-20, dinner €21-37;
⏱5-9.30pm Mon-Sat, 12.30-3pm & 5-9.30pm
Sun) 'No chips', reads the menu of this funky
blue-and-yellow, fishing-shack-style restaurant
on the waterfront. Despite its rustic surrounds,
this is one of Dingle's best restaurants, with an
intense devotion to fresh local seafood (and only
seafood); if they don't like the catch, they don't
open. With seafood this good, who needs chips?

### 🛏 Dingle Benner's Hotel    Hotel €€€

(📞066-915 1638; www.dinglebenners.com;
Main St; s/d from €104/159; 🅿 🛜) A Dingle
institution, melding Old World elegance, local
charm and modern comforts in the quiet
bedrooms, lounge, library, and (very popular)
Mrs Benner's Bar. Rooms in the 300-year-old
wing have the most character; those in the new
parts are quieter and more spacious.

## Glengarriff ⑨

### 🛏 Eccles Hotel    Historic Hotel €€

(📞027-63003; www.eccleshotel.com;
Glengarriff Harbour; d from €140, bar food €5-14,
restaurant mains €14-25; ⏱bar food noon-4pm,
restaurant 6-10pm Apr-Oct; closed Nov-Mar;
@) Just east of the centre, the grande-dame
Eccles has a long and distinguished history
(since 1745), counting the British War Office,
Thackeray, George Bernard Shaw and WB Yeats
as former guests. The decor retains some
19th-century grandeur; its 66 rooms are big and
bright. Ask for a bayside room on the 4th floor.

## Cork City ⑫

### ✖ Farmgate Cafe    Cafe, Bistro €

(📞021-427 8134; www.farmgate.ie; Princes St,
English Market; mains €8-13; ⏱8.30am-5pm
Mon-Sat) An unmissable experience at the heart
of the English Market, the Farmgate is perched
on a balcony overlooking the food stalls below,
the source of all that fresh local produce on your
plate – everything from crab and oysters to the
lamb for an Irish stew. Up the stairs and turn left
for table service, right for counter service.

### 🛏 River Lee Hotel    Hotel €€€

(📞021-425 2700; www.doylecollection.com;
Western Rd; r from €175; 🅿 🛜 🎿) This modern
riverside hotel brings a touch of luxury to the
city centre. It has gorgeous public areas with
huge sofas, a designer fireplace, a stunning five-
storey glass-walled atrium, and superb service.
There are well-equipped bedrooms (nice and
quiet at the back, but request a corner room for
extra space) and possibly the best breakfast
buffet in Ireland.

## Classic Trip

# Musical Landscapes

# 23

*From the busker-packed streets of Galway city, this rip-roaring ride takes you around County Clare and the Aran Islands to discover fine traditional-music pubs, venues and festivals.*

## TRIP HIGHLIGHTS

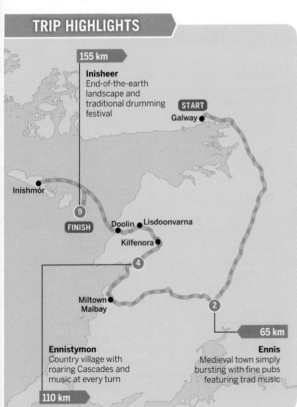

**155 km**

**Inisheer**
End-of-the-earth landscape and traditional drumming festival

**START**
Galway

Inishmór

**9**
**FINISH**

Doolin • Lisdoonvarna
Kilfenora

**4**

Miltown
Malbay

**2**

**65 km**

**Ennistymon**
Country village with roaring Cascades and music at every turn

**110 km**

**Ennis**
Medieval town simply bursting with fine pubs featuring trad music

**5 DAYS**
**155KM / 96 MILES**

### GREAT FOR...

### BEST TIME TO GO

The summer months, for outdoor *céilidh* (traditional dancing) and music festivals.

 **ESSENTIAL PHOTO**

Nightly set-dancing at the crossroads, in Vaughan's of Kilfenora.

 **BEST FOR SONG**

Ennis, on summer nights, where local musicians ply their wares.

**Doolin** A musician performs at Gus O'Connor's Pub

# Classic Trip

## 23 Musical Landscapes

Pick the big bawdy get-togethers of Galway's always-on music scene, the atmospheric small pub sessions in crossroad villages like Kilfenora or Kilronan on the Aran Islands, where nonplaying patrons are a minority, or the rollicking urban boozers in Ennis. Whatever way you like it, this region is undeniably one of Ireland's hottest for traditional music.

### 1 Galway City

Galway (Gaillimh) has a young student population and largely creative community that give a palpable energy to the place. Walk its colourful medieval streets, packed with heritage shops, sidewalk cafes and pubs, all ensuring there's never a dull moment. Galway's pub selection is second to none, and some swing to tunes every night of the week. **Crane Bar** (www.thecranebar.com; 2 Sea Rd; ⏰10.30am-11.30pm Mon-Fri, 10.30am-12.30am Sat, 12.30-11pm Sun), an atmospheric old pub west of the Corrib, is the best spot in Galway to catch an informal *céilidh* most

nights. Or for something more contemporary, **Róisín Dubh** (www.roisindubh.net; Upper Dominick St; ⏰5pm-2am Sun-Thu, till 2.30am Fri & Sat) is *the* place to hear emerging international rock and singer-songwriters.

🍴 🛏 p46, p74, p277

The Drive ›› From Galway city centre, follow either the coast road (R338) east out of town, or the inner R446, signposted Dublin or Limerick, as far as the N18 and then cruise south to Ennis, where your great musical tour of Clare begins.

TRIP HIGHLIGHT

### 2 Ennis

Ennis (Inis), a medieval town in origin, is packed with pubs featuring

trad music. **Brogan's** (24 O'Connell St; ⏰10.30am-11.30pm Mon-Thu, to 12.30am Fri & Sat, 12.30-11pm Sun), on the corner of Cooke's Lane, sees a fine bunch of musicians rattling even the stone floors almost every night in summer, and the plain-tile-fronted **John O'Dea** (66 O'Connell St; ⏰10.30am-11.30pm Mon-Thu,

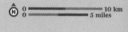

ATLANTIC OCEAN

Greatman's Bay

Gorumna Island  Carraroe
Lettermullen

Lettermullen Island

North Sound

Inishmór 8  ● Kilronan

Inishmaan
Aran Islands

Ⓝ 0 —————— 10 km
  0 —————— 5 miles

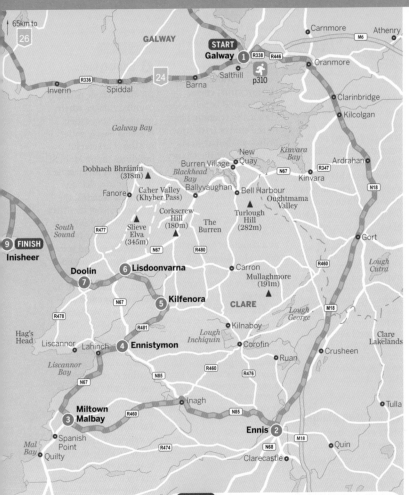

to 12.30am Fri & Sat, 12.30-
11pm Sun) is a hideout for
local musicians serious
about their trad sessions.
**Cois na hAbhna** (☏065-
682 0996; www.coisnahabhna.
ie; Gort Rd; ⏰shop 9am-5pm,
trad sessions 9pm Tue), a
pilgrimage point for
traditional music and
culture, has frequent
performances and a full

# LINK YOUR TRIP

**24** **Mountains & Moors**

From Galway take in
some of Connemara's
loveliest points.

**26** **North Mayo & Sligo**

Cruise up to Westport to
join this wondrous trail
around the hidden gems
of north Connaught.

*Classic Trip*

range of classes in dance and music; it's also an archive and library of Irish traditional music, song, dance and folklore. Traditional music aficionados might like to time a visit with **Fleadh Nua** (www.fleadhnua.com), a lively festival held in late May.

✗ ➤ p46, p269

**The Drive »** From the N85 that runs south of The Burren, you'll meet the smaller R460 at the blink-and-you'll-miss-it village of Inagh. Here you'll find the Biddy Early Brewery, which sells a draught ale, Red Biddy, made using local Burren plants and seaweeds for flavouring. Refuelled, it's a straight run into Miltown Malbay.

- - - - - - - - - -

### 3 Miltown Malbay

Miltown Malbay was a resort favoured by well-to-do Victorians,

though the beach itself is 2km south at **Spanish Point**. To the north of the Point, there are beautiful **walks** amid the low cliffs, coves and isolated beaches. A classically friendly place in the chatty Irish way, Miltown Malbay hosts the annual Willie Clancy Summer School, one of Ireland's great trad music events. **O'Friel's Bar** (Lynch's; The Square; ⏱2pm-midnight Sun-Wed, 6pm-1am Thu-Sat) is one of a couple of genuine old-style places with occasional trad sessions. The other is the dapper **Hillery's** (Main St; ⏱noon-12.30am Sun-Thu, to 1.30am Fri-Sat).

**The Drive »** Hugging the coast, continue north until you come to the small seaside resort of Lahinch, more or less a single street backing a wide beach renowned for its surfing. From here, it's only 4km up the road to the lovely heritage town of Ennistymon.

### THE PIED PIPER

Half the population of Miltown Malbay seems to be part of the annual **Willie Clancy Irish Summer School** (☎065-708 4148; www.scoilsamhraidhwillieclancy.com; ⏱Jul), a tribute to a native son and one of Ireland's greatest pipers. The eight-day **festival**, now in its fourth decade, begins on the first Saturday in July, when impromptu sessions occur day and night, the pubs are packed and Guinness is consumed by the barrel – up to 10,000 enthusiasts from around the globe turn up for the event. Specialist workshops and classes underpin the event; don't be surprised to attend a recital with 40 noted fiddlers.

- - - - - - - - - -

TRIP HIGHLIGHT

### 4 Ennistymon

Ennistymon (Inis Díomáin) is one of those country villages where people go about their business barely noticing the characterful buildings lining Main St. And behind this facade there's a surprise: the roaring **Cascades**, the stepped falls of the River Inagh. After heavy rain they surge, beer-brown and foaming, and you risk getting drenched on windy days in the flying drizzle. Not to be missed, **Eugene's** (Main St; ⏱10.30am-11.30pm Mon-Thu, 10.30am-12.30am Fri-Sat, 12.30-11pm Sun) is intimate and cosy and has a trademark collection of visiting cards covering its walls, alongside photographs of famous writers and musicians. The inspiring collection of whiskey (Irish) and whisky (Scottish) will have you smoothly debating their relative merits. Another great old pub is **Cooley's House** (☎065-707 1712; Main St; ⏱10.30am-11pm Mon-Sat, noon-11.30pm Sun), with music most nights in summer and on Wednesday (trad night) in winter.

➤ p269

**The Drive »** Heading north through a patchwork of green fields and stony walls on the R481, you'll land at the tiny village of Kilfenora, some 9km

**Kilfenora** Kilfenora Cathedral

later. Despite its diminutive size, the pulse of Clare's music scene beats strongly in this area.

------------

### ⑤ Kilfenora

Underappreciated Kilfenora (Cill Fhionnúrach) lies on the southern fringe of The Burren. It's a small place, with a diminutive 12th-century cathedral, and is best known for its **high crosses**. The town has a strong music tradition that rivals that of Doolin but without the crowds. The **Kilfenora Céili Band** (www.kilfenoraceiliband. com) is a celebrated community that's been playing for 100 years; its traditional music features fiddles, banjos, squeeze boxes and more.

**Vaughan's Pub** (www. vaughanspub.ie; Main St; mains €8-15; ⊙ kitchen 10am-9pm) has music in the bar every night during the summer and terrific set-dancing sessions in its barn on Thursday and Sunday nights.

The Drive ≫ From Kilfenora, the road meanders northwest 8km to Lisdoonvarna, home of the international matchmaking

# Classic Trip

## WHY THIS IS A CLASSIC TRIP
FIONN DAVENPORT, WRITER

To witness a proper traditional session in one of the music houses of Clare or the fine old pubs of Galway can be a transcendent experience, especially if it's appropriately lubricated with a pint (or few) of stout. Sure, there'll be plenty of tourists about, but this is authentic, traditional Ireland at its most evocative.

Top: Abandoned cottage, Inishmór
Left: Eugene's, Ennistymon
Right: Musician, Galway

MICHELLE MCMAHON/GETTY IMAGES ©

ROBIN BUSH/GETTY IMAGES ©

festival. Posh during Victorian times, the town is more down at heel today, but friendly, good-looking and far less overrun than Doolin.

- - - - - - - - - - - - -

## ⑥ Lisdoonvarna

Lisdoonvarna (Lios Dún Bhearna), often just called 'Lisdoon', is well known for its mineral springs. For centuries people have been visiting the local spa to swallow its waters. Down by the river at **Roadside Tavern** (www. roadsidetavern.ie; Kincora Rd; mains €11.50-20; ⊙noon-4pm & 6-9pm Mon-Fri, noon-9pm Sat, noon-8pm Sun), third-generation owner Peter Curtin knows every story worth telling. There are trad sessions daily in summer. Look for a trail beside the pub that runs 400m down to two **wells** by the river. One is high in sulphur, the other iron. Mix and match for a cocktail of minerals. Next door, **Burren Smokehouse** (☏065-707 4432; www.burren smokehouse.ie; Kincora Rd; ⊙9am-7pm May-Aug, 9am-6pm Apr, 10am-5pm Mar & Sep-Oct, shorter hrs winter; ℗) is where you can learn about the ancient Irish art of oak-smoking salmon.

**The Drive »** Just under 10 minutes' drive west of here is the epicentre of Clare's trad music scene, at Doolin. Also known for its setting – 6km north of the Cliffs of Moher – what's called Doolin is really three small neighbouring villages. There's Fisherstreet, right on the water, Doolin itself, about 1km east on the little River Aille, and Roadford, another 1km east.

## **7** Doolin

Doolin gets plenty of press as a centre of Irish traditional music, owing to a trio of pubs that have sessions through the year. **McGann's** (www.mcgannspubdoolin.com; Roadford; ◷10am-12.30am, kitchen 10am-9.30pm) has all the classic touches of a full-on Irish music pub; the action often spills out onto the street. Right on the water, **Gus O'Connor's Pub** (www.gusoconnorspubdoolin.net; Fisherstreet; ◷9am-midnight), a sprawling favourite, has a rollicking atmosphere. It easily gets the most crowded and has the highest tourist quotient. **MacDiarmada's** (Roadford; ◷bar 11am-midnight, kitchen 9am-9.30pm), also known as McDermott's, is a simple and sometimes rowdy red-and-white old pub popular with locals. When the fiddles get going, it can seem like a scene out of a John Ford movie.

🛏 p269

**The Drive »** You'll need to leave your car at one of Doolin's many car parks to board the ferry to the Aran Islands.

## **8** Inishmór

The Aran Islands sing their own siren song to thousands of travellers each year who find their desolate beauty beguiling. The largest and most accessible Aran, Inishmór, is home to ancient fort **Dún Aengus** (Dún Aonghasa; www.heritageireland.ie/en/west/dunaonghasa/; adult/child €4/2; ◷9.30am-6pm Apr-Oct, 9.30am-4pm Nov-Mar, closed Mon & Tue Jan & Feb), one of the oldest archaeological remains in Ireland. The island also has some lively pubs and restaurants, particularly in the only town, Kilronan. Irish remains the local tongue, but most locals speak English with visitors. **Tí Joe Watty's Bar** (www.joewattys.com; Kilronan; ◷kitchen 12.30-9pm) is the best pub in Kilronan, with traditional sessions most nights. Turf fires warm the air on the 50 weeks a year when this is needed. Informal music sessions, turf fires and a broad terrace with harbour views make **Tí Joe Mac's** (Kilronan) a local favourite, while jovial **Tigh Fitz** (Killeany), near the airport, has traditional sessions and set dancing every weekend. It's 1.6km from Kilronan (about a 25-minute walk).

🛏 p269, p309

**The Drive »** Ferries can be picked up between Aran Islands but tickets must be prebooked.

TRIP HIGHLIGHT

## **9** Inisheer

On Inisheer (Inis Oírr), the smallest of the Aran Islands, the breathtakingly beautiful end-of-the-earth landscape adds to the island's distinctly mystical aura. Steeped in mythology, traditional rituals are still very much respected here. Locals still carry out a pilgrimage with potential healing powers, known as the *Turas,* to the Well of Enda, an ever-burbling spring in the southwest. For a week in late June the island reverberates to the thunder of traditional drums during **Craiceann Inis Oírr International Bodhrán Summer School** (www.craiceann.com), which includes Bodhrán master classes, workshops and pub sessions as well as Irish dancing. Rory Conneely's atmospheric inn **Tigh Ruairí** (Strand House; ☎099-75020; www.tighruairi.com; r €50-90; @) hosts live music sessions and, here since 1897, **Tigh Ned** (meals €5-10) is a welcoming, unpretentious place, with harbour views and lively traditional music.

🛏 p269

# Eating & Sleeping

## Galway City ❶

### 🛏 Heron's Rest  B&B €€

(📞091-539 574; www.theheronsrest.com;
16a Longwalk; s/d from €80/140; 🛜) Ideally
located in a lovely row of houses on the banks of
the Corrib, the thoughtful hosts here give you
deck chairs so you can sit outside and enjoy the
scene. Other touches include holiday-friendly
breakfast times (8am to 11am), decanters of
port (enough for a glass or two) and more.
Rooms are small and cute, with double-glazed
windows and water views.

## Ennis ❷

### ✕ Zest  Cafe €

(www.zestfood.ie; Market Pl; meals €5-10;
🕐8am-6pm Mon-Sat, 10.30am-4.30pm Sun)
Zest combines a deli, bakery, shop and cafe.
Excellent prepared foods from the region are
offered along with salads, soups and much
more. It's ideal for a coffee or lunch.

### 🛏 Old Ground Hotel  Hotel €€

(📞065-682 8127; www.flynnhotels.com;
O'Connell St; s/d from €120/150; 🅿@🛜) A
seasoned, charming and congenial space of
polished floorboards, cornice-work, antiques
and open fires, the lobby is always a scene:
old friends sinking into sofas, deals cut at
the tables, and ladies from the neighbouring
church's altar society exchanging gossip over
tea. Parts of this smart and rambling landmark
date back to the 1800s. The 83 rooms vary
greatly in size and decor – don't hesitate to
inspect a few. On balmy days, retire to tables
on the lawn.

## Ennistymon ❹

### 🛏 Falls Hotel  Hotel €€

(📞065-707 1004; www.fallshotel.ie; off N67;
r from €95; 🅿🛜🏊) Built on the ruins of an
O'Brien castle, this handsome and sprawling
Georgian house was once Ennistymon House,
the family home of Caitlín MacNamara, who

married Dylan Thomas. With 140 modern
rooms and a large, enclosed pool, the hotel's
view of the Cascades from the entrance steps
is breathtaking, and there are 20 hectares of
wooded gardens.

## Doolin ❼

### 🛏 Cullinan's Guesthouse  Inn €€

(📞065-707 4183; www.cullinansdoolin.com; d
from €100; 🅿🛜) Owned by well-known fiddle-
playing James Cullinan, the eight rooms at this
smart place on the River Aille are very good-
looking, with power showers and comfortable
fittings. A couple of rooms are slightly smaller
than the others, but are right on the water.
There's a lovely back terrace for enjoying the
views.

## Inishmór ❽

### 🛏 Man of Aran Cottage  B&B €€

(📞099-61301; www.manofarancottage.com;
Kilmurvey; s/d from €55/80; 🕐Mar-Oct) Built
for the 1930s film of the same name, this
thatched B&B doesn't trade on past glories –
its authentic stone-and-wood interiors define
charming. The owners are avid organic
gardeners (the tomatoes are famous) and their
bounty can become your meal (mains €22).

## Inisheer ❾

### 🛏 Fisherman's Cottage &
### South Aran House  B&B €€

(📞099-75073; www.southaran.com; Castle
Village; s/d €49/80; 🕐Apr-Oct; 🛜) Slow-food
enthusiasts run this sprightly B&B and cafe
that's a mere five-minute walk from the pier;
look for the lavender growing in profusion at
the entrance. Meals (dinner mains €12 to €20)
celebrate local seafood and organic produce.
Nonguests can enjoy cakes by day and dinner at
night, but will need to book. Rooms are simple
yet stylish. Kayaking and fishing are among the
activities on offer.

# Mountains & Moors

# 24

*A whirl around Connemara's end-of-the-earth landscape of valleys, secret strands and even a fjord will leave you pining for more. So we've added cottages, abbeys and a quaint gastro village.*

## TRIP HIGHLIGHTS

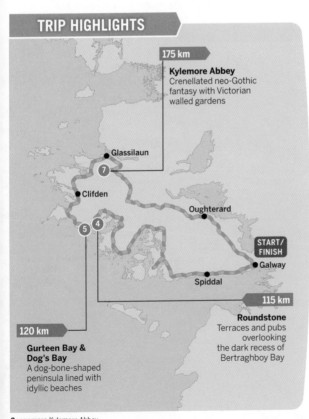

**175 km**

**Kylemore Abbey**
Crenellated neo-Gothic fantasy with Victorian walled gardens

Glassilaun

Clifden

Oughterard

**START/ FINISH**
Galway

Spiddal

**115 km**

**120 km**

**Gurteen Bay & Dog's Bay**
A dog-bone-shaped peninsula lined with idyllic beaches

**Roundstone**
Terraces and pubs overlooking the dark recess of Bertraghboy Bay

## 6 DAYS
## 206KM / 128 MILES

### GREAT FOR...

### BEST TIME TO GO
Winter, when the sea and landscape are at their wildest.

### ESSENTIAL PHOTO
Create your own historic movie still at the Quiet Man Bridge.

### BEST FOR DIVING
The turquoise water of Glassilaun Bay offers superb diving.

# 24 Mountains & Moors

West of Galway the scenery becomes increasingly wilder and more rugged. Crossing the Gaeltacht (Gaelic-speaking territory) beyond Spiddal, take in writer, poet and Easter 1916 leader Padraig Pearse's cottage, and sophisticated Roundstone for exceptional food and the impossibly blue waters of its adjoining bays. A spin through Connemara's heartland to gothic Kylemore Abbey takes you to pretty Oughterard and back on to Galway.

## ❶ Galway City

County Galway's namesake city is such a charmer you might not tear yourself away to the countryside. Arty, bohemian Galway city (Gaillimh) is renowned for its pleasures. Brightly painted pubs heave with live music, while cafes offer front-row seats for observing street performers, weekend hen parties run amok, lovers entwined and more. Steeped in history, the city nonetheless has a contemporary vibe. Walking the cobble-

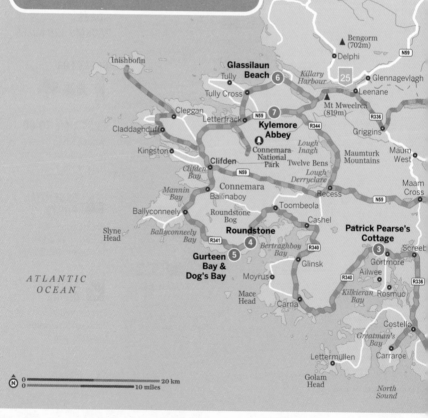

stone streets you'll find remnants of the medieval town walls between shops selling Aran sweaters, handcrafted Claddagh rings, and stacks of secondhand and new books.

🍴 🛏 p46, p74, p277

**The Drive ››** The slow coastal route between Galway and Connemara takes you past pretty seascapes and villages. Opposite the popular Blue Flag beach Silver Strand, 4.8km west of Galway on the R336, are the Barna Woods, a dense, deep-green natural oak forest perfect for rambling and picnicking before hitting Spiddal.

## ② Spiddal

Spiddal (An Spidéal) is a refreshingly untouched little village, and the start of the Gaeltacht region. On your right as you approach the village are the **Spiddal Craft & Design Studios** (www. spiddalcrafts.com; off R336; ⏰10am-5pm; shorter hours in winter), where you can watch woodworkers, leatherworkers, sculptors and weavers plying their crafts. Exceptional traditional music sessions take place at **Tigh Hughes** (⏰trad sessions 9pm Tue) – it's not uncommon for major musicians to turn up unannounced and join in the craic (fun).

🛏 p277

**The Drive ››** West of Spiddal, the scenery becomes more dramatic, with parched fields criss-crossed by low stone walls rolling to a ragged shore. Carraroe (An Cheathrú Rua) has fine beaches, including the Coral Strand. It's worth wandering the small roads on all sides of Greatman's Bay to discover tiny inlets and coves, often watched over by the local donkeys – the perfect scenic muse for a nationalist writer such as Pádraig Pearse.

## ③ Patrick Pearse's Cottage

Writer, poet and teacher Pádraig Pearse (1879–1916) led the Easter Rising with James Connolly and others in 1916; after the revolt

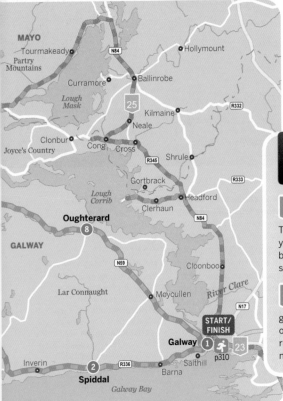

## 🔗 LINK YOUR TRIP

**23** **Musical Landscapes**

This rip-roaring ride takes you from Galway's music bars to the best trad sessions of Clare.

**25** **Loughs of the West**

Cruise Galway's gorgeous inland waterways on this tour of its lakes and rivers. Pick it up at Delphi, near Leenane.

he was executed by the British. Pearse wrote some of his short stories and plays in this small thatched **cottage** (Teach an Phiarsaigh; www.heritage ireland.ie; R340; adult/child €4/2; ⏰10am-6pm Easter & Jun–Aug) in a wonderfully picturesque location. Although the cottage was burned out during the War of Independence, it has been restored and contains an interesting exhibition about Pearse's life. It's near Gortmore, along the R340.

**The Drive** ›› The scenic R340 swings south along Kilkieran Bay, an intricate system of tidal marshes, basins and bogs containing an amazing diversity of wildlife. The R342 meanders past Cashel (where there's accommodation, see p277), skirting Cloonisle Bay. At Toombeola a short trip south on the R341 takes you to the picture-postcard village of Roundstone.

TRIP HIGHLIGHT

## 4 Roundstone

Clustered around a boat-filled harbour, Roundstone (Cloch na Rón) is one of Connemara's gems. Colourful terrace houses and inviting pubs overlook the dark recess of Bertraghboy Bay, which is home to lobster trawlers and traditional *currachs* (rowing boats with tarred canvas bottoms stretched over wicker frames). Wander the short **promenade** for views over the water to ribbons of eroded land.

Malachy Kearns' **Roundstone Musical Instruments** (www.bodhran.com; IDA Craft Park; ⏰9am-6pm) is just south of the village in the remains of an old Franciscan monastery. Kearns is Ireland's only full-time maker of traditional bodhráns (hand-held goatskin drums). Watch him work and buy a tin whistle, harp or booklet filled with Irish

ballads; there's also a small free folk museum and a cafe.

✕ p277

**The Drive** ›› The R341 shadows the coast from Roundstone to Clifden. Beaches along here have such beautiful white sand and turquoise water that, if you added 10°C to the temperature, you could be in Antigua. Don't believe us? Feast your eyes on the azure waters and brilliant white

**Roundstone** Buildings line the harbour

sand beaches of Gurteen Bay and Dog's Bay ahead.

TRIP HIGHLIGHT

### ❺ Gurteen Bay & Dog's Bay

About 2.5km from Roundstone, look for the turn to Gurteen Bay (sometimes spelt Gorteen Bay). After a further 800m there is a turn for Dog's Bay. Together, the pair form the two sides of a dog-bone-shaped peninsula lined with idyllic beaches. Park and enjoy a day strolling the grassy heads and frolicking on the hard-packed sand.

**The Drive »** Dusting the sand off, continue north to the village of Ballyconneely, renowned as a breeding ground for the famous Connemara pony. Although Connemara is a pearl necklace of sights, the north coast is diamond encrusted. Gorgeous beaches compete for your attention with stark, raw mountain vistas and views out to the moody sea. Heading from Clifden north on the N59, the nearby coast is a magnet for outdoors adventure seekers.

### ❻ Glassilaun Beach

Look for a turn to **Rosroe Quay**, where a truly magnificent crescent of sand awaits at Glassilaun

275

## BRIDGING THE QUIET MAN

Whenever an American cable TV station needs a ratings boost, they invariably trot out the iconic 1952 *The Quiet Man*. Starring John Wayne and filmed in lavish colour to capture the crimson locks of his co-star Maureen O'Hara, the film regularly makes the top-10 lists of aging romantic-comedy lovers for its portrayal of rural Irish life, replete with drinking and fighting, fighting and drinking etc. Director John Ford returned to his Irish roots and filmed the movie almost entirely on location in Connemara and the little village of Cong, just over the border in County Mayo. One of the most photogenic spots from the film, the eponymous **Quiet Man Bridge**, is just 3km west of Oughterard off the N59. Looking much as it did in the film, the picture-perfect arched span (whose original name was Leam Bridge) is a lovely spot. Purists will note, however, that the scene based here had close-ups done on a cheesy set back in Hollywood. That's showbiz. Hard-core fans will want to buy the superb *The Complete Guide to The Quiet Man* by Des MacHale. It's sold in most tourist offices in the area.

Beach, arguably one of Connemara's best beaches. If you're drawn to the beauty of the underwater world, **Scuba Dive West** (☏095-43922; www.scubadivewest.com), based at Glassilaun Beach, runs highly recommended courses and dives. Beginners are welcome.

**The Drive »** Continue southeast along the final 5km stretch of road that runs along Lough Fee. In spring when the gorse explodes in yellow bloom, the views here are, again, simply breathtaking. When you hit the N59 head south to the unmistakable, imposing beauty of Kylemore Abbey.

---

**TRIP HIGHLIGHT**

### ❼ Kylemore Abbey

Magnificently situated on the shores of a lake, the crenellated 19th-century neo-Gothic fantasy **Kylemore Abbey** (www.kylemoreabbeytourism.ie; off N59; adult/child €13/

free; ☉9am-6pm Apr-Sep, 10am-4.30pm Oct-Mar). was built for a wealthy English businessman, Mitchell Henry, who spent his honeymoon in Connemara. His wife died tragically young. Admission also covers the abbey's tranquil **Victorian walled gardens**. You can stroll around the lake and surrounding woods for free. Prepare for large volumes of visitors in high summer, when it's best to arrive in the early morning for uncluttered views.

**The Drive »** Heading back towards Galway, you'll cruise through a kaleidoscopic tapestry of typical Connemara valley scenery. It feels like the end of the earth, with large swaths of land – colours changing from lime green, to mustard to purple on the mountain side – only interrupted by dry-stone walls, the odd derelict cottage or oblivious sheep crossing your path.

### ❽ Oughterard

The writer William Makepeace Thackeray sang the praises of the small town of Oughterard (Uachtar Árd), saying: 'A more beautiful village can scarcely be seen'. Even if those charms have faded over the years, shadows of its former Georgian glory remain. And it is one of Ireland's principal angling centres. If you see tourists wandering around, talking with a drawl and calling people 'pilgrim', it's probably because they are here to relive the iconic film *The Quiet Man*.

**The Drive »** Heading east again, stop close by for a great photo op at 16th-century Aughnanure Castle, 3km east of Oughterard, off the N59. From here it's a quick run into Galway city for a well-deserved pint at Galway's finest, Tigh Neachtain.

# Eating & Sleeping

## Galway City ❶

### ✗ Aniar      Modern Irish €€€

(📞091-535 947; www.aniarrestaurant.ie;
53 Lower Dominick St; menus €90-120, with
wine pairings €140-190; 🕐6-10pm Tue-Thu,
5.30-10pm Fri & Sat) Deeply committed to the
flavours and food producers of Galway and West
Ireland, Aniar wears its Michelin star with pride.
There's no fuss, however. The casual spring-
green dining area is a relaxed place to taste
from the nightly, daily-changing menu. The wine
list favours small producers. Reserve.

### ✗ McCambridge's      Cafe €€

(www.mccambridges.com; 38/39 Shop St;
snacks from €4, mains €13-15; 🕐cafe 9am-
5.30pm Mon-Wed, 9am-9pm Thu-Sat, 10.30am-
6pm Sun, grocery 8am-7pm Mon-Wed, 8am-9pm
Thu-Sat, 10.30am-6pm Sun) The long-running
food hall here has some superb prepared
salads, hot foods and other more exotic treats.
Create the perfect picnic or enjoy your pickings
at the tables out front. All high ceilings, blond
wood and busy staff, the upstairs cafe is lovely,
with an ever-changing menu of modern Irish fare
plus gourmet sandwiches, salads, silky soups
and tip-top coffee.

### 🛏 House Hotel      Hotel €€€

(📞091-538 900; www.thehousehotel.ie; Spanish
Pde; r €140-220; 🅿🛜) There's a hip and cool
array of colour in the lobby at this smart and
stylish boutique hotel. Public spaces contrast
modern art with trad details and bold accents.
Cat motifs abound. The 40 rooms are small but
plush, with bright colour schemes and quality
fabrics.

### 🛏 Heron's Rest      B&B €€

(📞091-539 574; www.theheronsrest.com;
16a Longwalk; s/d from €80/140; 🛜) Ideally
located in a lovely row of houses on the banks of
the Corrib, the thoughtful hosts here give you
deck chairs so you can sit outside and enjoy the
scene. Other touches include holiday-friendly

breakfast times (8am to 11am), decanters of
port (enough for a glass or two) and more.
Rooms, with double-glazed windows and water
views, are small and cute.

## Spiddal ❷

### 🛏 Cloch na Scíth      B&B €€

(📞091-553 364; www.thatchcottage.com;
Kellough, Spiddal; d/tr from €76/90; 🅿) Set
in a story-book garden roamed by ducks and
chickens, this century-old thatched cottage
has a warm, friendly host, Nancy, who cooks
bread in an iron pot over the peat fire (as her
grandmother taught her and as she'll teach
you).

## Cashel ❸

### 🛏 Cashel House Hotel      Hotel €€

(📞095-31001; www.cashelhouse.ie; Cashel; s/d
from €75/170; 🅿🛜) At the head of Cashel Bay,
this flowered fantasy of a country mansion has
30 period rooms surrounded by 17 hectares of
woodland and gardens. It also has a stable of
Connemara ponies (riding lessons available),
a superb dining room and even a small private
beach.

## Roundstone ❹

### ✗ O'Dowd's      Seafood €€

(📞091-35809; www.odowdsseafoodbar.com;
Main St; mains €14-22, 2-course menus €20;
🕐restaurant noon-9.30pm Jun-Sep, to 9pm Oct-
May; 🛜) This well-worn, comfortable old pub
hasn't lost any of its authenticity since it starred
in the 1997 Hollywood flick *The Matchmaker*.
Specialities at its adjoining restaurant include
seafood sourced off the old stone dock right
across the street, while produce comes
from their garden. There's a good list of Irish
microbrews, too.

# Loughs of the West

**25**

*This trip takes you around beautiful, less-visited backwaters to see lakeside scenery at its most untarnished, with epic castles and intriguing islands en route.*

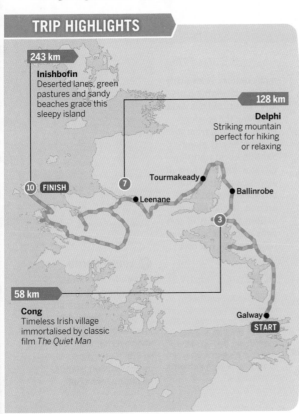

**243 km**

**Inishbofin**
Deserted lanes, green pastures and sandy beaches grace this sleepy island

**128 km**

**Delphi**
Striking mountain perfect for hiking or relaxing

Tourmakeady

Ballinrobe

Leenane

**10** FINISH

**7**

**3**

**58 km**

**Cong**
Timeless Irish village immortalised by classic film *The Quiet Man*

Galway
START

**3–4 DAYS**
**243KM / 151 MILES**

## GREAT FOR...

## BEST TIME TO GO

May, for ultimate fishing and the Inishbofin Arts Festival.

 **ESSENTIAL PHOTO**

Cong, with the spectacular vista of Ashford Castle and the lake as backdrop.

 **BEST FOR FISHING**

Loughs Corrib and Mask are world-renowned for their brown trout.

**Connemara National Park** Diamond Hill

# 25 Loughs of the West

Following the lay of the lakes, this panoramic waterside drive takes in the very best of Loughs Corrib and Mask. Pass the picture-postcard villages of Cong and Tourmakeady before crossing the barren beauty of Connemara to dramatic mountain-backed Delphi. Cruising Connemara's filigreed northern coast, you'll discover pretty strands and ancient remains both on shore and at the striking island of Inishbofin.

## ❶ Galway City

Galway's Irish name, Gaillimh, originates from the Irish word *gaill,* meaning 'outsiders' or 'foreigners', and the term resonates throughout the city's history. Colourful and cosmopolitan – many dark-haired, olive-skinned Galwegians consider themselves descended from the Spanish Armada – this small city is best explored by strolling its medieval streets. Bridges arc the salmon-filled River Corrib, and a long promenade leads to the seaside suburb of **Salthill**, on Galway Bay, the source of the area's fa-mous oysters. A favourite pastime for Galwegians and visitors alike is walking along the seaside **Prom**, running from the edge of the city along Salthill. Local tradition dictates 'kicking the wall' across from the diving boards before turning around. In and around Salthill are plenty of cosy pubs from where you can watch storms roll over the bay.

✕ 🛏 p46, p74, p277

**The Drive ≫** From Galway take the inspiringly named Headford Rd north onto the N84 into, well, Headford, skirting Lough Corrib, the Republic's biggest lake, which virtually cuts off western Galway from the rest of the country.

## ❷ Lough Corrib

Just under 7km west of Headford you can reach Lough Corrib at the pretty Greenfields pier. Over 48km long and covering some 200 sq km, it encompasses more than 360 islands, including **Inchagoill**,

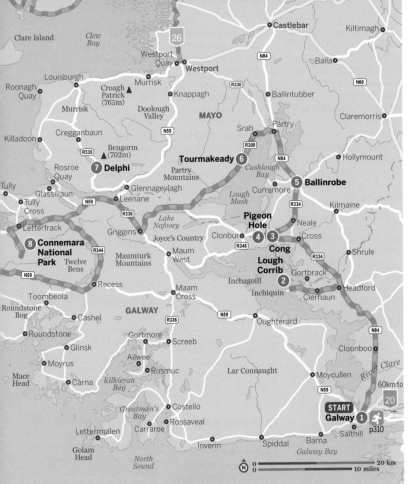

home to 5th-century monastic remains, a simple graveyard and Ogham stone. **Inchiquin** island, associated with St Brendan, can be accessed by road from the pier. It's world-famous for its salmon, sea trout and brown trout, with the highlight of the fishing

## LINK YOUR TRIP

### 20 Shannon River Route

From the waters to the wild, continue on the west's inland waterways at Portumna.

### 26 North Mayo & Sligo

Continue exploring the northwest's incredible coastline, joining the route at Westport.

calendar being mayfly season, when zillions of the small bugs hatch over a few days (usually in May) and drive the fish – and anglers – into a frenzy. Salmon begin running around June. Upstream is the curiosity **Ballycurrin Lighthouse**, built in 1772 when the lake may have seen more traffic – it's Europe's only inland lighthouse.

**The Drive »** From Headford, take the R334 north out of town as far as Cross, where you'll join the R346, which takes you into the outstanding village of Cong, some 16km later.

**TRIP HIGHLIGHT**

### 3 Cong

Sitting on a sliver-thin isthmus between Lough Corrib and Lough Mask, Cong complies with romantic notions of a traditional Irish village. Time appears to have stood still ever since the evergreen classic *The Quiet Man* was filmed here in 1951. Though popular on the tour-bus circuit, the wooded trails between the lovely 12th-century Augustinian abbey and stately Ashford Castle offer genuine quietude. **Ashford Castle** (☏094-954 6003; www.ashfordcastle.com; grounds adult/child €5/3.50; ⊙grounds 9am-dusk) was first built in 1228 as the seat of the de Burgo family. One-time owner Arthur Guinness (of stout fame) turned the castle into a regal hunting and fishing lodge, which it remains today. A range of **cruises** (www.corribcruises.com; adult/child €20/10) on Lough Corrib depart from the Ashford Castle pier.

✕ 🏠 p285

**The Drive »** From Cong take the R345 west out of town. After 2km or so in the woods you'll come to the famous sink hole, Pigeon Hole.

### 4 Pigeon Hole

The Cong area is honeycombed with 10 limestone caves, each with a colourful legend or story to its credit. Keep an eye out for the white trout of Cong, a mythical woman who turned into a fish to be with her drowned lover at **Pigeon Hole**, one of the best caves. Steep, slippery, stone steps lead down into the cave, where subterranean water flows in winter. Pigeon Hole can be reached by road or by the walking track from across the river.

**The Drive »** It's a 15-minute drive on the R345 and R334 north, veering left into Ballinrobe.

### 5 Ballinrobe

The small market town of Ballinrobe (Baile an Roba), on the River Robe, is a good base for exploring trout-filled Lough Mask, the largest lake in the county. **St Mary's Church** has an impressive collection of stained-glass windows by Ireland's renowned 20th-century artist, Harry Clarke.

## BOYCOTT BEGINNINGS

It was near the unassuming little village of Neale, near Cong, that the term 'boycott' first came into use. In 1880 the Irish Land League, in an effort to press for fair rents and improve the lot of workers, withdrew field hands from the estate of Lord Erne, who owned much of the land in the area. When Lord Erne's land agent, Captain Charles Cunningham Boycott, evicted the striking labourers, the surrounding community began a campaign to ostracise the agent. Not only did farmers refuse to work his land, people in the town refused to talk to him, provide services or sit next to him in church. The incident attracted attention from the London papers, and soon Boycott's name was synonymous with such organised, nonviolent protests. Within a few months, Boycott gave up and left Ireland.

**Connemara** Looking towards the Twelve Bens

One depicts St Brendan 'the Navigator', with oar in hand, who reputedly sailed to America long before Columbus. You can access Lough Mask at **Cushlough Bay**, just 5km west of town. Take the Castlebar road north and immediately on the left you'll see signs for Cushlough. For boat hire try **Lakeshore Angling Centre** (☎094-954 1389; www.lakeshoreholidays.com).

The Drive ›› Take the N84 north from Ballinrobe, veering west at Partry. The landscape is made up of mostly small farm holdings, rusty bogland and tumbledown dry-stone walls.

Follow the serene lakeside route (R300) through Srah to a great waterside pit stop to take in the lake at Tourmakeady.

- - - - - - - - - - -

### ❻ Tourmakeady

With the Partry Mountains acting as a picturesque backdrop to its west, the small village of Tourmakeady, on the shore of Lough Mask, is part of an Irish-speaking community. Once a flax-growing area, its name is derived from Tuar Mhic Éadaigh, meaning 'Keady's field', referring to the field where the flax was once laid out

to dry before spinning. Tourmakeady Woods, with a spectacular 58m-high **waterfall** at its centre, makes a wonderful spot for a picnic. Alternatively, you could water the horses at the cosy **Paddy's Thatched Bar**, overlooking the water.

The Drive ›› Follow the lakeside road, pulling in at stunning Lake Nafooey, at the foot of Maumtrasna, to take in the view. Head north on the R336 through Leenane and around the harbour, passing Assleagh Falls to Delphi, a scenic 45km in all.

## ❼ Delphi

Geographically just inside County Mayo, but administratively in County Galway, this swath of mountainous moorland is miles from any significant population, allowing you to set about the serious business of relaxing. At the southern extent of the Doolough Valley, the area was named by its most famous resident, the second marquis of Sligo, who was convinced that it resembled the land around Delphi, Greece. If you can spot the resemblance, you've a better imagination than most, but in many ways it's even more striking than its Mediterranean namesake. At the beautiful **Delphi Mountain Resort** (☎095-42208; www. delphiadventureresort.com; dm €40, d from €158; **P @**) opt for a day's surfing, kayaking or rock climbing, followed by a stay and some pampering spa treatments.

🛏 p285

**The Drive »** Return to Leenane and follow the N59 southwest to Letterfrack. Go through the crossroads to the turn-off for Connemara National Park.

## ❽ Connemara National Park

Spanning 2000 dramatic hectares of bog, mountain and heath, **Connemara National Park** (www. connemaranationalpark. ie; off N59; ☺visitor centre 9am-5.30pm Mar-Oct, park 24hr) encloses a number of the **Twelve Bens**, including Bencullagh, Benbrack and Benbaun. The heart of the park is **Gleann Mór** (Big Glen), through which the River Polladirk flows. There's fine walking up the glen and over the surrounding mountains. There are also short, self-guided walks and, if the Bens look too daunting, you can hike up **Diamond Hill** nearby. Various types of flora and fauna native to the area are explained, including the huge elephant hawkmoth, in the excellent **visitor centre**.

🛏 p285

**The Drive »** Join the R344 down through Lough Inagh Valley, on the eastern side of the brooding Twelve Bens, back to the N59 and on to Clifden. Following the jagged coastline north of Clifden brings you to the tiny village of Claddaghduff (An Cladach Dubh). If you turn west here down by the Catholic church, you'll come out on Omey Strand.

## ❾ Omey Strand

At low tide you can drive or walk across the sand at Omey Strand to **Omey Island** (population 20), a low islet of rock, grass, sand and a handful of houses.

**The Drive »** Double back to Claddaghduff and head north

to Cleggan to park up and take the 30-minute ferry to glorious Inishbofin.

## ❿ Inishbofin

By day sleepy Inishbofin is a haven of tranquillity. You can walk or bike its narrow, deserted lanes, green pastures and sandy beaches, with farm animals and seals for company. But with no *gardaí* (Irish Republic police) on the island to enforce closing times at the pub, by night – you guessed it – Inishbofin has wild craic (good times). Situated 9km offshore, Inishbofin is only 6km long by 3km wide, and its highest point is a mere 86m above sea level. Inishbofin's pristine waters offer superb scuba diving, sandy beaches and alluring trails that encourage exploring. The island well and truly wakes up during May's **Inishbofin Arts Festival** (www.inishbofin.com) which includes accordion workshops, archaeological walks, art exhibitions and concerts by such high-profile Irish bands as De Dannan and The Stunning. Ferries from Cleggan to Inishbofin are run by **Island Discovery** (☎095-45894/19; www. inishbofinislanddiscovery.com; adult/child return €20/10). Dolphins often swim alongside the boats.

🛏 p285

# Eating & Sleeping

## Cong ③

### ✗ Hungry Monk — Cafe €

(Abbey St; mains €6-14; ⏰10am-5pm Mon-Sat & bank holiday Sun; 🛜) This simple cafe with bright colours and artfully mismatched furniture is a perfect refuge on a misty day. Locally sourced ingredients make up the excellent sandwiches, soups and salads, the luscious cakes are homemade and the coffee is excellent.

### 🛏 Lodge at Ashford Castle — Hotel €€€

(📞094-954 5400; www.thelodgeac.com; The Quay; r from €240; 🛜) The lodge, built in the 1820s by Ashford Castle's owners, has rich, contemporary colours and is a good alternative to the actual **castle** (📞094-954 6003; www. ashford.ie; r from €400; @🛜). The 50 guest rooms and suites are lavishly decorated; some have copper bathtubs. It's on the grounds of Ashford Castle Estate.

## Delphi ⑦

### 🛏 Delphi Lodge — Resort €€€

(📞095-42222; www.delphilodge.ie; off R335; s/d/tr from €140/230/280; @) A wonderful 1830s Georgian mansion built by the Marquis of Sligo, Delphi Lodge is dwarfed by the mountain backdrop. This 13-room country hotel features beautiful interiors, vast grounds, lovely food (dinner €55) and a serious lack of pretension. It's popular with fishers (half day with fishing tutor €150) and with those simply aiming to relax.

## Connemara National Park ⑧

### 🛏 Lough Inagh Lodge — Lodge €€

(📞091-34706; www.loughinaghlodgehotel.ie; off R344; r from €148; dinner €44; P🛜) With walls stuffed with oil paintings hanging at odd angles, bowls of potpourri dotted about and the occasional Chinese ceramic, this atmospheric – and slightly haphazard – lodge has 13 grand rooms, with around five of them facing the water. Set in huge grounds against a hill, it's around midway up the gorgeous Lough Inagh Valley, 4.5km north of Recess.

## Inishbofin ⑩

### 🛏 Dolphin Hotel & Restaurant — Inn €€

(📞095-45991; www.dolphinhotel.ie; s/d from €45/90; ⏰Apr-Sep; @) Guest rooms are pleasant with large flat-screen TVs at this trim 11-room choice. Solar panels on the roof and an organic kitchen garden lend green cred. Local seafood and vegetarian dishes dominate the menu. There is a two-night minimum stay at weekends. Pick up from pier included.

### 🛏 Doonmore Hotel — Hotel €€

(📞095-45804; www.doonmorehotel.com; r €110; ⏰Apr-Sep; 🛜) Close to the harbour, Doonmore has comfortable, unpretentious rooms. Lunch (€15) and dinner (€35) in the dining room take advantage of the abundance of locally caught seafood, and the hotel can pack lunches for you to take while exploring the island.

# North Mayo & Sligo

# 26

*Travel from country-cosmopolitan Westport to nature at its most visceral on windswept Achill Island. Then, carry on through superb surfscapes to Sligo, Yeats' beloved adopted hometown.*

## TRIP HIGHLIGHTS

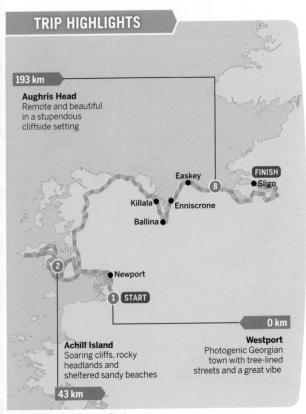

**193 km**

**Aughris Head**
Remote and beautiful in a stupendous cliffside setting

Eassey
Killala
Ballina
Enniscrone

**FINISH**
Sligo

**2**

Newport

**1** **START**

**0 km**

**Achill Island**
Soaring cliffs, rocky headlands and sheltered sandy beaches

**Westport**
Photogenic Georgian town with tree-lined streets and a great vibe

**43 km**

**4 DAYS**
**266KM / 165 MILES**

### GREAT FOR...

### BEST TIME TO GO
In early autumn crowds have abated and the sea is warmest.

### ESSENTIAL PHOTO

Wild Atlantic rollers at sunset on Easkey beach.

### BEST FOR OUTDOORS

Achill Island and Easkey offer surf and blustery beach walks.

**Achill Island** Surfer on Trawmore Beach

287

# 26 North Mayo & Sligo

This area has something quietly special – the rugged and remote Atlantic scenery of the west, but with fewer crowds. Grab a board and face off an invigorating roller at Achill, take a restorative seaweed bath at Enniscrone, walk in WB Yeats' footsteps round the 'Lake Isle of Innisfree' at the foot of Benbulben and enjoy the unpretentious company of lively Westport.

TRIP HIGHLIGHT

## ① Westport

Bright and vibrant even in the depths of winter, Westport is a photogenic Georgian town with tree-lined streets, a riverside mall and a great vibe. With an excellent choice of accommodation, and restaurants and pubs renowned for their music, it's an extremely popular spot yet has never sold its soul to tourism. A couple of kilometres west on Clew Bay, the town's harbour, Westport Quay

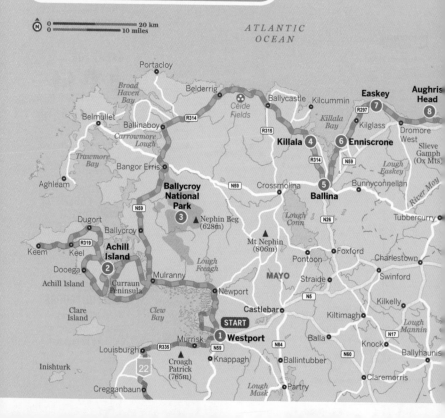

is a picturesque spot for a sundowner.

**Westport House**
(📞098-27766; www.west porthouse.ie; Quay Rd; house only adult/child €13/6.50, house & pirate adventure park €21/16.50; ⊙10am-6pm Jun-Aug, 10am-4pm Mar-May & Sep-Nov, hrs vary Dec, closed Jan & Feb; 👪), built in 1730 on the ruins of the 16th-century castle Grace O'Malley (p290), is a charming Georgian mansion that retains much of its original contents and has some stunning period-styled rooms. The house is set in glorious

gardens. Children will love the **Pirate Adventure Park**, complete with a swinging pirate ship, a 'pirate's playground' and a roller-coaster-style flume ride through a water channel.

✕ p258, p293

**The Drive »** A wiggling 12km drive north of Westport is the picturesque 18th-century village of Newport. Heading west look out for signs to Burrishoole Abbey and Rockfleet Castle, a 15th-century tower associated with 'pirate queen' Grace O'Malley. Mulranny village sits on a narrow isthmus overlooking the 365 or so islands of Clew Bay. Skip the main road to Achill Island in favour of the longer, narrower and infinitely more scenic Atlantic Dr.

----

TRIP HIGHLIGHT

**2 Achill Island**

Ireland's largest offshore island, Achill (An Caol), is connected to the mainland by a short bridge. Despite its accessibility, it has plenty of that far-flung-island feeling: soaring cliffs, rocky headlands, sheltered sandy beaches, broad

expanses of blanket bog and rolling mountains. **Slievemore Deserted Village** at the foot of Slievemore Mountain is a poignant reminder of the island's past hardships. In the mid-19th century, as the Potato Famine took hold, starvation forced the villagers to emigrate, or die. Except in the height of the holiday season, the Blue Flag beaches at **Dooega**, **Keem**, **Dugort** and **Golden Strand** are often deserted.

✕ 🛏 p293

**The Drive »** As you leave Achill (if you can), follow the R319 towards Mulranny and take the N59 north. From here the countryside throws out beautifully bleak boglands dotted with dry-stone walls and sheep. About 18km along the road, you might want to stop for a picnic lunch with a very fine backdrop at Ballycroy National Park.

----

**3 Ballycroy National Park**

Covering one of Europe's largest expanses of blanket

**LINK YOUR TRIP**

**22** **Best of the West**
The crème de la crème of Ireland's west coast; pick up this route in Westport for a scenic and cultural feast.

**27** **Sligo Surrounds**
Continue from Sligo to explore the county's rich megalithic remains, blustery beaches and Yeats' old stomping ground.

bog, **Ballycroy National Park** (⏱098-49888; www.
ballycroynationalpark.ie; off
N59, Ballycroy; ⊙visitor
centre 10am-5.30pm Apr-Sep)
is a gorgeously scenic
region, where the River
Owenduff wends its way
through intact bogs.

The park is home to a
diverse range of flora and
fauna, including pere-
grine falcons, corncrakes
and whooper swans. A
nature trail with inter-
pretation panels leads
from the visitor centre
across the bog with great
views to the surrounding
mountains. If you wish
to explore further, the
**Bangor Trail** crosses the
park and leads to some
of its most spectacular
viewpoints.

The Drive >> Ballycroy is
18km south of Bangor on the
N59. Continuing north from
here on the R314, you'll pass
the magnificent Stone Age
monument at Céide Fields
before heading through
Ballycastle and on to the historic
town of Killala.

### ④ Killala

The town itself is pretty
enough, but Killala is
more famous for its
namesake **bay** nearby,
and for its role in the
French invasion, when
in 1798 more than 1000
French troops landed at
Kilcummin in Killala Bay.
It was hoped that their
arrival would inspire the
Irish peasantry to revolt
against the English.

Lackan Bay **beach**
is a stunning expanse
of golden sand. There's
good surf here, but you'll
need to bring your own
equipment.

The Drive >> Back on the
R314, it's only 12km or so down
to the provincial hub of Ballina, a
busy market town.

### ⑤ Ballina

Mayo's second-largest
town, Ballina, is syn-
onymous with salmon. If
you're here during fishing
season, you'll see droves

RUNE JOHANSEN/GETTY IMAGES ©

of green-garbed waders,
poles in hand, heading
for the River Moy – one
of the most prolific rivers
in Europe for catching
the scaly critters – which
pumps right through the
heart of town. You'll also
spot salmon jumping in
the Ridge (salmon pool),
with otters and grey seals
in pursuit.

One of the best out-
door parties in the coun-
try, the weeklong **Ballina
Salmon Festival** (www.
ballinasalmonfestival.ie)
takes place in mid-July.

The Drive >> Taking the
N59 east out of town towards
Enniscrone, head back up to the
coast on the small R297, which

### THE PIRATE QUEEN

The life of Grace O'Malley (Gráinne Ní Mháille or
Granuaile; 1530–1603) reads like an unlikely work
of adventure fiction. Twice widowed and twice
imprisoned for acts of piracy, she was a fearsome
presence in the troubled landscape of 16th-century
Ireland, when traditional chieftains were locked in
battle with the English for control of the country.
Grace was ordered to London in 1593, whereupon
Queen Elizabeth I granted her a pardon and offered
her a title: she declined, saying she was already
Queen of Connaught. Westport House now resides
on the ruins of Grace's 16th-century castle.

Achill Island Sheep grazing near a stream

you'll meet just over 4km from Ballina.

- - - - - - - - - - - - -

### ⑥ Enniscrone

Enniscrone is famous for its traditional seaweed baths, which are some of the best and most atmospheric in the country. A stunning beach known as the **Hollow** stretches for 5km. Surf lessons and board hire are available from **Seventh Wave Surf School** (📱087 971 6389; www.surfsligo.com; Beach, Enniscrone; lessons adult/child from €30/25; ⊙Apr-Oct).

🛏 p351

**The Drive »** Some 14km north you'll come to the little village of Easkey.

- - - - - - - - - - - - -

### ⑦ Easkey

Easkey seems blissfully unaware that it's one of Europe's best year-round surfing destinations. Pub conversations revolve around hurling and Gaelic football, and the road to the beach isn't even signposted (turn off next to the childcare centre). Facilities are few; most surfers camp (free) around the castle ruins by the sea.

**The Drive »** From Easkey, you'll hug the winding coast

road (R297) until you see signs for Aughris Head.

- - - - - - - - - - - - -

TRIP HIGHLIGHT

### ⑧ Aughris Head

An invigorating 5km walk traces the cliffs around remote Aughris Head, where dolphins and seals can often be seen swimming into the bay. Birdwatchers should look out for kittiwakes, fulmars, guillemots, shags, storm petrels and curlews along the way. In a stupendous setting on the lovely beach by the cliff walk, the Beach Bar (p293) is tucked inside a 17th-century thatched

# IRELAND'S SEAWEED BATHS

Ireland's only native spa therapy is the stuff of mermaid (or merman) fantasies. Part of Irish homeopathy for centuries, steaming your pores open then submerging yourself in a seaweed bath is said to help rheumatism and arthritis, thyroid imbalances, even hangovers. Certainly it leaves your skin feeling baby-soft: seaweed's silky oils contain a massive concentration of iodine, a key presence in most moisturising creams.

Seaweed baths are prevalent along the west coast, but two places stand out. **Kilcullen's Seaweed Baths** (☎096-36238; http://homepage.eircom.net/~seaweedbaths/frame.htm; Cliff Rd, Enniscrone; baths from €25; ⊙10am-10pm Jun-Aug, noon-8pm Mon-Fri, 10am-8pm Sat & Sun Apr, May, Sep & Oct, noon-8pm Mon & Thu, 10am-8pm Sat & Sun Nov-Mar), in Enniscrone, is the most traditional and has buckets of character. Set within a grand Edwardian structure, it seems perfectly fitting to sit with your head exposed and your body ensconced in an individual cedar steam cabinet before plunging into one of the original gigantic porcelain baths filled with amber water and seaweed.

For an altogether more modern setting, try **Voya Seaweed Baths** (☎071-916 8686; www.voyaseaweedbaths.com; Shore Rd, Strandhill; baths from €25; ⊙10am-8pm), which has a beachfront location.

If too much relaxation is barely enough, both establishments also offer the chance to indulge in various other seaweed treatments, including body wraps and massages.

cottage, with cracking traditional music sessions and superb seafood.

✗ p293

**The Drive »** From Aughris follow the N59 southeast and onto the N4 towards Sligo until you see a sign for Dromahair (R287). Take this small, leafy road east, skirting the south of Lough Gill and on through Dromahair, making sure to stop at Cheese Etc for some excellent picnic supplies.

- - - - - - - - - - - - - -

### ❾ Lough Gill

The mirrorlike 'Lake of Brightness', Lough Gill is home to as many legends as fish. One that can be tested easily is the story that a silver bell from the abbey in Sligo was thrown into the lough and only those free from sin can hear it peeling. (We didn't hear it.)

Two magical swaths of woodland – **Hazelwood** and **Slish Wood** – have loop trails; from the latter, there are good views of Innisfree Island, subject of WB Yeats' poem 'The Lake Isle of Innisfree'. You can take a cruise on the lake from **Parke's Castle**.

**The Drive »** Having soaked up the atmosphere of Yeats' backyard, make your way a few kilometres north to the hub of Yeats country, Sligo town.

- - - - - - - - - - - - - -

### ❿ Sligo Town

Sligo town is in no hurry to shed its cultural traditions but it doesn't sell them out, either. Pedestrian streets lined with inviting shop fronts, stone bridges spanning the River Garavogue, and *céilidh (*sessions of traditional music and dancing) spilling from pubs contrast with contemporary art and glass towers rising from prominent corners of the compact town. A major draw of Sligo's **County Museum** (☎071-911 1679; Stephen St; ⊙9.30am-12.30pm Tue-Sat year-round, 2-4.50pm Tue-Sat May-Sep) is the Yeats room, which features photographs, letters and newspaper cuttings connected with the poet WB Yeats, as well as drawings by his brother Jack B Yeats, one of Ireland's most important modern artists.

✗ 🛏 p293, p301

# Eating & Sleeping

## Westport ❶

### ✗ An Port Mór  Modern Irish €€

(☎098-26730; www.anportmor.com; 1 Brewery
Pl; mains €15-28; ⊘5-9.30pm Tue-Sat) Hidden
down a lane off Bridge St, proprietor-chef
Frankie Mallon's little restaurant packs quite
a punch. It's an intimate place with a series of
long narrow rooms and a menu that features
excellent meats and much-lauded seafood
(try the Clew Bay scallops). Most everything is
procured from the region.

## Achill Island ❷

### ✗ Chalet  Seafood €€

(☎098-43157; www.keembayfishproducts.ie;
Keel; mains €16-29; ⊘6-10pm daily summer,
shorter hours rest of year) The proprietors of
Keem Bay Fish Products have been serving up
their acclaimed smoked local salmon and other
delicacies at this restaurant for decades. The
menu changes with what's fresh, but expect a
meal of the very best seafood.

### ⌗ Bervie  B&B €€

(☎098-43114; www.bervie-guesthouse-achill.
com; Keel; s/d from €85/110; [P]) Once a
coastguard station, this delightful B&B is a
wonderfully friendly place with views over the
ocean and direct access to the beach from the
well-tended garden. The 14 rooms are bright but
cosy. There's a playroom with a pool table for
wet days. Lauded evening meals are available
on request.

## Aughris Head ❽

### ✗ Beach Bar  Seafood €€

(☎071-917 6465; www.thebeachbarsligo.com;
mains €10-25, tent/van sites from €12/22,
s/d from €50/80; ⊘ food served 1-8pm daily

summer, Fri-Sun winter; 🛜) In a sheltered
setting on the lovely beach by the cliff walk, the
pub in this 17th-century thatched cottage hosts
cracking traditional-music sessions and serves
superb seafood, including creamy chowder and
poached salmon. The owners also operate the
**Aughris House B&B** next door, with seven
comfy rooms and adjacent campsites.

## Sligo Town ❿

### ✗ Hargadons  Pub €€

(☎071-915 3709; www.hargadons.com; 4/5
O'Connell St; mains €8-20; ⊘11am-11pm Mon-
Thu & Sun, to 12.30am Fri & Sat, food noon-9pm
Mon-Sat) You'll have a hard time leaving this
superb 1864 pub with its winning blend of
Old World fittings and gastropub style. Its
uneven floors, peat fire, antique signage, snug
corners and bowed shelves laden down with
ancient bottles give it a wonderful charm. The
great-value food is renowned, combining local
ingredients such as oysters with continental
flair.

### ✗ Lyons Cafe  Modern European €

(☎071-914 2969; www.lyonscafe.com; Quay
St; mains €7-15; ⊘9am-6pm Mon-Sat) Sligo's
flagship department store, Lyons, opened in
1878 – with original leadlight windows and
squeaky timber floors – and has been going
strong since 1923. Its airy 1st-floor cafe is
anything but stodgy, and acclaimed chef (and
cookbook author) Gary Stafford offers a fresh
and seasonal menu that's inventive yet casual.

### ⌗ Pearse Lodge  B&B €€

(☎071-916 1090; www.pearselodge.com; Pearse
Rd; s/d from €50/80; [@][🛜]) Welcoming owners
Mary and Kieron have four stylish guest rooms
with hardwood floors. The breakfast menu
includes smoked salmon, French toast with
bananas and homemade muesli. A sunny sitting
room opens to a garden. It's 700m southwest
of the centre.

# Sligo Surrounds

## 27

*Sligo is as varied as a county this size gets. On top of its exceptional beaches, there's a wealth of prehistoric sites and Yeats literary heritage, along with fine traditional bars.*

## TRIP HIGHLIGHTS

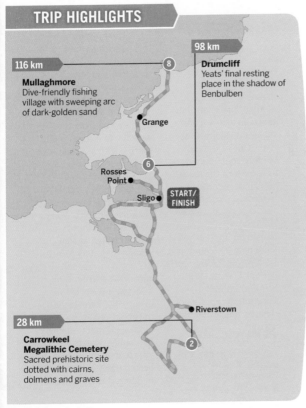

**116 km**

**Mullaghmore**
Dive-friendly fishing village with sweeping arc of dark-golden sand

**98 km**

**Drumcliff**
Yeats' final resting place in the shadow of Benbulben

**28 km**

**Carrowkeel Megalithic Cemetery**
Sacred prehistoric site dotted with cairns, dolmens and graves

**5 DAYS**
**155KM / 96 MILES**

## GREAT FOR...

### BEST TIME TO GO
May, June or September, when the weather is best and crowds less.

### ESSENTIAL PHOTO
Drumcliff cemetery with Benbulben in the background.

### BEST FOR ANCIENT HISTORY
South Sligo is awash with megalithic dolmens and burial grounds.

**Sligo** Mullaghmore's coastline

# 27 Sligo Surrounds

Sligo offers wild beauty, but with quietude, too. Lush fields, lakes and flat-topped mountains provided inspiration for William Butler Yeats. And among the stretches of golden sands and legendary breaks that lure the surfing cognoscenti, you'll find a bounty of prehistoric sites, elegant Georgian towns, little fishing villages and good old-fashioned country hospitality.

## ❶ Sligo Town

For a small provincial hub, Sligo, with its galleries, museum and atmospheric old-man pubs, is quite the cultural magnet. Thanks largely to WB Yeats' childhood affection for, and his association with, the area, Sligo attracts visitors keen to learn more about the poet's formative environment. In the **Yeats Memorial Building** (☎071-914 2693; www. yeatssociety.com; Hyde Bridge; adult/child €2/free; ⊙10am-5pm Tue-Fri, to 2pm Sat), in a pretty setting near Hyde Bridge, you can visit the **WB Yeats Exhibition**, with a video presentation and valuable draft manuscripts; the €2 exhibition catalogue makes a good souvenir of Sligo. The charming **tearoom** has outdoor tables overlooking the river. One of Ireland's leading contemporary-arts centres, the **Model** (☎071-914 1405; www. themodel.ie; The Mall; admission varies; ⊙10am-5.30pm Tue-Sat, 10.30am-3.30pm Sun) houses an impressive collection of contemporary Irish art, including works by Jack B Yeats (WB's brother), as well as a program of experimental theatre, music and film.

✕ ⊨ p293, p301

The Drive ≫ Heading south and west off the N4 road, Carrowkeel Megalithic Cemetery is closer to Boyle than Sligo

TRIP HIGHLIGHT

## ❷ Carrowkeel Megalithic Cemetery

With a God's-eye view of the county from high in the Bricklieve Mountains, it's little wonder this hilltop site was sacred in prehistoric times. The windswept location is simultaneously eerie and uplifting, its undeveloped, spectacular setting providing a momentous atmosphere. Dotted with around 14 cairns, dolmens and the scattered remnants of other graves, Carrowkeel dates from the late Stone Age (3000 to 2000 BC). Climbing up from the car park the first tomb you'll reach is Cairn G. Above its entrance is a roofbox aligned with the midsummer sunset which illuminates the inner chamber. The only other such roofbox known in Ireland is that at Newgrange in County Meath. Everywhere you look across the surrounding hills you'll see evidence of early life here, including about 140 **stone circles**, all that remain of the foundations of a large village thought to have been inhabited by the builders of the tombs.

**The Drive ❯❯** Head south from Carrowkeel and into Kesh (sometimes spelt Keash), around 6km south of Ballymote. The Caves of Kesh are rich with mythology and are believed to extend for miles. From here continue till you meet the R295 and turn right for Ballymote and across the N4 to Riverstown.

- - - - - - - - - - - - - - -

### ❸ Riverstown

The endearing **Sligo Folk Park** (📞071-916 5001; www.sligofolkpark.com; Millview House, Riverstown; adult/child €5/3; ☺noon-5pm Sun & bank holidays year-round, 10am-5.30pm Mon-Sat Jun-Aug, 10am-5pm Mon-Fri Sep-May) revolves around a lovingly restored 19th-century cottage. Humble thatched structures complement this centrepiece, along with scattered farm tools and an exhibit that honours the old country life. Another fine reason

### LINK YOUR TRIP

**25** **Loughs of the West**
From the northwest's wild coast, turn it down a little for a tour of the west's serene lakelands, from Sligo on the N17.

**32** **Northwest on Adrenalin**
There's plenty more surf to be found on Donegal's beach beauties. From Grange stick north on the N15.

to come here is to attend a course on permaculture, bee-keeping or even solar-panel building at the green-roofed **Gyreum** (☎071-916 5994; www.gyreum. com; Corlisheen, Riverstown; dm €17-21, d €50-54; **P**), a pudding-shaped building hidden by the surrounding hills. You can also give your own sermon on a Sunday morning, volunteer to help out or stay in the simple rooms.

**The Drive »** Returning to the N4, follow the Sligo road for some 15km till you veer off onto the R292 to the seaside resort of Strandhill.

DEB SNELSON/GETTY IMAGES ©

## ❹ Strandhill

The great Atlantic rollers that sweep the shorefront of Strandhill make this long, red-gold **beach** unsafe for swimming. They have, however, made it a surfing mecca. Gear hire and lessons can be arranged through **Perfect Day Surf Shop** (☎087 202 9399; www.perfectdaysurfing. ie; Airport Rd; lessons adult/child from €30/20; ☻Apr-Oct). Alternatively, take a gentler, warmer dip in the **Voya Seaweed Baths** (p292). A few kilometres towards Sligo, you can walk – at low tide only! – to **Coney Island**. Its New York namesake was supposedly named by a man from Rosses Point. The island's wishing well is reputed to have been dug by St Patrick (who, if all these tales are to be

trusted, led a *very* busy life). Check tide times to avoid getting stranded.

✗ ⊨ p301

**The Drive »** Continue along the R292 and then follow the R291 out of town and along the coast to Rosses Point, 8km northwest of Sligo. This road can get busy with holidaymakers in summer.

## ❺ Rosses Point

Rosses Point has two wonderful beaches and one of Ireland's most challenging and renowned golf links, **County Sligo Golf Course** (☎071-917 7171; www.countysligogolfclub.

ie; green fees €125-140; ☻Apr-Oct), which attracts golfers from all over the world. Fringed by the Atlantic and lying in the shadow of Benbulben, this is one of Ireland's greatest and most picturesque golf links. Offshore, the odd **Metal Man** beacon dates from 1821. **Harry's Bar** (on your right as you enter town) has a historic well, aquarium and maritime bric-a-brac. It's been in the same family since 1870 and serves good, classic fare.

⊨ p301

**The Drive »** Returning via the R291 you'll pick up the busy N15,

**Drumcliff** Benbulben

where you head north to the quaint town of Drumcliff, at the foot of Benbulben, Yeats' final resting place.

TRIP HIGHLIGHT

### ⑥ Drumcliff

Visible right along Sligo's northern coast, **Benbulben** (525m) resembles a table covered by a pleated cloth: its limestone plateau is uncommonly flat, and its near-vertical sides are scored by earthen ribs. Benbulben's beauty was not lost on WB Yeats. Before the poet died in Menton, France, in 1939, he had requested that should he die there that 'after a year or so' he be dug up and brought to Sligo. Someone was buried here, but there is an ongoing debate as to whether it was actually Yeats or not. Still, **Yeats' grave** is next to the doorway of the Protestant church in Drumcliff, and his youthful bride Georgie Hyde-Lee is buried alongside. Historic **Lissadell House**, west of Drumcliff off the N15 just past Yeats Tavern, was recently restored to its former glory by its private owners but is not open to visitors.

**The Drive »** The light on Benbulben looming in the distance inland often changes it from dark blue, to purple or a mossy shade of green. Continue on the N15 less than 9km into the small village of Grange.

### ⑦ Grange

From the village of Grange, signs point towards **Streedagh Beach**, a grand crescent of sand that saw some 1100 sailors perish when three ships from the Spanish Armada were wrecked nearby. Views extend from the beach to the cliffs at Slieve League in Donegal. Locals regularly swim here, even in winter. Don't leave

## MICHAEL QUIRKE: WOODCARVER OF WINE STREET

The inconspicuous studio of Michael Quirke, woodcarver, raconteur and local character, is filled with the scents of locally felled timbers and offcuts of beech stumps. A converted butcher shop on Wine St in Sligo town, it retains some of the implements of the butcher's trade, including an electric bone saw. Quirke, himself formerly a butcher, began to use his tools for cutting and carving wood in 1968. He divided his time between his twin callings for 20 years, after which he gave up meat, so to speak. Quirke's art is inspired by Irish mythology, a subject about which he is passionate and knowledgable, and as he carves he readily chats with the customers and the curious who enter his shop and end up staying for hours. He draws unforced connections between Ireland's shifting myths, music, history, flora, fauna and contemporary events, as well as comparisons in the wider world, such as Australian Aboriginal and Native North American lore. As he talks and carves, Quirke frequently pulls out a county map, pointing to places that spring from the conversation, leading you on your own magical, mystical tour of the county.

Grange without stopping into **Langs Pub** (☑071-916 3105; www.langs.ie; ⊙noon-11.30pm Mon & Wed-Thu, from 5pm Tue, noon-12.30am Fri & Sat) for a bite or to water the horses in the well-preserved front bar, with its bottles of Guinness among the old washing powder and cereal boxes. It's one of the county's finest old grocery-draper-bars.

The Drive » Keep heading north on the N15 till you reach the sleepy crossroads of Cliffony. Take a left at the church, onto the R279 to Mullaghmore.

TRIP HIGHLIGHT

### 8 Mullaghmore

The sweeping arc of dark-golden sand and the safe shallow waters make the pretty fishing village of Mullaghmore a popular family destination. It was a favoured holiday spot of Lord Mountbatten, who was killed here when the IRA rigged his boat with explosives in 1979. Take time to drive the scenic road looping around Mullaghmore Head, where wide shafts of rock slice into the Atlantic surf. En route you'll pass **Classiebawn Castle** (closed to the public), a neo-Gothic tur-reted pile built for Lord Palmerston in 1856 and later home to the ill-fated Lord Mountbatten. Mullaghmore Head is becoming known as one of Ireland's premier **big wave surf** spots, with swells of up to 17m allowing for Hawaiian-style adventure. Mullaghmore's clear waters, rocky outcrops and coves are also ideal for diving.

🛏 p301

The Drive » It's a straight run back on the N15 some 27km back to Sligo, where you can enjoy a creamy pint in a snug at one of the region's finest traditional pubs, Connolly's on Holborn St.

# Eating & Sleeping

## Sligo Town ❶

### ✗ Kate's Kitchen
Cafe €

(www.kateskitchen.ie; Castle St; mains from €6; ◷8.30am-5.30pm Mon-Sat) Only the best local foodstuffs are sold at this lovely, contemporary shop. All the fixings for a prime picnic are combined with prepared foods. It also does a big lunchtime trade.

### ✗ Montmartre
French €€

(☏071-916 9901; www.montmartrerestaurant. ie; 1 Market Yard; mains €20-25; ◷5-11pm Tue-Sat) Tucked away on a quiet back road by the market, this excellent French restaurant is unpretentious, simply decorated and good value if you get one of the set-meal specials. The menu offers local seafood, but meat lovers and vegetarians are well catered for, too. Book ahead.

### ⌂ Sligo Park Hotel
Hotel €€

(☏071-919 0400; www.sligoparkhotel.com; Pearse Rd/R287; r from €90; [P][🖥][🛜][♿]) Set 3km south of the centre in landscaped gardens with mature trees, this modern hotel is large but tranquil. The pretty, tastefully decorated rooms are bright and modern.

## Strandhill ❹

### ✗ Trá Bán
Modern Irish €€

(☏071-912 8402; www.trabansligo.ie; Shore Rd; mains €18-25; ◷5-9.30pm; [👶]) This justifiably popular 1st-floor restaurant above the Strand Bar serves excellent pasta, steaks and seafood. The crab-claws starter is all briney joy. It has a relaxed atmosphere and is popular with local families who've something to celebrate. Book in advance.

### ⌂ Strandhill Lodge & Suites
Guesthouse €€

(☏071-912 2122; www.strandhilllodgeandsuites. com; Top Rd/R292; s/d from €65/100; [🛜]) Up

the hill, this excellent guesthouse offers 22 bright, spacious rooms with king-size beds, hotel-quality design and trendy neutral styling. Room sizes vary, but most have fabulous views down to the ocean and terraces or balconies.

### ⌂ Surf & Stay Lodge & Hostel
Lodge €

(☏071-916 8313; www.surfnstay.ie; Shore Rd; dm from €20, s/d from €40/60; [🛜]) Surfers thaw out by the open fire in the common room of the 34-bed hostel portion of this two-building complex. Rooms in the adjoining house are B&B style and, while small, are comfy. Some share bathrooms. The beach is close and there is an on-site surf school.

## Rosses Point ❺

### ⌂ Yeats Country Hotel
Hotel €€

(☏071-917 7211; www.yeatscountryhotel.com; s/d from €69/90) There isn't a town centre as such, so this huge three-star hotel more or less stands in for the heart of Rosses Point. It has a commanding presence overlooking a beach and the County Sligo golf course, and attracts golfers and families. Rooms are large, and many afford sea views. There's a popular restaurant; food is also served at its two bars.

## Mullaghmore ❽

### ⌂ Pier Head Hotel
Hotel €€

(☏071-916 6171; www.pierheadhotel.ie; Mullaghmore; s/d from €50/80; ◷closed late Dec; [🛜][♿]) Enjoy magnificent views from this hotel by the harbour. The 40 rooms are clean and crisp (request one with a view across Donegal Bay), and there's a panoramic rooftop terrace with hot tub, indoor pool and decent food (mains from €10 to €21) in the bar.

# County Clare

**28**

*Experience scenic coastline including the breathtaking Cliffs of Moher, the Aran Islands, market towns with cracking pubs, and Clare's jewel, the geological wonder of The Burren.*

## TRIP HIGHLIGHTS

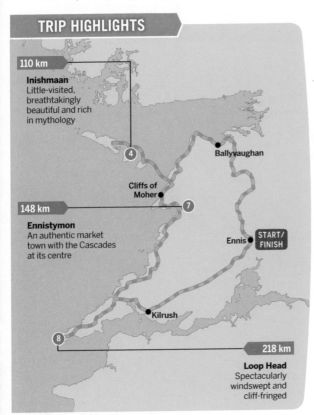

**110 km**

**Inishmaan**
Little-visited, breathtakingly beautiful and rich in mythology

**④**

**Ballyvaughan**

**Cliffs of Moher**

**148 km**
**⑦**

**Ennistymon**
An authentic market town with the Cascades at its centre

**Ennis** **START/ FINISH**

**Kilrush**

**⑧**

**218 km**

**Loop Head**
Spectacularly windswept and cliff-fringed

**7 DAYS**
**299KM / 185 MILES**

**GREAT FOR...**

**BEST TIME TO GO**
Spring, for the awakening of nature in The Burren.

**ESSENTIAL PHOTO**

A sunset shot over the Atlantic from Dún Aengus, Inishmór.

**BEST FOR RAMBLING**

Take blustery cliff walks, or cross The Burren on foot.

**Cliffs of Moher** The cliffs rise to a height of 203m

# 28 County Clare

From friendly market towns Ennis and Ennistymon down the cliff-fringed coast of Clare to its southernmost tip, the raggedly beautiful Loop Head, you'll encounter sandy strands and quiet coves just begging for company. Cruise out to the Aran Islands for their historic relics and a taste of a simpler life before returning to the mainland's homely resorts of Kilrush and Kilkee.

## ❶ Ennis

Ennis (Inis) is the busy commercial centre of Clare. It lies on the banks of the smallish River Fergus, which runs east, then south into the Shannon Estuary. It's the place to stay if you want a bit of urban flair; short on sights, the town's strengths are its food, lodging and traditional entertainment. The town's medieval origins are indicated by its irregular, narrow streets. Its most important historical site is **Ennis Friary**, founded

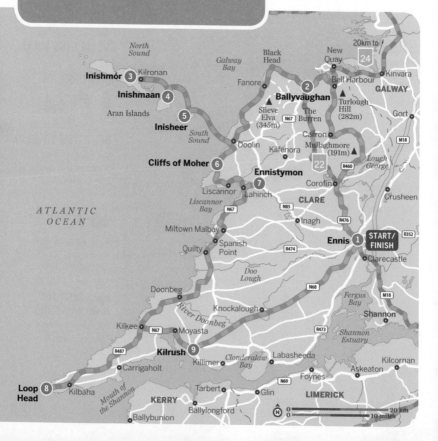

in the 13th century by the O'Briens, kings of Thomond, who also built a castle here.

 p46, p269, p309

**The Drive >>** A jaunt north on the R476 through Corofin finds you in wondrous karst limestone Burren heartland. Make sure you stop and take in primroses and other flora dotted in the crevices in spring. Skirting the Burren National Park, you'll turn left onto the N67 to get to Ballyvaughan. It's 55km from Ennis to Ballyvaughan taking this route.

## ❷ Ballyvaughan

Something of a hub for the otherwise dispersed charms of The Burren, Ballyvaughan (Baile Uí Bheacháin) sits between the hard land of the hills and a quiet leafy corner of Galway Bay. Just west of the village's junction is the **quay**, built in 1829 at

## LINK YOUR TRIP

**Best of the West**
**22** Having sampled the delicious Clare coast, take a wild southerly bite of Kerry and West Cork from Limerick down.

**Mountains & Moors**
**24**
If you like The Burren, you'll love Connemara. Join this trip at Ballyvaughan and wander west at Galway.

a time when boats traded with the Aran Islands and Galway, exporting grain and bacon and bringing in turf – a scarce commodity in the windswept rocks of Burren.

 p309

**The Drive >>** From Ballyvaughan it's a leisurely 40-minute coastal route down to Doolin, with splendid views over to the Aran Islands on your right. From here, park up and catch the ferry (p308) to Inishmór, the first of the three splendid Aran Islands.

## ❸ Inishmór

Most visitors who venture out to the islands don't make it beyond 14.5km long Inishmór (Árainn) and its main attraction, **Dún Aengus** (Dún Aonghasa; www.heritageireland.ie/en/west/dunaonghasa/; adult/child €4/2; ⊘9.30am-6pm Apr-Oct, 9.30am-4pm Nov-Mar, closed Mon & Tue Jan & Feb), the stunning stone fort perched perilously on the island's towering cliffs. The arid landscape west of Kilronan (Cill Rónáin), Inishmór's main settlement, is dominated by stone walls, boulders, scattered buildings and the odd patch of deep-green grass and potato plants. It gets pretty crowded in summer, but on foot or on bike (for hire at the pier), you can happily set your own pace. There's an EU Blue Flag white-sand beach

(awarded for cleanliness) at **Kilmurvey**, peacefully situated west of bustling Kilronan.

 p269, p309

**The Drive >>** It's easy to travel between the Aran Islands, but you'll need to prebook your ticket with one of the ferry companies and check their timetables for crossing times.

TRIP HIGHLIGHT

## ❹ Inishmaan

The least-visited of the islands, with the smallest population, Inishmaan (Inis Meáin) is a rocky respite. Early Christian monks seeking solitude were drawn to Inishmaan, as was the author JM Synge, who spent five summers here over a century ago. The island they knew largely survives today: stoic cows and placid sheep, impressive old forts and warm-hearted locals, who may tell you with a glint in their eye that they had a hard night on the whiskey the previous evening. Inishmaan's scenery is breathtaking, with a jagged coastline of startling cliffs, empty beaches, and fields where the main crop seems to be stone. **Teach Synge** (☑099-73036; admission €3; ⊘by appointment), a thatched cottage on the road just before you head up to the fort, is where JM Synge spent his summers.

 p309

### ⑤ Inisheer

Inisheer (Inis Oírr), the smallest of the Aran Islands with a population of only 200, has a palpable sense of enchantment, enhanced by the island's deep-rooted mythology, its devotion to traditional culture and its ethereal landscapes. Wandering the lanes, with their ivy-covered stone walls, and making discoveries here and there is the best way to experience the island. At **O'Brien's Castle**, a 100m climb to the island's highest point yields dramatic views over clover-covered fields to the beach and harbour. Dating from 1960, an iconic island sight is a freighter, **Plassy**, that was thrown up on the rocks in bad weather. An aerial shot of the wreck was used in the opening sequence of the seminal TV series *Father Ted*.

🛏 p309

**The Drive** ⟩⟩ From Doolin, it's a pleasurable 10-minute cruise on the coastal R478 to the famed, unmistakable Cliffs of Moher.

### ⑥ Cliffs of Moher

Star of a million tourist brochures, the Cliffs of Moher (Aillte an Mothair, or Ailltreacha Mothair) is one of the most popular sights in Ireland. But like many an ageing star, you have to look beyond the famous facade to appreciate the inherent attributes behind the postcard image. The entirely vertical cliffs rise to a height of 203m, their edge falling away abruptly into the constantly churning sea. A series of heads, the dark limestone seems to march in a rigid formation that amazes, no matter how many times you look. Such appeal comes at a price: mobs. But, if you're willing to walk

**Aran Islands** Black Fort wall, Inishmór

for 10 minutes past the end of the 'Moher Wall' south, there's still a **trail** along the cliffs to Hag's Head – few venture this far. A vast **visitor centre** (www.cliffsofmoher.ie; admission to site adult/child €6/ free; ⏱9am-9pm Jul & Aug, to 7.30pm June, to 7pm May & Sep, to 6.30pm Apr, to 6pm Mar & Oct, to 5pm Nov-Feb; 🛜) is set back into the side of a hill, Teletubbies style. For uncommon views of the cliffs and wildlife you might consider a **cruise**. The boat operators in Doolin offer popular tours of the cliffs.

The Drive » A short drive takes you to the small seaside resort of Lahinch and from there up the proverbial hill (in this case the N67) to a more traditional, authentic rural experience, at the market town of Ennistymon.

- - - - - - - - - - - - -

TRIP HIGHLIGHT

**7 Ennistymon**

Ennistymon (Inis Díomáin) is a genuinely charming market town. On the first Monday of each month **Ennistymon Horse Market** is one of Clare's great spectacles: the horse market literally takes over the town's streets as people from around the region come to buy and sell donkeys, mares, thoroughbreds and old nags.

The town's biggest draw, though, is the roaring Cascades, the stepped falls of the River Inagh, which accompany languorous walks downstream.

🛏 p309

The Drive » It's about a 74km scenic trip down the coastal N67 and then the R487. The land from the old-fashioned resort of Kilkee south to Loop Head has subtle undulations that suddenly end in dramatic cliffs falling off into the Atlantic. It's a windswept place with timeless striations of old stone walls.

# GETTING TO & FROM THE ARAN ISLANDS

Doolin is one of two ferry departure points to the Aran Islands (from April to October); the other is at Rossaveal in County Galway, from where there are year-round crossings. Various ferry companies offer departures in season from Doolin. It takes around half an hour to cover the 8km to Inisheer; a boat to Inishmór takes at least 1½ hours with an Inisheer stop. Ferries to Inishmaan are infrequent. Rates vary, but Inisheer should cost about €20 to €25 return. Each boat has an office at Doolin Pier at the harbour, or you can book online. Most of the boats also offer various Cliffs of Moher tours, which are best done late in the afternoon when the light is from the west.

**Cliffs of Moher Cruises** (☏065-707 5949; www.mohercruises.com; Doolin Pier; ◷Apr-Oct) Offers combined Aran Islands trips with Cliffs of Moher cruises on the *Jack B*.

**O'Brien Line** (☏065-707 5618; www.obrienline.com) Usually has the most sailings; also offers cliff cruises and combo tickets.

The following ferry company services the islands year-round from Rossaveal, 38km west of Galway:

**Aran Island Ferries** (☏091-568 903; www.aranislandferries.com; 19 Eyre Sq, Galway Ticket Office; adult/child return from €25/13; ◷8am-5pm) Up to five return crossings daily in high season (three in low) to Inishmór and twice daily to Inishmaan and Inisheer. Shuttle bus available from Galway.

Alternatively you can pick up an eight-minute flight from Connemara airport at Inverin (also known as Minna airport), 27km west of Galway, on a nine-seater plane.

**Aer Arann** (☏091-593 034; www.aerarannislands.ie; return adult/child €49/27) Up to 25 return flights daily in high season (10 in low) to each of the islands. Seats cost €45 return.

---

**TRIP HIGHLIGHT**

## 8 Loop Head

Discriminating travellers are coming here for coastal views that in many ways are more dramatic than the Cliffs of Moher. On a clear day, Loop Head (Ceann Léime), Clare's southernmost point, has magnificent views south to the Dingle Peninsula crowned by Mt Brandon (951m), and north to the Aran Islands and Galway Bay. There are bracing walks in the area, and a long hiking trail runs along the cliffs to Kilkee.

A working **lighthouse** (complete with Fresnel lens) is the punctuation on the point.

The Drive ›› A scenic 40km drive north on the R487 and west on the N67 brings you to the bustling local resort of Kilrush.

---

## 9 Kilrush

Kilrush (Cill Rois) is a small, atmospheric town that overlooks the Shannon Estuary and the hills of Kerry to the south. It has the western coast's biggest **marina** (www.kilrushcreekmarina.ie) at Kilrush Creek, and offers various opportunities to experience the bottlenose

dolphins living in the Shannon. The remarkable 'lost' **Vandeleur Walled Garden** (www.vandeleurwalledgarden.ie; Killimer Rd; ◷10am-7pm daily Apr-Sep, 9.30am-5pm Mon-Sat Oct-Mar) was the private domain of the wealthy Vandeleur family – merchants and landowners. The gardens are just east of the town centre and have been redesigned and planted with colourful tropical and rare plants.

✗ p309

The Drive ›› After all that sea air and seafood you'll be ready for a straight 40-minute jaunt (on the N68) inland back to Ennis.

# Eating & Sleeping

## Ennis ❶

### 🛏 Old Ground Hotel · Hotel €€

(☏065-682 8127; www.flynnhotels.com; O'Connell St; s/d from €120/150; ⓟ@🛜) A seasoned, charming and congenial space of polished floorboards, cornice-work, antiques and open fires, the lobby is always a scene: old friends sinking into sofas, deals cut at the tables, and ladies from the neighbouring church's altar society exchanging gossip over tea. Parts of this smart and rambling landmark date back to the 1800s.

## Ballyvaughan ❷

### 🛏 Gregan's Castle Hotel · Hotel €€€

(☏065-707 7005; www.gregans.ie; N67; s/d/ste from €220/280/345; ⓟ🛜) This hidden Clare gem is housed in a grand estate dating to the 19th century, some 6km south of Ballyvaughan at Corkscrew Hill. The 21 rooms and suites are plush, with enough modern flair to make them stylish (but there are no TVs). Some have private garden areas. Inventive fresh fare sourced locally is served in the restaurant.

## Inishmór ❸

### 🛏 Kilmurvey House · B&B €€

(☏099-61218; www.kilmurveyhouse.com; Kilmurvey; s/d from €50/90; ☷mid-Apr–mid-Oct) On the path leading to Dún Aengus is this grand 18th-century stone mansion. It's a beautiful setting, and the 12 rooms are well maintained. Hearty meals (dinner €30) incorporate vegetables from the garden and local fish and meats. You can swim at a pretty beach that's a short walk from the house.

## Inishmaan ❹

### 🛏 Inis Meáin · Inn €€€

(☏086 826 6026; www.inismeain.com; r per 2 nights €480-960; ☷Mar-Sep; 🛜) An anomaly on the island, where almost everything is as basic as a rock – or is a rock – this smart boutique inn has five lovely suites crafted from local materials (rocks). Views go on forever, and you can grab a bike and spend your day exploring in blessed isolation. Rates – minimum two-night stay – include many extras. The restaurant serves a changing menu of exquisite dishes made from local foods (dinner mains €15 to €35). It's open to nonguests, but book.

## Inisheer ❺

### 🛏 Fisherman's Cottage & South Aran House · B&B €€

(☏099-75073; www.southaran.com; Castle Village; s/d €49/80; ☷Apr-Oct; 🛜) Slow-food enthusiasts run this sprightly B&B and cafe that's a mere five-minute walk from the pier; look for the lavender growing in profusion at the entrance. The meals celebrate local seafood and organic produce (dinner mains €12 to €20). Nonguests can enjoy cakes by day and dinner by night, but will need to book.

## Ennistymon ❼

### 🛏 Falls Hotel · Hotel €€

(☏065-707 1004; www.fallshotel.ie; off N67; r from €95; ⓟ🛜🏊) Built on the ruins of an O'Brien castle, this handsome and sprawling Georgian house was once Ennistymon House, the family home of Caitlín MacNamara, who married Dylan Thomas. With 140 modern rooms and a large, enclosed pool, the hotel's view of the Cascades from the entrance steps is breathtaking, and there are 20 hectares of wooded gardens.

## Kilrush ❾

### ✕ Quayside Restaurant · Irish €€

(17 Frances St; meals €5-11; ☷9.30am-5.15pm Mon-Sat) Local gossip is dissected each morning here, amid the smells of fresh coffee and the wondrous baked treats emerging from the oven. Tables overlook the town-side bustle or boats moored out back.

# STRETCH YOUR LEGS
# GALWAY CITY

**Start/Finish** Spanish Arch

**Distance** 1.8km

**Duration** 2 hours

The best way to soak up Galway's convivial atmosphere is to wander its cobblestoned streets. This walk takes you from the city's medieval roots, through its cafe- and bar-lined heart to some of its finest historic buildings.

Take this walk on Trips

## Spanish Arch & Medieval Walls

Framing the river east of Wolfe Tone Bridge, the Spanish Arch (1584) is thought to be an extension of Galway's medieval walls. The arch appears to have been designed as a passageway through which ships entered the city to unload goods, such as wine and brandy from Spain. Today, the lawns and riverside form a gathering place for locals and visitors on any sunny day.

**The Walk »** A mere step from the Spanish Arch, you can't miss the modernist Galway City Museum. For cake and coffee before you go, Ard Bia, right opposite, will hit the spot beautifully.

## Galway City Museum

The **Galway City Museum** (www.galway citymuseum.ie; Spanish Pde; ⊗10am-5pm Tue-Sat year-round, noon-5pm Sun Easter-Sep) is in a glossy, glassy building that reflects the old walls. Exhibits trace aspects of daily life through Galway's history; especially good are the areas dealing with life – smelly and otherwise – during medieval times. Look for the photos of President John F Kennedy's 1963 visit to Galway, including one with dewy-eyed nuns looking on adoringly.

**The Walk »** A few minutes' walk from here, crossing the plaza and heading up bustling Quay St, take the first right at the Quays Pub onto Druid Lane, also home to the acclaimed Druid Theatre.

## Hall of the Red Earl

Back in the 13th century when the de Burgo family ran the show in Galway, Richard – the Red Earl – had a large **hall** (www.galwaycivictrust.ie; Druid Lane; ⊗9am-5pm Mon-Fri year-round, 10am-1pm Sat May-Sep) built as a seat of power. The hall fell into ruin and was lost until 1997 when expansion of the city's Custom House uncovered its foundations. It now gives a fascinating sense of Galway life some 900 years ago.

**The Walk »** Back on Quay St walk up as far as Neachtain's pub, and turn left onto Upper Cross St where you continue for 50m. You'll spot the Church of St Nicholas on your right.

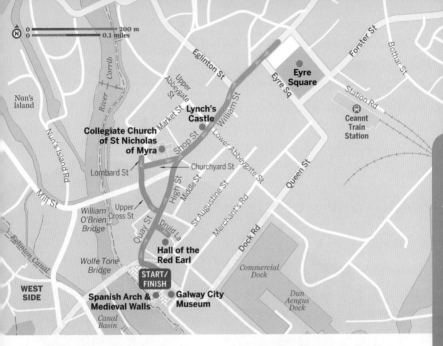

## Collegiate Church of St Nicholas of Myra

Crowned by a pyramidal spire, the **Collegiate Church of St Nicholas of Myra** (Market St; admission by donation; ⏱9am-5.45pm Mon-Sat, 1-5pm Sun Apr-Sep, 10am-4pm Mon-Sat, 1-5pm Sun Oct-Mar) is Ireland's largest medieval parish church still in use. Dating from 1320, the church has been rebuilt and enlarged over the centuries. St Nicholas is the patron saint of sailors – Christopher Columbus reputedly worshipped here in 1477.

The Walk ⟩⟩ Outside on Lombard St, head east along Churchyard St to Shop St and straight up to Eyre Sq, 600m from the church.

## Eyre Square

Galway's central public square is an open space with sculptures and pathways. The eastern side is taken up almost entirely by the Hotel Meyrick, an elegant grey limestone pile. Guarding the upper side of the square, **Browne's Doorway** (1627), a classy, if forlorn, fragment is from the home of one of the city's merchant rulers.

The Walk ⟩⟩ From north of the square, make your way back down Shop St. Not far down on the right-hand side you'll spot the stone facade of Lynch's Castle, now a bank.

## Lynch's Castle

Considered the finest town castle in Ireland, the old stone house **Lynch's Castle** (cnr Shop & Upper Abbeygate Sts; ⏱10am-4pm Mon-Wed & Fri, 10am-5pm Thu) was built in the 14th century. The Lynch family was the most powerful of the 14 ruling Galway 'tribes'. Stonework on the castle's facade includes ghoulish gargoyles and many coats of arms.

The Walk ⟩⟩ It may take you a while to navigate the pleasant bustle of Shop St with its many buskers and shoppers. Return to the Spanish Arch via High St, stopping at Murphy's pub for a sup.

# Belfast & the North of Ireland

**IRELAND'S NORTH IS MADE FOR ROAD TRIPS.** Routes swoop from hard, stark hills to soft, sandy shores, and cliff-clinging roads snake into wild lands peppered with loughs, glens and bogs.

These epic routes link blockbuster sights. The Giant's Causeway, romantic castles and stately homes are just an exhilarating drive from surfing, hiking or horseback riding across golden sand. Within easy reach are Belfast and Derry, once crippled by sectarian violence but now inspirational in their progress towards peace.

In this compelling corner of Ireland you might get a little lost, but that's more than made up for by what you'll find.

**Giant's Causeway** A 60-million-year-old rock formation
GARETH MCCORMACK/GETTY IMAGES ©

# Belfast & the North of Ireland

**The North in a Nutshell 10 Days**
Big cities, big-name sights, hidden beaches, tiny islands – an epic drive. (p317)

**Delights of Donegal 7 Days**
Brooding mountains, exquisite beaches, boat trips, tradition: the best of the northwest. (p329)

**Inishowen Peninsula 3 Days**
An off-the-map adventure; compelling for its heritage, scenery and sheer sense of space. (p337)

**Northwest on Adrenalin 4 Days**
An activity-rich trip of surfing, hiking and thrilling mountain-to-sea drives. (p345)

**From Bangor to Derry 4 Days**
Rich heritage and remarkable scenery; one for the landscape and culture connoisseur. (p353)

**The Antrim Coast 3 Days**
Blockbuster sights, plus plenty of depth; the best of the northeast's shore. (p361)

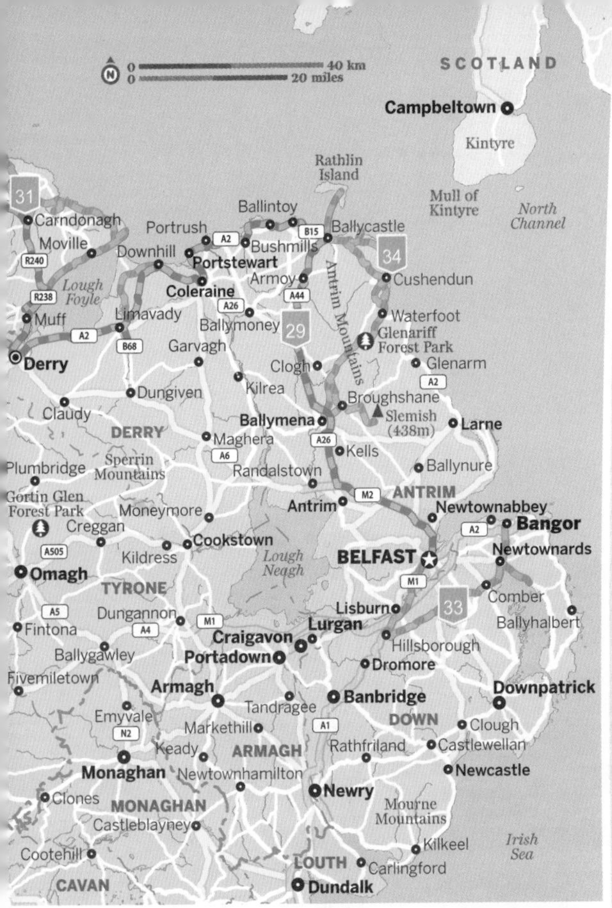

Map labels (Northern Ireland and surrounding area):

SCOTLAND

Campbeltown

Kintyre

Rathlin Island

Mull of Kintyre

North Channel

Ballintoy
Ballycastle
Portrush
Carndonagh
Moville
Downhill
Bushmills
Armoy
Cushendun
Portstewart
Coleraine
Waterfoot
Glenariff Forest Park
Limavady
Ballymoney
Glenarm
Muff
Garvagh
Clogh
Derry
Dungiven
Kilrea
Broughshane
Claudy
DERRY
Ballymena
Slemish (438m)
Larne
Maghera
Plumbridge
Sperrin Mountains
Randalstown
Kells
Ballynure
Gortin Glen Forest Park
Moneymore
Antrim
ANTRIM
Newtownabbey
Creggan
Kildress
Cookstown
Lough Neagh
BELFAST
Bangor
Omagh
Newtownards
TYRONE
Dungannon
Lisburn
Comber
Fintona
Craigavon
Lurgan
Ballyhalbert
Ballygawley
Portadown
Hillsborough
Fivemiletown
Dromore
Armagh
Banbridge
Downpatrick
Emyvale
Tandragee
DOWN
Clough
Markethill
Rathfriland
Castlewellan
Monaghan
Keady
ARMAGH
Newcastle
Newtownhamilton
Newry
Clones
MONAGHAN
Mourne Mountains
Castleblayney
Irish Sea
Cootehill
Kilkeel
CAVAN
LOUTH
Carlingford
Dundalk

Lough Foyle
Antrim Mountains

# DON'T MISS

### Arranmore Island

Ancient pubs, turf fires and late-night music sessions make overnighting special. Do a Robinson Crusoe on Trip 29

### Glenariff Forest Park

Many visitors bypass this dramatic gorge. Let them. It will make your wander beside waterfalls even more tranquil on Trip 34

### Belfast

When previously warring communities have the courage to strive for peace, it's inspiring. Witness that transformation on Trips 29 33

### Malin Head

Don't miss beachcombing for semiprecious stones near Ireland's most northerly point. Try your luck on Trip 31

### Enniscrone's Seaweed Baths

This Edwardian spa will have you steaming and soaking amid therapeutic seaweed on Trip 32

**Enniscrone** Old Cliff Baths

315

## Classic Trip

# The North in a Nutshell

# 29

*The North's must-do trip takes in unmissable cities and big-name sights. It also heads off the tourist trail, revealing secret beaches, quaint harbours, waterfalls and music-filled pubs.*

## TRIP HIGHLIGHTS

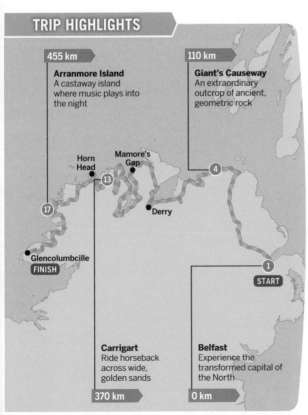

**455 km**
**Arranmore Island**
A castaway island where music plays into the night

**110 km**
**Giant's Causeway**
An extraordinary outcrop of ancient, geometric rock

Horn Head

Mamore's Gap

13

17

Derry

Glencolumbcille
FINISH

1
START

**Carrigart**
Ride horseback across wide, golden sands

**Belfast**
Experience the transformed capital of the North

**370 km**

**0 km**

**10 DAYS**
**470KM / 292 MILES**

### GREAT FOR...

### BEST TIME TO GO

March to June and September mean good weather but fewer crowds.

### ESSENTIAL PHOTO

Crossing the Carrick-a-Rede Rope Bridge as it swings above the waves.

### BEST FOR SCENERY

Stops 16 to 20 head into the heart of wild, wind-whipped Donegal.

**Ballycastle** Sunset on the harbour

# Classic Trip

## 29 The North in a Nutshell

On this road-trip-to-remember you'll drive routes that cling to cliffs, cross borders and head high onto mountain passes. You'll witness Ireland's turbulent past and its inspiring path to peace. And you'll also explore rich faith, folk and music traditions, ride a horse across a sandy beach, cross a swaying rope bridge and spend a night on a castaway island. Not bad for a 10-day drive.

TRIP HIGHLIGHT

## ❶ Belfast

In bustling, big-city Belfast, the past is palpably present – walk the city's former sectarian battlegrounds (p368) for a profound way to start exploring the North's story. Next, cross the River Lagan and head to the Titanic Quarter. Dominated by the towering yellow Harland and Wolff (H&W) cranes, it's where RMS *Titanic* was built. **Titanic Belfast** (www.titanicbelfast. com; Queen's Rd; adult/child £17.50/7.25; ⊙9am-7pm Jun-Aug, to 6pm Apr, May & Sep, 10am-5pm Oct-Mar) is a stunning multisensory experience: see bustling shipyards, join crowds at *Titanic's* launch, feel temperatures drop as she strikes that iceberg, and look through a glass floor at watery footage of the vessel today. Slightly to the west, don't miss the **Thompson Graving Dock** (www.titanicsdock. com; Queen's Rd; graving dock admission free, pump house adult/child £5/3.50; ⊙10am-5pm Sat-Thu, 9.30am-5pm Fri), where you descend into the immense dry dock where the liner was fitted out.

**The Drive »** As you drive the M3/M2 north, the now-familiar H&W cranes recede. Take the A26 through Ballymena; soon the Antrim Mountains loom large to the right. Skirt them along the A44 into Ballycastle, 96km from Belfast.

✗ 🛏 p60, p359

## ❷ Ballycastle

Head beyond the sandy beach to the harbour at the appealing resort of Ballycastle. From here, daily **ferries** (☏028-2076 9299; www.rathlinballycastle ferry.com; adult/child/bicycle return £12/6/3.30) depart for Rathlin Island, where you'll see sea stacks and thousands of guillemots, kittiwakes, razorbills and puffins.

🛏 p327

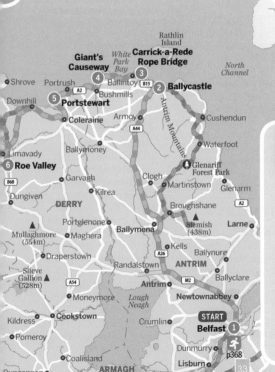

**LINK YOUR TRIP**

### 33 From Bangor to Derry

Encounter seaside fun, a grand stately home and the Queen's official residence. Begin 20km east of Belfast at Bangor.

### 3 Tip to Toe

Take in the best of Irish music and poetry. Start where this trip stops: Glencolumbcille.

Classic Trip

**The Drive »** Pick up the B15 towards Ballintoy, which meanders up to a gorse-dotted coastal plateau where hills part to reveal bursts of the sea. As the road plunges downwards, take the right turn to the Carrick-a-Rede Rope Bridge (10km).

## ③ Carrick-a-Rede Rope Bridge

The **Carrick-a-Rede Rope Bridge** (www.nationaltrust. org.uk; Ballintoy; adult/child £5.90/3; ⏰9.30am-7pm Apr-Aug, to 6pm Mar, Sep & Oct, to 3.30pm Nov-Feb) **loops** across a surging sea to a tiny island 20m offshore. This walkway of planks and wire rope sways some 30m above the waves, testing your nerve and head for heights. The bridge was originally put up each year by salmon fishermen to help them set their nets, and signs along the 1km clifftop

hike to the bridge detail the fascinating process. Declining stocks have put an end to fishing, however.

**The Drive »** The B15, then the A2, snake west along clifftops and past views of White Park Bay's sandy expanse. Swing right onto the B146, passing Dunseverick Castle's fairy-tale tumblings, en route to the Giant's Causeway (11km).

TRIP HIGHLIGHT

## ④ Giant's Causeway

Stretching elegantly out from a rugged shore, the **Giant's Causeway** (www. nationaltrust.org.uk; ⏰dawn-dusk) is one of the world's true geological wonders. Clambering around this jetty of fused geometric rock chunks, it's hard to believe it's not man-made. Indeed, legend says Irish giant Finn Mc-Cool built the Causeway to cross the sea to fight Scottish giant Benan-donner. More prosaically, however, scientists tell us the 60-million-year-old rocks were formed

when a flow of molten basaltic lava cooled and hardened from the top and bottom inwards. It contracted, and the hexagonal cracks spread as the rock solidified.

Entry to the Causeway site is free, but to use the National Trust car park you'll need to buy a ticket that includes entrance to the excellent new **Giant's Causeway Visitor Experience** (☎028-2073 1855; www. nationaltrust.org.uk; adult/child with parking £9/4.50, without parking £7/3.25; ⏰9am-7pm Apr-Sep, to 6pm Feb, Mar & Oct, to 5pm Nov-Jan).

✗ p60

**The Drive »** Continue west, through Bushmills, with its famous distillery, picking up the A2 Coastal Causeway route towards Portrush. You'll pass wind-pruned trees, crumbling Dunluce Castle and Portrush's long sandy beaches before arriving at Portstewart (16km).

## ⑤ Portstewart

Time for some unique parking. Head through resort-town Portstewart, following signs for the **Strand** (beach). Ever-sandier roads descend to an immense shoreline that doubles as a car park for 1000 vehicles. It's a decidedly weird experience to drive and park (£5) on an apparently endless expanse of hard-packed sand. It's also at your own risk, which doesn't deter the locals (but do stick to cen-

## CAUSEWAY COAST WALKS

The official **Causeway Coast Way** (www.walkni.com) stretches for 53km from Ballycastle to Portstewart, but individual chunks can be walked whenever you feel like stretching your legs. Day hikes include the supremely scenic 16.5km section between Carrick-a-Rede and the Giant's Causeway – one of the finest coastal walks in Ireland. Shorter options also abound, including a 2km ramble around Portrush, a 1.5km stroll on sandy White Park Bay and a 300m scramble around ruined Dunluce Castle.

tral, compacted areas). Nearby, a 1km **walking trail** meanders up a sand ladder, through huge dunes and past marram grass and occasional orchids.

🛏 p327

The Drive ≫ Take the A2 west, through Coleraine towards Downhill. About 1km after the Mussenden Temple's dome appears, take the Bishop's Rd left up steep hills with spectacular Lough Foyle views. Descend, go through Limavady and onto the B68 (signed Dungiven). Soon a brown Country Park sign points to Roe Valley (42km).

## 6 Roe Valley

This beguiling **country park** (🕙9am-dusk) is packed with rich reminders of a key Irish industry: linen production. The damp valley was ideal for growing the flax that made the cloth; the fast-flowing water powered the machinery. The **Green Lane Museum** (🕙1-4.30pm Sat-Thu May-Aug, Sat & Sun Sep), near the car park, features sowing fiddles, flax breakers and spinning wheels. Look out for nearby watchtowers, built to guard linen spread out to bleach in the fields, and Scutch Mills, where the flax was pounded.

The Drive ≫ Head back into Limavady to take the A2 west to Derry (28km). Green fields give way to suburbs, then city streets.

# TOP TIP:
## THE BORDER

Driving 20 minutes north out of Derry will see you entering another country: the Republic of Ireland. Be aware that road sign speed limits will suddenly change from mph to km/h, while wording switches from English to Irish and English. Stock up on euros in Derry or visit the first post-border ATM.

## 7 Derry

Northern Ireland's second city offers another powerful insight into the North's troubled past and the remarkable steps towards peace. It's best experienced on foot (p370). Partway round, drop into the **Tower Museum** (www.derrycity.gov.uk/museums; Union Hall Pl; adult/child £4/2; 🕙10am-5.30pm). Its imaginative Story of Derry exhibition leads you through the city's history, from the 6th-century monastery of St Colmcille (Columba) to the 1960s Battle of the Bogside.

🍴 🛏 p327, p359

The Drive ≫ The A2 heads north towards Moville. Soon speed-limit signs switch from mph to km/h: welcome to the Republic of Ireland. Shortly after Muff take the small left turn, signed Iskaheen, up the hill. Park beside Iskaheen church (11km).

## 8 Iskaheen

It's completely off the tourist trail, but Iskaheen church's tiny **graveyard** offers evidence of two of Ireland's most significant historical themes: the poverty that led to mass migration and the consequences of sectarian violence. One gravestone among many is that of the McKinney family, recording a string of children dying young: at 13 years, 11 months, nine months, and six weeks. It also bears the name of 34-year-old James Gerard McKinney, one of 13 unarmed civilians shot dead when British troops opened fire on demonstrators on Bloody Sunday, 1972.

The Drive ≫ Rejoin the R238 north, turning onto the R240 to Carndonagh, climbing steeply into rounded summits. After quaint Ballyliffin and Clonmany, pick up the Inis Eoghain (Scenic Route) towards Mamore's Gap, before parking at the Glen House Tea Rooms (40km).

## 9 Glenevin Waterfall

Welcome to Butler's Bridge – from here a 1km trail winds beside a stream through a

*Classic Trip*

### WHY THIS IS A CLASSIC TRIP
ISABEL ALBISTON, WRITER

Starting in Belfast, a city whose turbulent history seems finally to be coming second to its flourishing future, this trip gives a sense of the north's past and present while showcasing a stunning and ancient natural landscape – the striking hexagonal rocks of the Giant's Causeway date back 60 million years.

Top: Portstewart Strand
Left: Tower Museum, Derry
Right: Lighthouse, Arranmore Island

wooded glen to Glenevin Waterfall, which cascades 10m down the rock face. It's an utterly picturesque, gentle, waymarked route that's the perfect spot for a leg stretch.

🛏 p327

**The Drive** » The Inis Eoghain snakes south up to Mamore's Gap, a high-altitude, white-knuckle mountain pass that climbs 260m on single-lane, twisting roads, past shrines to the saints. After a supremely steep descent (and glorious views), go south through Buncrana, and on to Fahan (37km), parking beside the village church.

### ⑩ Fahan

St Colmcille founded a monastery in Fahan in the 6th century. Its creeper-clad ruins sit beside the church. Among them, hunt out the beautifully carved **St Mura Cross**. Each face of this 7th-century stone slab is decorated with a cross in intricate Celtic weave. The barely discernible Greek inscription is the only one known in Ireland from this early Christian period and is thought to be part of a prayer dating from 633.

**The Drive** » Take the N13 to Letterkenny, where you'll pick up the R245 to Rathmelton (aka Ramelton), a 10km sweep north through the River Swilly valley. Turn off for the village, heading downhill to park beside the water in front of you (50km).

## ⓫ Rathmelton

In this picture-perfect town, rows of Georgian houses and rough-walled stone warehouses curve along the River Lennon. Strolling right takes you to a string of three-storey, three-bay Victorian warehouses; walking back and left up Church Rd leads to the ruined **Tullyaughnish Church**, with its Romanesque carvings in the eastern wall. Walking left beside the river leads past Victorian shops to the three-arched, late-18th-century Rathmelton Bridge.

🛏 p327

**The Drive »** Cross the town bridge, turning right (north) for Rathmullan. The hills of the Inishowen Peninsula rise ahead and Lough Swilly swings into view – soon you're driving right beside the shore. At Rathmullan (11km), make for the harbour car park.

- - - - - - - - - - - - - - - -

## ⓬ Rathmullan

Refined, tranquil Rathmullan was the setting for an event that shaped modern Ireland. In 1607 a band of nobles boarded a ship here, leaving with the intention of raising an army to fight the occupying English. But they never returned. Known as the Flight of the Earls, it marked the end of the Irish (Catholic) chieftains' power. Their estates were confiscated, paving the way for the Plantation of Ulster with British (Protestant) settlers. Beside the sandy beach, look for the striking modern **sculpture** depicting the departure of the earls, waving to their distressed people as they left.

**The Drive »** Head straight on from the harbour, picking up Fanad/Atlantic Dr, a roller-coaster road that surges up Lough Swilly's shore, round huge Knockalla, past the exquisite beach at Ballymastocker Bay and around Fanad Head. It then hugs the (ironically) narrow Broad Water en route to Carrigart (74km), with its village-centre horse-riding centre.

- - - - - - - - - - - - - - - -

TRIP HIGHLIGHT

## ⓭ Carrigart

Most visitors scoot straight through laid-back Carrigart, heading for the swimming beach at Downings (there's also accommodation there; see p327). But they miss a real treat: a horse ride on a vast beach. The **Carrigart Riding Centre** (☏ 087 227 6926; per hr adult/child €20/15) is just across the main street from sandy, hill-ringed Mulroy Bay, meaning you can head straight onto the beach for an hour-long ride amid the shallows and the dunes. Trips go on the hour, but it's best to book.

**The Drive »** Head south for Creeslough. An inlet with a creamy, single-towered castle soon pops into view. The turn-off comes on the plain, where brown signs point through narrow lanes and past farms to Doe Castle (12km) itself.

- - - - - - - - - - - - - - - -

## ⓮ Doe Castle

The best way to appreciate the charm of early-16th-century Doe Castle is to wander the peaceful grounds, admiring its slender tower and crenellated battlements. The castle was the stronghold of the Scottish

## NORTH WEST 200 ROAD RACE

Driving this delightful coast can have its challenges, so imagine doing it at high speed. Each May the world's best motorcyclists do just that, going as fast as 300km/h in the **North West 200** (www.northwest200.org), which is run on a road circuit taking in Portrush, Portstewart and Coleraine. This classic race is Ireland's biggest outdoor sporting event and one of the last to take place on closed public roads anywhere in Europe. It attracts up to 150,000 spectators; if you're not one of them, it's best to avoid the area on the race weekend.

MacSweeney family until it fell into English hands in the 17th century. It's a deeply picturesque spot: a low, water-fringed promontory with a moat hewn out of the rock.

**The Drive** ›› Near Creeslough, the bulk of Muckish Mountain rears up before the N56 to Dunfanaghy undulates past homesteads, loughs and sandy bays. Once in Dunfanaghy, with its gently kooky vibe, welcoming pubs and great places to sleep (see p327), look out for the signpost pointing right to Horn Head (25km).

**Belfast** Titanic Belfast

## 15 Horn Head

This headland provides one of Donegal's best clifftop drives: along sheer, heather-clad quartzite cliffs with views of an island-dotted sea. A circular road bears left to the coastguard station – park to take the 20-minute walk due north to the signal tower. Hop back in the car, continuing east – around 1km later a viewpoint tops cliffs 180m high. There's another superb vantage point 1km further round – on a fine day you'll see Ireland's most northerly point, Malin Head.

**The Drive** ›› The N56 continues west. Settlements thin out, the road climbs and the pointed peak of Mt Errigal fills more and more of your windshield before the road swings away. At tiny Crolly, follow the R259 towards the airport, then turn right, picking up signs for Leo's Tavern (35km).

## 16 Meenaleck

You never know who'll drop by for one of the legendary singalongs at **Leo's Tavern** (☎074-954 8143; www.leostavern.com; off R259, Crolly; ☉kitchen 1-8.45pm Jun-Sep, 5-8.45pm Thu-Fri, 1-8.45pm Sat, 1-8pm Sun Oct-May; 🛜🅿) in Meenaleck. It's owned by Bartley Brennan, brother of Enya and her siblings Máire, Ciaran and Pól (aka the group Clannad). The pub glitters with gold, silver and platinum discs and is packed with musical mementos – there's live music nightly in the summer.

**The Drive** ›› Continue west on the R259 as it bobbles and twists besides scattered communities and a boggy, then sandy, shore. Head on to the pocket-sized port of Burtonport, following ferry signs right, to embark for Arranmore Island (25km).

TRIP HIGHLIGHT

## 17 Arranmore Island

Arranmore (Árainn Mhór) offers a true taste of Ireland. Framed by dramatic cliff faces, cavernous sea caves and clear sandy beaches, this 9km-by-5km island sits 5km offshore. Here you'll discover a prehistoric triangular fort and an offshore bird sanctuary fluttering with corncrakes, snipes and seabirds. Irish is the main language spoken, pubs put on turf fires, and trad-music sessions run late into the night. To get the full castaway experience, stay overnight (book). The **Arranmore Ferry** (☎074-952 0532; www.arranmoreferry. com; Burtonport; return adult/ child/car & driver €15/7/30; ☉4-8 daily sailings year-round) takes 20 minutes.

🛏 p327

*Classic Trip*

**The Drive** ≫ The R259 bounces down to Dungloe, where you take the N56 south into a rock-strewn landscape that's backed by the Blue Stack Mountains. After a stretch of rally-circuit-esque road, the sweep of Gweebarra Bay emerges. Take the sharp right towards peaceful Narin (R261), following signs to the beach *(trá)*, 45km from Arranmore Island.

## 18 Narin

You've now entered the beautiful Loughrea Peninsula, which glistens with tiny lakes cupped by undulating hills. Narin boasts a spectacular 4km-long, wishbone-shaped Blue Flag beach, the sandy tip of which points towards **Iniskeel Island**. You can walk to the island at low tide along a 500m sandy

causeway. Your reward? An intimate island studded with early Christian remains: St Connell, a cousin of St Colmcille, founded a monastery here in the 6th century.

🛏 p327

**The Drive** ≫ Continue south on the R261 through tweed-producing Ardara. Shortly after leaving town, take the right, signed 'Waterfall', following a road wedged between craggy hills and an increasingly sandy shore. In time the Assarancagh Waterfall (14km) comes into view.

## 19 Assarancagh Waterfall

Step out of the car and you immediately feel what an enchanting spot this is. As the waterfall streams down the sheer hillside, walk along the road (really a lane) towards the sea. This 1.5km route leads past time-warp farms – sheep bleat and the tang of

peat smoke scents the air. At tiny Maghera, head through the car park, down a track, over a boardwalk and onto a truly stunning expanse of pure-white sand. This exquisite place belies a bloody past. Some 100 villagers hid from Cromwell's forces in nearby caves – all except one were discovered and massacred.

**The Drive** ≫ Drive west through Maghera on a dramatic route that makes straight for the gap in the towering hills. At the fork, turn right, heading deeper into the remote headland, making for Glencolumbcille (20km).

## 20 Glencolumbcille

The welcome in the scattered, pub-dotted, bayside village of Glencolumbcille (Gleann Cholm Cille) is warm. This remote settlement also offers a glimpse of a disappearing way of life. **Father McDyer's Folk Village** (www.glenfolkvillage. com; Doonalt; adult/child €4.50/2.50; ⊙10am-6pm Mon-Sat, noon-6pm Sun Easter-Sep) took traditional life of the 1960s and froze it in time. Its thatched cottages re-create daily life with genuine period fittings, while the Craft Shop sells wines made from such things as seaweed, as well as marmalade and whiskey truffles – a few treats at your journey's end.

🛏 p74, p335

## DETOUR: FINTOWN RAILWAY

**Start:** 17 **Arranmore Island (p325)**

You've been driving for days now – time to let the train take the strain. The charming **Fintown Railway** (☎074-954 6280; www.antraen.com; off R250, Fintown; adult/child €8/5; ⊙11am-4pm Mon-Sat, 1-5pm Sun Jun–mid-Sep) runs along a rebuilt 5km section of the former County Donegal Railway track beside picturesque Lough Finn. It's been lovingly restored to its original condition, and a return trip in the red-and-white, 1940s diesel railcar takes around 40 minutes. To get to the railway, head east on the R252, off the N56 south of Dungloe. Then settle back to enjoy the ride.

# Eating & Sleeping

## Ballycastle ②

### 🛏 An Caislean
**Guesthouse**      Guesthouse ££

(☎028-2076 2845; www.ancaislean.co.uk; 42 Quay Rd; s/d from £45/60; 🅿 📶) An Caislean has a luxurious lounge, a summer tea room and restaurant, and a welcoming atmosphere. It's just a few minutes' walk from the beach.

## Portstewart ⑤

### 🛏 Strandeen
B&B ££

(☎028-7083 3872; www.strandeen.com; 63 Strand Rd; d from £110) Set on a hilltop and more like a boutique hotel than a B&B, Strandeen has four beautiful rooms, scrumptious organic and/or free-range breakfasts, bike rental (per day £15), and an ocean-facing terrace.

## Derry ⑦

### 🛏 Merchant's House
B&B ££

(☎028-7126 9691; www.thesaddlershouse.com; 16 Queen St; s/d/tr/f from £40/65/90/100; @ 📶) This historic, Georgian-style town house has an elegant lounge and dining room and home-made marmalade at breakfast. Some rooms share a bathroom. Call at **Saddler's House** (36 Great James St) first to pick up a key.

## Glenevin Waterfall ⑨

### 🛏 Glen House
Guesthouse €€

(☎074-937 6745; www.glenhouse.ie; Straid, Clonmany; r €70-100; 🅿 📶) Despite the grand surroundings and luxurious rooms, you'll find neither pretension nor high prices at this gem of a guesthouse. The rooms are a lesson in restrained sophistication, and the setting is incredibly tranquil. The walking trail to Glenevin Waterfall starts next to the **Rose Tea Room** (mains from €6; ⊙10am-6pm daily Jul-Aug, Sat & Sun only Mar-Jun & Sep-Oct), which opens to a deck.

## Rathmelton ⑪

### 🛏 Frewin House
B&B €€

(☎074-915 1246; www.frewinhouse.com; Rectory Rd; d €110-150; 🅿) Set in secluded grounds, this fine Victorian rectory combines antique furniture with contemporary style. You can arrange for a communal dinner by candlelight.

## Downings ⑬

### 🛏 Beach
Hotel €€

(Óstán na Trá; ☎074-915 5303; www.beachhotel.ie; s/d €80/120; 🅿) Many of the bright, modern rooms at this large family-run hotel have ocean views. You can refuel in its restaurant (three courses for €27.50) or bar (mains €10 to €22). It's in Downings, 4km north of Carrigart.

## Dunfanaghy ⑭

### 🛏 Corcreggan Mill
Guesthouse €

(☎074-913 6409; www.corcreggan.com; off N56; camp sites from €12, s/d from €60/75; @ 📶) Spotless four-bed dorms and private guest rooms are tucked into cosy corners of this lovingly restored former mill house, Continental breakfast is included in the room rates. Some rooms have private bathrooms. The mill is 2.5km southwest of town on the N56.

## Arranmore Island ⑰

### 🛏 Claire's Bed & Breakfast
B&B €

(☎074-952 0042; www.clairesbandb.wordpress.com; Leabgarrow; s/d €35/60; 📶) This modern house with simple rooms is right by the ferry port.

## Narin ⑱

### 🛏 Carnaween House
B&B €€

(☎074-954 5122; www.carnaweenhouse.com; Narin; s/d €60/120, cottage from €210, mains €15-25; ⊙kitchen 6-9pm Thu-Sun, 1-4pm Sun Jun-Sep, shorter hrs rest of year; 📶) Carnaween House glows with brilliant white bedrooms in a luxury beach-house style. The restaurant serves modern Irish fare.

# Delights of Donegal

**30**

*Supremely scenic (sometimes scary) roads lead from sandy shores to exposed mountains, taking in horse rides, boat trips and world-class art along the way.*

## TRIP HIGHLIGHTS

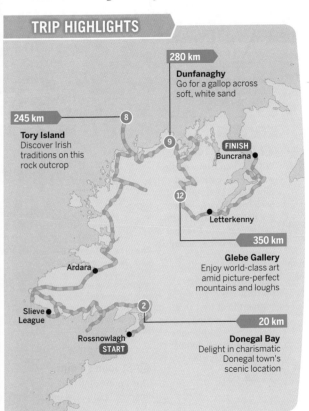

**280 km**

**Dunfanaghy**
Go for a gallop across soft, white sand

**245 km** — ⑧

**Tory Island**
Discover Irish traditions on this rock outcrop

⑨

**FINISH**
Buncrana

⑫

Letterkenny

**350 km**

**Glebe Gallery**
Enjoy world-class art amid picture-perfect mountains and loughs

Ardara

Slieve League

Rossnowlagh
**START**

②

**20 km**

**Donegal Bay**
Delight in charismatic Donegal town's scenic location

**7 DAYS**
**423KM / 263 MILES**

**GREAT FOR...**

**BEST TIME TO GO**

Easter to October, when sights and activities are open and the weather is better.

 **ESSENTIAL PHOTO**

Horses galloping on Dunfanaghy beach.

 **BEST TWO DAYS**

From tweed town via mountain to classic Irish island: stops 6 to 8 deliver the essence of Donegal.

**Dunfanaghy** Boats reflected in calm water

329

# 30 Delights of Donegal

This trip evokes a range of diverse sensations: looming Mt Errigal is overwhelming; a beach horse ride feels liberating; and driving the high mountain passes is heart-in-the-mouth stuff. Relax on boat trips around Donegal Bay to 600m-high sea cliffs and an island, then encounter international art, Ireland's traditional industries and piles of hand-cut peat beside the road. On this trip you gain a true insight into delightful Donegal.

## ❶ Rossnowlagh

There's more to the happy-go-lucky resort of Rossnowlagh than its superb 3km sandy beach. Deep in a forest (signed off the R231 south of town), a **Franciscan Friary** (☎071-985 1342; www.franciscans.ie; off R231; ⊙11am-5.30pm Mon, Wed-Sat, to 8pm Tue, 11.45am-5.30pm Sun) offers tranquil gardens, a small museum and the Way of the Cross walk, which meanders up a hillside covered with rhododendrons for spectacular views.

✕ ⊨ p351

The Drive » The R231 heads north through a gently rolling landscape, joining the N15 for a smooth run into Donegal town (19km). Head for the waterfront, parking near the pier.

TRIP HIGHLIGHT

## ❷ Donegal Town

With its handsome castle, waterside location and Blue Stack Mountains backdrop, Donegal town is a delightful stop. Drink in the beauty of Donegal Bay on the **Donegal Bay Waterbus** (☎074-972 3666; www.donegalbaywaterbus.com; Donegal Pier; adult/child €20/7; ⊙Easter-Oct), a 1¼-hour boat tour that will see you gazing at historic sites, seal-inhabited coves, an island manor and a ruined castle.

✕ ⊨ p351

The Drive » Take the N56 west. The Blue Stack Mountains retreat in your wing mirror, an open coast road unfurls, and soon the wafer-thin St John's peninsula comes into view. Turn off left, heading out to its tip (32km).

## ❸ St John's Point

This improbably thin finger of land pokes into

the sea, culminating at
St John's Point. Driving
the 11km lane to the tip
feels like driving into the
ocean. The point itself
has a small sandy beach,
rich bird and plant life,
total tranquillity and
(inevitably) remarkable,
wrap-around views.

🛏 p335

# LINK YOUR TRIP

## 27 Sligo Surrounds

A five-day
meander through
culture-packed Sligo.
Head for Sligo town,
50km south of this trip's
start.

## 31 Inishowen Peninsula

An exhilarating trip to a
remote headland. Start
in Derry, 20km southeast
of this trip's finish.

**The Drive »** Continue west on the N56, then take the R263 through fish-scented Killybegs. After its harbour full of trawlers, signs appear for Slieve League, the towering mountains that loom ever closer ahead. After Carrick comes tiny Teelin (Tieleann), 34km from St John's Point.

## ④ Slieve League

From the road so far, Slieve League has looked like an impressive mountain range, but these sheer 600m-high sea cliffs are utterly awe-inspiring when seen from the water at their base. Boats leave from Teelin; book with **Nuala Star** (☎074-973 9365; www.sliabhleagueboattrips.com; Teelin Pier; tours per person €20-25; ⏱hrs vary Apr-Oct).

**The Drive »** Back at Carrick, edge west on the R263 before turning left on the minor route signed Malin Beg (Málainn Bhig). It cuts behind Slieve League's massive peaks, threading through an increasingly remote landscape, dotted with isolated farms and scored with strips of hand-cut turf (peat). It's 12km to Malin Beg.

## ⑤ Malin Beg

Malin Beg is one of Donegal's wildest spots, which is quite something in a county crammed with them. An undulating sea-monster-like headland snakes into the waves, Sligo's coast appears distant to the south, and a lighthouse sits just offshore. The

bay below appears to be bitten out of low cliffs; descend 60 steps to firm, red-tinged sand, a spot sheltered from Malin Beg's howling winds.

**The Drive »** Go north through Glencolumbcille (Gleann Cholm Cille), with its sleeping options (p335), picking up signs for Glengesh Pass. A steep climb past bogs and wandering sheep leads to a plunging road, winding into the valley below. Go north onto the N56 to reach Ardara (34km).

## ⑥ Ardara

Heritage-town Ardara is the heart of Donegal's traditional tweed industry; the **Heritage Centre** (☎087 286 8657; Main St; ⏱ 10am-5pm Mon-Fri, 11am-4pm Sat Easter-Sep; hrs may vary) charts its transformation from cottage industry to global product. Turn right out of the centre and stroll up the hill to **Eddie Doherty Handwoven Tweed** (☎074-954 1304; www.handwoventweed.com; Main St; ⏱10am-6pm Mon-Sat, sometimes Sun) to see a vast loom, piles of rugs and rolls of cloth. Staff will happily explain more.

**The Drive »** The N56 sweeps north towards Dungloe (signed Glenties). After Maas it narrows into a bucking, twisting road: subsidence of bogs has created a suspension-testing ride. After Dungloe, Mt Errigal's pyramidal peak rears from a lough-studded landscape. Turn onto the R251, climbing steadily towards it and Dunlewey (70km).

## ⑦ Dunlewey

Isolated, exposed lough-side Dunlewey (Dún Lúiche) offers a true taste of mountain life. The scenery overwhelms everything here; human habitation seems very small. Get the landscape's full impact on a boat trip run by the **Dunlewey Centre** (Ionad Cois Locha; ☎074-953 1699; www.dunleweycentre.com; combined ticket adult/child €10.30/7.50; ⏱10.30am-5.30pm Easter-Sep, to 4.45pm Oct; ⊕), as a storyteller expounds on ghoulish folklore.

🛏 p335

**The Drive »** Rejoin the N56, heading briefly west before taking the R258 around Bloody Foreland (Cnóc Fola), a spectacular shore so named because sunsets turn its rocks crimson. Turn towards the tiny harbour (Magheraroarty; 32km) that eventually swings into view. From Magheraroarty, the 35-minute crossing to Tory Island with **Donegal Coastal Cruises** (Turasmara Teo; ☎074-953 1320; www.toryislandferry.com; adult/child return €26/13; ⏱1-3 daily Apr-Oct, less often Nov-Mar) can be wild.

TRIP HIGHLIGHT

## ⑧ Tory Island

Some 11km offshore, craggy Tory Island (Oileán Thóraí) is a fiercely independent community with its own Irish dialect, elected 'king' and style of 'naïve' art, plus

**Glengesh Pass** The road between Ardara and Glencolumbcille

early Christian remains and 100 seabird species.

**The Drive »** Back on the mainland, the N56 undulates north past loughs to Dunfanaghy in a sheep-grazed landscape, where the ever-present bulk of Muckish Mountain looms to the right. Once in Dunfanaghy (37km), make for the central Arnolds Hotel.

TRIP HIGHLIGHT

### ⑨ Dunfanaghy

Along with chilled-out pubs and arty shops, cheerful Dunfanaghy offers the chance to ride along pristine sweeps of white sand. **Dunfanaghy Stables** (☏074-910 0980;

www.dunfanaghystables.com; Arnolds Hotel, Main St; adult/child per hr €32/27; ☉Easter-Oct) at Arnolds Hotel are just across the road from the beach; book for an unforgettable ride.

✕ ⊨ p60, p327, p335

**The Drive »** Continue east through Dunfanaghy; 5km later turn left into Ards Forest Park.

### ⑩ Ards Forest Park

From the main car park at **Ards Forest Park** (www. coillteoutdoors.ie; off N56; parking €5 (in €1 & €2 coins only); ☉8am-9pm Apr-Sep, 10am-4.30pm Oct-Mar), pick up the trail that

meanders east through ash and oak towards a Capuchin Friary. Follow the path further down still and you'll stumble upon the exquisite Isabella's Cove then Lucky Shell Bay. Allow two hours return.

**The Drive »** Rejoin the N56 east, before taking the R245, an increasingly windy road backed by the rugged hills of the Fanad Peninsula, to Carrigart (Carraig Airt). Head through amiable Carrigart to Downings, 24km from Ards Forest Park.

### ⑪ Downings

The **beach** at Downings (or Downies) is simply

## TOP TIP:
## GLENVEAGH NATIONAL PARK

Glebe Gallery sits beside the stunning **Glenveagh National Park** (Páirc Náisiúnta Ghleann Bheatha; www. glenveaghnationalpark.ie). This 16,500-sq-km wilderness features forests, mountains, shimmering lakes and green-gold bogs and makes for magnificent walking. The **visitor centre** (☑076-100 2537; www. glenveaghnationalpark.ie; off R251; ⊙9am-6pm Apr-Oct, to 5pm Nov-Mar, cafe 10.30am-5.30pm) provides free maps.

superb: rolling green hills meet an immense curl of bright-white sand. It's also, unlike many local beaches, safe to swim here; the Atlantic makes for a chilly, but memorable, dip.

🛏 p327

**The Drive »** Return to the N56, turning towards Letterkenny, with the Derryveagh Mountains gathering ahead. Turn onto the R255 (signed Glenveagh National Park), climbing towards those peaks. Turn left onto the R251, which descends, revealing a glittering Lough Gartan. At the water's edge, follow Glebe Gallery signs right (40km).

TRIP HIGHLIGHT

### ⑫ Glebe Gallery

This is a true treat: the top-notch artwork at **Glebe Gallery** (☑074-913 7071; www.heritageireland.ie; Church Hill; adult/child €4/2; ⊙11am-6.30pm daily Easter & Jul-Aug, Sat-Thu Jun & Sep,

last admission 5.30pm) belonged to English painter Derrick Hill. Works include pieces by Tory Island's 'naive' artists, plus Picasso, Landseer, Hokusai, Jack B Yeats and Kokoschka.

**The Drive »** The R251 winds south through woodland, hugging the lough shore. Turn onto the R250 towards Letterkenny (where there is accommodation; see p335). Soon you'll see Newmills Corn and Flax Mills signed on your right (11km).

### ⑬ Newmills Corn and Flax Mills

A whirring, creaking, gushing delight, this restored three-storey, water-powered **corn mill** (☑074-912 5115; www. heritageireland.ie; R250; ⊙10am-6pm late May-Sep) is full of in-motion grinding stones, drive shafts, cogs and gears.

**The Drive »** After Letterkenny join the N13 east towards Derry. The River Swilly uncurls to your left. Take the R238/239 turn, then the left towards Inch Island (signed 'Wildfowl Reserve'). Once over the causeway, the (signed) road to Inch Pier (53km) snakes along tranquil, tree-lined lanes.

### ⑭ Inch Island

At Inch's tiny pier, park on the right (don't block the fishers' track to the left). Few tourists make it to this compact crescent of sand. It's a place to rest, skim stones and watch waves.

**The Drive »** Return to the R238, which sweeps north past a 5km sandy beach to Buncrana. By now Lough Swilly is stretching far ahead. Head for Buncrana's shoreline, parking beside the Leisure Centre (20km).

### ⑮ Buncrana

Bustling Buncrana provides a fitting trip finale, courtesy of stunning sunsets; locals will tell you the ones over Lough Swilly are the best around. A path leads beside the water to pint-sized, 1718 **Buncrana Castle** – it and neighbouring **O'Doherty's Keep** provide ideal sun-going-down vantage points.

✕ 🛏 p335, p343

# Eating & Sleeping

## St John's Point ③

### 🛏 Castle Murray — Boutique Hotel €€

(📞074-973 7022; www.castlemurray.com; s/d from €90/120, set menu €41; ⏰6.30-9pm Mon-Sat, 1-3pm & 6.30-9pm Sun Jul & Aug, closed Mon & Tue Sep-Jun, closed Jan; 🛜) Overlooking the ruins of the 15th-century McSwyne's Castle, Castle Murray is not a castle itself, but a boutique hotel in a sprawling modern beach house. Most of the 10 guest rooms have great sea and castle views. It's best known for its fine French restaurant, and its signature dish of prawns and monkfish in garlic butter is a must-try. Castle Murray is 1.5km south of Dunkineely on a minor road leading to St John's Point.

## Glencolumbcille ⑤

### 🛏 Dooey Hostel — Hostel €

(📞074-973 0130; www.independenthostels ireland.com; Dooey; campsites per person €10, dm/d €16/32) Built into a hillside with a corridor carved out of the plant-strewn rock face and amazing views of the ocean and hills below, this 32-bed hostel is a charmer. Facilities are rustic, but clean and comfortable. Driving, turn left just after the Glenhead Tavern and continue for 1.5km; walkers can hike up a path behind the folk village. Cash only.

## Dunlewey ⑦

### 🛏 Glen Heights B&B — B&B €

(📞074-956 0844; www.glenheightsbb.com; d €70; 🛜) The three rooms are cosy, the Donegal charm is in full swing, and there are breathtaking views of Dunlewey Lake and the Poisoned Glen from the conservatory.

## Dunfanaghy ⑨

### ✕ Muck 'n' Muffins — Cafe €

(📞074-913 6780; The Square; mains €4-10; ⏰9.30am-5pm Mon-Sat, 10.30am-5pm Sun

Sep-Jun, to 6pm Jul & Aug; 🛜) A 19th-century stone grain store houses this 1st-floor cafe and crafts shop. Even on rainy days, it's packed with locals tucking into sandwiches, breakfast, hot specials, cakes and, of course, muffins.

### 🛏 Arnolds Hotel — Hotel €€

(📞074-913 6208; www.arnoldshotel.com; Main St; s/d from €80/110; ⏰Apr-Oct; 🅿🛜) Open since 1922, this family-run hotel at the east end of the village has 30 comfortable but very red corporate-style rooms. The hotel's Whiskey Fly bar serves up traditional Irish pub grub (mains €10 to €25).

### 🛏 Whins — B&B €€

(📞074-913 6481; www.thewhins.com; off N56; s/d €50/80; 🛜) The colourful, individually decorated rooms at the Whins have patchwork quilts and a real sense of character. A wide choice of breakfasts is served upstairs in a room with a view towards Horn Head. It's about 750m east of the town centre opposite the golf course.

## Letterkenny ⑫

### 🛏 Pearse Road B&B — Guesthouse €

(📞074-912 3002; www.pearseroadguesthouse. com; Pearse Rd; r €60-70; 🛜) This tidy guest-house has rooms spread over two buildings close to Main St. Breakfast is not included, but rooms are well-equipped. There's a speedy laundry right next door.

## Buncrana ⑮

### 🛏 Caldra Bed & Breakfast — B&B €€

(📞074-936 3703; www.caldrabandb.com; Lisnakelly; s/d from €50/80; 🅿🛜) This large, modern B&B has four spacious rooms ideal for families. The public rooms feature impressive fireplaces and gilt mirrors, while the guest rooms are more sedate. The garden and patio overlook Lough Swilly and the mountains.

# Inishowen Peninsula

## 31

*This thrilling route heads deep into Ireland's wild lands. You'll encounter clifftop hikes, shipwrecks, a fort and superb seafood, then return, exhilarated, to the comforts of town.*

## TRIP HIGHLIGHTS

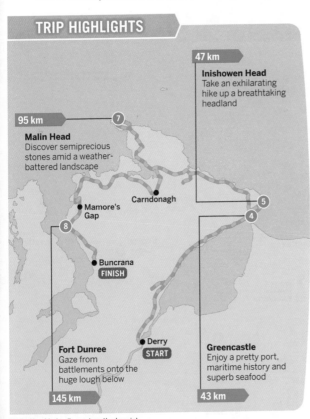

**47 km**

**Inishowen Head**
Take an exhilarating hike up a breathtaking headland

**95 km**

**Malin Head**
Discover semiprecious stones amid a weather-battered landscape

Carndonagh

Mamore's Gap

7

5

4

Buncrana
FINISH

8

**Fort Dunree**
Gaze from battlements onto the huge lough below

**145 km**

● Derry
START

**Greencastle**
Enjoy a pretty port, maritime history and superb seafood

**43 km**

**3 DAYS**
**165KM / 103 MILES**

**GREAT FOR...**

**BEST TIME TO GO**
Easter to October should have better weather, and more things are open.

 **ESSENTIAL PHOTO**

The gorgeous sandy-bay views from Inishowen Head.

**BEST DRIVE**
The white-knuckle ascent up mountainous Mamore's Gap.

**Malin Head** Ireland's most northerly point

This trip isn't about skimming Ireland's surface through big-name sights. Instead it's a route to the heart of the country's compelling narratives: faith, poverty, mass migration, territorial disputes, the Troubles. With unsigned, cliffside roads that look more like farm tracks, you'll probably get a little lost. But locals are helpful if you do – and asking for directions is a great conversation starter.

## 1 Derry

Kick-start your Inishowen trip by exploring the story of one of the coast's most famous victims: *La Trinidad Valenciera*. This Venetian trader was the second-biggest vessel in the Spanish Armada and was shipwrecked at Kinnagoe Bay in 1588 – a spot you'll see later. Derry's award-winning **Tower Museum** (www.derrycity.gov.uk/museums; Union Hall Pl; adult/child £4/2; ⊙10am-5.30pm) tells the vessel's story and features poignant wreck finds: pewter tableware, wooden combs, olive jars, shoe soles. There are also impressive bronze guns. Look out for the 2.5-tonne siege gun bearing the arms of Phillip II of Spain. They show him as king of England – factually accurate because of his marriage to Queen Mary I, but perhaps also indicative of the ambitions that launched the Armada. Make time to explore vibrant, fascinating Derry, Northern Ireland's second city.

**The Drive** » Take the A2 north towards Moville, where there's a luxury resort (see p343). Derry's retail parks quickly give way to fields and mountain views, and the silvery Lough Foyle emerges to your right. Soon road signs switch from mph to km/h as you transition to the Republic of Ireland. Shortly after Muff, turn left to Iskaheen (11km), head up the hill and park beside the village church.

 p327, p359

## LINK YOUR TRIP

### 29 The North in a Nutshell

The best of the North in one glorious route; pick it up from this trip's end at Buncrana.

### 33 From Bangor to Derry

Belfast and the sight-packed Antrim Coast. It stops where this trips starts: Derry.

## 2 Iskaheen

Head across the road, through the creaking gate and into the old graveyard. There you'll see evidence of spectres that have long stalked Ireland: poverty, high death rates and the Troubles. Among many gravestones recording multiple deaths, hunt out the broad memorial to the McKinney family. Its losses include a 24-year-old woman, a nine-month-old boy and three girls, aged 13 years, 11 months and six weeks. It also commemorates 34-year-old James Gerard McKinney, one of 13 unarmed demonstrators shot dead by British troops in Derry on 30 January 1972 – Bloody Sunday.

**The Drive** » Head back to the R238 drinking in the panorama of Lough Foyle as you go. Next comes a 15-minute, scenic shoreside cruise north to Moville. Just before town, take the left turn, signed Cooley Cross, which appears next to a small lay-by (shoulder) on the right, 20km from Iskaheen.

## 3 Cooley Cross

The 3m-high cross you've parked beside has an unusual ringed head – through it negotiating parties are said to have shaken hands to seal agreements. The atmospheric tumbling of ruins beyond features the remnants of an early monastery founded by St Patrick. At the foot of the enclosure, set against some great lough views, sits the tiny, hut-like **Skull House**. This roofed, gabled structure is a tomb-shrine associated with St Finian, an abbot of the early monastery.

**The Drive** » Rejoin the R238, heading left for the 10-minute drive along the shore to Greencastle. Opposite, Magilligan Point's sandy beaches curl into view. Soon after entering Greencastle (5km) take the right to the Maritime Museum.

TRIP HIGHLIGHT

## 4 Greencastle

Packed with boats and top seafood restaurants, the thriving port of Greencastle also boasts a fine **Maritime Museum** (www.inishowenmaritime.com; adult/child €5/3; ☺9.30am-5.30pm Mon-Sat, noon-5.30pm Sun Easter-Sep, 9.15am-5.30pm Mon-Fri Oct-Easter). It reveals the part this area played in one of Ireland's most powerful stories: mass emigration to America and Australia. It started in 1718 and continued until 1939, but peaked in the mid-1800s. At one stage Derry was Ireland's premier emigration port, and the initial route those vessels took echoes your own – from the city, up the length of Lough Foyle to the sea.

 p343

**The Drive** » Continue north. Just after the Fisheries College take the right, following signs to Stroove. Houses thin out and the road narrows before the black-and-white Inishowen lighthouse edges into your windscreen (windshield). Park just beyond, beside Stroove Beach (5km).

TRIP HIGHLIGHT

### ⑤ Inishowen Head

From Stroove Beach's curling sands, join the footpath that winds north, initially on the road and then onto a track, up towards Inishowen Head itself. This stiff 2.5km climb reveals spectacular views over Lough Foyle to the immense ribbon of sand framing Magilligan Point. On clear days you can spot Scotland's islands to the northeast. Edge high enough and you'll see the jagged rocks and golden sands of Kinnagoe Bay – where *La Trinidad Valenciera* came to grief.

**The Drive** » Motor north, initially along your walk route, before curving left. Opposite the Maritime Museum turn-off, head up an unsigned, steep, narrow, roller-coaster road (it even has grass in the middle) to Culdaff, where there's a guesthouse with a restaurant (see p343). At Culdaff, take the R238 towards Gleneely. Turn right 1km along, opposite the modern church. Cloncha Church (30km) appears 1km later.

### ⑥ Cloncha Church

The towering gable ends and huge windows of the roofless shell of 17th-century Cloncha Church frame views of the Donegal mountains. Inside sits the intricately carved tombstone of Scott Magnus Mac-Orristin – spot the carved writing sloping down the side, and the sword and hurling-stick motifs. Outside, a tall cross stands in a field; clamber down to decipher the depiction of the loaves-and-fishes miracle on its weathered face, amid ornate swirls and zigzags.

**The Drive** » The R238/R243 leads from Culdaff to quaint Malin village, with its excellent sleeping options (see p343). Next make for Malin Head (25km from Cloncha Church), a spectacular drive through Trawbreaga Bay's lowlands, past massive dunes at Five Fingers Strand and the hulk of Knockamany. You emerge onto a rugged coast dotted with whitewashed cottages. Take the right, signed Banba's Crown.

TRIP HIGHLIGHT

### ⑦ Malin Head

Open your car door at Malin Head and step into a weather-battered landscape of tumbling cliffs and sparse vegetation – welcome to Ireland's most northerly point. The clifftop tower beside you was built in 1805 by the British admiralty and

BILDAGENTUR ZOONAR GMBH/ SHUTTERSTOCK ©

**Derry** *Reconciliation/Hands Across the Divide*, by sculptor Maurice Harron

## INISHOWEN'S TREASURES

Beachcombers love Inishowen's postglacial strand lines and raised beaches. They're littered with semiprecious stones such as agate and jasper. Ballyhillin Beach, just east of Malin Head, is a great hunting ground. From Banba's Crown car park, go back down the hill, take the rough farm track left towards a terracotta-coloured cottage and go over the ladder stile.

You can also buy the polished stones at **Malin Pebbles** (www.malinpebbles.com) in Greencastle.

later used as a Lloyds signal station. WWII lookout posts are dotted around. To the west a path leads to Hell's Hole, a chasm where the incoming waters crash against rock formations. Just to the east of the head sits Ballyhillin Beach, one of the best places locally to hunt for semiprecious stones.

**The Drive »** From Malin village take the R238 through Carndonagh (where there's a stop-worthy cafe; see p343) to Clonmany. Then follow signs to Mamore's Gap, heading straight for the by-now-large-looming mountains. At the crossroads the Inis Eoghain (Scenic Route) goes up what looks like a farm track. Wayside shrines and another first-and-second-gear ascent follow, before a brake-burning descent. At the plain, head right to Dunree Head (50km).

TRIP HIGHLIGHT

### 8 Fort Dunree

Dunree Head overlooks Lough Swilly, a highly strategic stretch of water that's been navigated by Norsemen, Normans, Ireland's fleeing aristocracy and part of Britain's WWI naval fleet. The 19th-century **Fort Dunree** (☎074-936 1817; www.dunree. pro.ie; Dunree Head; adult/ child €7/5; ⊙10.30am-6pm Mon-Sat, 1-6pm Sun Jun-Sep, 10.30am-4.30pm Mon-Fri, 1-6pm Sat & Sun Oct-May) commands the water. Along with some menacing artillery, films explore the fort's past, while an underground bunker conjures up daily life. The scenery and the bird life are stunning, too.

**The Drive »** Head south to Buncrana, past the mountains of Bulbin and Aghaweel, rising up to your left. The waters of Lough Swilly sweep off to the right, backed by the ranges of the Fanad Peninsula. At the appealing town of Buncrana (19km), head for the shore, initially signed Swilly Ferry, and park beside the leisure centre.

### 9 Buncrana

From the car park a path leads across the grass and along the coast, with Lough Swilly and the Fanad Peninsula's hills stretching out in front of you. John Newton, the composer of 'Amazing Grace', was inspired to write his legendary anti-slavery song after his ship, the *Greyhound,* sheltered from a storm in these waters in 1748. It was a near-death experience that started his spiritual journey from slave trader to antislavery campaigner.

Make for **Buncrana Castle**, built in 1718. Wolfe Tone was imprisoned here following the unsuccessful French invasion in 1798. Beside the castle you'll find **O'Doherty's Keep**, a 15th-century tower built by the local O'Doherty chiefs, but burned by the English and rebuilt for their own use.

✕ ⌫ p335, p343

# Eating & Sleeping

## Moville ❶

### 🛏 Redcastle Hotel & Spa
Hotel €€

(☎074-938 5555; www.redcastlehoteldonegal.com; R238, Redcastle; s/d from €90/140; 🛜🏊) The peninsula's flashiest luxury resort is on the coast 7km southwest of Moville. Tucked away off the main road, the 93 rooms are comfortable and classy. Restaurants include the **Edge**, which has good views and modern Irish cuisine. Facilities include a nine-hole golf course.

## Greencastle ❹

### ✕ Kealy's Seafood Bar
Seafood €€

(☎074-938 1010; www.kealysseafoodbar.ie; The Harbour; mains €10-50, set menu €36; ⏱12.30-9.30pm Tue-Sun Jul & Aug, Thu-Sun Sep-Jun) This bistro offers locally caught seafood so fresh you almost have to fight the harbourside seals for it. Its unpretentious nautical-style decor belies its numerous culinary awards. It's a splendid spot for anything from a bowl of chowder to a lobster feast, and every meal comes with a great view.

## Culdaff ❺

### 🛏 McGrory's of Culdaff
Guesthouse €€

(☎074-937 9104; www.mcgrorys.ie; R238; s/d from €65/100, mains €12-24; ⏱bar food noon-9pm daily, restaurant 6-9pm Fri-Sun; 🛜) This celery- and plum-hued village landmark has 17 stylish rooms. Of the three bars, catch live music in the **Backroom**, which books international singer-songwriters and traditional music. McGrory's classic Irish cuisine, served in the **Front Room**, is the best for miles around.

## Malin Village ❻

### 🛏 Village B&B
B&B €

(☎074-937 0763; www.malinvillagebandb.com; The Green, Malin; s/d €40/70) Right on the village green, this lovely B&B has a choice of rooms – some traditional with antique furniture, others more contemporary. Although you'll get breakfast here, guests also have use of a kitchen.

### 🛏 Whitestrand B&B
B&B €

(☎086 822 9163; www.whitestrand.net; off R242, Middletown; s/d €32/64; 🛜) Perfectly placed amidst the bluffs and hills leading to Malin Head, this comfy B&B has three fine bedrooms. As a welcome you'll receive a hot beverage and tasty home-baked treats.

## Carndonagh ❼

### ✕ Patisserie de Pascal/Café Donagh
Cafe €

(☎074-937 4191; www.patisseriedepascal.com; The Diamond; mains from €4; ⏱9.30am-5pm Mon-Sat) Stop in for a French-accented light lunch or stock up on beautiful baked goods and sandwiches for a fabulous picnic.

## Buncrana ❾

### ✕ Beach House
Modern Irish €€

(☎074-936 1050; www.thebeachhouse.ie; Swilly Rd; mains lunch €9-13, dinner €17-27; ⏱5-9pm Thu-Sun, 12.30-4pm Sat & Sun, plus Tue & Wed Jul & Aug; 👶) With picture windows overlooking the lough, this cafe-restaurant can easily be your destination for the day. The seasonal menu focuses on simple flavours superbly executed. There's everything from burgers to seafood right off the boats. The wine list is excellent.

### 🛏 Tullyarvan Mill
Hostel €

(☎074-936 1613; www.tullyarvanmill.com; off R238; dm/d/f €15/40/60; 🛜) This 51-bed hostel is housed in a modern building attached to the historic Tullyarvan Mill. Set amid riverside gardens, it also hosts regular cultural events and art exhibitions. It's just north of town.

### 🛏 Westbrook House
B&B €

(☎074-936 1067; www.westbrookhouse.ie; Westbrook Rd; s/d from €40/70; 🛜) A handsome Georgian house set in beautiful gardens, Westbrook features chandeliers and antique furniture, giving it a refined sophistication. The honey served at breakfast comes from the bees kept in the lush garden.

# Northwest on Adrenalin

**32**

*This high-octane trip sees you surfing, hiking and gazing at 600m-high cliffs, driving through mountain passes and along remote, rugged roads – it's an action-packed, unforgettable drive.*

## TRIP HIGHLIGHTS

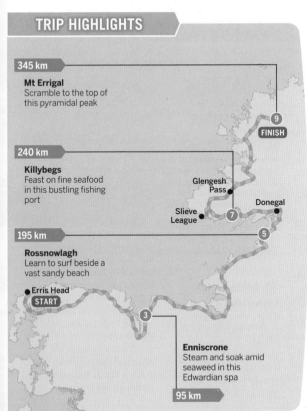

**345 km**

**Mt Errigal**
Scramble to the top of this pyramidal peak

**240 km**

**Killybegs**
Feast on fine seafood in this bustling fishing port

Glengesh
Pass

Donegal

Slieve
League

**9**
**FINISH**

**7**

**5**

**195 km**

**Rossnowlagh**
Learn to surf beside a vast sandy beach

● **Erris Head**
**START**

**3**

**Enniscrone**
Steam and soak amid seaweed in this Edwardian spa

**95 km**

**4 DAYS**
**345KM / 214 MILES**

**GREAT FOR...**

**BEST TIME TO GO**
Easter to October means better weather and opening hours.

**ESSENTIAL PHOTO**
The 600m-high sea cliffs at Slieve League are a photographer's dream.

 **BEST FOR OUTDOORS**
Stops 3 to 8 for surfing, clambering around cliffs and soaking in seaweed baths.

**Slieve League** Sea kayakers explore the cliffs

If you're after an Irish adventure, this trip delivers in spades. Along with adrenalin-fuelled surfing and hiking, you'll take in Donegal's highest mountain, Europe's highest sea cliffs and the world's largest Stone Age monument. Other heritage crowds in, too: an abbey, a castle and a seafaring past. And then there's the drive itself, from sand-dusted seaside lanes to exhilarating mountain roads – it's a roller-coaster ride.

## 1 Erris Head

Where better to start a road trip than at the end of the road – literally. The parking area for Erris Head appears where the rough lane peters out. From there waymarks (black posts with purple arrows) direct you on a two-hour, 5km loop walk around this wind-buffeted headland. The path leads over footbridges and earth banks, across fields and along sheep tracks. The views from the high cliffs are spectacular, taking in islands, sea stacks and rock arches.

**Belmullet Tourist Office** (☎097-20494; www.visiterris. ie; cnr Main St & Chapel St, Belmullet; ☺9am-4pm Mon-Sat Jun-Aug, 9am-4pm Mon-Fri Sep-May) has free guides; to get to the lay-by, follow trailhead signs from Belmullet.

**The Drive ›› **Motor southeast across the narrow neck of land that fuses Belmullet to the rest of County Mayo. Soon, turn left onto the R314, towards Ballycastle. After the road climbs a lush ravine and attaches itself to the coast, a wood-and-glass pyramid suddenly pops up on the right. It's your next stop: Céide Fields (45km).

## 2 Céide Fields

**Céide Fields** (☎096-43325; www.heritageireland. ie; off R314; adult/child €4/2; ☺visitor centre 10am-6pm Jun-Sep, to 5pm Easter-May & Oct, last tour 1hr before closing) is the world's most extensive Stone Age monument. Half a million tonnes of rock make up its field boundaries, houses and megalithic tombs. Today it's a barren, wind-blasted spot, but five millennia ago a thriving farming community lived here, growing wheat and barley and grazing sheep and cattle. Although important,

ATLANTIC
OCEAN

this story is hard to tell engagingly (to the uninitiated the site could resemble tumbles of stone) but a sleek, award-winning visitor centre cleverly re-creates life in early farming communities. Better still, take a guided tour of the site.

The Drive » The R314 heads east, revealing a vast sea stack

## LINK YOUR TRIP

### 3 Tip to Toe

Wind south to Wexford, past the pick of Ireland's historic sites. Join it at stop 4: Sligo town.

### 30 Delights of Donegal

Head further north for exquisite beaches and a sandy horseback ride. Pick it up where this trip stops: towering Mt Errigal.

at Downpatrick Head. Gradually, exposed hills give way to rolling fields. After one-street Ballycastle comes congested Ballina, where you take the N59 north (signed 'Sligo'). Soon the R297 peels off to Enniscrone, 56km from Céide Fields. Drive up Main St, then follow the Hot Seaweed Baths signs left.

TRIP HIGHLIGHT

### ❸ Enniscrone

Right beside Enniscrone's stunning 5km beach sits **Kilcullen's Seaweed Baths** (☎096-36238; http://homepage.eircom.net/~seaweedbaths/frame.htm; Cliff Rd; baths from €25; ⏰10am-10pm Jun-Aug, noon-8pm Mon-Fri, 10am-8pm Sat & Sun Apr, May, Sep & Oct, noon-8pm Mon & Thu, 10am-8pm Sat & Sun Nov-Mar). Step into this Edwardian spa and soon you'll be steaming away in a cedar cabinet, then submerging yourself in a gigantic porcelain bath filled with orangey water and bits of seaweed. It's used to treat arthritis and rheumatism, but the baths' high iodine content means this traditional natural therapy also acts as an intense moisturiser. It's also a great way to recover from, and prepare for, this trip's adventures.

🛏 p351

**The Drive »** You could head south back to the N59, but it's more fun to stay on the R297 as it bobbles and twists beside flat coastal fields. Eventually it rejoins the N59 to sweep east to Ballysadare. From there take the N4 to Sligo (56km); Sligo Abbey is signed from the ring road.

### ❹ Sligo Town

Sligo is an inviting stop: stone bridges frame the river; pedestrian streets are lined with attractive shops; and pub music sessions overflow onto the footpath. In the centre sits **Sligo Abbey** (www.heritageireland.ie; Abbey St; adult/child €4/2; ⏰10am-6pm Easter–mid-Oct), a Dominican friary founded around 1252. The abbey survived the worst ravages of the Tudor era, and it has the only sculpted altar to survive the Reformation. The doorways reach only a few feet high at the abbey's rear – the ground around it was swollen by mass graves from years of famine and war.

🍴 p293, p301, p351

**The Drive »** Heading north out of Sligo on the N15 sees the mountains of Benbulben and Truskmore looming ever larger. At Ballyshannon take the R231 to Rossnowlagh. When sand starts edging onto the road, you know you're near the resort's Blue Flag beach. Make for the graffiti-art designs of Fin McCool's Surf School (53km).

TRIP HIGHLIGHT

### ❺ Rossnowlagh

Rossnowlagh's spectacular 3km-long beach is a wide, sandy stretch beloved by families, walkers and surfers throughout the year. The gentle rollers are great for learning to ride the waves, or to hone your skills. **Fin Mc-**

ROLF G WACKENBERG/SHUTTERSTOCK ©

**Cool Surf School** (☎071-985 9020; www.finmccoolsurf-school.com; Beach Rd; gear rental per day €39, 2hr lessons incl gear €35; ⏰10am-5pm dailyJun-Aug, 10am-5pm Sat & Sun Sep-May) offers tuition and gear hire; the waters of Donegal Bay offer an exhilarating ride.

🍴 🛏 p351

**The Drive »** From Rossnowlagh's sand-dusted road, the R231 winds north

**Rossnowlagh** Bellal Strand

through rolling fields before rejoining the N15. This sweeps on towards Donegal town, with the Blue Stack Mountains now appearing behind. On the roundabout on its fringes, pick up the signs for Donegal Castle (20km).

## 6 Donegal Town

Mountain-backed, pretty Donegal town was for centuries the stamping grounds of the chiefs who ruled northwest Ireland from the 15th to 17th centuries: the O'Donnells. They built **Donegal Castle** (☏074-972 2405; www.heritageireland.ie; Castle St; adult/child €4/2; ☉10am-6pm daily Easter–mid-Sep, 9.30am-4.30pm Thu-Mon mid-Sep–Easter) in 1474, and it served as the seat of their formidable power until 1607, when the English ousted Ireland's chieftains. Rory O'Donnell torched his own castle before leaving for France in the infamous Flight of the Earls. Their departure paved the way for the Plantation of Ulster by thousands of Scots and English Protestants, creating divisions still felt today. The castle was rebuilt in 1623, and it's a wonderfully atmospheric place to visit, with rooms furnished with French tapestries and Persian rugs.

## TOP TIP: GAELTACHT

This part of Ireland is the Donegal Gaeltacht, one of many areas where Irish culture and language are championed. Initially you'll notice it most in road signs, as here they tend to be in Irish only (elsewhere it's Irish and English). We use English transliterations with Irish names included in brackets.

✕ ⊨ p351

**The Drive »** As the N56 heads west, the Blue Stacks range to your right and more mountains shade the horizon ahead. For now, though, it's a gently rolling road that leads towards Killybegs. Take the R263 into town (30km); the Maritime and Heritage Centre is signed soon after the fishing-boat-packed harbour.

- - - - - - - - - - - - - - - -

TRIP HIGHLIGHT

### ❼ Killybegs

Killybegs is a sensory summation of the sea – the scent of fish hangs in the air, and seagulls wheel overhead in this, Ireland's largest fishing port. So a visit to the **Maritime and Heritage Centre** (www.visitkillybegs. com; Fintra Rd; admission €4; ☺10am-6pm Mon-Fri year-round, plus 1-5pm Sat Jul & Aug) is a must. You'll hear the personal accounts of local fishers and see evocative sepia images of the industry's heyday. The best bit, though, is to step aboard the simulation of a fishing-trawler wheelhouse, where you'll try navigating into port

amid choppy seas – driving seems easy after that.

✕ ⊨ p351

**The Drive »** The R263 heads west, tracing the shore before cutting inland to a peak-lined landscape threaded with rough stone walls. Gradually the brooding Slieve League mountains come to dominate the view. At Carrick turn left, following signs for Slieve League, and nudge round the mountain edge to the lower car park (16km).

- - - - - - - - - - - - - - - -

### ❽ Slieve League

The Cliffs of Moher get more publicity, but the spectacular polychrome sea cliffs at Slieve League are higher – the highest in Europe, plunging 600m to the sea. From the lower car park, a path skirts up around the near-vertical rock face to the aptly named **One Man's Pass** – look out for two rocks nicknamed the 'school desk and chair'. Sunset can be stunning, with waves crashing dramatically far below and the ocean reflecting the day's last rays. It's a strenuous hike to the summit, and rain and mist can appear

unexpectedly, making conditions slippery. You can now drive all the way to the top – be aware it can involve reversing up/ down the steep, one-car-wide, cliffside road.

**The Drive »** Pick up the (signed) Glengesh Pass road, a long climb into a wild landscape that crests to reveal sweeping valley views. A dizzying, hairpin descent lurches to the N56 and towards Mt Errigal, the massive pointed peak that edges ever nearer. The R251 climbs through Dunlewey village; when Errigal is directly on your left, turn into the small, walled parking area (83km).

- - - - - - - - - - - - - - - -

TRIP HIGHLIGHT

### ❾ Mt Errigal

Towering Mt Errigal (752m) seemingly dares you to attempt the tough but beautiful climb to its pyramid-shaped peak. Watch the weather: it's a dangerous trek on misty or wet days, when visibility is minimal. The easiest path to the summit covers 5km and takes around three hours (two up, one back); the **Dunlewey Centre** (Ionad Cois Locha; ☎074-953 1699; www.dunleweycentre. com; Dunlewey; combined ticket adult/child €10.30/7.50; ☺10.30am-5.30pm Easter-Sep, to 4.45pm Oct; ♿) can direct you to the starting point. Even if you don't climb, drink in this remarkably exposed, re-mote landscape of peaks, loughs and bogs.

⊨ p351

# Eating & Sleeping

## Enniscrone ❸

### 🛏 Waterfront House — Lodge €€

(📞096-37120; www.waterfronthouse.ie; Cliff Rd; s/d from €55/90; 🛜) Perched on the knoll overlooking the broad beach and surf, the 16 rooms are done up in ubiquitous maroon, but considering the views, they are a bargain. The bar and restaurant will keep you otherwise occupied.

## Sligo Town ❹

### 🍴 Lyons Cafe — Modern European €

(📞071-914 2969; www.lyonscafe.com; Quay St; mains €7-15; ⏱9am-6pm Mon-Sat) At this airy 1st-floor cafe, acclaimed chef (and cookbook author) Gary Stafford offers a fresh and seasonal menu that's inventive yet casual.

## Rossnowlagh ❺

### 🍴 Gaslight Inn — Irish €€

(📞071-985 1141; www.gaslight-rossnowlagh. com; mains €8-35; ⏱11am-late daily Jun-Sep, 5pm-late Fri, 11am-late Sat & Sun Oct-May) Set on the clifftop, the Gaslight Inn offers an extensive menu of well-cooked comfort food and spectacular views over the bay. The owners also run the **Ard na Mara** (📞071-985 1141; www. ardnamara-rossnowlagh.com; r €70-100; 🛜) guesthouse, which has five bright rooms.

### 🛏 Smugglers Creek — B&B €€

(📞071-985 2367; www.smugglerscreekinn.com; Cliff Rd; r €50-100; mains €8-25; ⏱daily Apr-Sep, Thu-Sun Oct-Mar; 🛜) This combined pub/ restaurant/guesthouse perches on the hillside above the bay. It's justifiably popular for its excellent food and sweeping views (room 4 has the best vantage point and a balcony). There's live music on summer weekends.

## Donegal Town ❻

### 🍴 Olde Castle Bar — Irish €€

(📞074-972 1262; www.oldecastlebar.com; Castle St; mains €9-29; ⏱kitchen noon-9pm;

🍴) This ever-busy pub off the Diamond serves some of the area's best food. Look for upmarket classics such as Donegal Bay oysters, Irish stew, seafood platters (the €29 one is spectacular), plus steaks and burgers. The pub is always rollicking with locals and serves its own excellent pale ale: Red Hugh Brew.

### 🛏 Ard na Breatha — B&B €€

(📞074-972 2288; www.ardnabreatha.com; Drumrooske Middle; r €90-160; ⏱Feb-Oct; 🛜🍴) In an elevated setting 1.5km north of town, this boutique guesthouse on a working farm has tasteful rooms with wrought-iron beds. The six rooms are in a building separate from the main house. It has a full bar and restaurant (three-course dinner €39) with organic food sourced from the farm or locally, where possible. You must pre-book dinner.

## Killybegs ❼

### 🍴 Kitty Kelly's — Modern Irish €€

(📞074-973 1925; www.kittykellys.com; off R263, Largy; dinner mains €17-25; ⏱12.30-3pm & 6.30-9.30pm Mon-Sat, 1.30-3.30pm Sun Jun-Sep, closed Mon & Tue Oct-May, closed Jan) Dining at this restaurant in a 200-year-old farmhouse feels more like attending an intimate dinner party. The menu is a modern take on Irish favourites with an emphasis on seafood. It's on the coast road, 5km west of Killybegs – you can't miss the lurid pink-and-green paint job. Bookings essential.

### 🛏 Tara Hotel — Hotel €€

(📞074-974 1700; www.tarahotel.ie; Main St; s/d from €65/120; 🅿🛜) This modern hotel across from and overlooking the harbour has 31 comfortable, minimalist rooms, a decent bar and a small gym with spa bath, sauna and steam room.

## Mt Errigal ❾

### 🛏 Glen Heights B&B — B&B €

(📞074-956 0844; www.glenheightsbb.com; Dunlewey; d €70; 🛜) The three rooms are cosy, and there are breathtaking views of Dunlewey Lake from the conservatory.

# From Bangor to Derry

**33**

*From seaside to mountainside, via ruined castles, stately homes, museums and the Giant's Causeway – this trip blends cracking coastal scenery with blockbuster historic sights.*

## TRIP HIGHLIGHTS

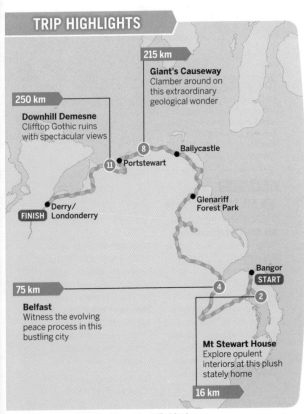

**215 km**

**Giant's Causeway**
Clamber around on this extraordinary geological wonder

**250 km**

**Downhill Demesne**
Clifftop Gothic ruins with spectacular views

**8** Portstewart **Ballycastle**

**11**

**Derry/**
**FINISH** **Londonderry**

**Glenariff**
**Forest Park**

**Bangor**
**START**

**4** **2**

**75 km**

**Belfast**
Witness the evolving peace process in this bustling city

**Mt Stewart House**
Explore opulent interiors at this plush stately home

**16 km**

### 4 DAYS
### 295KM / 183 MILES

### GREAT FOR...

### BEST TIME TO GO

March to October brings better weather; avoid August to dodge holiday crowds.

### 📷 ESSENTIAL PHOTO

The spectacular Giant's Causeway, your must-have north-coast snap.

### ☑ BEST TWO DAYS

Stops 8 to 11 take in the Causeway, castles, ruins and golden sands.

**Carrick-a-Rede Rope Bridge** Tourists crossing to the island

## 33 From Bangor to Derry

This drive delivers a true taste of Ireland's gloriously diverse north: the must-see stops of the Giant's Causeway and Carrick-a-Rede; castles and historic homes at Mt Stewart, Hillsborough, Dunluce and Downhill; and superb scenery, from Slemish to sea-sprayed cliffs and immense sand dunes. While in Belfast and Derry, you'll experience two vibrant cities progressing beyond a painful past.

### ① Bangor

Start your journey through the North's scenic and historic highlights at a stop with a pop-culture twist. Pedal round the ornamental lake at Bangor's kitsch-rich **Pickie Family Fun Park** (http://pickiefunpark. com; Marine Gardens; family pass £10-35; ☺9am-7.30pm mid-Mar–May, to 9pm Jun-Aug, to 4pm Sep & Oct, 9am-4pm Sat & Sun Nov–mid-Mar) in one of its famous swan-shaped boats, then do a road trip warm-up by putting a track full of electric cars through their paces.

**The Drive »** From Bangor's pastel-painted seafront terraces, pick up the A21 south to Newtownards. From there the A20 runs south towards Mt Stewart (initially signed Portaferry). Soon the vast, island-dotted Strangford Lough emerges to your right; the road clings to its winding shore to Mt Stewart House (16km).

TRIP HIGHLIGHT

### ② Mt Stewart House

Magnificent 18th-century **Mt Stewart House** (www. nationaltrust.org.uk; Portaferry Rd; adult/child £8.50/4.25; ☺house 11am-4.30pm mid-Apr–late Oct, to 3pm Sat & Sun Nov-Mar, gardens 10am-5pm mid-Mar–late Oct, to 4pm Nov–Mar) is one of Northern Ireland's grandest stately homes. Lavish plaster-work combines with antiques and artworks that include a painting of the racehorse Hambletonian by George Stubbs. Garden highlights include griffin and mermaid statues on the Dodo Terrace, and the **Temple of the Winds** (☺2-5pm Sun Mar-Sep), a mock-Gothic ruin with great views of the Strangford Lough.

**The Drive »** Go north, back along the A20 beside

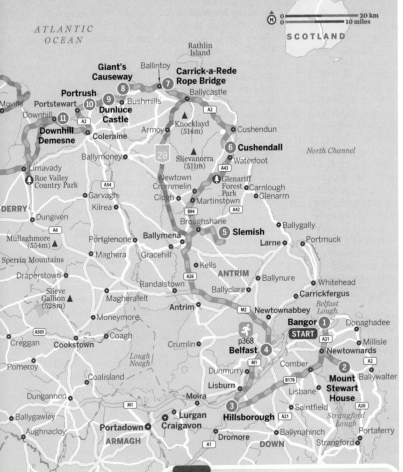

scenic Strangford Lough into Newtownards. There, take the A21 southwest through Comber. Soon the B178 to Hillsborough (40km) cuts off to the right, across a lush pastoral landscape.

- - - - - - - - - - - -

### ❸ Hillsborough

Set in elegant Hillsborough, the rambling, late-Georgian **Hillsborough Castle** (☎028-9268

**LINK YOUR TRIP**

**29 The North in a Nutshell**

Head west to wild Donegal for sandy shores, live-music sessions and a castaway island. Pick it up at this trip's end in Derry.

**31 Inishowen Peninsula**

Drive north onto a remote headland boasting exquisite scenery, shipwrecks and white-knuckle drives. Start in Derry.

1300; www.hrp.org.uk; Main St; guided tour of castle & access to gardens adult/child £7.50/5.50, gardens only adult & child £3.50; ☺gardens 9.30am-6pm Mar-Oct, to 4pm Mon-Sat Nov-Feb; castle hours vary Mar-Sep) is the Queen's official residence in Northern Ireland. Book ahead for guided tours taking in opulent state drawing and dining rooms and the Lady Grey Room, where former UK prime minister Tony Blair and former US president George W Bush had talks on Iraq. Garden delights include yew and lime tree walks, an ice house and a lake.

✕ ⊨ p359

**The Drive »** Head north on the A1 then join the M1 for Belfast. Exit onto the A55/Outer Ring, then follow signs for Queens University, Botanic Gardens or your destination, Ulster Museum (16km).

TRIP HIGHLIGHT

### ④ Belfast

Bustling Belfast has big-city appeal. As well as walking through its former sectarian strongholds (p368), drop by

the **Ulster Museum** (www. nmni.com; Botanic Gardens; ☺10am-5pm Tue-Sun). Completely revamped in 2009, it's now one of Northern Ireland's don't-miss attractions. Highlights of its beautifully designed displays are the Armada Room; Takabuti, a 2500-year-old Egyptian mummy; the Bann Disc; and the Snapshot of an Ancient Sea Floor.

✕ ⊨ p60, p359

**The Drive »** Head into Belfast, passing the Grand Opera House (which was bombed by the IRA in the 1990s). Take the M2 north, then the A26 to Ballymena, and then the A42 to Broughshane. There, turn right after James McNeil Hardware, following the hard-to-see sign to Slemish. Follow another sign, which points left almost immediately, before the mountain itself emerges, an immense, hump-topped plateau of rock (67km).

### ⑤ Slemish

Craggy Slemish (438m) is where Ireland's patron saint St Patrick is said to have tended goats. On St Patrick's Day, thousands make a pilgrimage to its

summit. It's a steep but pleasant 30-minute climb that's rewarded with fine views.

**The Drive »** Go back to Broughshane, then peel off right onto the B94 towards Clogh. Next take the A43 north towards Waterfoot. In time the road suddenly rises, settlements thin out and you're in the glens: sweeping ridges of steep-sided hills. After a steep valley descent, emerge at the coast to go north to Cushendall (32km), parking beside its beach.

### ⑥ Cushendall

From Cushendall's beach, walk 1km north, scrambling up the coast path to the picturesque ruins of **Layde Old Church**. Here views stretch as far as the Scottish coast. Founded by the Franciscans, Layde was used as a parish church from the early 14th century. Today the picturesque ruins have grand memorials to the MacDonnells (earls of Antrim from 1620) in the graveyard and an ancient, weathered ring-cross by the gate.

⊨ p359

**The Drive »** The A2 heads north, through pretty Cushendun, before climbing steeply to open heathland. At the holiday resort of Ballycastle, pick up the B15, which winds beside fields and windswept cliffs to the Carrick-a-Rede Rope Bridge (34km).

# TOP TIP:
## GIANT'S CAUSEWAY

The causeway is stunning but it can get overwhelmed by visitor numbers. If you can, visit midweek or out of season to experience it at its most evocative. Sunset in spring and autumn is the best time for photographs.

**Portrush** Dunluce Castle

## ⑦ Carrick-a-Rede Rope Bridge

A wobbling bridge is an unusual spot to stretch your legs, but it's unforgettable nonetheless. The **Carrick-a-Rede Rope Bridge** (www.nationaltrust. org.uk; Ballintoy; adult/child £5.90/3; ⏱9.30am-7pm Apr-Aug, to 6pm Mar, Sep & Oct, to 3.30pm Nov-Feb) is a 20m-long, 1m-wide contraption of wire and planks that stretches 30m above rock-strewn water. It sways and bounces beneath your feet before you emerge onto a tiny island dotted with reminders of its past as a salmon fishery.

The Drive » Rejoin the B15, then the A2 before turning right onto the scenic B146, which clings to the coast, passing ruined Dunseverick Castle en route to the Giant's Causeway (11km).

`TRIP HIGHLIGHT`

## ⑧ Giant's Causeway

The **Giant's Causeway** (⏱dawn-dusk) is this coast's must-see sight: a remarkable, ragged ribbon of regular, closely packed, hexagonal stone columns that dips gently beneath the waves. The spectacular rock formation is Northern Ireland's only Unesco World Heritage site and is one of Ireland's most impressive and atmospheric landscape features. To park on-site you'll need to buy a ticket to the **Giant's Causeway Visitor Experience** (☎028-2073 1855; www.nationaltrust.org. uk; adult/child with parking £9/4.50, without parking £7/3.25; ⏱9am-7pm Apr-Sep, to 6pm Feb, Mar & Oct, to 5pm Nov-Jan), the superb new visitor centre.

 p60

The Drive » Head through Bushmills, with its historic distillery and great sleeping options, onto the A2 to Portrush. Soon sea views flood in, then Dunluce Castle's ragged ruins (8km) springs into view. Be aware: the castle turn-off comes immediately afterwards, down a sloping track on the right.

## ⑨ Dunluce Castle

The atmospheric remains of **Dunluce Castle** (87 Dunluce Rd; adult/ child £5/3; ⏱10am-5pm, 4.30pm) cling to a dramatic basalt crag. Built between the 15th and 17th centuries, it was once the coast's finest castle and the seat of the powerful MacDonnell family. A narrow bridge leads from the mainland courtyard across a dizzying gap to the main fortress, where you can roam the shells of buildings and listen to the sea pounding on the cliffs.

## DERRY OR LONDONDERRY?

Derry is a town with two names. Nationalists/
Republicans (mostly Catholics who want the North
to be part of the Irish Republic) use Derry; Unionists/
Loyalists (mostly Protestants who want to preserve
the union with Britain) use Londonderry, which is still
the city's official name. Northern Ireland road signs
point to Londonderry (as you drive you might well
see the 'London' part of the name defaced), while
Republic road signs point to Derry. Politics aside, the
city's name is often shortened to Derry in everyday
speech.

**The Drive »** Taking the A2 towards Portrush, you're soon sandwiched between cliffs and a huge golden beach far below. At Portrush (6km), sand dunes dotted with golf courses take over; head for the central East (Curran) Strand car park.

### 🔟 Portrush

You can't leave the Antrim coast without some head-clearance time beside the sea. The East Strand car park borders the 3km Curran Strand, a dune-backed golden ribbon of sand that makes for a glorious walk. Or make for nearby **Troggs Surf School** (☎028-7082 5476; www.troggs.com; 88 Main St; ◷10am-5.30pm Mon-Sat, noon-5.30pm Sun), which runs lessons (bookings advised) and hires out bodyboards/surfboards (per day £7.50/10) and wetsuits (per day £7).

🍴 🛏 p359

**The Drive »** The A2 heads west, passing through seaside Portstewart and shop-packed Coleraine. Next the cupola of Downhill Demesne's Mussenden Temple eases into view. Go past the Bishop's Gate entrance, turning off into the Lion's Gate (24km).

**TRIP HIGHLIGHT**

### 1️⃣1️⃣ Downhill Demesne

In 1774 the eccentric Bishop of Derry built himself a palatial, clifftop home: **Downhill Demesne** (www.nationaltrust.org. uk; adult/child £4.50/2.30; ◷dawn-dusk). It burnt down in 1851, was rebuilt in 1876 and was finally abandoned after WWII. Today it features follies (ornamental buildings), mausoleums and a giant, ruined house. Trails lead past a dovecote onto a grassy headland and the elegant **Mussenden Temple**. From inside,

the cliff-edge views are extraordinary, reaching from Portrush (where you strolled on the sand) round to the shores of Lough Foyle (where you're headed).

**The Drive »** The A2 continues west, through the fertile lowlands that frame Lough Foyle, and on to the city of Derry (41km).

### 1️⃣2️⃣ Derry

Northern Ireland's second city surprises some with its riverside setting and impressive, 17th-century walls. The best way to explore them, and the city's inspiring progress beyond sectarian violence, is by walking (p370). Make sure you drop into **St Columb's Cathedral** (www.stcolumbscathedral. org; 17 London St; admission by donation; ◷9am-5pm Mon-Sat). This stately church was completed in 1633, making it Derry's oldest building. In the porch look for the hollow mortar shell fired into the churchyard during the Great Siege of 1688. Inside the shell were the terms of a surrender that never came.

🍴 🛏 p327, p359

# Eating & Sleeping

## Hillsborough ③

### ✕ Plough Inn     Bistro ££

(☎028-9268 2985; http://ploughgroup.com; 3 The Square; mains lunch £9.50-12, dinner £11.50-20; ⊙noon-2.30pm & 5-9pm Mon-Thu, to 9.30pm Fri & Sat, noon-8pm Sun; ⊕) This fine old pub, with its maze of dark, wood-panelled nooks and crannies, has been offering 'beer and banter' since 1758. It serves gourmet bar lunches and also offers fine dining in the upstairs restaurant, where stone walls, low ceilings and a roaring fireplace make a cosy setting for a menu ranging from whiskey-cured salmon to braised brisket of beef.

### ⨇ Fortwilliam Country House   B&B ££

(☎028-9268 2255; www.fortwilliamcountry house.com; 210 Ballynahinch Rd; s/d £50/70; 🅿🛜) The Fortwilliam's four luxurious rooms include the Victorian room, with rose wallpaper, huge antique mahogany wardrobe and view over the garden. Breakfast includes fresh eggs from the chickens in the yard, and the smell of home-baked wheaten bread wafts from the Aga. From Hillsborough, take the B177 towards Anahilt; it's 5.6km along on the right.

## Belfast ④

### ✕ Café Conor     Cafe ££

(☎028-9066 3266; www.cafeconor.com; 11a Stranmillis Rd; mains £9-19; ⊙9am-10pm Mon-Sat, to 9pm Sun) Set in the glass-roofed former studio of William Conor, a Belfast artist, this light-filled, laid-back bistro offers a range of pastas, salads, burgers and stir-fries, along with favourites such as fish and chips with mushy peas. The breakfast menu is served till 5pm.

## Cushendall ⑥

### ⨇ Village B&B     B&B ££

(☎028-2177 2366; www.thevillagebandb.com; 18 Mill St; s/d/f from £40/65/95; 🅿🛜) Right in the middle of town, the Village offers three spotless rooms with private bathrooms

and fireplaces, and huge hearty breakfasts (including a vegetarian option).

## Portrush ⑩

### ✕ 55 Degrees North    International ££

(☎028-7082 2811; www.55-north.com; 1 Causeway St; mains £10-19; ⊙12.30-2.30pm & 5-8.30pm Mon-Fri, to 9pm Sat, noon-8.30pm Sun; ⊕♿) Floor-to-ceiling windows allow you to soak up a spectacular panorama of sand and sea from this stylish restaurant. The food concentrates on clean, simple flavours. Downstairs, licensed **Café North** (lunch mains £6-8, dinner mains £10-14; ⊙9am-9pm Mon, Tue & Sat, to 6pm Wed-Fri Easter-Sep, reduced hrs Oct-Easter) has a beach-facing terrace.

### ⨇ Clarmont     B&B ££

(☎028-7082 2397; www.clarmontguesthouse. com; 10 Landsdowne Cres; d £50-70; 🛜) The pick of Portrush's guesthouses, the refurbished Clarmont has great views and a decor that tastefully mixes Victorian and modern styles. Ask for one of the bay-window bedrooms with sea views and spa.

## Derry ⑫

### ✕ Custom House    Modern Irish ££

(☎028-7137 3366; http://customhouse restaurant.com; Custom House St, Queen's Quay; mains lunch £8-10, dinner £13-19; ⊙noon-9.30pm Wed-Sun) You can just drop in for a drink in the bar – fitted out with pewter, copper and walnut wood – but the 1876-built Custom House is a superb spot to dine on seared monkfish, slow braised belly of pork and whiskey-cured salmon. Service goes above and beyond.

### ⨇ Saddler's House     B&B ££

(☎028-7126 9691; www.thesaddlershouse. com; 36 Great James St; s/d from £55/60; 🛜) Centrally located within a five-minute walk of the walled city, this friendly B&B is set in a lovely Victorian town house. All seven rooms have private bathrooms, and you get to enjoy a huge breakfast in the family kitchen.

# The Antrim Coast

**34**

*This trip encompasses Antrim's big sights (causeway, rope bridge, distillery) and some surprises: a hideaway island, a gorgeous glen and a clifftop walk where you'll hardly see another soul.*

## TRIP HIGHLIGHTS

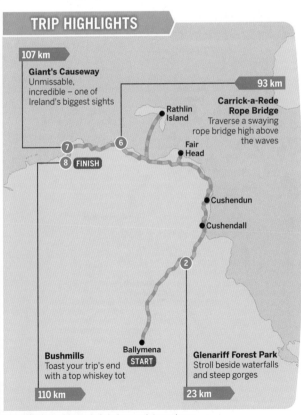

**107 km**

**Giant's Causeway**
Unmissable, incredible – one of Ireland's biggest sights

**93 km**

**Carrick-a-Rede Rope Bridge**
Traverse a swaying rope bridge high above the waves

Rathlin Island

Fair Head

7

8 FINISH

6

2

Cushendun

Cushendall

**Bushmills**
Toast your trip's end with a top whiskey tot

**110 km**

Ballymena
START

**Glenariff Forest Park**
Stroll beside waterfalls and steep gorges

**23 km**

### 3 DAYS
### 110KM / 68 MILES

### GREAT FOR...

### BEST TIME TO GO
Avoiding August means less crowded sights; Easter to July and September should mean brighter days.

### ESSENTIAL PHOTO
You, standing on the basalt columns of the Giant's Causeway.

### BEST FOR SOLITUDE
Stops 4 and 5 see you well away from the crowds.

**Giant's Causeway** Tourists climb the hexagonal stone columns

# 34 The Antrim Coast

Many visitors cram the Antrim coast's big-name sights into a day. But take this trip slowly and you'll have time to marvel at less obvious sights. From exploring a thought-provoking museum to overnighting on an island, you'll discover an Antrim many people miss. This mystical landscape's extraordinary rock formations, ruined castles and wooded glens have made the region an atmospheric backdrop for the TV series *Game of Thrones*, with numerous filming locations here.

## ❶ Ballymena

Start exploring the Antrim coast with the superb potted history offered by the **Braid Museum** (📞028-2563 5077; www.thebraid.com; 1-29 Bridge St; ⏰10am-5pm Mon-Fri, to 4pm Sat). Interactive, audiovisual displays evoke a rich history stretching from the county's prehistoric inhabitants to the present. Prepare for stories of Irish chiefs, the mass settlement of Scottish and English Protestants (called Plantation) and the historic

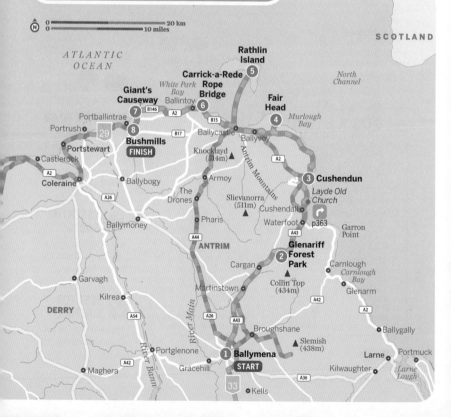

events behind the island's political banners – both Unionist/Loyalist (mostly Protestants who want to preserve the union with Britain) and Nationalist/Republican (mostly Catholics who want the North to be part of the Irish Republic). The *Modern Times* film montage is another highlight, encompassing the *Titanic*, WWI, the Depression, Civil Rights, footballer George Best and former US president Bill Clinton.

**The Drive »** As the A43 heads north towards Waterfoot, the Antrim Mountains rise into view. Suddenly, there's a landscape shift: houses peter away, the road climbs and trees thin out, revealing rock ridges and plunging valleys. The road climbs abruptly, exposing plummeting hills.

# LINK YOUR TRIP

**29** **The North in a Nutshell**

Head west to Donegal's wild, beach-fringed coast. Begin where this trip ends: Bushmills.

**33** **From Bangor to Derry**

Take in seaside fun, history-rich Belfast and two stately homes. Start 60km southeast of Ballymena, at Bangor.

# DETOUR: LAYDE OLD CHURCH

**Start: ❷ Glenariff Forest Park**

In a coast full of big sights, it's worth hunting out some hidden delights. In central Cushendall, turn right to park beside its beach. Then walk 1km north up the coast path, enjoying views across to the Scottish coast. The path leads to Layde Old Church. Founded by the Franciscans, the church was in use from the early 14th century until 1790. The graveyard features grand memorials to the MacDonnells (earls of Antrim from 1620) and an ancient, weathered ring-cross, much older than the 19th-century inscription on its shaft.

TRIP HIGHLIGHT

## ❷ Glenariff Forest Park

The pick of the trails at Glenariff Forest Park is the **Red Waterfall Walk**. From the car park (surely one of the North's most scenic; parking £5) this 3km, waymarked, circular trail goes beside the Glenariff River and past the Ess-na-Larach and Ess-na-Crub waterfalls, along paths cut into the sheer gorge sides, up stairways and along boardwalks set on stilts on the water. The forest is a mix of native species (look out for oak, elm and hazel) and introduced trees, notably pine and Douglas fir. You've a fair chance of spotting red squirrels, hen harriers and Irish hares darting among the trees. The tea house beside the car

park offers the chance to refuel and take in more stunning gorge views.

 p367

**The Drive »** Continue on the A43, descending steeply through hairpin bends into a wide, U-shaped glacial valley with suddenly revealed sea views. Follow the A2 north along the shore, through the busy resort of Cushendall to Cushendun (17km).

## ❸ Cushendun

Follow the shoreline to the right, past the fisherman's cottage on the south side of pretty Cushendun, until you reach a series of caves sculpted from porous-looking rock; *Game of Thrones* fans will recognise this as a filming location for the Stormlands. Head back along the seafront and over the bridge, this time going straight on to the village itself. Its central cluster of Cornish-style cottages was built between 1912 and 1925 and designed by Clough Williams-Ellis, the architect of Portmeirion in north Wales. They were commissioned by Lord Cushendun and his Cornish wife, Maud. Her grave in the village churchyard bears the inscription, 'To a Cornish woman who loved the Glens and their people'.

✕ 🛏 p367

**The Drive** ›› Pick up the (signed) Torr Head Scenic Route, a heart-in-the-mouth route of winding first-gear gradients that clings to increasingly stark cliffs. Ignore the Torr Head turn-off and instead peel off right to Murlough Bay, passing a National Trust welcome sign before reaching a car park 300m further on (16km).

MNHETEC/GETTY IMAGES ©

### ④ Fair Head

By now the 180m-high basalt cliffs of Fair Head rear to your left. Walk towards them, following a 1km moderate clifftop path (waymarked by yellow circles) to the top. Once there, look out for rock climbers (this is one of the region's best climbing sites) and the spectacular gully bridged by a fallen rock, called Grey Man's Path. A stunning panorama sweeps from Rathlin Island in the west to Scotland's Mull of Kintyre in the east. Keep an eye out, too, for whales and dolphins swimming offshore.

**The Drive** ›› Heading west on the A2, the landscape becomes steadily less rugged. Soon golf courses replace sheep-grazed hills, and sandy beaches replace that precipitous shore. At the cheery resort of Ballycastle (20km), park in the ferry-terminal car park or in a harbourside, free, long-stay bay (some have time limits, so double-check).

### ⑤ Rathlin Island

Time to leave the car behind and overnight on Rathlin Island (Reachlainn; www.rathlincommunity.org), a 6.5km-by-4km windswept slab of rock that's 6km offshore. From mid-April to August it's home to hundreds of seals and thousands of nesting

**Glenariff Forest Park** Mill wheel and waterfall

seabirds. The Royal Society for the Protection of Birds' **Rathlin Seabird Centre** (www.rspb.org.uk; adult/child £5/2.50; ☉10am-5pm Mar-Sep) provides extraordinary views of sea stacks thick with guillemots, kittiwakes, razorbills and puffins.

Scottish hero Robert the Bruce hid here in 1306 after being defeated by the English. Inspired by a spider's determined web-spinning, he subsequently triumphed at Bannockburn. His cave is beneath the East Lighthouse.

It takes 25 to 45 minutes to cross to the island by **ferry** (☎028-2076 9299; www.rathlinballycastleferry.com; adult/child/bicycle return £12/6/3.30). In July and August there are 10 ferries each day, eight daily in April, May and September and five daily from October to March. Book in advance.

🛏 p367

**The Drive** ≫ From the Rathlin Island ferry terminal the B15 climbs north towards Ballintoy. As Rathlin Island recedes behind you, a coastal plateau of rugged heathland unfurls. The plateau runs along then steeply down to the Carrick-a-Rede Rope Bridge turn (19km) on the right.

TRIP HIGHLIGHT

## 6 Carrick-a-Rede Rope Bridge

The **Carrick-a-Rede Rope Bridge** (www.nationaltrust. org.uk; Ballintoy; adult/child £5.90/3; ⊙9.30am-7pm Apr-Aug, to 6pm Mar, Sep & Oct, to 3.30pm Nov-Feb) is a 20m-long, 1m-wide assemblage of wire rope and planks that sways 30m above rock-strewn water. It spans a chasm between cliffs and a tiny island that sustained a salmon fishery for centuries – fishers used the bridge to stretch their nets out from the island's tip to intercept migrating salmon. Declining stocks have now put an end to fishing, however.

It's a heart-in-the-mouth walk across the bridge. Once on the island the panorama includes last night's stop, Rathlin Island, and the site of your walk the day before: the sheer cliffs of Fair Head.

The Drive >> Heading west, the B15 and then the A2 deliver more bursts of rugged coastal driving – the golden beach unfurling below is White Park Bay. Turn onto the B146, getting even closer to the shore. This road glides past ruined Dunseverick Castle en route to the coast's big draw: the Giant's Causeway (11km).

TRIP HIGHLIGHT

## 7 Giant's Causeway

When you first see it you'll understand why the ancients believed the **causeway** (www.national trust.org.uk; ⊙dawn-dusk) couldn't be a natural feature. The spectacular expanse of regular, closely packed, hexagonal stone columns dipping gently beneath the waves looks for all the world like the handiwork of giants. The phenomenon is explained in the **Giant's Causeway Visitor Experience** (☑028-2073 1855; www.nationaltrust.org.uk; adult/child with parking £9/4.50, without parking £7/3.25; ⊙9am-7pm Apr-Sep, to 6pm Feb, Mar & Oct, to 5pm Nov-Jan), a superb new ecofriendly building half-hidden in a hillside above the sea.

It's a sloping 1km walk to the causeway. Once you've clambered around on the geometric rocks, don't miss the stack of pipe-like basalt columns known as the **Organ** – access them on the lower coastal path that heads towards the **Amphitheatre Viewpoint** at Port Reostan.

Visiting the causeway itself is free of charge, but you pay to use the car park and the visitor centre.

✘ p60

The Drive >> Rejoin the A2 for a 3km uphill drive inland to the small town of Bushmills. Signs point towards the world-famous distillery on its western edge.

TRIP HIGHLIGHT

## 8 Bushmills

What better way to finish a trip full of the flavour of the Antrim coast than with a true taste of Ireland: Bushmills Irish Whiskey? **Old Bushmills Distillery** (☑028-2073 3218; www.bushmills.com; 2 Distillery Rd; tours adult/child £7.50/4; ⊙9.15am-4.45pm Mon-Sat, noon-4.45pm Sun Mar-Oct, 10am-4.45pm Mon-Sat, noon-4.45pm Sun Nov-Feb) is the world's oldest legal distillery. During ageing, the alcohol content drops from around 60% to 40%. The spirit lost through evaporation is known as 'the angels' share'. Tastings (£7.50, every 30 minutes from 11am to 4pm) include a sample of a 12-year-old Single Malt Distillery Reserve, only available on-site.

✘ ⤶ p367

# Eating & Sleeping

## Glenariff Forest Park ❷

### ✖ Laragh Lodge — Pub Food £

(☎028-2175 8221; 120 Glen Rd; mains £8.50-16, 4-course Sun lunch £20; ☺10.30am-9pm May-Jul, to 7.45pm Aug-Apr) A renovated Victorian tourist lodge with assorted bric-a-brac dangling from the rafters, the Laragh dates from 1890 and serves hearty pub-grub-style meals like cottage pie, steak sandwiches and fish and chips, as well as a traditional roast lunch on Sunday. It's on a side road off the A43, 3km northeast of the main park entrance.

## Cushendun ❸

### ✖ Mary McBride's Pub — Pub Food ££

(☎028-2176 1511; 2 Main St; bar snacks £4-10, dinner mains £12-19.50; ☺food noon-7pm Wed, 11am-5pm & 6-9.30pm Thu-Sat, 11am-6pm Sun) The original bar here (on the left as you go in) is the smallest in Ireland (2.7m by 1.5m), but there's plenty of elbow-bending room in the rest of the pub. The pub grub served in the downstairs bar is good and there's Guinness on tap, as well as live music at weekends. Upstairs the **Little Black Door** seafood bistro is open from 6pm to 9.30pm, Thursday to Saturday.

### ⌂ Cloneymore House — B&B ££

(☎028-2176 1443; ann.cloneymore@btinternet.com; 103 Knocknacarry Rd; s/d £50/65; Ⓟ🛜) A traditional family B&B on the B92 road 500m southwest of Cushendun, Cloneymore has three spacious and spotless rooms named after Irish and Scottish islands – Aran is the biggest. There are wheelchair ramps and a stairlift, and rooms are equipped for visitors with limited mobility.

### ⌂ Villa Farmhouse — B&B ££

(☎028-2176 1252; www.thevillafarmhouse.com; 185 Torr Rd; s/d £35/60; Ⓟ🛜) This lovely old whitewashed farmhouse is set on a hillside, 1km north of Cushendun, with great views over the bay and the warm atmosphere of a family home, decorated with photos of children and grandchildren. The owner is an expert chef

and breakfast will be a highlight of your stay – possibly the best scrambled eggs in Northern Ireland!

## Rathlin Island ❺

### ⌂ Coolnagrock B&B — B&B ££

(☎028-2076 3983; Coolnagrock; s/d from £40/70; ☺closed Dec; 🛜) Views stretch across the sea to Kintyre from this well-appointed guesthouse in the eastern part of the island. It's a 15-minute walk from the ferry, but you can arrange for the owner to pick you up.

### ⌂ Rathlin Island Hostel — Hostel £

(☎07563 814378; http://rathlinhostel.com; dm £18) Just a five-minute walk south of the harbour, this hostel opened in 2014. The five simple but bright rooms have four to 12 beds, with the option to book each as a private room (£67 to £200). All share bathrooms (including one for visitors with limited mobility). There's a self-catering kitchen and fantastic ocean-view terrace. Cash only.

## Bushmills ❽

### ✖ Bushmills Inn — Irish ££

(9 Dunluce Rd; mains lunch £11-16, dinner £12.50-23.50; ☺noon-5pm & 6-9.30pm Mon-Sat, noon-2.30pm & 6-9.30pm Sun; 🛜) Set in the old 17th-century stables of the Bushmills Inn, this haven has intimate wooden booths and blazing fires, and uses fresh Ulster produce in dishes like onion-and-Guinness soup, haunch of venison, and traditional Dalriada Cullen Skink (wood-smoked haddock poached in cream, with poached eggs and new potatoes). Book ahead.

### ⌂ Bushmills Inn Hotel — Hotel £££

(☎028-2073 3000; www.bushmillsinn.com; 9 Dunluce Rd; d/ste from £170/300; Ⓟ@🛜) The Bushmills is an old coaching inn complete with peat fires, gas lamps and a round tower with a secret library. The old part of the hotel has been given over to the restaurant – the luxurious modern accommodation is in the neighbouring, modern Mill House complex.

# STRETCH YOUR LEGS
# BELFAST

**Start/Finish** Belfast City Hall

**Distance** 5km

**Duration** 3 hours

For decades Belfast's murals were powerful symbols of a violent sectarian divide. On this walk you'll see those passions painted large, but you'll also witness remarkable progress towards peace. Note that, although safe, this walk crosses West Belfast's Peace Lines (walls with gates), which are best avoided after dark.

Take this walk on Trips

## City Hall

Start at the 1906 classical Renaissance **City Hall** (www.belfastcity.gov.uk; Donegall Sq; ⊙ guided tours 11am, 2pm & 3pm Mon-Fri, noon, 2pm & 3pm Sat & Sun), fronted by a dour Queen Victoria accompanied by bronzes symbolising Belfast's textile and ship-building industries.

The Walk » Go up Donegall Pl, turning left on Castle St, which becomes the Falls Rd; you've entered Republican, Catholic West Belfast. After the huge murals of the Solidarity Wall, which champion global Civil Rights Movements, stop at Sevastopol St.

## Sinn Féin Headquarters

This red-brick building is the base of the Irish Republican party, which is committed to ending British rule in Northern Ireland. It features a vast mural of Bobby Sands, the West Belfast MP who died on hunger strike in 1981.

The Walk » Pass the Royal Victoria Hospital, which developed expertise in treating gunshot wounds during the Troubles. The Cultúrlann McAdam Ó Fiaich comes soon after, on the left.

## Cultúrlann McAdam Ó Fiaich

The welcoming **Cultúrlann McAdam Ó Fiaich** (www.culturlann.ie; 216 Falls Rd; ⊙ 9am-5.30pm Mon-Sat, 10am-4.30pm Sun) features a shop selling Ireland-related books and crafts and a good cafe-restaurant.

The Walk » At nearby Islandbawn St the Plastic Bullet Mural commemorates 17 people, including eight children, killed by security-service plastic-baton rounds. Beechmount Ave is two streets on.

## Beechmount Avenue

Absorbed by Beechmount Ave's murals, most visitors miss the hand-painted 'RPG Avenue' sign beside the street name. 'RPG' stands for 'rocket-propelled grenade', a nickname awarded because the street offered sight lines for IRA rocket attacks on security forces based nearby.

The Walk » Go back up Falls Rd, noticing dual Irish-English street names. After 1km, turn left into North Howard St and go through the gate in the tall steel fencing. Turn left beside it, walking 150m.

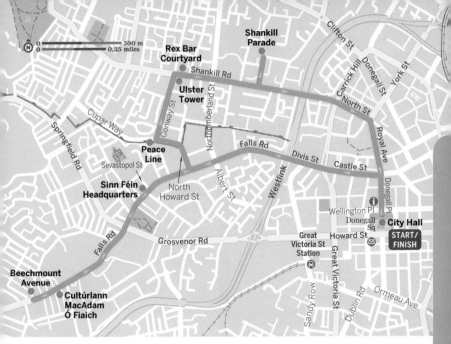

## Peace Line

This imposing 6m-high, 4km-long barrier has divided West Belfast's Catholic and Protestant communities for more than four decades. Now sections are a focus for reconciliation; here you'll find local people's testimonies and spaces for adding your own peace message.

The Walk » Turn off the main road into residential (unsigned) Conway St. You're now in Loyalist, Protestant West Belfast. Stop at the junction of Shankill Rd.

## Ulster Tower

The huge mural depicting a creamy, poppy-fringed fort is on the Ulster Tower, emphasising Protestant loyalty to Britain by highlighting Ulster regiments' catastrophic WWI losses.

The Walk » Cross Shankill Rd to the photograph-filled courtyard beside the Rex Bar.

## Rex Bar Courtyard

Photographic and textual displays here describe the signing of the Ulster Cov-enant, a mass petition against limited Irish self-government in 1912, and the formation of the Ulster Volunteer Force in 1913.

The Walk » Head down Shankill Rd, passing batches of murals, tributes to the Queen and masses of red, white and blue. After the Gospel Hall, turn left into Shankill Pde.

## Shankill Parade

Murals covering the entire gable ends of houses pack this housing estate. The Protestant King William III rides a prancing white horse on the left, while on the right sits **Remember, Respect, Resolution**, three metal columns representing the communities' willingness to embrace Northern Ireland's future. Several paramilitary murals have now been replaced by local community artworks.

The Walk » Shankill Rd crosses the dual carriageway. Head straight on, turning right down Royal Ave and on to City Hall.

# STRETCH YOUR LEGS
# DERRY

**Start/Finish** Butcher's Gate

**Distance** 3km

**Duration** 3 hours

Winding along 17th-century city walls and past former sectarian battlegrounds, this walk reveals a vivid history, startling political murals and the inspiring steps being taken towards peace.

Take this walk on Trips

## Butcher's Gate

Derry's immense **city walls** (www.derryswalls.com) were built in 1619 to secure the settlement of immigrant Protestants. In 1688 they helped residents repel a 105-day siege by Catholic forces. The Protestants' slogan, 'No Surrender', remains a Loyalist battle cry today.

The Walk ≫ Climb the gateside steps, walking downhill along the top of the walls, high above the streets, to the first corner.

## Magazine Gate

The **Tower Museum** (www.derrycity.gov.uk/museums; Union Hall Pl; adult/child £4/2; ⏰10am-5.30pm) rears up to the right. On the left, the red-brick, neo-Gothic **Guildhall** (☏028-7137 6510; www.derrycity.gov.uk/Guildhall; Guildhall St; ⏰10am-5.30pm) was formerly home to the Londonderry Corporation, which institutionalised anti-Catholic discrimination over housing and jobs.

The Walk ≫ After the next corner, the wall-top walk climbs steeply, passing bastions occupied by huge cannons. As you near the crest of the rise, look down left over the wall.

## Fountain Housing Estate

You're now looking onto the last significant Protestant community on the River Foyle's western bank. Immediately obvious is the massive slogan, 'West Bank Loyalists Still Under Siege. No Surrender'. Looking closer reveals kerb-stones and lamp posts painted in Unionist (British) red, white and blue.

The Walk ≫ After more bastions and massive cannons, the walls widen, revealing a plinth that's been empty since the IRA blew up a statue of one of Derry's siege-era governors. Go down the Butcher's Gate steps, through the arch, into Waterloo St.

## Peadar O'Donnell's

Time to refuel. **Peadar O'Donnell's** (www.peadars.com; 59-63 Waterloo St; ⏰11.30am-1.30am Mon-Sat, 12.30pm-12.30am Sun) is done up as a typical Irish pub-cum-grocer. It's alive with traditional music on weekend afternoons (and every night), too.

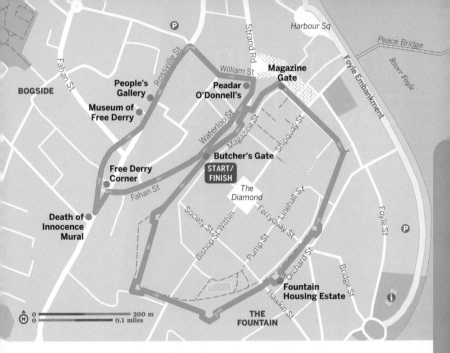

The Walk » William St cuts left to Rossville St, a junction dubbed Agro Corner, where security forces and residents of the Catholic Bogside housing estate routinely clashed. Some 120m on, the Bloody Sunday Memorial commemorates where British soldiers shot dead 13 unarmed demonstrators in 1972.

## People's Gallery

The huge murals you can now see are part of the People's Gallery and were painted by three Bogsiders who lived through the Troubles. Ahead is a huge monochrome **Civil Rights** mural; behind you a rioter and armoured car clash in **Saturday Matinee**.

The Walk » Cut between these murals, into the Museum of Free Derry.

## Museum of Free Derry

This **museum** (www.museumoffreederry.org; 55 Glenfada Park; adult/child £3/2; 9.30am-4.30pm Mon-Fri year-round, plus 1-4pm Sat Apr-Sep, 1-4pm Sun Jul-Sep) chronicles the Bogside's history, the Civil Rights Movement and the events of Bloody Sunday.

The Walk » Pass more murals: the sledgehammer drama of *Operation Motorman; Bloody Sunday,* where a priest tries to shepherd one of the dying to safety; and a boy in a gas mask (*Petrol Bomber*). Look to the left.

## Free Derry Corner

The roundabout contains a house remnant bearing the words 'You Are Now Entering Free Derry'. This stems from the late 1960s, when Bogsiders declared themselves independent of the authorities and barricaded the streets.

The Walk » Continue down Rossville St, looking back up to the gable ends to your right.

## Death of Innocence Mural

This mural depicts 14-year-old Annette McGavigan, who was killed in crossfire between the IRA and the British Army in 1971. The downward-pointing, broken rifle symbolises the failure of violence; the butterfly symbolises the peace process.

The Walk » Return to Free Derry Corner then head up Fahan St, back to Butcher's Gate.

# ROAD TRIP ESSENTIALS

## IRELAND DRIVING GUIDE .....373

Driving Licence & Documents...................... 373
Insurance ...................................................... 373
Hiring a Car .................................................. 373
Bringing Your Own Vehicle........................... 374
Maps .............................................................. 374
Roads & Conditions ..................................... 374
Road Distances............................................. 374
Road Rules ....................................................375
Parking ..........................................................375
Fuel ................................................................375
Safety ............................................................ 376
Border Crossings .......................................... 376
Radio.............................................................. 376
Road Trip Websites........................................ 376

## IRELAND TRAVEL GUIDE...... 378

GETTING THERE & AWAY ............................ 378
Air.................................................................. 378
Sea................................................................. 378
Arriving in Ireland........................................ 379
DIRECTORY A–Z ........................................... 379
Accommodation ........................................... 379
Electricity......................................................380
Food...............................................................380
Gay & Lesbian Travellers..............................381
Health ........................................................... 382
Internet Access ............................................ 382
Money............................................................ 382
Opening Hours.............................................. 383
Photography ................................................. 383
Public Holidays............................................. 383
Safe Travel ................................................... 383
Taxes & Refunds .......................................... 384
Telephone ..................................................... 384
Tourist Information....................................... 385
Travellers with Disabilities .......................... 385
Visas.............................................................. 385

# Ireland Driving Guide

*The motorway system makes for easy travelling between major towns, but the spidery network of secondary and tertiary roads makes for the most scenic driving.*

## DRIVING LICENCE & DOCUMENTS

EU licences are treated like Irish ones. Holders of non-EU licences from countries other than the USA or Canada should obtain an International Driving Permit (IDP) from their home automobile association.

You must carry your driving licence at all times.

## INSURANCE

All cars on public roads must be insured. Most hire companies quote basic insurance in their initial quote.

If you are bringing your own vehicle, check that your insurance will cover you in Ireland. When driving your own car, you'll need a minimum insurance known as third-party insurance.

## HIRING A CAR

Compared with many countries (especially the USA), hire rates are expensive in Ireland; you should expect to pay around €250 a week for a small car (unlimited mileage), but rates go up at busy times and drop off in quieter seasons. The main players:

**Avis** (www.avis.ie)

**Budget** (www.budget.ie)

**Europcar** (www.europcar.ie)

**Hertz** (www.hertz.ie)

**Sixt** (www.sixt.ie)

**Thrifty** (www.thrifty.ie)

### Driving Fast Facts

➡ **Right or left?** Drive on the left

➡ **Manual or automatic?** Manual

➡ **Legal driving age** 18

➡ **Top speed limit** 120km/h (motorways; 70mph in Northern Ireland)

➡ **Best radio station** Newstalk 106-108

The major car-hire companies have different web pages on their websites for different countries, so the price of a car in Ireland can differ from the same car's price in the USA or Australia. You have to surf a lot of sites to get the best deals. **Nova Car Hire** (www.novacarhire.com) acts as an agent for Alamo, Budget, European and National, and offers greatly discounted rates.

Other tips:

➡ Most cars are manual; automatic cars are available, but they're more expensive to hire.

➡ If you're travelling from the Republic into Northern Ireland, it's important to be sure that your insurance covers journeys to the North.

➡ The majority of hire companies won't rent you a car if you're under 23 and haven't had a valid driving licence for at least a year.

➡ Some companies in the Republic won't rent to you if you're aged 74 or over; there's no upper age limit in the North.

➡ Motorbikes and mopeds are not available for hire in Ireland.

## BRINGING YOUR OWN VEHICLE

It's easy to take your own vehicle to Ireland and there are no specific procedures involved, but you should carry a vehicle registration document as proof that it's yours.

## MAPS

You'll need a good road map; we recommend getting one even if you have a sat-nav system.

Michelin's 1:400,000-scale *Ireland* map (No 923) is a decent single-sheet map, with clear cartography and most of the island's scenic roads marked. The four maps – North, South, East and West – that make up the Ordnance Survey Holiday map series at 1:250,000 scale are useful if you want more detail. Collins also publishes a range of maps covering Ireland.

The Ordnance Survey Discovery series covers the whole island in 89 maps at a scale of 1:50,000.

These are all available at most big bookshops and tourist centres throughout Ireland as well as at www.osi.ie.

## ROADS & CONDITIONS

Irish road types and conditions vary wildly. The road network is divided into the following categories:

**Regional Roads** Indicated by an R and (usually) three numbers on a white background, these are the secondary and tertiary roads that make up the bulk of the road network, generally splintering off larger roads to access even the smallest hamlet. Blind corners, potholes and a width barely enough for two cars are the price for some of the most scenic routes in all of Ireland; whatever you do, go slowly. In Northern Ireland, these are classified as B-roads.

**National Roads** Indicated by an N and two numbers against a green background, these were, until the construction of the motorway network, the primary roads in Ireland. They link most towns and are usually single lane in

## Road Distances (Km)

| | Athlone | Belfast | Cork | Derry | Donegal | Dublin | Galway | Kilkenny | Killarney | Limerick | Rosslare Harbour | Shannon Airport | Sligo | Waterford |
|---|---|---|---|---|---|---|---|---|---|---|---|---|---|---|
| Belfast | 227 | | | | | | | | | | | | | |
| Cork | 219 | 424 | | | | | | | | | | | | |
| Derry | 209 | 117 | 428 | | | | | | | | | | | |
| Donegal | 183 | 180 | 402 | 69 | | | | | | | | | | |
| Dublin | 127 | 167 | 256 | 237 | 233 | | | | | | | | | |
| Galway | 93 | 306 | 209 | 272 | 204 | 212 | | | | | | | | |
| Kilkenny | 116 | 284 | 148 | 335 | 309 | 114 | 172 | | | | | | | |
| Killarney | 232 | 436 | 87 | 441 | 407 | 304 | 193 | 198 | | | | | | |
| Limerick | 121 | 323 | 105 | 328 | 296 | 193 | 104 | 113 | 111 | | | | | |
| Rosslare Harbour | 201 | 330 | 208 | 397 | 391 | 153 | 274 | 98 | 275 | 211 | | | | |
| Shannon Airport | 133 | 346 | 128 | 351 | 282 | 218 | 93 | 135 | 135 | 25 | 234 | | | |
| Sligo | 117 | 206 | 336 | 135 | 66 | 214 | 138 | 245 | 343 | 232 | 325 | 218 | | |
| Waterford | 164 | 333 | 126 | 383 | 357 | 163 | 220 | 48 | 193 | 129 | 82 | 152 | 293 | |
| Wexford | 184 | 309 | 187 | 378 | 372 | 135 | 253 | 80 | 254 | 190 | 19 | 213 | 307 | 61 |

## Local Expert: Driving Tips

Conor Faughnan, Director of Consumer Affairs with the Automobile Association, shares his tips for hassle-free driving in Ireland:

➡ The motorway network is excellent, but there aren't nearly enough rest areas so check that you have a full tank of fuel before setting off. Off the motorway network there is a good supply of service stations, often open 24 hours, but less so in more remote areas.

➡ The real driving fun is on Ireland's network of secondary roads, where road conditions vary – make sure you're equipped with a good map along with your sat-nav, and beware of potholes, poor road surfaces and corners obscured by protruding hedges! You may also encounter farm machinery and even livestock on rural roads.

➡ Although it rarely snows, winter conditions can be testing (particularly with ice).

➡ A driver may flash their hazard lights once or twice as an informal way to say 'thank you' for any kind of road courtesy extended to them.

either direction, widening occasionally to double lane (usually on uphill stretches to allow for the overtaking of slower vehicles). In Northern Ireland, these are classified as A-roads.

**Motorways** Indicated by an M and a single digit against a blue background, the network is limited to the major routes and towns. Most motorways are partially tolled. Motorways in Northern Ireland are not tolled.

## ROAD RULES

A copy of Ireland's road rules is available from tourist offices. Following are the most basic rules:

➡ Drive on the left, overtake to the right.

➡ Safety belts must be worn by the driver and all passengers.

➡ Children aged under 12 aren't allowed to sit on the front seats.

➡ Motorcyclists and their passengers must wear helmets.

➡ When entering a roundabout, give way to the right.

➡ Speed limits are 120km/h on motorways (70mph in Northern Ireland), 100km/h on national roads (60mph in Northern Ireland), 80km/h on regional and local roads (60mph in Northern Ireland) and 50km/h (30mph in the North) or as signposted in towns.

➡ The legal alcohol limit is 50mg of alcohol per 100ml of blood or 22mg on the breath (roughly two units of alcohol per hour for a man and one for a woman); in Northern Ireland the limit is 80mg of alcohol per 100ml of blood.

## PARKING

All big towns and cities have covered, short-stay car parks that are conveniently signposted.

➡ On-street parking is usually by 'pay and display' tickets available from on-street machines or disc parking (discs, which rotate to display the time you park your car, are available from newsagencies). Costs range from €1.50 to €5 per hour; all-day parking in a car park will cost around €28.

➡ Yellow lines (single or double) along the edge of the road indicate restrictions. You can usually park on single yellow lines between 7pm and 8am, while double yellow lines mean no parking at any time. Always look for the nearby sign that spells out when you can and cannot park.

➡ In Dublin, Cork and Galway, clamping is rigorously enforced; it'll cost you €85 to have the yellow beast removed. In Northern Ireland, the fee is £100 for removal.

## FUEL

The majority of vehicles operate on unleaded petrol; the rest (including many hire cars) run on diesel.

**Cost** In the Republic, petrol costs range from €1.30 to €1.50 per litre, with diesel usually €0.10 cheaper. Fuel is marginally more expensive in Dublin. In Northern Ireland, petrol costs between £1.05 and £1.15 per litre, but diesel is slightly more expensive (between £1.10 and £1.20 per litre).

**Service Stations** These are ubiquitous on all national roads, usually on the outskirts of towns. They're increasingly harder to find in cities, and the motorway network has only three or four spread across the entire system. In the North, the big supermarket chains have gotten into the fuel business, so you can fill your car before or after you shop. There are service stations along the North's motorway network.

## SAFETY

Although driving in Ireland is a relatively pain-free experience, hire cars and cars with foreign registrations can be targeted by thieves looking to clean them of their contents. Don't leave any valuables, including bags and suitcases, on display. Overnight parking is safest in covered car parks.

## BORDER CROSSINGS

Border crossings between Northern Ireland the Republic are unnoticeable; there are no formalities of any kind.

### Ireland Playlist

Virtually every parish and hamlet has a song about it. Here are our favourites:

**Carrickfergus** Traditional Irish folk song

**Galway Girl** Steve Earle

**Raglan Road** Luke Kelly

**Running to Stand Still** U2

**The Fields of Athenry** Paddy Reilly

**The Town I Loved So Well** The Dubliners (about Derry)

## RADIO

The Irish love radio – up to 85% of the population listens in on any given day. Following are the national radio stations:

**Newstalk 106-108** (106-108FM) News, current affairs and lifestyle.

**RTE Radio 1** (88.2-90FM) Mostly news and discussion.

**RTE Radio 2** (90.4-92.2FM) Lifestyle and music.

**RTE Lyric FM** (96-99FM) Classical music.

**Today FM** (100-102FM) Music, chat and news.

Regional or local radio is also very popular, with 25 independent local radio stations available, depending on your location.

In Northern Ireland, the BBC rules supreme, with BBC Radio Ulster (92.7-95.4FM) flying the local flag in addition to the four main BBC stations.

## ROAD TRIP WEBSITES

### Automobile Associations

**Automobile Association** (AA; www.theaa.ie) Roadside assistance and driving tips.

**Royal Automobile Club** (RAC; www.rac.co.uk) Roadside assistance, route planner and accommodation.

### Road Rules

**Road Safety Authority** (www.rsa.ie) Rules, tips and information in case of accident.

### Conditions & Traffic

**AA Roadwatch (www.theaa.ie)** Up-to-date traffic info.

**Traffic Watch Northern Ireland (www.trafficwatchni.com)** Traffic news, maps and live cameras.

### Maps

**AA Route Planner** (www.theaa.ie) Map your route for the whole island.

### Apps

Both the AA and the RAC have mobile apps for Android and IOS that track traffic and allow you to report breakdowns.

# Driving Problem-Buster

**What should I do if my car breaks down?** Call the service number of your car-hire company and a local garage will be contacted. If you're bringing your own car, it's a good idea to join the Automobile Association Ireland, which covers the whole country, or, in Northern Ireland, the Royal Automobile Club (RAC), which can be called to attend breakdowns at any time.

**What if I have an accident?** Hire cars usually have a leaflet in the glovebox about what to do in case of an accident. Exchange basic information with the other party (name, insurance details, driver's licence number, company details if the car's a rental). No discussion of liability needs to take place at the scene. It's a good idea to photograph the scene of the accident, noting key details (damage sustained, car positions on the road, any skid markings). Call the police (☎999) if required.

**What should I do if I get stopped by police?** Always remain calm and polite: police are generally courteous and helpful. They will want to see your passport (or valid form of ID), licence and proof of insurance. In the Republic, breath testing is mandatory if asked.

**What if I can't find anywhere to stay?** If you're travelling during the summer months, always book your accommodation in advance. If you're stuck, call the local tourist office's accommodation hotline.

**How do I pay for tollways?** Tolls are paid by putting cash in the bucket as you pass. If you don't have exact change, at least one booth is staffed.

# Ireland Travel Guide

## GETTING THERE & AWAY

### AIR

Ireland's main airports:

**Cork Airport** (ORK; ☑021-431 3131; www.
cork-airport.com) Airlines servicing the airport
include Aer Lingus and Ryanair.

**Dublin Airport** (DUB; ☑01-814 1111; www.
dublinairport.com) Ireland's major international gateway airport, with direct flights from
the UK, Europe, North America and the Middle
East.

**Shannon Airport** (SNN; ☑061-712 000;
www.shannonairport.com; ☎) Has a few direct
flights from the UK, Europe and North America.

Northern Ireland's airport:

**Belfast International Airport** (BFS;
☑028-9448 4848; www.belfastairport.com)
Has direct flights from the UK, Europe and
North America.

Car-hire firms are well represented at all
major airports. Regional airports will have
at least one internationally recognised firm
as well as local operators.

### Book Your Stay Online

For more accommodation reviews
by Lonely Planet authors, check
out http://hotels.lonelyplanet.com.
You'll find independent reviews, as
well as recommendations on the
best places to stay. Best of all, you
can book online.

### SEA

The main ferry routes between Ireland and
the UK and mainland Europe:

➡ Belfast to Liverpool (England; eight hours)

➡ Belfast to Cairnryan (Scotland; 1¾ hours)

➡ Cork to Roscoff (France; 14 hours; April to
October only)

➡ Dublin to Liverpool (England; fast/slow
four/8½ hours)

➡ Dublin & Dun Laoghaire to Holyhead (Wales;
fast/slow two/3½ hours)

➡ Larne to Cairnryan (Scotland; two hours)

➡ Larne to Troon (Scotland; two hours; March
to October only)

➡ Larne to Fleetwood (England; six hours)

➡ Rosslare to Cherbourg/Roscoff (France;
18/20½ hours)

➡ Rosslare to Fishguard & Pembroke (Wales;
3½ hours)

Competition from budget airlines has
forced ferry operators to discount heavily
and offer flexible fares.

A useful website is www.ferrybooker.
com, which covers all sea-ferry routes and
operators to Ireland.

Main operators include the following:

**Brittany Ferries** (www.brittanyferries.com)
Cork to Roscoff; April to October.

**Irish Ferries** (www.irishferries.com) Dublin
to Holyhead (up to four per day year-round)
and France to Rosslare (three times per week).

**P&O Ferries** (www.poferries.com) Daily sailings year-round from Dublin to Liverpool, and
Larne to Cairnryan. Larne to Troon runs March
to October only.

**Stena Line** (www.stenaline.com) Daily
sailings from Holyhead to Dublin Port, from
Belfast to Liverpool and Cairnryan, and from
Rosslare to Fishguard.

## ARRIVING IN IRELAND

**Dublin Airport** Private coaches run every 10 to 15 minutes to the city centre (€7). Taxis take 30 to 45 minutes and cost €20 to €25.

**Dublin Port Terminal** Buses are timed to coincide with arrivals and departures; costs €3 to the city centre.

**Dun Laoghaire Ferry Port** Public bus takes around 45 minutes to the centre of Dublin; DART (suburban rail) takes about 25 minutes.

**Belfast International Airport/George Best Belfast City Airport** A bus runs to the centre every 15 to 20 minutes from both airports; a taxi from the international airport costs around £30, or £10 from George Best City Airport.

# DIRECTORY A–Z

## ACCOMMODATION

Accommodation options range from bare and basic to pricey and palatial. The spine of the Irish hospitality business is the ubiquitous B&B, in recent years challenged by a plethora of midrange hotels and guesthouses. Beyond Expedia, Booking.com, Trivago and other hotel price comparison sites, Ireland-specific online resources for accommodation include the following:

**www.daft.ie** Online classified paper for short- and long-term rentals.

**www.elegant.ie** Specialises in self-catering castles, period houses and unique properties.

**www.familyhomes.ie** Lists family-run guesthouses and self-catering properties.

**www.imagineireland.com** Modern cottage rentals throughout the whole island, including Northern Ireland.

**www.irishlandmark.com** Not-for-profit conservation group that rents self-catering properties of historical and cultural significance, such as castles, tower houses, gate lodges, schoolhouses and lighthouses.

**www.stayinireland.com** Lists guesthouses and self-catering options.

### B&Bs & Guesthouses

Bed and breakfasts are small, family-run houses, farmhouses and period country houses with fewer than five bedrooms. Standards vary enormously, but most have some bedrooms with private bathroom at a cost of roughly €35 to €40 (£25 to £30) per person per night. In luxurious B&Bs, expect to pay €55 (£40) or more per person. Off-season rates – usually October through to March – are usually lower, as are midweek prices.

Guesthouses are like upmarket B&Bs, but bigger – the Irish equivalent of a boutique hotel. Facilities are usually better and sometimes include a restaurant.

Other tips:

➡ Facilities in B&Bs range from basic (bed, bathroom, kettle, TV) to beatific (whirlpool baths, rainforest showers) as you go up in price. Wi-fi is standard and most have parking (but check).

---

### A 'Standard' Hotel Rate?

There is no such thing. Prices vary according to demand – or have different rates for online, phone or walk-in bookings. B&B rates are more consistent, but virtually every other accommodation will charge wildly different rates depending on the time of year, day, festival schedule and even your ability to do a little negotiating. The following price ranges have been used in our reviews of places to stay. Prices are all based on a double room with private bathroom in high season.

| Budget | Republic | Northern Ireland |
| --- | --- | --- |
| Budget (€) | <€80 | <£50 |
| Midrange (€€) | €80–180 | £50–120 |
| Top end (€€€) | >€180 | >£120 |

→ Most B&Bs take credit cards, but the occasional rural one might not have facilities; check when you book.

→ Advance reservations are strongly recommended, especially in peak season (June to September).

→ Some B&Bs and guesthouses in more remote regions only operate from Easter to September or other months.

→ If full, B&B owners may recommend another house in the area (possibly a private house taking occasional guests, not in tourist listings).

→ To make prices more competitive at some B&Bs, breakfast may be optional.

## Camping & Caravan Parks

Camping and caravan parks aren't as common in Ireland as they are elsewhere in Europe. Some hostels have camping space for tents and also offer house facilities, which makes them better value than the main camping grounds. At commercial parks the cost is typically somewhere between €12 and €20 (£8 to £14) for a tent and two people. Prices given for campsites are for two people unless stated otherwise. Caravan sites cost around €15 to €25 (£10 to £18). Most parks are open only from Easter to the end of September or October.

## Hostels

Prices quoted for hostel accommodation apply to those aged over 18. A high-season dorm bed generally costs €10 to €25 (£7 to £18). Many hostels now have family and double rooms.

Hostel associations:

**An Óige** (www.anoige.ie) Hostelling International (HI)–associated national organisation with 26 hostels scattered around the Republic.

**HINI** (www.hini.org.uk) HI-associated organisation with five hostels in Northern Ireland.

**Independent Holiday Hostels of Ireland** (www.hostels-ireland.com) Fifty-five tourist-board approved hostels throughout all of Ireland.

**Independent Hostel Owners of Ireland** (www.independenthostelsireland.com) Independent hostelling association.

## ELECTRICITY

220V/50Hz

## FOOD

In the past decade Ireland has 'rediscovered' its own native cuisine. A host of chefs and producers have led a foodie revolution that, at its heart, is about bringing to the table the kind of meals that have long been taken for granted on well-run Irish farms.

Coupled with the growing sophistication of the Irish palate – by now well used to the varied flavours of worldwide cuisines – it's relatively easy to eat well on all budgets. Needless to say, this has been a boon to the tourist industry, which no longer has to explain why so many Irish meals are so memorable – for completely the wrong reasons.

### When to Eat

Irish eating habits have changed over the past couple of decades, and there are differences between urban and rural practices.

**Breakfast** Usually eaten before 9am (although hotels and B&Bs will serve until 11am Monday to Friday, and to noon at weekends in urban areas), as most people rush off to work. Weekend brunch is popular in bigger towns and cities.

**Lunch** Urban workers eat on the run between 12.30pm and 2pm (most restaurants don't begin to serve lunch until at least midday). At weekends, especially Sunday, the midday lunch is skipped in favour of a substantial mid-afternoon meal (called dinner), usually between 2pm and 4pm.

**Tea** Not the drink, but the evening meal – also confusingly called dinner – is the main meal of the day for urbanites, usually eaten around 6.30pm. Rural communities eat at the same time but with a more traditional tea of bread, cold cuts and, yes, tea. Restaurants follow international habits, with most diners not eating until at least 7.30pm.

**Supper** A before-bed snack of tea and toast or sandwiches is still enjoyed by many Irish, although urbanites increasingly eschew it for health reasons. Not a practice in restaurants.

### Dining Etiquette

The Irish aren't big on restrictive etiquette, preferring friendly informality to any kind of stuffy to-dos. Still, the following are a few tips on dining with the Irish:

**Children** All restaurants welcome kids up to 7pm, but pubs and some smarter restaurants don't allow them later in the evening. Family restaurants have children's menus; others have reduced portions of regular menu items.

**Returning a dish** If the food is not to your satisfaction, it's best to politely explain what's wrong with it as soon as you can; any respectable restaurant will endeavour to replace the dish immediately.

**Paying the bill** If you insist on paying the bill for everyone, be prepared for a first,

second and even third refusal to countenance such an exorbitant act of generosity. But don't be fooled: the Irish will refuse something several times even if they're delighted with it. Insist gently but firmly and you'll get your way!

### Vegetarians & Vegans

Ireland has come a long, long way since the days when vegetarians were looked upon as odd creatures; nowadays, even the most militant vegan will barely cause a ruffle in all but the most basic of kitchens. Which isn't to say that travellers with plant-based diets are going to find the most imaginative range of options on menus outside the bigger towns and cities – or in the plethora of modern restaurants that have opened in the past few years – but you can rest assured that the overall quality of the homegrown vegetables is top-notch and most places will have at least one dish that you can tuck into.

## HEALTH

No jabs are required to travel to Ireland. Excellent health care is readily available. For minor, self-limiting illnesses, pharmacists can give valuable advice and sell over-the-counter medication. They can also advise when more specialised help is required and point you in the right direction.

EU citizens with a European Health Insurance Card (EHIC), available from health centres or, in the UK, post offices, will be covered for most medical care – but not non-emergencies or emergency repatriation. While other countries, such as Australia, also have reciprocal agreements with Ireland and Britain, many do not.

In Northern Ireland, everyone receives free emergency treatment at accident and emergency (A&E) departments of state-run NHS hospitals, irrespective of nationality.

## INTERNET ACCESS

If using a laptop, tablet, phablet or smartphone to get online, the vast majority of hotels, B&Bs, hostels, bars and restaurants offer wi-fi access, usually for free (though there may be a charge in a minority of hotels).

Internet cafes are increasingly disappearing. The survivors generally charge up to €6/£5 per hour.

---

### Eating Price Ranges

The folllowing price indicators, used throughout this guide, represent the cost of a main dish:

| Budget | Republic | Northern Ireland |
|---|---|---|
| Budget (€) | <€12 | <£12 |
| Midrange (€€) | €12–25 | £12–20 |
| Top end (€€€) | >€25 | >£20 |

## GAY & LESBIAN TRAVELLERS

Ireland is a pretty tolerant place for gays and lesbians. Bigger cities such as Dublin, Galway and Cork have well-established gay scenes, as do Belfast and Derry in Northern Ireland. In 2015 Ireland overwhelmingly backed same-sex marriage in a historic referendum. Nonetheless, you'll still find pockets of homophobia throughout the island, particularly in smaller towns and rural areas. Resources include the following:

**Gaire** (www.gaire.com) Message board and info for a host of gay-related issues.

**Gay & Lesbian Youth Northern Ireland** (www.cara-friend.org.uk/projects/glyni) Voluntary counseling, information, health and social space organisation for the gay community.

**Gay Men's Health Project** (☎01-660 2189; http://hse.ie/go/GMHS) Practical advice on men's health issues.

**National Lesbian & Gay Federation** (NLGF; ☎01-671 9076; http://nxf.ie) Publishes the monthly *Gay Community News* (http://theoutmost.com).

**Northern Ireland Gay Rights Association** (Nigra; ☎9066 5257; http://nigra.org.uk)

**Outhouse** (☎01-873 4932; www.outhouse.ie; 105 Capel St, Dublin; ☐all city centre) Top gay, lesbian and bisexual resource centre. Great stop-off point to see what's on, check noticeboards and meet people. It publishes the free *Ireland's Pink Pages*, a directory of gay-centric services, also accessible on the website.

**The Outmost** (www.theoutmost.com) Excellent and resourceful for gay news, entertainment, lifestyle and opinion.

## MONEY

The currency in the Republic of Ireland is the euro (€). The island's peculiar political history means that the six Ulster counties that make up Northern Ireland use the pound sterling (£). Although notes issued by Northern Irish banks are legal tender throughout the UK, many businesses outside of Northern Ireland refuse to accept them and you'll have to swap them in British banks.

### ATMs

Usually called 'cash machines', ATMs are easy to find in cities and all but the smallest of towns. Watch out for ATMs that have been tampered with; card-reader scams ('skimming') have become a real problem.

### Credit & Debit Cards

Visa and MasterCard credit and debit cards are widely accepted in Ireland. American Express is only accepted by the major chains, and very few places accept Diners or JCB. Smaller businesses, such as pubs and some B&Bs, prefer debit cards (and will charge a fee for credit cards), and a small number of rural B&Bs only take cash.

### Exchange Rates

The Republic of Ireland uses the euro.

| Australia | A$1 | €0.68 |
|---|---|---|
| Canada | C$1 | €0.69 |
| Japan | Y100 | €0.88 |
| New Zealand | NZ$1 | €0.64 |
| UK | £1 | €1.19 |
| USA | US$1 | €0.90 |

Northern Ireland uses the pound sterling.

| Australia | A$1 | £0.48 |
|---|---|---|
| Canada | C$1 | £0.57 |
| Republic of Ireland | €1 | £0.84 |
| Japan | Y100 | £0.74 |
| New Zealand | NZ$1 | £0.54 |
| USA | US$1 | £0.75 |

For current exchange rates see www.xe.com.

### Tipping

You're not obliged to tip if the service or food was unsatisfactory (even if it's been automatically added to your bill as a 'service charge').

**Hotels** Only for bellhops who carry luggage, then €1/£1 per bag

**Pubs** Not expected unless table service is provided, then €1/£1 for a round of drinks

**Restaurants** 10% for decent service, up to 15% in more expensive places

**Taxis** 10% or rounded up to the nearest euro/pound

**Toilet attendants** €0.50/50p

## OPENING HOURS

Opening hours in both the Republic and Northern Ireland are roughly the same.

**Banks** 10am to 4pm Monday to Friday (to 5pm Thursday).

**Offices** 9am to 5pm Monday to Friday.

**Post offices** Northern Ireland: 9am to 5.30pm Monday to Friday, 9am to 12.30pm Saturday; Republic: 9am to 6pm Monday to Friday, 9am to 1pm Saturday. Smaller post offices may close at lunch and one day per week.

**Pubs** Northern Ireland: 11.30am to 11pm Monday to Saturday, 12.30pm to 10pm Sunday. Pubs with late licences open until 1am Monday to Saturday and midnight Sunday. Republic: 10.30am to 11.30pm Monday to Thursday, 10.30am to 12.30am Friday and Saturday, noon to 11pm Sunday (30 minutes of 'drinking up' time allowed). Pubs with bar extensions open to 2.30am Thursday to Saturday. All pubs close Christmas Day and Good Friday.

Pubs that serve food often have more limited kitchen hours, so while the pub observes regular pub opening hours its kitchen might stop serving a few hours before closing time.

**Restaurants** Noon to 10.30pm in Dublin, and till 9pm outside of Dublin (aim to be seated by 8pm at the latest); many close one day of the week.

**Shops** 9am to 5.30pm or 6pm Monday to Saturday (until 8pm on Thursday and sometimes Friday), noon to 6pm Sunday (in bigger towns only). Shops in rural towns may close at lunch and one day per week.

**Tourist offices** 9am to 5pm Monday to Friday, and 9am to 1pm Saturday. Many extend their hours in summer and open fewer hours/days or close from October to April.

**Tourist sights** Some sights only open from Easter through to September or October.

## PHOTOGRAPHY

➤ Natural light can be very dull, so use higher ISO speeds than usual, such as 400 for daylight shots.

➤ In Northern Ireland, get permission before taking photos of fortified police stations, army posts or other military or quasi-military paraphernalia.

➤ Don't take photos of people in Protestant or Catholic strongholds of West Belfast without permission; always ask and be prepared to accept a refusal.

## PUBLIC HOLIDAYS

Public holidays can cause road chaos as everyone tries to get somewhere else for the break. It's wise to book accommodation in advance for these times.

The following are public holidays in both the Republic and Northern Ireland:

**New Year's Day** 1 January

**St Patrick's Day** 17 March

**Easter** (Good Friday to Easter Monday inclusive) March/April

**May Holiday** 1st Monday in May

**Christmas Day** 25 December

**St Stephen's Day** (Boxing Day) 26 December

When they fall on a weekend, St Patrick's Day and St Stephen's Day holidays are taken on the following Monday. In the Republic, nearly everywhere closes on Good Friday even though it isn't an official public holiday. In the North, most shops open on Good Friday, but close the following Tuesday.

### Northern Ireland

**Spring Bank Holiday** Last Monday in May

**Orangemen's Day** 12 July

**August Holiday** Last Monday in August

### Republic

**June Holiday** 1st Monday in June

**August Holiday** 1st Monday in August

**October Holiday** Last Monday in October

## SAFE TRAVEL

Ireland is safer than most countries in Europe, but normal precautions should be observed.

Northern Ireland is as safe as anywhere else, but there are areas where the sectarian divide is bitterly pronounced, most notably in parts of Belfast. It's probably

## Practicalities

➜ **Smoking** Smoking is illegal in all indoor public spaces, including restaurants and pubs.

➜ **Time** Ireland uses the 12-hour clock and is on Western European Time (UTC/GMT November to March; plus one hour April to October).

➜ **TV & DVD** All TV in Ireland is digital terrestrial; Ireland is DVD Region 2.

➜ **Weights & Measures** In the Republic, both imperial and metric unites are used for most measures except height, which is in feet and inches only. Distance is measured in kilometres, but people can refer to it colloquially in miles. In the north, it's imperial all the way.

best to ensure your visit to Northern Ireland doesn't coincide with the climax of the Orange marching season on 12 July; sectarian passions are usually inflamed and even many Northerners leave the province at this time.

## TAXES & REFUNDS

Non-EU residents can claim Value Added Tax (VAT, a sales tax of 21% added to the purchase price of luxury goods – excluding books, children's clothing and educational items) back on their purchases, so long as the store operates either the Cashback or Taxback refund program (they should display a sticker). You'll get a voucher with your purchase that must be stamped at the *last point of exit* from the EU. If you're travelling on to Britain or mainland Europe from Ireland, hold on to your voucher until you pass through your final customs stop in the EU; it can then be stamped and you can post it back for a refund of duty paid.

VAT in Northern Ireland is 20%; shops participating in the Tax-Free Shopping refund scheme will give you a form or invoice on request to be presented to customs when you leave. After customs have certified the form, it will be returned to the shop for a refund and the cheque sent to you at home.

## TELEPHONE

Area codes in the Republic have three digits and begin with a 0; eg ✆021 for Cork, ✆091 for Galway and ✆061 for Limerick. The only exception is Dublin, which has a two-digit code (✆01). Always use the area code if calling from a mobile phone, but you don't need it if calling from a fixed-line number within the area code.

In Northern Ireland, the area code for all fixed-line numbers is ✆028, but you only need to use it if calling from a mobile phone or from outside Northern Ireland. To call Northern Ireland from the Republic, use ✆048 instead of ✆028, without the international dialling code.

Other codes:

➜ ✆1550 or ✆1580 – premium rate

➜ ✆1890 or ✆1850 – local or shared rate

➜ ✆0818 – calls at local rate, wherever you're dialling from within the Republic

➜ ✆1800 – free calls

Free-call and low-call numbers are not accessible from outside the Republic. Other tips:

➜ Prices are lower during evenings after 6pm and weekends.

➜ If you can find a public phone that works, local calls in the Republic cost €0.30 for around three minutes (around €0.60 to a mobile), regardless of when you call. From Northern Ireland local calls cost about 40p, or 60p to a mobile, although this varies somewhat.

➜ Prepaid phonecards can be purchased at both newsagencies and post offices, and work from all payphones for both domestic and international calls.

### Directory Enquiries

For directory enquiries, a number of agencies compete for your business.

➜ In the Republic, dial ✆11811 or ✆11850; for international enquiries it's ✆11818.

➜ In the North, call ✆118 118, ✆118 192, ✆118 500 or ✆118 811.

➜ Expect to pay at least €1/£1 from a land line and up to €2/£2 from a mobile phone.

## International Calls

To call out from Ireland dial ☎00, then the country code (☎1 for USA, ☎61 Australia etc), the area code (you usually drop the initial zero) and then the number. Ireland's international dialling code is ☎353; Northern Ireland's is ☎44.

## Mobile Phones

➡ Ensure your mobile phone is unlocked for use in Ireland.

➡ Pay-as-you-go mobile phone packages with any of the main providers start around €40 and usually include a basic handset and credit of around €10.

➡ SIM-only packages are also available, but make sure your phone is compatible with the local provider.

## TOURIST INFORMATION

In both the Republic and the North there's a tourist office or information point in almost every big town; most can offer a variety of services, including accommodation and attraction reservations, currency-changing services, map and guidebook sales, and free publications.

In the Republic, the tourism purview falls to **Fáilte Ireland** (☎Republic 1850 230 330, UK 0800 039 7000; www.discoverireland.ie); in Northern Ireland, it's the **Northern Irish Tourist Board** (NITB; ☎head office 028-9023 1221; www.discovernorthernireland.com). Outside Ireland, Fáilte Ireland and the NITB unite under the banner Tourism Ireland (www.tourismireland.com).

**Cork & Kerry** (☎021-425 5100; www.discoverireland.ie/corkcity; Grand Pde, Cork; ◷9am-6pm Mon-Sat year-round, plus 10am-5pm Sun Jul & Aug)

**Dublin** (www.visitdublin.com; Arrivals Hall; ◷8am-10pm)

**East Coast & Midlands** (☎044-934 8761; East Coast & Midlands Tourism, Dublin Rd, Mullingar)

**Ireland North West & Lakelands** (☎071-916 1201; Temple St, Sligo)

**Ireland West** (☎091-537 700; Ireland West Tourism, Áras Fáilte, Forster St, Galway)

**Shannon Region** (☎061-361 555; Shannon Development, Shannon, Clare)

**South East** (☎051-875 823; www.discoverwaterfordcity.ie; 120 Parade Quay; ◷9.15am-5.30pm Mon-Sat)

## TRAVELLERS WITH DISABILITIES

All new buildings have wheelchair access, and many hotels have installed lifts, ramps and other facilities. Others, especially B&Bs, have not adapted as successfully so you'll have far less choice. Fáilte Ireland and NITB's accommodation guides indicate which places are wheelchair accessible.

In big cities, most buses have low-floor access and priority space on board, but the number of kneeling buses on regional routes is still relatively small.

Trains are accessible with help. In theory, if you call ahead, an employee of Irish Rail (Iarnród Éireann) will arrange to accompany you to the train. Newer trains have audio and visual information systems for visually impaired and hearing-impaired passengers.

The **Citizens' Information Board** (☎0761 079 000; www.citizensinformationboard.ie) in the Republic and **Disability Action** (☎028-9066 1252; www.disabilityaction.org) in Northern Ireland can give some advice to travellers with disabilities.

Lonely Planet's free Accessible Travel guide can be downloaded here: http://lptravel.to/AccessibleTravel.

## VISAS

If you're a European Economic Area (EEA) national, you don't need a visa to visit (or work in) either the Republic or Northern Ireland. Citizens of Australia, Canada, New Zealand, South Africa and the USA can visit the Republic for up to three months, and Northern Ireland for up to six months. They are not allowed to work unless sponsored by an employer.

Full visa requirements for visiting the Republic are available online at www.dfa.ie; for Northern Ireland's visa requirements see www.gov.uk/government/organisations/uk-visas-and-immigration.

To stay longer in the Republic, contact the local *garda* (police) station or the **Garda National Immigration Bureau** (☎01-666 9100; www.garda.ie; 13-14 Burgh Quay, Dublin). To stay longer in Northern Ireland, contact the Home Office (www.gov.uk/government/organisations/uk-visas-and-immigration).

# Language

Irish (Gaeilge) is the country's official language. In 2003 the government introduced the Official Languages Act, whereby all official documents and street signs must be either in Irish or in both Irish and English. Despite its official status, Irish is really only spoken in pockets of rural Ireland known as the Gaeltacht, the main ones being Cork (Corcaigh), Donegal (Dún na nGall), Galway (Gaillimh), Kerry (Ciarraí) and Mayo (Maigh Eo).

Ask people outside the Gaeltacht if they can speak Irish and nine out of 10 of them will probably reply, '*ah, cupla focal*' (a couple of words), and they generally mean it – but many adults also regret not having a greater grasp of it. Irish is a compulsory subject in schools for those aged six to 15. In recent times, a new Irish curriculum has been introduced cutting the hours devoted to the subject but making the lessons more fun, practical and celebratory.

Irish divides vowels into long (those with an accent) and short (those without), and also distinguishes between broad (a, á, o, ó, u) and slender (e, é, i and í), which can affect the pronunciation of preceding consonants. Other than a few clusters, such as mh and bhf (both pronounced as w), consonants are generally pronounced the same as in English.

Irish has three main dialects: Connaught Irish (in Galway and northern Mayo), Munster Irish (in Cork, Kerry and Waterford) and Ulster Irish (in Donegal). Our pronunciation guides are an anglicised version of modern standard Irish, which is essentially an amalgam of the three – if you read them as if they were English, you'll be able to get your point across in Gaeilge without even having to think about the specifics of Irish pronunciation or spelling.

## BASICS

**Hello.**
*Dia duit.*　　　　deea gwit

**Hello.** (reply)
*Dia is Muire duit.*　　deeas moyra gwit

**Good morning.**
*Maidin mhaith.*　　mawjin wah

**Good night.**
*Oíche mhaith.*　　eekheh wah

**Goodbye.** (when leaving)
*Slán leat.*　　slawn lyat

**Goodbye.** (when staying)
*Slán agat.*　　slawn agut

**Yes.**
*Tá .*　　taw

**No.**
*Níl.*　　neel

**It is.**
*Sea.*　　sheh

**It isn't.**
*Ní hea.*　　nee heh

**Thank you (very) much.**
*Go raibh (míle)*　　goh rev (meela)
*maith agat.*　　mah agut

**Excuse me.**
*Gabh mo leithscéal.*　　gamoh lesh scale

**I'm sorry.**
*Tá brón orm.*　　taw brohn oruhm

**Do you speak (Irish)?**
*An bhfuil (Gaeilge) agat?*　　on wil (gaylge) oguht

**I don't understand.**
*Ní thuigim.*　　nee higgim

**What is this?**
*Cad é seo?*　　kod ay shoh

### Want More?

For in-depth language information and handy phrases, check out Lonely Planet's *Irish Language & Culture*. You'll find it at **shop.lonelyplanet.com**, or you can buy Lonely Planet's iPhone phrasebooks at the Apple App Store.

## Signs

| | |
|---|---|
| **Dúnta** | Closed |
| **Fir** | Men |
| **Gardaí** | Police |
| **Leithreas** | Toilet |
| **Mná** | Women |
| **Ná Caitear Tobac** | No Smoking |
| **Oifig An Phoist** | Post Office |
| **Oifig Eolais** | Tourist Information |
| **Oscailte** | Open |
| **Páirceáil** | Parking |

**What is that?**
*Cad é sin?* — kod ay shin

**I'd like to go to ...**
*Ba mhaith liom dul go dtí ...* — baw wah lohm dull go dee ...

**I'd like to buy ...**
*Ba mhaith liom ... a cheannach.* — bah wah lohm ... a kyanukh

**another/one more**
*ceann eile* — kyawn ella

**nice**
*go deas* — goh dyass

## MAKING CONVERSATION

**Welcome.**
*Ceád míle fáilte.* — kade meela fawlcha
(lit: 100,000 welcomes)

**Bon voyage!**
*Go n-éirí an bóthar leat!* — go nairee on bohhar lat

**How are you?**
*Conas a tá tú?* — kunas aw taw too

**I'm fine.**
*Táim go maith.* — thawm go mah

**... please.**
*... más é do thoil é.* — ... maws ay do hall ay

**Cheers!**
*Slainte!* — slawncha

**What's your name?**
*Cad is ainm duit?* — kod is anim dwit

**My name is (Sean Frayne).**
*(Sean Frayne) is ainm dom.* — (shawn frain) is anim dohm

**Impossible!**
*Ní féidir é!* — nee faydir ay

**Nonsense!**
*Ráiméis!* — rawmaysh

**That's terrible!**
*Go huafásach!* — guh hoofawsokh

**Take it easy.**
*Tóg é gobogé .* — tohg ay gobogay

## DAYS OF THE WEEK

| | | |
|---|---|---|
| **Monday** | *Dé Luaín* | day loon |
| **Tuesday** | *Dé Máirt* | day maart |
| **Wednesday** | *Dé Ceádaoin* | day kaydeen |
| **Thursday** | *Déardaoin* | daredeen |
| **Friday** | *Dé hAoine* | day heeneh |
| **Saturday** | *Dé Sathairn* | day sahern |
| **Sunday** | *Dé Domhnaigh* | day downick |

## NUMBERS

| | | |
|---|---|---|
| 1 | haon | hayin |
| 2 | dó | doe |
| 3 | trí | tree |
| 4 | ceathaír | kahirr |
| 5 | cúig | kooig |
| 6 | sé | shay |
| 7 | seacht | shocked |
| 8 | hocht | hukt |
| 9 | naoi | nay |
| 10 | deich | jeh |
| 11 | haon déag | hayin jague |
| 12 | dó dhéag | doe yague |
| 20 | fiche | feekhe |
| 21 | fiche haon | feekhe hayin |

# BEHIND THE SCENES

## SEND US YOUR FEEDBACK

We love to hear from travellers – your comments help make our books better. We read every word, and we guarantee that your feedback goes straight to the authors. Visit **lonelyplanet. com/contact** to submit your updates and suggestions.

Note: We may edit, reproduce and incorporate your comments in Lonely Planet products such as guidebooks, websites and digital products, so let us know if you don't want your comments reproduced or your name acknowledged. For a copy of our privacy policy visit lonelyplanet.com/privacy.

## WRITERS' THANKS

### FIONN DAVENPORT

Thanks to my editor at Lonely Planet and all those who worked on the guide. A huge thanks to Laura, who's the best support team any guidebook author could hope for.

### CATHERINE LE NEVEZ

*Sláinte* first and foremost to Julian, and to all of the Irish locals, fellow travellers and tourism professionals in the southwest. Huge thanks too to Destination Editor James Smart and everyone at Lonely Planet. As ever, *merci encore* to my parents, brother, *belle-sœur* and *neveu*.

## ACKNOWLEDGMENTS

Climate map data adapted from Peel MC, Finlayson BL & McMahon TA (2007) 'Updated World Map of the Köppen-Geiger Climate Classification', *Hydrology and Earth System Sciences*, 11, 163344.

Front cover photographs (clockwise from top): Fanad Head lighthouse, Donegal, Olimpio Fantuz/ 4Corners©; Celtic cross, Inishmór, Aran Islands, Danita Delimont Stock/AWL©; Vintage Morris Mini Cooper, culture-images GmbH/Alamy©

Back cover photograph: Donegal countryside, Olimpio Fantuz/4Corners©

## THIS BOOK

This 2nd edition of Lonely Planet's *Ireland's Best Trips* guidebook was researched and written by Fionn Davenport, Isabel Albiston and Catherine Le Nevez. The previous edition was written by Fionn Davenport, Belinda Dixon, Catherine Le Nevez and Oda O'Carroll. This guidebook was produced by the following:

**Destination Editor** James Smart

**Product Editors** Grace Dobell, Alison Ridgway, Luna Soo

**Senior Cartographer** Mark Griffiths

**Book Designer** Jessica Rose

**Assisting Editors** Andrew Bain, Judith Bamber, Pete Cruttenden, Kate James, Fionnuala Twomey

**Cover Researcher** Lucy Burke

Thanks to Dan Corbett, Liz Heynes, Andi Jones, Indra Kilfoyle, Catherine Naghten, Mazzy Prinsep, Rob Rachowiecki, Kirsten Rawlings, Luc Tétreault, Angela Tinson, Saralinda Turner, Anna Tyler, Jerry Watson, Lauren Wellicome, Tracy Whitmey, Juan Winata

# INDEX

## A

abbeys
  Black Abbey 169
  Duiske Abbey 142
  Dunbrody Abbey 148
  Hore Abbey 110, 240
  Jerpoint Abbey 110, 140
  Kylemore Abbey 276
  Mellifont Abbey 100-2
  Mt Melleray Cistercian
    Abbey 156
  Muckross Abbey 186
  Sligo Abbey 348
  Tintern Abbey 147-8
accessible travel 385
accommodation 23, 378,
  379-80, see also individual
  locations
Achill Island 289, 293
activities 21, see also
  individual activities
Adare 230, 233, 255, 258-9
Adare Castle 230
Ahakista 224
air travel 378
Allihies 224
Altamont Gardens 132
ancient sites & ruins 19, 20,
  see also abbeys, churches
  & cathedrals, castles,
  stone circles
  Athassel Priory 239
  Battle of the Boyne Site 100

Browne's Hill Dolmen 132
Brú na Bóinne 17, 83, 99,
  103, 106-7, 111, 164
Carrowkeel Megalithic
  Cemetery 296-7
Céide Fields 250-1, 346-8
Cooley Cross 339
Corlea Trackway 118
Dún Aengus 56, 92, 268,
  305
Gallarus Oratory 194
Kells Priory 139-40
Kilree High Cross 140
Kilree Round Tower 140
Loughcrew Cairns 107-8
Monasterboice 102
Reginald's Tower 148, 150
Riase Monastic
  Settlement 194
Saltee Islands 148
Slea Head 192
Spanish Arch 310
St Mura Cross 323
Antrim Coast 361-7
apps 376
Aran Islands 308
Ardara 332
Ardgroom 224
Ardmore 58, 150, 151, 156
Ards Forest Park 333
area codes 384
Arranmore Island 325, 327
Arthurstown 148
Ashford Castle 282

Askeaton 231
Assarancagh Waterfall 326
Athassel Priory 239
Athenry 70
Athlone 70-1, 74, 119
ATMs 382
Aughris Head 291-2, 293
automobile associations 376
Avondale House 126

## B

Bagenalstown 134
Ballaghbeama Gap 184
Ballina 228, 290
Ballinrobe 282-3
Ballon 135
Ballycarbery Castle 181
Ballycastle 319, 327
Ballycroy National Park
  289-90
Ballycurrin Lighthouse 282
Ballyduff Upper 158
Ballyferriter 194
Ballyhillin Beach 342
Ballymaloe House 216
Ballymena 362-3
Ballysaggartmore Towers 158
Ballyvaughan 305, 309
Baltimore 214, 222
Bangor 354
Bansha 237-8
Bantry 203-5, 209, 223-4,
  225

Bantry House 203-4
Barleycove Beach 222
Battle of the Boyne Site 100
B&Bs 379-80
beaches
Achill Island 289
Ballyhillin Beach 342
Barleycove Beach 222
Glassilaun Beach 275-6
Omney Strand 284
Portrush 358
Portstewart Strand 320
Rossbeigh Strand 180
Strandhill 298
Streedagh Beach 299-300
Youghal 154
Beara Peninsula 224, 225
beer 50, 134
Belfast 12, 27, 51-2, 319, 356, 368-9
accommodation 60
food 60, 359
Belfast City Hall 368
Belvedere House & Gardens 117-18
Belvelly 216
Benbulben 299
Bennettsbridge 139
Birr 71, 75, 108, 111, 116-17, 119
Birr Castle 71, 116
Bishop's Palace 150
Black Abbey 169
Black Castle 134
Blackwater River 157
Blackwater Valley 153-9
Blarney Castle 207
Blarney Stone 207
Blasket Centre 193
Blasket Islands 192
Blennerville 196
Blessington 85, 87
boat travel 253, 378
Book of Kells 36
Booley House 158

border crossings 376
Borris 133, 135
Boycott, Captain Charles Cunningham 282
Boyne Valley 97-103
Braid Museum 362-3
Brandon Point 194
Brandon Regatta 195
Brow Head 223
Browne's Hill Dolmen 132
Brú Ború 240
Brú na Bóinne 17, 83, 99, 103, 106-7, 111, 164
Buncrana 334, 335, 342, 343
Buncrana Castle 334, 342
Bunratty 232
Bunratty Castle 232
Burren 55-6, 93
Bushmills 366, 367
business hours 383
Butcher's Gate 370
Butter Museum 214
Butter Slip 168

C

Caherconnell Fort 57
Caherdaniel 44-5, 184, 202-3
Cahergall 181
Cahersiveen 181-3, 202
Cahir 237
Cahir Castle 237
camping 380
Cappoquin 154-6, 159
Cappoquin House & Gardens 155-6
car hire 22, 373
car insurance 373
caravan parks 380
Carlingford 166, 167
Carlow Brewing Company 134
Carlow County 129-35
Carlow County Museum 130
Carlow Garden Trail 134

Carlow Town 130, 135
Carndonagh 343
Carrick-a-Rede Rope Bridge 52, 320, 357, 366
Carrigart 324
Carrowkeel Megalithic Cemetery 296-7
cars, see driving
Cashel 109, 111, 240, 241, 277
Cashel Folk Village 240
Castlebar 70, 74
Castlebellingham 102
Castlegregory 195, 197
castles
Adare Castle 230
Ashford Castle 282
Ballycarbery Castle 181
Birr Castle 71, 116
Black Castle 134
Blarney Castle 207
Buncrana Castle 334, 342
Bunratty Castle 232
Cahir Castle 237
Classiebawn Castle 300
Desmond Castle 214, 231, 255
Doe Castle 324-5
Donegal Castle 67, 349
Dungarvan Castle 150, 208
Dunguaire Castle 94
Dunluce Castle 357-8
Dunseverick Castle 52
Hillsborough Castle 355-6
Huntington Castle 132-3
Kilkenny Castle 71-2, 168
King John's Castle 230
Lismore Castle 157
Lynch's Castle 311
Mullin's Castle 140
O'Brien's Castle 306
Parke's Castle 292
Portumna Castle & Gardens 228

Ross Castle 186
Termonfeckin Castle 102
Trim Castle 98-9, 163-4
Tynte's Castle 208
Castletown House 83-4, 114
Castletownbere 224
Castletownshend 256-7
Cathedral of the
    Assumption 130
Causeway Coast Way 52,
    320
Céide Fields 250-1, 346-8
Celbridge 83-4, 114
cell phones 23, 385
Celtic & Prehistoric Museum
    192
Charles Fort 220-1
Charlie Chaplin Comedy Film
    Festival 183
Chester Beatty Library 170
Christ Church Cathedral 170
churches & cathedrals
    Cashel Cathedral 109
    Cathedral of the
        Assumption 130
    Christ Church Cathedral
        170
    Church of St Mary 140
    Cloncha Church 340
    Clonfert Cathedral 92
    Collegiate Church of
        St Nicholas of Myra 311
    Franciscan Friary
        (Clonmel) 237
    Franciscan Friary
        (Killarney) 201-2
    Franciscan Friary
        (Rossnowlagh) 330
    Layde Old Church 356, 363
    St Anne's Church 243
    St Canice's Cathedral 169
    St Carthage's
        Cathedral 157
    St Colman's Cathedral 207
    St Columb's Cathedral 358

St Declan's Church 150
St Fin Barre's Cathedral
    242
St Gobban's Church 52
St Mary's Cathedral
    (Killarney) 201
St Mary's Cathedral
    (Limerick) 230
St Mary's Church 282-3
St Mary's Church of
    Ireland 231
St Mary's Collegiate
    Church 208
St Patrick's Cathedral 170
Tullyaughnish Church 324
Church Island 183
Church of St Mary 140
Clare, County 303-9
Clarinbridge 94, 253-5
Classiebawn Castle 300
Claycastle 154
Clifden 38, 46, 92, 95
Cliffs of Moher 19, 38-41,
    306-7
climate 22
Cloghane 194-5
Clogherhead 102
Clonakilty 213-14, 217, 221-2
Cloncha Church 340
Clonegal 132-3
Clonfert Cathedral 92
Clonmacnoise 91, 95, 108-9,
    111, 117
Clonmel 236-7, 241
Cobh 207-8, 209
Coleman Irish Music Centre
    69
Collegiate Church of
    St Nicholas of Myra 311
Collins, Michael 213, 221-2
Cong 282, 285
Connemara 12, 257
Connemara National Park
    284, 285
Connor Pass 195

cooking schools 150, 216
Cooley Cross 339
Cork 13, 28-9, 58, 205-6,
    214-16, 242-3, 257
    accommodation 61, 209,
        217, 259
    festivals 205, 206
    food 61, 209, 217, 259
Cork Butter Museum 243
Cork City Gaol 206
Cork Film Festival 206
Corlea Trackway 118
costs 23
County Clare 303-9
County Donegal 329-35
County Sligo 295-301
County Sligo Golf
    Course 298
Craiceann Inis Oírr
    International Bodhrán
    Summer School 268
Crawford Municipal Art
    Gallery 242
credit cards 382
Croagh Patrick 252
Cromane Peninsula 180
Cromwell, Oliver 100
Crookhaven 223
crystal 150
Cúirt International Festival of
    Literature 252
Culdaff 343
Cultúrlann McAdam
    Ó Fiaich 368
currency 22
Cushendall 356, 359
Cushendun 363-4, 367
Cushlough Bay 283

- - - - - - - - - - - -

# D

dangers, see safety
Death of Innocence Mural 371
Delphi 284, 285
Delta Sensory Gardens 131-2

Derry 64, 321, 338-9, 358, 370-1
  accommodation 327, 359
  food 359
Derrynane House 203
Derrynane National Historic Park 44-5, 202-3
Desmond Castle 214, 231, 255
Diamond Hill 284
Dingle Oceanworld 192
Dingle Peninsula 17, 57, 189-97
Dingle Peninsula Museum 194
Dingle Town 42, 192, 256
  accommodation 47, 61, 197, 259
  food 47, 61, 197, 259
disabilities, travellers with 385
Doe Castle 324-5
Dog's Bay 275
dolphin-watching 192, 256
Donegal Castle 67, 349
Donegal, County 329-35
Donegal Gaeltacht 350
Donegal Town 330, 349, 351
Doolin 56, 94, 95, 268, 269
Downhill Demesne 358
Downings 327, 333-4
driving 373-7
  automobile associations 376
  car hire 22, 373
  documents 373, 374
  driving licences 373
  fuel 22, 257, 375-6
  insurance 373
  maps 374, 376
  parking 375
  road rules 374, 375
  safety 374-5, 376
  websites 376
driving licences 373

Drogheda 100, 103, 166, 167
Druid Theatre 253
Drumcliff 299
Dublin 10, 36, 50-1, 90-1, 162-3, 170-1
  accommodation 46, 60, 95, 167
  food 46, 60, 95, 167
Dublin Zoo 162
Duckett's Grove 132
Duiske Abbey 142
Dún Aengus 56, 92, 268, 305
Dún an Óir Fort 194
Dunbeg Fort 42, 192
Dunbrody Abbey 148
Dunbrody Country House 148
Dunbrody Famine Ship 72
Dunfanaghy 53, 60, 327, 333, 335
Dungarvan 150, 151, 208
Dungarvan Castle 150, 208
Dunguaire Castle 94
Dunlewey 66, 74, 332, 335
Dunluce Castle 357-8
Dunmore Cave 139
Dunseverick Castle 52
Dunquin 193
Durrus 212-13
Dursey Island 224
DVDs 384

E

Easkey 291
electricity 380
emergencies 22, 377, 382
English Market 214-15, 242
Ennis 41-2, 46-7, 262-4, 269, 304-5, 309
Ennis Friary 304-5
Enniscorthy 72, 75, 146-7, 151
Enniscrone 291, 348, 351
Enniskerry 86, 87, 122, 127
Ennistymon 264, 269, 307, 309

Ennistymon
  Horse Market 307
Erris Head 346
exchange rates 382
Eyeries 224
Eyre Square 311

F

Fahan 323
Fahan beehive huts 193
Fair Head 364
Father Mathew Statue 243
Father McDyer's Folk Village 326
festivals & events
  Ballina Salmon Festival 290
  Brandon Regatta 195
  Carlingford Oyster Festival 166
  Charlie Chaplin Comedy Film Festival 183
  Clarinbridge Oyster Festival 94, 253
  Cork Film Festival 206
  Craiceann Inis Oírr International Bodhrán Summer School 268
  Cúirt International Festival of Literature 252
  Galway Film Fleadh 252
  Galway International Arts Festival 252
  Galway International Oyster & Seafood Festival 252
  Galway Race Week 252
  Guinness Jazz Festival 206
  Inishbofin Arts Festival 284
  Kilmore Quay Seafood Festival 147
  Kinsale Gourmet Festival 214
  Laytown Races 165
  Lughnasa 194-5

North West 200 Road Race 324
Puck Fair 180, 202
Rose of Tralee 196
Seafood Festival 214
Taste of West Cork Food Festival 213
Town of Books Festival 142
Waterford Festival of Food 150
West Cork Chamber Music Festival 205
West Waterford Drama Festival 158
Willie Clancy Irish Summer School 264
film locations 276, 282
Fintown Railway 326
fishing 155-6
Flagstaff Viewpoint 166
folk music 15, 21
food 21, 23, 380-1
Fort Dunree 342
forts
Caherconnell Fort 57
Charles Fort 220-1
Dún Aengus 56, 92, 268, 305
Dún an Óir Fort 194
Dunbeg Fort 42, 192
Fort Dunree 342
Grianán of Aileách 65-6
Fota House 206-7
Fota Wildlife Park 206-7
Fountain Housing Estate 370
Foynes 231
Franciscan Friary (Clonmel) 237
Franciscan Friary (Killarney) 201-2
Franciscan Friary (Rossnowlagh) 330
Free Derry Corner 371

Front Strand 154
fuel 22, 257, 375-6

**G**

Gaeilge 386
Gallarus Oratory 194
galleries, see museums & galleries
Galtee Mountains 240
Galway City 12, 26, 36-8, 70, 92, 253, 262, 272-3, 280, 310-11
accommodation 46, 74, 95, 258, 269, 277
festivals 252
food 46, 258, 277
Galway City Museum 70, 310
Gap of Dunloe 185
gardens, see parks & gardens
Garinish Island (Ilnacullin) 224, 256
gas 22, 257, 375-6
gay travellers 382
gemstones 342
Giant's Causeway 18, 52-3, 60, 320, 356, 357, 366
Glandore 257
Glanteenassig Forest Recreation Area 196
glass 132
Glassilaun Beach 275-6
Gleann Mór 284
Glebe Gallery 334
Glebe Gardens 214
Glen of Aherlow 238
Glenariff Forest Park 363, 367
Glencolumbcille 67, 74, 326, 335
Glencree 122-4
Glendalough 15, 85-6, 87, 110, 125-6, 127
Glendalough Valley 125

Glenevin Waterfall 321-3, 327
Glengarriff 224, 225, 256, 259
Glengesh Pass 66-7
Glenmacnass Valley 124
Glenmacnass Waterfall 124
Glenmalure 126, 127
Glenveagh National Park 66, 334
golf 141, 183, 298
Gougane Barra Forest Park 206
Graiguenamanagh 142, 143
Grange 299-300
Green Lane Museum 321
Greencastle 339, 343
Grianán of Aileách 65-6
Guinness Jazz Festival 206
Guinness Storehouse 50
Gurteen 69-70
Gurteen Bay 275

**H**

Hall of the Red Earl 310
Hazelwood 292
health 381
Healy Pass 58
highlights 10-19, 33
Hill of Slane 107
Hill of Tara 99, 107
Hillsborough 355-6, 359
Hillsborough Castle 355-6
holidays 383
Hollow 291
Hore Abbey 110, 240
Horn Head 53, 325
hostels 380
House of Waterford Crystal 150
Howth 82, 87
Hunt Museum 230
Huntington Castle 132-3

# I

Ilnacullin (Garinish Island) 224, 256
Inch 191
Inch Island 334
Inchagoill 280-1
Inchiquin 281
Inisfallen 186
Inishbofin 284, 285
Inishbofin Arts Festival 284
Inisheer 268, 269, 306, 309
Inishmaan 305, 309
Inishmór 56, 92-3, 268, 305
    accommodation 61, 95, 269, 309
Inishowen Head 340
Inishowen Peninsula 337-43
Iniskeel Island 326
Inistioge 141-2, 143
insurance 373, 382
internet access 23, 381
Iskaheen 321, 339

# J

James Joyce Museum 86
Jameson Whiskey 208, 216
Jerpoint Abbey 110, 140
Jerpoint Glass Studio 132

# K

Kells 139-40
Kenmare 43-4, 57-8, 184, 203
    accommodation 47, 61, 187, 209
    food 47, 61, 187
Kenmare Heritage Centre 203
Kenmare Lace & Design Centre 203
Kerry Bog Village Museum 180
Kerry County Museum 196
Kilcrohane 224

Kilfenora 265
Kilgraney House Herb Gardens 134
Kilkee 232, 233
Kilkenny 71-2, 75, 138-9, 143, 168-9
Kilkenny Castle 71-2, 168
Killala 290
Killaloe 228
Killarney 43, 178-9, 190-1, 201-2
    accommodation 47, 187, 197
    food 47, 197
Killarney National Park 43, 185, 201
Killary Harbour 252
Killashee 118
Killorglin 45, 180, 187, 202, 209
Killybegs 350, 351
Kilmore Quay 73, 75, 147, 151
Kilmore Quay Seafood Festival 147
Kilmurvey 93, 305
Kilree High Cross 140
Kilree Round Tower 140
Kilrush 232, 308, 309
Kinsale 214, 217, 220-1
Kinsale Gourmet Festival 214
Kinvara 93-4
Knocknadobar 181
Kylemore Abbey 276

# L

Lackan Bay 290
languages 22, 386-7
Layde Old Church 356, 363
Laytown Races 165
Leacanabuile 181
Leenane 252-3, 258
Leighlinbridge 134
lesbian travellers 382
Letterkenny 74, 335

Lewis Glucksman Gallery 242, 257
Limerick City 229-31, 233
Limerick City Gallery of Art 230
Lisdoonvarna 267
Lismore 156-8, 159
Lissadell House 299
Londonderry 358, *see also* Derry
Loop Head 232, 308
Lord Brandon's Cottage 185
Lough Corrib 280-2
Lough Gill 292
Loughcrew Cairns 107-8
Loughrea Peninsula 66
Luggala 124
Lughnasa 194-5
Lynch's Castle 311

# M

Magan's 118
Magazine Gate 370
Malin Beg 332
Malin Head 340-2
maps 374, 376
Maritime & Heritage Centre 350
Maritime Museum 339
markets 159, 214-15, 233, 242, 307
Mathew, Father Theobald 243
measures 384
medical services 382
Medieval Museum 150
Meenaleck 325
Mellifont Abbey 100-2
Michael Collins Centre 221-2
Midleton 208, 216
Millmount Museum 100, 166
Miltown Malbay 264
Mizen Head Peninsula 222-3, 225
mobile phones 23, 385

Model 296
Monasterboice 102
money 22, 23, 382-3
motorcycles, see driving
Mount Juliet 141
Moville 343
Mt Brandon 194
Mt Errigal 350, 351
Mt Leinster 133
Mt Melleray Cistercian Abbey 156
Mt Mweelrea 252
Mt Stewart House 354
Muckross Abbey 186
Muckross Estate 186
Muckross Traditional Farms 186
Mullaghmore 300, 301
Mullingar 119
Mullin's Castle 140
Museum of Free Derry 371
museums & galleries
  Bishop's Palace 150
  Blasket Centre 193
  Braid Museum 362-3
  Brú Ború 240
  Butter Museum 214
  Carlow County Museum 130
  Céide Fields Interpretive Centre 250
  Celtic & Prehistoric Museum 192
  Cobh, the Queenstown Story 207
  Cork Butter Museum 243
  Crawford Municipal Art Gallery 242
  Dingle Peninsula Museum 194
  Foynes Flying Boat Museum 231
  Galway City Museum 70, 310
  Glebe Gallery 334

  Green Lane Museum 321
  Hunt Museum 230
  James Joyce Museum 86
  Kenmare Heritage Centre 203
  Kenmare Lace & Design Centre 203
  Kerry Bog Village Museum 180
  Kerry County Museum 196
  Lewis Glucksman Gallery 242, 257
  Limerick City Gallery of Art 230
  Maritime & Heritage Centre 350
  Maritime Museum 339
  Medieval Museum 150
  Michael Collins Centre 221-2
  Millmount Museum 100, 166
  Model 296
  Museum of Free Derry 371
  National 1798 Rebellion Centre 72, 147
  National Craft Gallery & Design Centre 168
  National Museum of Country Life 70
  National Museum of Ireland – Archaeology & History 90-1, 171
  National Museum of Ireland – Natural History 171
  Nore View Folk Museum 139
  Old Barracks Heritage Centre 202
  Old Market House Arts Centre 208
  People's Gallery 371
  Rothe House & Garden 169
  Skibbereen Heritage Centre 222

  Sligo County Museum 67-8, 292
  South Tipperary County Museum 237
  Spiddal Craft & Design Studios 273
  Strokestown Park House & Famine Museum 118
  Tarbert Bridewell Jail & Courthouse 232
  Tower Museum 64, 321, 370
  Ulster Museum 356
  Waterford County Museum 208
  Waterford Museum of Treasures 148-50
  Yeats Memorial Building 296
music 15, 21, 261-9, 376
Mussenden Temple 358
Myrtle Grove 208

N

Narin 326, 327
National 1798 Rebellion Centre 72, 147
National Craft Gallery & Design Centre 168
National Museum of Country Life 70
National Museum of Ireland – Archaeology & History 90-1, 171
National Museum of Ireland – Natural History 171
national parks, see also parks & gardens
  Ballycroy National Park 289-90
  Connemara National Park 284, 285
  Derrynane National Historic Park 44-5, 202-3
  Glenveagh National Park 66, 334

national parks *continued*
  Gougane Barra Forest Park 206
  Killarney National Park 43, 185, 201
Neale 282
New Ross 72
Newgrange 164
Newgrange Farm 165
Newmills Corn & Flax Mills 334
Newtown 238-9, 241
Nore View Folk Museum 139
North West 200 Road Race 324

# O

O'Brien's Castle 306
Old Barracks Heritage Centre 202
Old Bushmills Distillery 366
Old Market House Arts Centre 208
O'Malley, Grace 290
Omey Island 284
Omey Strand 284
One Man's Pass 350
opening hours 383
Organ 366
Oughterard 276
outdoor activities 21, *see also* individual activities
oysters 94, 166, 252, 253

# P

Parke's Castle 292
parking 375
parks & gardens, *see also* national parks
  Altamont Gardens 132
  Ards Forest Park 333
  Belvedere House & Gardens 117-18
  Bishop Lucey Park 215
  Cappoquin House & Gardens 155-6
  Carlow Garden Trail 134
  Delta Sensory Gardens 131-2
  Derrynane National Historic Park 202-3
  Fota House arboretum 207
  Garinish Island 256
  Glebe Gardens 214
  Glenariff Forest Park 363, 367
  Kilgraney House Herb Gardens 134
  Kylemore Abbey 276
  Muckross Estate 186
  Portumna Castle & Gardens 228
  Rothe House & Garden 169
  Vandeleur Walled Garden 232, 308
Passage Coast Road 150
Patrick Pearse's Cottage 273-4
Peace Line 369
Peadar O'Donnell's 370
Pearse, Pádraig 273-4
People's Gallery 371
petrol 22, 257, 375-6
photography 383
Pickie Family Fun Park 354
Pigeon Hole 282
Plassy 306
police 377
Port Chorrúch 93
Portbradden 52
Portmagee 45
Portrush 358, 359
Portstewart 320-1, 327
Portumna 228
Portumna Castle & Gardens 228
Powerscourt Estate 86, 122
Powerscourt Waterfall 86

prehistoric sites 19, 20, *see also* ancient sites & ruins
public holidays 383
Puck Fair 180, 202

# Q

Quiet Man Bridge 276
*Quiet Man, The* 276
Quirke, Michael 300

# R

radio 373, 376
Raleigh, Sir Walter 208
Rathlin Island 319, 364-6, 367
Rathlin Seabird Centre 365
Rathmelton 324, 327
Rathmullan 324
refunds 384
Reginald's Tower 148, 150
Republic of Ireland 321
Riasc Monastic Settlement 194
Ring of Kerry 18, 57, 177-87
Riverstown 297-8
road distances 374
road rules 373, 374, 375
roads, best for driving 13
roads, types of 374-5
Rock of Cashel 17, 71, 109, 240
Roe Valley 321
Rose of Tralee 196
Ross Castle 186
Rossbeigh Strand 180-1
Rosses Point 298, 301
Rossnowlagh 330, 348, 351
Rothe House & Garden 169
Rough Point Peninsula 195
Roundstone 38, 274, 277
ruins, *see* ancient sites & ruins
Russborough House 84, 85

# S

safety 374-5, 376, 383-4
sailing 253
Saltee Islands 73, 148
Salthill 280
Sandycove 86, 87
Seafood Festival 214
seaweed baths 292, 298, 348
Shannon River 227-33
Shannonbridge 119
Sheep's Head Peninsula 224
Sinn Féin Headquarters 368
Skellig Michael 44
Skellig Ring 181
Skibbereen 213, 222, 225
Skibbereen Heritage Centre 222
Sky Road 38
Slane 107
Slea Head 42, 192-3
Slemish 356
Slieve Bloom Mountains 116
Slieve League 67, 332, 350
Slievemore Deserted Village 289
Sligo Abbey 348
Sligo, County 295-301
Sligo County Museum 67-8, 292
Sligo Folk Park 297-8
Sligo Town 53, 67-9, 292, 296, 348, 351
    accommodation 61, 293, 301
    food 60-1, 74, 293, 301
Slish Wood 292
smoking laws 384
Sneem 184, 187
Sonairte 164-5
South Tipperary County Museum 237
Spanish Arch 310

speed limit 373
Spiddal 273, 277
Spiddal Craft & Design Studios 273
St Anne's Church 243
St Canice's Cathedral 169
St Carthage's Cathedral 157
St Colman's Cathedral 207
St Columb's Cathedral 358
St Declan's Church 150
St Fin Barre's Cathedral 242
St John's Point 330-2, 335
St Mary's Cathedral (Killarney) 201
St Mary's Cathedral (Limerick) 230
St Mary's Church 282-3
St Mary's Church of Ireland 231
St Mary's Collegiate Church 208
St Mullins 133-4, 135
St Mura Cross 323
St Patrick's Cathedral 170
stone circles
    Ahakista 224
    Ardgroom 224
    Carrowkeel Megalithic Cemetery 296-7
    Kenmare 184
Stonyford 132
Strandhill 298, 301
Streedagh Beach 299-300
Strokestown 118
surfing 300, 348, 358
Synge, JM 305

# T

Tarbert 232
Taste of West Cork Food Festival 213
taxes 384
Teach Synge 305
telephone services 23, 384-5

Temple of the Winds 354
Termonfeckin 102
Tholsel 168
Thomastown 140, 143
Thompson Graving Dock 319
time 384
Tintern Abbey 147-8
tipping 23, 382-3
Titanic Belfast 51-2, 319
Titanic Experience Cobh 207
tollways 375, 377
Torc Waterfall 186
Tory Island 332-3
tourist information 385
Tourmakeady 283
Tower Museum 64, 321, 370
Town of Books Festival 142
traditional music 15, 21
traffic information 376
Tralee 196, 197
transport 23, 378-9, see also driving
Trim 98-9, 103, 163-4, 167
Trim Castle 98-9, 163-4
Trinity College 36, 170
Tullamore 115-16, 119
Tullyaughnish Church 324
Tulsk 108
TV 384
Twelve Bens 284
Tynte's Castle 208

# U

Ulster Museum 356
Ulster Tower 369
Union Hall 257

# V

vacations 383
Valentia Island 45, 181
Vandeleur Walled Garden 232, 308
Vee Gap 158

vegetarian travellers 381
Ventry 192-6
views 20
Vinegar Hill 146-7
visas 22, 385

# W

waterfalls
  Assarancagh Waterfall 326
  Glenevin Waterfall 321-3
  Glenmacnass Waterfall 124
  Powerscourt Waterfall 86
  Torc Waterfall 186
  Tourmakeady Waterfall 283
Waterford City 148-50, 151
Waterford County Museum 208

Waterford Festival of Food 150
Waterford Museum of Treasures 148-50
Waterville 183-4, 187
weather 22
websites 23, 376
weights 384
West Cork Chamber Music Festival 205
West Waterford Drama Festival 158
Westport 53-5, 251-2, 258, 288-9, 293
Westport House 252, 289
Wexford Town 72-3, 75
whiskey
  Jameson Whiskey 208, 216
  Old Bushmills Distillery 366

Tullamore Dew Whiskey 115-16
White Park Bay 52
Wicklow Gap 126
Wicklow Mountains 121-7
wi-fi 23, 381
Willie Clancy Irish Summer School 264
winter solstice 164
woodcarving 300

# Y

Yeats' grave 299
Yeats Memorial Building 296
Yeats, WB 296, 299
Youghal 154, 159, 208